SOU FUJIMOTO RECENT PROJECT

Edited by Yoshio Futagawa

Copyright ©2013 A.D.A. EDITA Tokyo Co., Ltd.
3-12-14 Sendagaya, Shibuya-ku, Tokyo 151-0051, Japan
All rights reserved. No part of this publication may be reproduced,
stored in a retrieval system, or transmitted,
in any form or by any means, electronic, mechanical,
photocopying, recording, or otherwise,
without permission in writing from the publisher.

Copyright of photographs
©2013 GA photographers
Copyright of drawings, renderings
©2013 Sou Fujimoto Architects

Printed and bound in Japan

ISBN 978-4-87140-684-0 C1052

SOU FUJIMOTO
RECENT PROJECT

A.D.A. EDITA Tokyo

SOU FUJIMOTO
RECENT PROJECT

008

AN ARCHITECT'S INDIVIDUALITY IS DERIVED FROM RELATIONSHIPS
INTERVIEW
建築家としての個は，関係性において生まれてくる

022

HOUSE K
2010-12 | Hyogo, Japan | RESIDENCE
House K | 兵庫県

032

LA SMALL HOUSE
2010- | Los Angeles, California, U.S.A. | GUEST HOUSE
ロサンゼルス・スモール・ハウス | アメリカ，カリフォルニア州，ロサンゼルス

035

NUBE ARENA
2010- | Las Torres de Cotillas, Spain | AUDITORIUM / PUBLIC SPACE
Nube Arena | スペイン，ラス・トレス・デ・コティラス

040

KULTUR PROJEKTE BERLIN
2010- | Berlin, Germany | EXHIBITION SPACE
カルチャー・プロジェクト・ベルリン | ドイツ，ベルリン

044

PUBLIC TOILET IN ICHIHARA
2011-12 | Ichihara, Chiba, Japan | PUBLIC LAVATORY
市原の公衆トイレ | 千葉県市原市

046

NORMANDY RENOVATION PROJECT
2011- | Normandy, France | RESIDENCE
ノルマンディー改築計画 | フランス，ノルマンディー

048

BETON HALA WATERFRONT CENTER
2011- | Belgrade, Serbia | COMMERCIAL BUILDING COMPLEX
ベトン・ハラ・ウォーターフロントセンター | セルビア，ベオグラード

054

TAIWAN TOWER
2011- | Taichung, Taiwan | OBSERVATORY / MUSEUM
台湾タワー | 台湾，台中市

060

RIZHAO CITY CLUB CHINA
2011- | Rizhao, Shandong, China | CLUBHOUSE
日照シティクラブ | 中華人民共和国，山東省，日照市

064

SMALLEST/LARGEST ART MUSEUM
2011- | Château La Coste, Aix-en-Provence, France | MUSEUM
Smallest/Largest Art Museum | フランス，エクサンプロヴァンス，シャトー・ラ・コスト

068

VITAMIN SPACE ART GALLERY
2011- | Guangzhou, China | ART GALLERY
ヴィタミン・スペース・アートギャラリー | 中華人民共和国，広州

073

ALL IS ONE, ONE IS ALL
INTERVIEW
すべては一つであり，一つはすべてである

086

SERPENTINE GALLERY PAVILION 2013
2012-13 | Kensington Gardens, London, U.K. | PAVILION
サーペンタイン・ギャラリー・パヴィリオン 2013 | イギリス，ロンドン，ケンジントン・ガーデン

100

GEOMETRIC FOREST – SOLO HOUSES PROJECT
2012- | Cretas, Spain | RESIDENCE
ジオメトリック・フォレスト―ソロ・ハウス・プロジェクト | スペイン，クレタス

104

TAIWAN PAVILION
2012- | Tainan, Taiwan | PAVILION / SHOWROOM
台湾パヴィリオン | 台湾，台南市

107

CONNECTICUT POOL HOUSE
2012- | Connecticut, U.S.A. | POOL HOUSE
コネチカット・プール・ハウス | アメリカ，コネチカット州

112

CATALUNYA HOUSE
2012- | Caldes de Malavella, Spain | RESIDENCE
カタルーニャ・ハウス | スペイン，カルデス・デ・マラベーリャ

117
21ST CENTURY RAINFOREST ARCHITECTURE
2012 | Libreville, Gabon | CONFERENCE CENTER
21st Century Rainforest Architecture | ガボン共和国, リーブルヴィル

122
ENERGY FOREST
2012- | URBAN PLANNING
Energy Forest

126
TREE SKYSCRAPER
2012- | URBAN PLANNING
ツリー・スカイスクレイパー

128
LOUISIANA CLOUD
2012- | URBAN PLANNING
ルイジアナ・クラウド

130
MUSEUM IN THE FOREST
2012- | Taoyuan County, Taiwan | MUSEUM
森の中の美術館 | 台湾, 桃園県

134
CENTER OF TRADITIONAL PERFORMING ARTS IN IZUNOKUNI
2012- | Izunokuni, Shizuoka, Japan | AUDITORIUM
伊豆の国市伝統芸能会館 | 静岡県伊豆の国市

136
YUZ MUSEUM
2012- | Shanghai, China | MUSEUM
YUZ Museum | 中華人民共和国, 上海

140
FUTUROSPEKTIVE ARCHITEKTUR
2012 | Kunsthalle Bielefeld, Bielefeld, Germany | EXHIBITION
「Futurospektive Architektur」展 | ドイツ, ビーレフェルト, ビーレフェルト美術館

141
ARCHITECTURE AS FOREST
2012-13 | SICLI Pavilion, Geneva, Switzerland | EXHIBITION
「Architecture as Forest」展 | スイス, ジュネーヴ, SICLIパヴィリオン

142
MOUNTAIN HOTEL
2012- | China | HOTEL
マウンテン・ホテル | 中華人民共和国

150
GINZA BUILDING
2012- | Tokyo, Japan | OFFICE / RESIDENCE
銀座ビル | 東京都中央区

154
JJ99 YOUTH HOSTEL
2012-13 | Tainan, Taiwan | HOTEL
JJ99ユース・ホステル | 台湾, 台南市

156
SETONOMORI HOUSES
2012-13 | Coastal Area of the Seto Inland Sea, Japan | TOWNHOUSE
せとの森住宅 | 瀬戸内海沿岸地区

165
TAIWAN CAFE
2013- | Tainan, Taiwan | CAFE
台湾のカフェ | 台湾, 台南市

170
CHILE HOUSE
2013- | Los Vilos, Chile | RESIDENCE
チリ・ハウス | チリ, ロス・ビロス

176
SOUK MIRAGE / PARTICLES OF LIGHT
2013- | COMMERCIAL BUILDING COMPLEX
スーク・ミラージュ/パーティクル・オブ・ライト

182
OUTLOOK TOWER
2013- | OBSERVATORY / WATER PLAZA
アウトルック・タワー

190
LIST OF PROJECTS
2010-
プロジェクト・リスト

INTERVIEW
AN ARCHITECT'S INDIVIDUALITY IS DERIVED FROM RELATIONSHIPS
建築家としての個は，関係性において生まれてくる

IS SERPENTINE AN ARCHITECTURE?

GA After a series of in-depth talks for our publication of *The Sou Fujimoto Reader* in 2011, you have been more and more engaged in projects that call for reality for the past two years, including the Serpentine Gallery Pavilion (2013, p.86-) that came to be completed in June this year. Up to now you have been tackling given themes in an innocent way (laughs) which had a charm to it, but looking at you now we notice a certain evolution taking place in the process of adjusting your ideas to reality.

A while ago in a conversation with Tadao Ando I said that the type of things Fujimoto does is different from conventional architecture. Your work is regarded as a sort of detonator, or architectural art, which is, of course, what the clients are asking for, but there's this innocence of yours as a given (laughs). Traditionally, there's been a notion that architecture is a totality of mixture between ideas and methods, the hot and the cool. But maybe that's not the case anymore.

Your success with Serpentine is symbolic. In spite of the fact that everybody sees that as architecture, I see it as an architectural situation, not architecture. I think it's too early to call it an architecture. It works because it's pure, without frills. And as I said, the way it emerged was definitely different from the age-old tradition of architecture. So for me, it was a significant phenomenon in the sense that new circumstances are beginning to emerge in architecture.

Do you personally identify yourself as being closer to the traditional architect, or would continue working your way to being a sort of a trickster in society?

Sou Fujimoto (SF) Serpentine was indeed a case of peculiarity. With a rather flexible program of a pavilion, you have an absolute mission to make it the talk of the town, and it inevitably becomes a certain kind of statement. But my first thought was that I didn't want to get carried away in the situation and create something superficial and flashy, just spinning my wheels. The client first told me: "it's a Barcelona Pavilion of today that you're going to create here" (laughs). An incredibly challenging situation, in which I had to transcend architecture while to that end the result had to be an architecture, from top to bottom.

A trickster in society might be a good way of putting it. For better or for worse, in order to have that sort of

Final Wooden House (Mokuban, 2008)

power, the result has to be linked to 'architecture.' If you create something outlandish outside the frame of architecture, you'll just make people say "oh isn't that peculiar?" and that's it. It's got to be an architecture that will give people a whole new understanding on architecture.

For me, the basis of such 'architecture' is 'a place for people to spend some time' — in a rather loosely-knit situation, where people gather. Regardless of the size of the group, what matters is to create a cue for people to spend some time there. That's been the basis of my idea of architecture for over ten years, to which I've been trying to give shape.

GA When I saw your Final Wooden House (2008) some time ago I saw it as something close to a playground equipment or folly, and because it's not architecture it possesses a certain freedom that creates a situation which makes it easier to have people get involved.

SF I'd be against calling it a playground equipment, but if you ask me the reason why it's not, I can't exactly tell (laughs).

For me, what makes an architecture is the quality of time spent in a place that's defined by an object, rather than a place to play with that object. Unlike play equipments or art, that object or space itself is not the end result: there's this place, in which spatial constituents have little presence and don't bother people as they come and sit, have a chat with friends, and spend some time there. That imagery has always been with me, as the very first step of architecture.

With the right amount of variety of spatial density — nicely enclosed or comfortably open — the space becomes an architecture, not just a vast extent of 'place.' Looking back on Serpentine I think that the idea of a straightforward realization of what I believe is the starting point of architecture has always been at the back of my mind. Luckily, the site's public character and the history of past annual pavilions naturally lead to a social situation in which crowds of people would visit the place on their own and enjoy as they please, even if it were a 'primordial architecture' type of place. So in a sense, I took advantage of that.

Society as I believe it should be is, basically, full of people who love to spend their time having fun in their own different ways in various places of comfort. And it's when I say this type of thing that people think

しまう。人々の建築というものへの理解を一変させてしまうような建築，でなくてはならない。

ぼくにとってその「建築」であるためのベースは，人が過ごす場所，ということです。緩い状況ながらも人が集まってきて，人が群れていたり，2〜3人ぐらいであっても，とにかく人々が過ごす手がかりをここにつくること。それは，この10数年，自分が考えている建築の根幹だと思います。それにどう形を与えるかをずっと考えたわけです。

GA 以前「モクバン／くまもとアートポリス次世代木造バンガロー」（2008年）を見た時に，これは遊具とかフォリーのようなものであって，建築じゃないがゆえにある自由さを獲得していて，だから人々がそれと付き合いやすい状況ができているのだと思ったことがありました。

藤本 遊具だと言われると，反論したくなるんだけど，「なぜ遊具じゃないの？」と聞かれると，よく判らないところもある（笑）。

単にモノと戯れるというよりは，モノがつくり出す場で時間を過ごすというクオリティが建築になってくるとぼくは思うのです。遊具やアートと違って，そのモノや空間が目的なのではなく，空間を構成しているものが気にならないぐらいに場所ができていて，そこに身を置くとか，友達とおしゃべりするとか，時間を過ごす場所になっている。それが建築のまず最初の一歩，という意識は原風景としてぼくの中に多分ずっとありました。

場所の濃淡みたいなものが程よくできていて，程よく囲まれていたりオープンになっていると，ただの茫漠とした場所じゃなくて建築になってきたなあと感じるわけです。「サーペンタイン」は，自分の考える建築の始まりをいかにそのまま立ち上げることができるか，と無意識に考えていた気がします。幸い敷地はパブリックな場所なのと，毎年のパヴィリオンの歴史があるので，そういう建築の原初のような場所だったとしても，大勢の人が勝手に入って来て，どんどん勝手に楽しんでくれるという社会的な状況が必然的に生まれていた。だからそこに乗っかったとも言える。

ぼくが考える社会というものは，基本的に快適な場所でいろいろに楽しく過ごすのが好きな人々であふれていると思っているんです。こういうことを言うと，だからお前は無邪気だと言われるのかもしれないけど（笑）。

GA ある条件がベースにあることで成り立っているというのはすごくよく判ります。藤本さんの無邪気さは，ある何かに守られて成立している。それが，今後どうなっていくんでしょうね？

今どんどんリアリティに対して進んでいる貴方の建築はどうなるのか。社会的な責任についてどう考えるのか。そういうこと

I'm innocent (laughs).

GA We can really see that it's based on particular circumstances. You have this innocence because someone or something is protecting it. And I wonder what will become of it in the years to come. What will become of your architecture, which is today progressing more toward reality?

What will be your approach to social responsibilities? It seems to me that up to now you haven't been much conscious about those things. Will you keep it that way and let your work blow up in scale as the complexity of circumstances around you increases?

One of your current large-scale project is Taiwan Tower (2011-, p.54-) which is now on its way to realization. How are you planning to reflect/materialize in a tower building your idea of 'creating a cue for people to gather' that you tried to embody in Serpentine?

SF I feel that there are different versions of myself in me who think different things all at the same time. But I guess they're all connected at the root.

Serpentine and Wooden House are my attempts to reconstruct/redefine architecture on a scale that is closer to our body. Using a size of scale in which a small, partial change would radically affect the significance of the entire architecture, I found myself concentrating on making small discoveries one after another. On the other hand, in the case of a large-scale project such as Taiwan Tower, changes on floors or walls are just minor manipulations within the whole picture. So I try to reinterpret/rediscover architecture in my own way, on a massive scale. The notion of people gathering under a different scale means a totally different relationship between people's motions and behaviors and architecture. For example, I see House NA (2011) and Taiwan Tower from totally different dimensions in terms of relationship with the city. Although today I am still trying to see what powers my proposals can demonstrate in larger scale projects.

GA Looking at your works, I sometimes find you taking models from other projects and simply scaling them up for reuse.

SF You're right (laughs). But not any model can be enlarged. It depends on whether or not by changing the scale something interesting will happen in terms of architecture. If it will, whatever I found interesting in the first place will be expressed in a giant format. An enlarged version of Serpentine's grid concept would be

って，今までは，あまり考えてこなかったようにも見える。これからもそんなことは考えず，ブロウアップして，今の状況が複雑になって大きくなって成り立っていくのか。

大きなものとしては「台湾タワー」(2011年〜，p.54〜)が進行中ですね。今ちょうど実現化に向かっている途中で，「サーペンタイン」に託していた，「人が集まってくる手がかりをつくる」という考え方は，どうやって高層ビルで反映，実現していこうと考えているんでしょう？

藤本 自分の中では分裂症的にいくつかの自分がいて，いろいろと別なことを同時に考えているんです。根っこではつながっているんでしょうけど。

「サーペンタイン」や「モクバン」は，身体に近いスケールで建築を再構築，再定義しようとしていました。一つの部分を変えると建築全体の意味合いががらっと変わっていくようなスケールを使っていて，小さな発見をひたすら続けていく自分がいた。一方で「台湾タワー」など規模の大きいプロジェクトの場合，床，壁を変えても，全体のスケールにしたらささいな操作だったりする。その時には，巨大スケールの中で自分なりの建築の再解釈，再発見をしようとするわけです。人が集まってくるという同じ言葉でもスケールが違えば，人々の動きや振る舞いと建築の関係の仕方がまったく違う。例えば，「House NA」(2011年)と「台湾タワー」の都市との関係は，まったく違う次元で見ているところがある。デカいスケールになった時に，自分の提案がどういう力を持ち得ているのかは，まだ試行錯誤中なところもありますが。

GA 藤本さんの仕事を見ていると，時々，すごく簡単に別のプロジェクトのモデルが巨大化されて使われていたりしますね。

藤本 確かにそうですね(笑)。ただ，どんなモデルでも拡大できるわけではないんです。スケールが変わることで，そこで建築的に面白いことが起こっているかどうか。面白いと思ったものがデカくなって現れてきます。「サーペンタイン」の格子のアイディアが大きくなったのが中東の商業施設のプロジェクト(「スーク・ミラージュ」p.176〜/「アウトルック・タワー」p.182〜，共に2013年〜)と言えるかもしれませんが，大きくなることで解像度が高くなって，積層されているセル自体が異なる意味を持ってくる。その場合でもセルを積層するアイディアが通用するかどうかがポイントでした。

「サーペンタイン」は建築のスケールを再解釈して40cmと80cmというスパンにしていますが，中東のプロジェクトは5mとごく普通のスパンになっています。小さいセルをつなぎ合わせてつくっている点は共通しているけれど，中東のプロジェクトでは，そのセルはごく普通の構造スパン，階高になってしまっ

the commercial facilities projects in the Middle East (Souk Mirage, p.176-, 2013- / Outlook Tower, p.182-, 2013-). Increase in size results in higher resolution and different meanings in those layered cells. In this case the key point was whether or not the idea of layering cells would still hold effective.

While Serpentine's 40 cm x 80 cm span is a reinterpretation of architectural scale, the project in the Middle East adopts a quite normal span of 5 m. Both share the same idea of connecting small cells together, but in the Middle Eastern project the cells have normal structural span and ceiling height, as if it were a self-denial of Serpentine's rediscovery of scale. What attracted my interest was the fact that because the cells are all made of round arches, natural light that passes through these cells is percolated in a complex, three-dimensional manner. I found it interesting that the relationship between the space wrapped in such light introduced in the enormous multi-level void in the center and the tiered layering of small-scaled activity spaces around it is neither architectural nor urban in terms of scale, making up an intermediate public space.

In other words, in this case, rather than the appeal on the cells themselves, what captured me was the layer of light cut through round arches and through three-dimensional layering of various round shapes, the diversity of views of the sky through them and the enormous public space enveloped in all of them that create a place where multilayered scales overlap with one another, which seemed to demonstrate a new type of architectural quality. People might think "all that this guy does is just apply grids in different scales and mass produce" but in fact I'm having different ideas.

GA　For me it doesn't look like mass production but I definitely appreciate your ability to deliver a variety of interpretations from a single model (laughs).

SF　You may call it unscrupulous (laughs).

GA　I'd call it an ability, in a good sense.

SF　We've been testing a tremendous amount of ideas, most of which being useless, but now and then some get to grow out it. When Serpentine is placed in a context of different scale, the seeds start to grow differently, to offer different architectural values even if the seeds are the same. It's like growing countless crops. Watching the genes transform through generations, I sift through them picking up those that look interesting and throw-

て，「サーペンタイン」でのスケールの再発見を自ら否定するようなつくりになっているわけです。では，何故面白いと思ったかというと，セルがすべて丸いアーチでつくられていることで，セルを通して入ってくる光が複雑に立体的に濾過されるのです。真ん中の巨大な吹き抜けに入ってくる複層的な光に包まれた空間と，その廻りに広がる段階的で重層的なスケールの小さなアクティビティ空間との関係が，建築のスケールでも都市のスケールでもない，ちょうどその中間的な公共空間として面白そうだと思いました。

つまりこの場合は，セルが面白いというよりは，丸いアーチゆえに切られる光の重なり，三次元的にいろんな丸型が重なってそれで切り取られる光，見える空の面白さと，それらに包まれる巨大な公共空間が，多層的なスケールの重なり合いの場になっているという点が，新しい建築の質を持っているのではないかと思った。「こいつ，グリッドをいろんなスケールに適用してただ大量生産しているんじゃないか」と見られるかもしれないけど，考えていることは違うんです。

GA　大量生産には見えないけど，一つのモデルに対していろいろな解釈を持ち込めるというその能力に対しては，すごいと思う（笑）。

藤本　悪く言うと節操がないというか（笑）。

GA　良い意味で，能力だと思います。

藤本　ぼくたちは，本当にたくさんのアイディアを試していて，そのほとんどは使えないものですが，たまにそこから進化してくるものがある。「サーペンタイン」が違うスケールのコンテクストに置かれると，その種が最初に蒔かれた時とはまったく違う進化をし始めて，種は一緒でもそこに現れてくる建築的な価値観は違ってくるのです。無数の作物を育てながら，世代ごとに遺伝子が変わっていくのを見て，面白そうなやつだなあ，とかやっぱりこれはダメだなあ，といった作業を繰り返す……，だから自分がどこに向かっているか自分でも判らない（笑）。

GA　スケールの違う模型を置いてみて「あっ，面白い」と思うわけですね。

藤本　単純にスケールが違う場合もあるし，プログラムだったり文化的なコンテクストが違う場合もある。中東じゃなかったら丸いアーチなんてやらないけど，やってみたら意外な発見がある。これを普通のラーメンでやってもしょうがないかもしれない。

そう考えると，一つのアイディアと思われるもののなかにも，単純な形式とか形のタイポロジーでは語れない幾つものレイヤーがいっぱいあって，あるプロジェクトでは，その中の一番見えやすいレイヤーが表に出てくる。だけどそのアイディアが持って

ing away those that are no good — so I can't tell where I'm headed myself (laughs).

GA So you start with putting models in different scales in front of you and go "oh, this one looks interesting."

SF Sometimes it's a difference in just the scale, but in other times it's the program or the cultural context. If it wasn't for the Middle East, I wouldn't opt for round arches, but I tried it anyway and came by an unexpected discovery. Though it wouldn't work like that with regular rigid frame structures.

So when you come to think of it, what appears to be a single idea includes a lot of layers that can't be simply categorized in styles or in the typology of shapes, and in a project you only see the most obvious layer on the surface. In fact the values of an idea are not only in the visible parts — they are expressed under different forms, when placed in a different location or combined with different things.

When I observe an idea grow, I do it from a traditional architect's point of view. Because you have to have an architectural perspective to be able to tell if a growth is good or bad. I think about its relationship with the city, its context, history of architecture, its programs and functions. I can tell where it creates a new path and what it renovates, from an architectural point of view. Just making it interesting or original won't take you to the depths of an idea. But when I see something being updated and a bit of a progress in architecture being made, then I feel like going further with it. So depending on circumstances, a good number of my ideas would grow as regular, normal architecture. I then become anxious (laughs) and start to want to make it pretentious and interesting, but such superficial charm will never reach the essence. So I have to be patient. On the other hand, at times when there seems to be no way out I may bring up a fanciful idea trying to stir things up just to make the situation better — like throwing in an idea from another project on a different scale, as I mentioned earlier. Sometimes that can help you get further.

AFTER SERPENTINE

GA Now that you've finished Serpentine, is there a rediscovery of certain things that's been on your mind or do you feel any change in yourself over the past two years?

SF To be honest, I feel myself not yet ready for a calm

いる価値は見えている部分だけじゃなくて，違うところに置いてみたり，他のものと結び合わさった時に別の形で浮かび上がってくる。

育っていくアイディアを見ている時は，旧態然とした建築家の視点のはずなんです。よく育っているか悪く育っているかという判断は，建築的な視点がないと上手くできないのではないかと思う。その時にはプログラムや機能，建築の歴史やコンテクストや都市との関係を考えます。建築的にみて，どこを切り拓いているのか，何を新しくしているのか，という判断が働く。単に面白いとか変わっているというだけでは，アイディアの深層までは行き着けない気がする。それで，何かが少しでも新しく更新されていて建築のあり方が一歩前進できていると思ったら，進めてみようかという気持ちになる。だから，状況によっては本当に普通の建築の状態で進んでいくものも多い。そういう時には，不安になってきて（笑），はったりでも何か面白い感じにしなくちゃいけない気もしてくるけれど，そういう表面的な面白さは結局本質的にはなり得ない。だからじっと我慢しなくちゃいけない。一方で，出口が見えないときに，状況を打開するために突飛なアイディアで揺さぶりをかけるときもある。さっきお話しした，別のプロジェクトのアイディアを違うスケールでぶつけるとか。そこから先が見えてくるときもあります。

「サーペンタイン」以後

GA「サーペンタイン」ができてみて，それまで自分が考えてきたことの再発見や，この2年間の変化など感じたことはありませんか。

藤本 正直，まだあまり冷静に検証できてない気がします。とにかく何とかしてこのミッションをコンプリートさせることがとても重要だと思っていました。プロジェクトをやっていた半年間ぐらいは，最初はいろいろ考えていましたが，途中からは，言語的な思考で整理することを超えた何かができつつある感じになってきて，最後は動物的嗅覚で決めていたような気がします。自分の理解を超えつつあるものと格闘しているような感覚でした。

そんななかで「とにかくなんだか判らないけれど圧倒的にすごい！」というようなものでないと絶対ダメだという思いはあった。なんというか，理解不可能性の淵を覗き込むような感覚というか……，こちら側とあちら側が繋がる感じというか……，建築のクオリティを決めるのはそこなんじゃないかと。「何かすごい」という感覚は万国の人に通じる気がします。

GA それは本当にそうだと思います。アントン・ガルシア＝アブリルやBIGのビャルケ・インゲルスといった同世代の人たち

House NA (2011)

examination of recent events. What mattered most was to complete this mission, one way or the other. I've been on the project for about six months. First I did a lot of thinking and then gradually something — that can't be elaborated with verbal thought — started to build up, and in the end I was making decisions by animal instinct. It was like wrestling with something that was beyond my understanding. And all the while I had this belief that it's got to have people say "I don't really understand it but it's utterly amazing!" no matter how. Make them feel like gazing into the depth of the incomprehensible..... A feeling that this side here and that side over there come to be connected..... And that's what determines the quality of architecture. A sense of incomprehensible awe can be shared among people of all nations.

GA No doubt about it. Contemporary architects such as Anton Garcia-Abril and BIG's Bjarke Ingels are all working hard to create such impression. Their mission is different from that of old traditional architecture. However, not everyone is able to dive in and rush that way. I sometimes think they should just go for it.

SF I do sometimes think that way, that I should just go for it.....

GA Yes. Hence the notion that the situation of architecture is beginning to change, as I talked with Mr. Ando.

SF If that change is so new that people would call it a phenomenon as you said, then I think I should just go for it head-on..... But truth is, I'm not totally letting myself go.

GA Maybe a part of you is still concerned with traditional architectural common ground and thinking that Yukio Futagawa called old and outdated (laughs).

SF His remark's been staying with me for a long time. There's a part of me who wants to get over it, while the other thinks that trying to get over it would be just right. Use of the word 'balance' might be superficial, but I believe that keeping balance is important in the true sense. I'm of the old breed who, left alone, would naturally sink 100 meters below water surface so in order to maintain a good balance I constantly need to struggle just to keep my face out of the water.

I also must admit I have a "so-what" attitude: if an architect's mission were to churn out "awe-inducing" buildings, I'll give my best shot now, for good or for bad, and leave judgement to history. And with the piece

は，そういう見え方をいかにつくるかを考えているわけです。それがいわゆる旧態然とした建築が負っている使命とは違うんだなと。しかし，皆，そのまま突っ走れているわけでもない。もっと突っ走ってもいいんじゃないかとも思ったりする。

藤本 ぼく自身，突っ走っちゃってもいいのかなと，思うときもあります……。

GA そう。だから建築の状況は変わってきたんじゃないでしょうか，と安藤さんとは話をしたんです。

藤本 二川さんがおっしゃったように，それが事件と言われるくらい新しい変化なのだとしたら，突っ走って行くべきだと思いますが……。実際には，まだ振り切れてない感じもあるんですけどね。

GA 旧態然とした建築的な落としどころや思考にこだわるという，二川幸夫が古いと言っていた部分があるのかもしれません（笑）。

藤本 その発言はぼくの中でずっと残ってます。それを振り切りたい自分がいて，一方で，振り切ろうと頑張ってるぐらいでちょうどいいんじゃないかなとも思う。バランスというと表層的かもしれませんが，本当の意味で調和は大事だと思います。自分はそもそもが古いから，放っておくと水深100メートルぐらいのところに沈んじゃうので，そのバランスを取るためには無我夢中になって，もがいてギリギリ水面に顔が出るぐらいの感じでちょうどいいんじゃないかと。

「とにかくすごい！」というものをボコボコ建ち上げていくのが建築家だとすれば，今良いか悪いかは判らないけど，あとは歴史が決めてくれるはずだから，やれるだけやってやる，みたいな開き直りの気持ちもあります。もちろん建築的良心は残っているから，表面的な面白さには走らないようにはしたい。

GA その線引きはすごく難しいと思う。自分が相手にする社会や都市がどんどんマスになってきて，それを巻き込むということに対して，もっとポリフォニックに対応しないといけなくなってくるんじゃないでしょうか。そこがアーティストと建築家との違いになってくるのでしょう。マスに対して建築家の責任をどういう風に摺り合わせられるのかなと。今後の問題として興味を持つところです。

建築家の社会性は個が結ぶ関係性によりつくられる

藤本 陸前高田の「みんなの家」（2012年）をつくっていた時，伊東豊雄さんが「個としての建築家はもう終わった」とさかんに言われました。「個を超えた個」だと。最初，何を言ってるんだろうな？という感じだったんです。「自分を消して三角屋根にすれ

of architectural conscience that's left in me, I'll try not to get away with superficial appeal.

GA Drawing a line there would be an extremely tough thing to do. You'll have to deal with larger societies and cities, so your approach to getting them involved has to be more polyphonic. And that's what makes the difference between an artist and an architect. I'd be interested in seeing how you'd manage to adjust an architect's responsibility to the mass in the years to come.

AN ARCHITECT'S SOCIALITY IS DERIVED FROM RELATIONSHIPS BETWEEN INDIVIDUALS

SF Back when I was working on Home For All (2012) in Rikuzentakata, Toyo Ito used to say repeatedly that "architect as an individual is a dead issue already." That it is now an "individual that transcends the individual." My first impression was "what's he talking about?" Akihisa Hirata, Kumiko Inui and I used to say "does he mean we should leave our selves behind and opt for the triangular roof?" "no kidding." It took about two years to complete Home For All, and the other day I heard Ito say at a recent lecture that "the modern-era individual is Descartes' individual." "Descartes had said 'I think therefore I am' but that's no longer the case today" he also said. He didn't give a definition of what happens next, but when I heard this a thought crossed my mind.

For Descartes who regards himself as an independent existence, the individual is something that's defined by itself: the individual is self-contained. It is closed in itself, so once society is born they are bound to conflict. Then what does transcending the individual mean? If it means to be neutral by losing the self, the idea has no appeal at all for me. Instead, when I think about what I do as an architect, there in the picture is a particular person that is myself, as well as a particular person that is the client. Circumstances are also quite particular. A project begins by establishing a relationship between them. Meaning that my self is defined by this relationship. No matter how hard I'd try to claim "this is me," it can never be a definition of myself. I am defined within such relationships as between a person and a person or a person and a situation. And such relationships can only be defined by the uniqueness of such unique characters. If one of them loses its uniqueness, that relationship can never be established. I would take part in it with my

ばいいのかな？」「それはないでしょう」といったやりとりを平田晃久くんや乾久美子さんとしていました。「みんなの家」は2年ほど掛かって完成して，この前伊東さんは講演会で，「近代の個はデカルトの個だ」と言われていました。「デカルトは『我思う，ゆえに我あり』と言った。でもこれからは違うんだ」と。違ってどうなるという定義はありませんでしたが，それを聞いた時にふと思ったことがありました。

デカルトにとって，自分は独立した存在だと思っているから，個は自分自身によって定義されるわけです。個が完結している。自分の中で閉じていて，だから社会が出てきた時には対立する。では，個を超えるとはどういうことなのか？　自分を捨ててニュートラルにするという意味ではまったく魅力的に感じられなかった。むしろぼく自身が建築家としてやっていることは何なのかと考えると，ここに自分というかなり特殊な人間がいて，クライアントというやはり特殊な人間がいる。状況も結構特殊である。それらの関係を取り結ぶことでプロジェクトが始まる。そうすると自分はその関係の中でしか定義されないわけです。いくらこれが自分だと言っても自分の定義にはなっていなくて，人と人，人と状況といった，ある関係の中で初めて自分は定義される。しかもとてもユニークなキャラクターのユニークネスによってしかその関係は定義されない。そのユニークネスを捨てたら，そもそも関係自体が成り立たないわけで，自分は自分の個を持って参加するけれど，自分が何者かは，廻りの人や状況によって定義されていく。

それは考えてみれば自然な話で，住宅をつくる場合，クライアントと土地と藤本という関係において初めて出てくるアイディアが必ずある。当たり前の話ですが，特に陸前高田のプロジェクトを通して，徐々に意識的になった感があって，伊東さんの言われていることが2年たった今になって，そういうことだったのか！と自分なりに腑に落ちたんです。伊東さんには「そういうことじゃないんだ」と言われそうだから直接そのことは話していないんですが……（笑）。だから勝手な自分なりの理解なんですけどね。

GA それが藤本さんが考える現代の社会性であると。

藤本 そうですね。社会という巨大で曖昧なものに巨大で曖昧なスローガンを投げつけるんじゃなくて，そもそも社会は巨大な敵なのではない，むしろ顔の見える個性的な人間同士がお互いに関係を取り結んで相互作用しながら，徐々に巻き込まれていく中で物事が動いていく，という感覚でしょうか。公共的な建物の場合は，直接関係を結ぶ相手が大勢です。そのスケールだと一対一の関係を取り結ぶのは無理ですが，でもその場

own individuality, but who I am is defined by the people and situation that surround me.

Which is, when you come to think of it, quite natural — in the case of a private residence, there always are ideas that can only be derived.

GA So that's your idea of sociality today.

SF Yes. Rather than throwing a huge and ambiguous slogan in the face of something huge and ambiguous that is the society, I see society not as a huge enemy, but as a series of interactions within relationships established between people with a real face and character, whose involvement drives certain things to happen. In the case of public buildings, you have to establish a direct relationship with a lot of people. On that scale it's impossible to forge a one-on-one relationship, but what we create can only be defined inside our relationship with a specific general public. In that sense, even if the projects get bigger and more social, I'll be constantly affected by what's happening to the others, drawing my inspiration from that in my attempt to respond to them and interacting with them over specific matters, and be swept away in the big tide. Although I have to transform myself within the relationship of a particular situation, it doesn't necessarily mean that I am losing myself. I'm just moving around, driven by my own reactions. I'd feel most comfortable working in such state of mind when dealing with society.

GA You don't have an intention to lead the society?

SF No, I'm not the type to do that.

GA And yet what you do isn't marketing either.

SF I do propose but that's different from marketing. I'd throw my "how about something like this?" and when things work out financially or people show up to support my idea, it becomes a reality. Even if it doesn't make it to reality, by turning it into images and models I can reach not only those who are in front of me but people who are far away through magazines and books and Internet. Then I would start something new, a different type of relationship, that might appeal to someone who'd want to imitate it, might inspire people to draw a proposal on their own, or might bring in new clients. If the new client has a different type of site, the result will be completely different, with an appeal that is specific to that project. For me, that's what sociality is all about.

GA That's what people would call optimistic (laughs) but certainly demonstrative of your personality. And not

所にぼくらがつくるものは，ある不特定多数の人との関係性の場の中でしか定義され得ないわけです。そういう意味では，大きな社会的なプロジェクトになってきたとしても，相手に今起こっていることから自分は絶えず影響を受けているし，そこから発想して何かを返してみて，具体的なやりとりを交わしながら，大きな波に自分も流されていく。ある状況の中の関係性で自分も変化せざるを得ないけれども，自分を捨てるわけではなくて，今の自分ならっではの反応であちこち動いていく。そのぐらいの立ち位置で社会と接していくのがぼくにとっては一番自然かなと。

GA 社会を牽引しようという姿勢ではない？

藤本 そうですね。牽引という感じではない。

GA だからといって，マーケティングでもない。

藤本 提案はしますが，マーケティングとは違います。「こういうのどうですかねえ？」と投げかける。経済的なことや，賛同してくれる人がいたりいくつかの状況が上手くいくと，実現するわけです。実現しないとしても，イメージにしたり模型にすると，目の前の人だけじゃなくて，さらに遠くの人たちに雑誌や本やインターネットを通して広がっていく。それでまた何がしかの違った関係を取り結び始めて，面白いと思って真似する人がいるかもしれないし，触発されて別の提案をする人がいるかもしれないし，仕事を頼んでくる人がいるかもしれない。仕事を頼んでくる人が別の敷地を持っていたら，また全然違うものになってまた個別の面白さが生まれてくる。それが自分の中では，社会性なんじゃないかなと。

GA 人はそれを楽天的と呼ぶかもしれない（笑）。でも藤本さんのパーソナリティを浮かび上がらせていますね。それに今の状況ともフィットしているし，ぼくらが危機感として持っている意識を完全に打棄している。藤本さんの大らかさが功を奏している部分がありますね。

藤本 もちろん提案を社会が受け入れてくれない場合も多くて，ちょっと腹は立つわけです。ただ，だからといって社会が悪いということではなく，だいたいは判ってくれないよな，と思い直して，ちょっと面白いものができたら，性懲りもなくまた見せる。誰も判ってくれなかったらさすがにグレるかもしれないけど，判ってほしいなと思う人には伝わることが多いと感じられる。例えば世界中に散らばっている自分が信頼できる10人ぐらいの人は何となく判ってくれる。そうすると，いわゆる一般社会が，すぐこれを建てようとか，すごいと言ってくれなくても，可能性があると自分では思えるし，そういうことを繰り返していくうちに，徐々に大陸が移動していくように，気がついたら知らない

only it fits the current situation, it also tosses aside the sense of crisis that we have. Your easygoing nature seems to play an important part in it.

SF Of course, many a time society wouldn't appreciate my proposals, which makes me a bit angry. But instead of blaming it on society I usually don't feel bad about it and take the occasion to give it a second thought. As soon as I come up with something interesting I'd show it to people, again and again. If no one ever understands me I might get pissed, but most of the time I feel myself capable of getting across to those whom I wish could understand. For example, there are about 10 people scattered around the world that I can rely on who would more or less understand. Then, even if society in general won't be impressed nor agree on building it right away, that's enough reason to believe it's got potentials. And as long as you don't stop, like a continent that moves slowly, a great change can be brought about, as if you found yourself in an unfamiliar place without knowing. Although I won't try to lead the society on my own, I do wish to bring some help in moving, quietly but definitely, what may be called the essence of values or the foundation of the entire society.

Despite the fact that there have been a lot of great architects in the course of history, we always refer to a handful of giants such as Mies or Le Corbusier. Hidden behind them are many extraordinary architects who may have influenced Mies and Le Corbusier. Each one of them is a small but irreplaceable piece of stone that makes up the wall of history. Even if I'm not good enough I'm still bound to be that small piece of stone in history, so I'd better go for it (laughs). And face that mission. I believe that, as long as there's hope that someone in the future would find me out and think "there was this guy in the past who used to do this type of crap" there'd be some value. My notion of sociality also has temporal and historical aspects, in that the individual, in its slow travel across past, present and future, transforms within relationships as it comes to be exposed to different interpretations from time to time (laughs).

GA Back when I started to get to know you, I once told you that you are fundamentalist, but I'll take that back (laughs). Although there's something that's vaguely fundamentalist at the very base of you, it's already lost substance — you've now become someone extremely versatile.

SF I agree that the category of fundamentalist doesn't

ところに移動していた，といった大きな変化が起こるんじゃないかなと思っています。その意味では，直接社会を牽引する訳ではないけれど，でも社会全体が載っている基盤というか価値観のおおもとのようなものを，静かに，でも確実に動かしていく役に立ちたいとは思っているんです。

歴史上すごい建築家がたくさんいたにもかかわらず，ぼくらは，ミース，コルビュジエといった巨匠を話題にすることが多い。でもその陰にいろんな建築家が隠れていて，ミースやコルビュジエに影響を与えたすごい人も多分たくさんいる。彼らも歴史を一つひとつ積み重ねていくかけがえのない石ころの一つなんです。ぼく自身どんなにダメでもとにかく歴史の一つの石ころにはならざるを得ないわけだから，それは精一杯やった方がいいんじゃないかと思ってる（笑）。そのミッションから逃げちゃいけないなと。とにかく未来の誰かに，「こういうしょうもないことをやっていたヤツがいたんだ」とでも見つけてもらえば，価値があるような気がしています。過去現在未来の中をゆったりと流れていく個が，その時々でいろいろな解釈にさらされて，その関係の中で変化していく，そういう時間的，歴史的な社会性でもある（笑）。

GA 昔，藤本さんと付き合い始めた頃に，原理的であると言いましたけど，訂正します（笑）。手がかりとして原理みたいなのはあるけれど，それはもう形骸化して，融通無碍に変化する人ですね，もはや。

藤本 原理主義者としてカテゴライズされるのは違うなあとぼくも思ってます（笑）。確かに5年ぐらい前はもう少し形式にこだわっていましたが，だんだん変わってきて，多分それは実際のプロジェクトが増えてきて，たとえば「武蔵野美術大学図書館」（2010年）だと相手が20人ぐらいいるから，原理だけじゃとても立ち行かない。しかも，ダメと言われて考え直した案の方が良かったりする。考え直すチャンスを貰えて結果的には有り難かった，といったことがあるんです。

だいたいぼくの場合は，最初はあんまり良い形を出せなくて，いろいろ言われるうちに，プロジェクトのコアにあらためて気づいたりするのです。「サーペンタイン」も最初，ダメ出しされて，考え直す中で自分たちのやっているものの本質を理解していけた。摺り合わせるというより見つけ出していくんでしょうね。最初掘っていたところが，全貌かなと思ってたら実は端っこで，ダメと言われて別の場所を掘ってみたら本体がこっちにあった，でも全体はつながってた，という具合に試行錯誤を続けることで自分自身にとっても発見が連鎖していく。一つのプロジェクトの中での多層的な連鎖もそうですし，それがまた別のプロジ

quite fit me (laughs). About 5 years ago I was indeed a bit more concerned with style, but that gradually changed probably because I became involved more with real projects. For example in Musashino Art University Library (2010) I had to deal with about 20 people, so the fundamentals weren't enough to get me through. What's more, it happens that refined versions after being rejected are more likely to be better: sometimes, having the chance to think over turns out to be a blessing.

In my case my earlier attempts usually prove to be fruitless. With a lot of remarks and criticisms being made, I'd finally become aware of the project's core. Serpentine was no exception: our first design was rejected, and as we reconsidered our plan we managed to develop our understanding on the essence of what we were about to create. I'm seeing that process as a discovery rather than adjustment. As we started to dig up, what we thought to be the entire picture was in fact just a piece in the corner. Then after being told that it's no good we picked another place to dig then we stumbled upon the real thing. But in fact everything was connected under the ground. In this way through constant trial and error we get to achieve a chain of discoveries. Same thing happens with multilayered sequences within a project, which in turn hold the promise of developing into other projects.

You've mentioned earlier about polyphony, and I imagine that it's expected to emerge, little by little, from such chain of events in a multilayered manner. Instead of a one-dimensional diversity of a strong individual, a polyphony generated by multilayered interaction. A place in which each individual melody stands out separately in order to emphasize the entirety and its multi-tiered profile. A polyphonic architecture that is receptive of the era of relationships. I'm probably vaguely conscious about such authentic "architecture of diversity." And again, I might appear much too innocent when I say something like this..... (laughs)

July 30, 2013, Sou Fujimoto Architects
Inteview by Yoshio Futagawa

ェクトにも展開していく可能性も秘めている。

先ほどお話しされたポリフォニックというものも，そういう中から多層的に徐々に湧き上がってくることを期待している気がします。一つの強い個による一元的な多様性というよりも，多層的な相互作用によって湧き上がる多重奏。個々の旋律がそれぞれ際立つことで全体が複層的な輪郭をもって引き立つような場所。ポリフォニックな，あるいは関係性の時代を受け止める多重層的な建築。そういう真の「多様性の建築」というものをぼんやりと意識しているのかもしれません。そんなことを言うと，また無邪気すぎるのかもしれませんが……（笑）。

2013年7月30日，藤本壮介建築設計事務所にて
聞き手：二川由夫

SOU FUJIMOTO
RECENT PROJECT
2010-/2011-

HOUSE K
Hyogo, Japan, 2010-12
RESIDENCE

View from northwest: entrance on left
北西より見る：左手に玄関

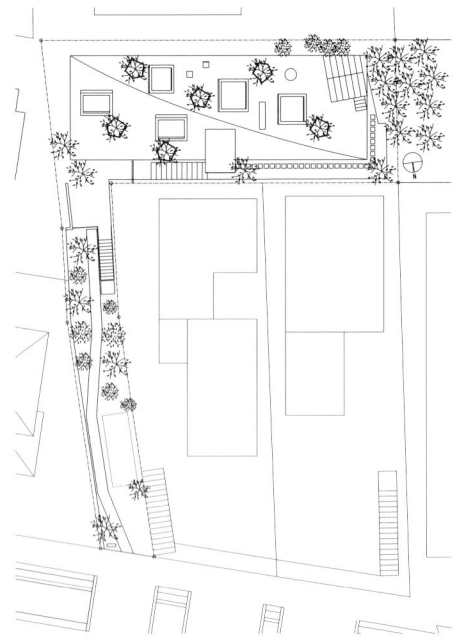

1 ENTRANCE
2 LIVING ROOM
3 DINING ROOM
4 KITCHEN
5 MASTER BEDROOM
6 BATHROOM
7 CHILDREN'S ROOM

Site Plan S=1:500

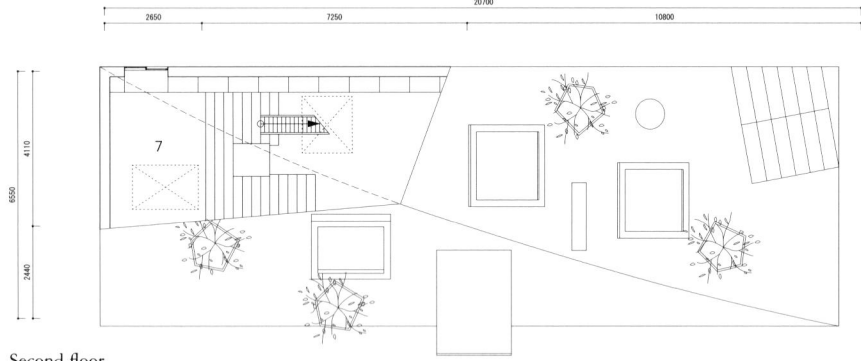

Second floor

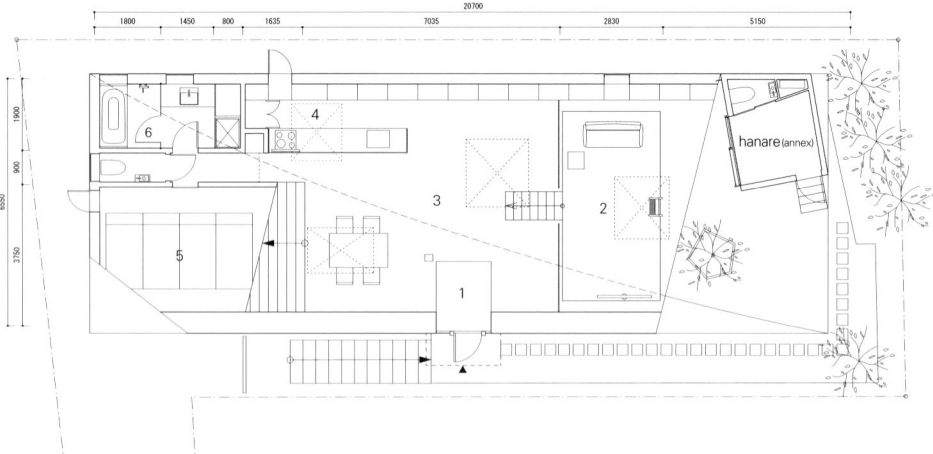

First floor S=1:200

The residence stands on a serene site enclosed by houses in a residential district in Nishinomiya, Hyogo. The idea of diagonally stretching roofs, which serve as a garden, was generated as a result of opening up a view towards a forest that stretches on the west side and planning a life that garden and interior are elaborately connected. A gradually rising roof is like a garden of slanting slope and at the same time it creates a freely extending living space under it. On the roof, pots of trees that are planted as if floating in the air dot and so the scenery is like half-artificial and half-natural mountain. Many openings are perforated on the slope. Taking in gentle light, they clearly cut out forest and sky's scenes in an unexpected distance.

Three different floor levels were set in one-room interior space; living space at a half underground level digging down the ground for 1.5 m, a kitchen and dining space at a ground level extending from an entrance hall and a living and children's room that appear after climbing up 2.5 m high steps that can be sit on variously. A master bedroom, a bathroom and other spaces were arranged under the steps. By the continuous space in various heights and the overlapping windows randomly opened in the space, eye levels differ and the extent of the space and calmness variously change.

It was very important to connect the interior and the roof garden in the residence. Moreover, if connections are more than one and residents can come and go the inside and outside at many different height levels, the life that cross the mountain-like garden and living space should become very amusing. At the end of the design it was possible to create routes to access to the garden at all three above-mentioned different levels. By crossing over inside and outside in such a way, we considered to create a relationship between in and out that is more topographical and close to nature, differing from ordinal architecture that a garden and floors are separated.

A small shed was built on the sloped garden. It is a shed that supplements a life in the garden similar to an arbor and is like a small country villa. Jointly with several furniture attached on the roof, we hope it serves as an opportunity to use the new-style garden with pleasure.

Downward view from the top of roof garden 屋根の庭から見下ろす

Approach: entrance on left　アプローチ：左は玄関

兵庫県西宮市の住宅地，周囲を家々に囲まれた落ち着きのある敷地に建つ住宅。西側に広がる森に向かって視線を開いて，庭と室内が豊かに連続するような生活を構想した結果，この斜めに伸び上がる屋根＝庭のアイディアが生まれた。緩やかに上昇する屋根は丘の斜面のような庭であり，同時にその下に伸びやかに広がる住空間を生み出す。屋根には浮いているかのように鉢植えされた樹木が点在し，半人工半自然の山のような風景である。斜面には幾つもの開口が開けられて柔らかい光を取り込みながら，意外な距離感で森や空の風景を鮮やかに切り取る。

ワンルームの室内空間には，異なる三つの床レベルを用意した。1.5メートル掘り込んだ半地下レベルのリビングスペース，エントランスから広がるキッチンとダイニングのある地上レベル，さまざまに座ることができる段々を約2.5メートル上った先にはリビング兼子供部屋。段々の下には主寝室や浴室などを収めた。これらの異なる高さのスペースが連続し，そこにランダムに穿たれた窓が重なることで，さまざまな視線の高さの違いゆえに空間の広がりや落ちつきが多様に変化する。

この家では室内と屋根の庭を繋ぐことがとても重要だった。それも1カ所ではなく，異なる幾つもの高さレベルで内と外を行き来することができれば，この山のような庭と住空間を行き交う生活がとても豊かになるに違いない。最終的には，上記の三つの異なるレベルの全てからこの庭にアクセスするルートをつくることができた。そうやって内外を自由に行き来することで，庭と階が分かれた通常の建築とは異なる，もっと地形的で自然的な内外の関係をつくり出すことを考えた。

斜面の庭の上には小さな小屋を一つ設置した。それは東屋のように庭での生活を補完する小屋でもあるし，小さな別荘のようでもある。屋根に据え付けた幾つかの家具とともに，この新しい形の庭を楽しく使ってもらえるきっかけになればと思っている。

View of dining room from living room: entrance on left　居間からの食堂の眺め：左は玄関

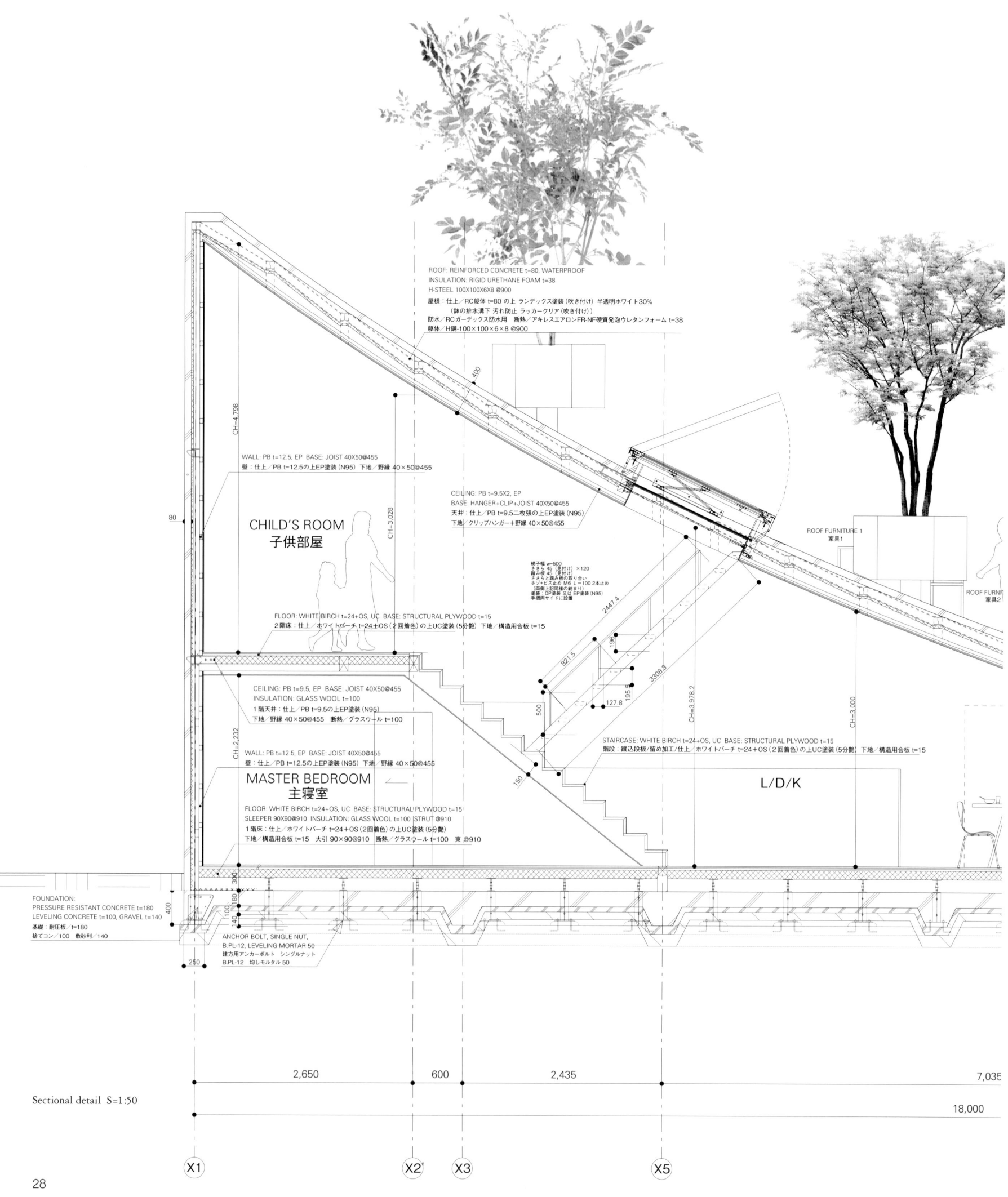

Sectional detail S=1:50

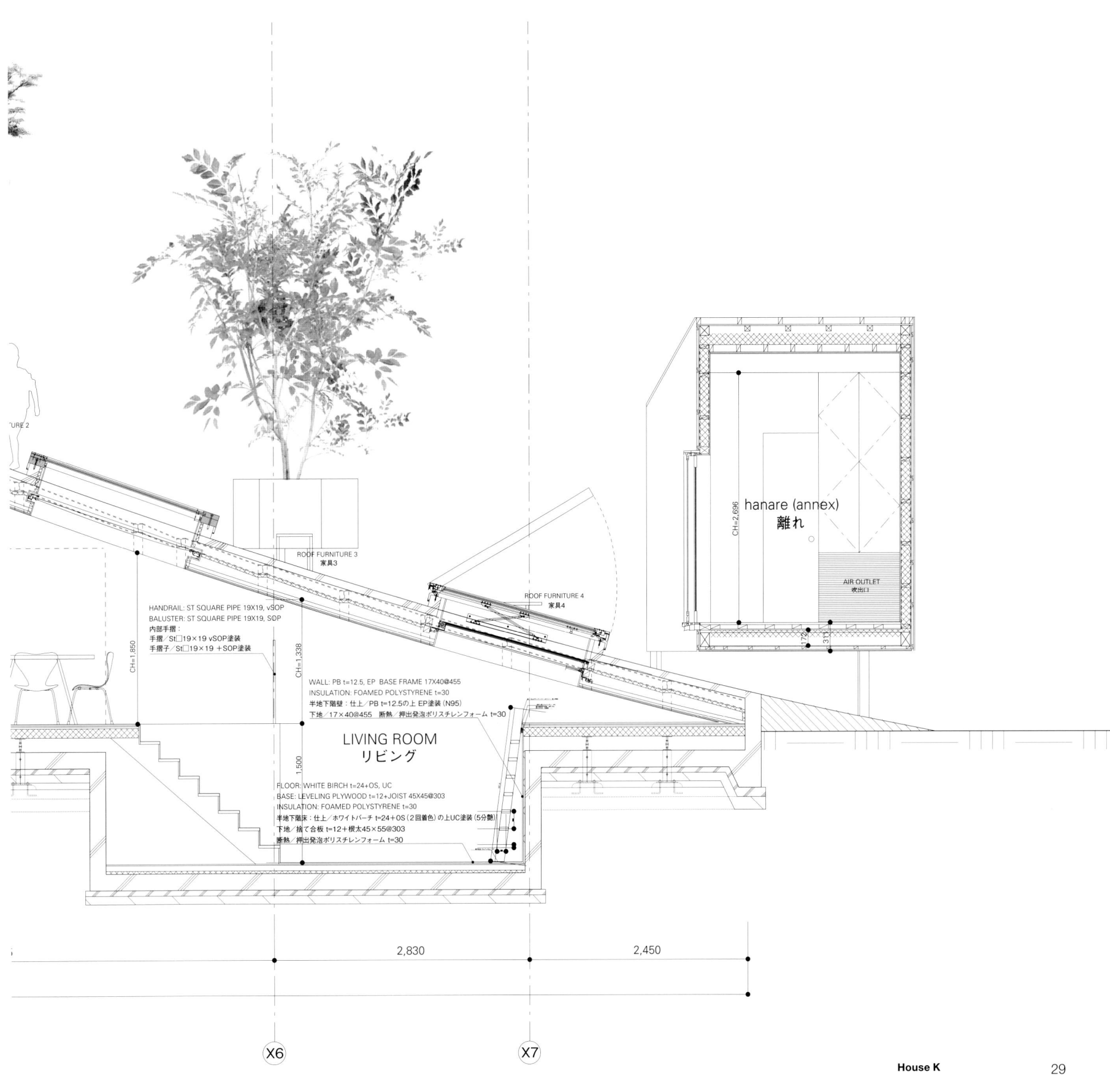

Downward view from child's room　子ども部屋からの見下ろし

Hanare (annex) 離れ

View of roof garden from hanare (annex) 離れから屋根の庭を見る

LA SMALL HOUSE

Los Angeles, California, U.S.A., 2010-
GUEST HOUSE

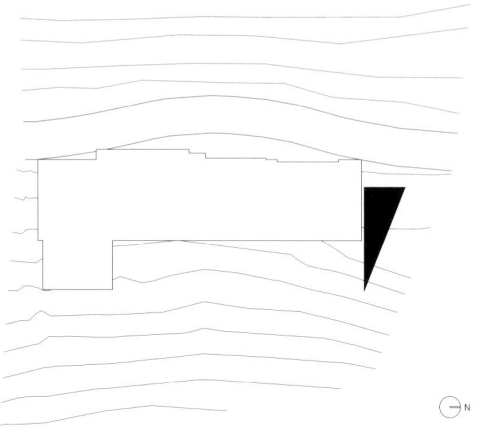

Site plan S=1:600

Level 5

Level 4
access to rooftop garden

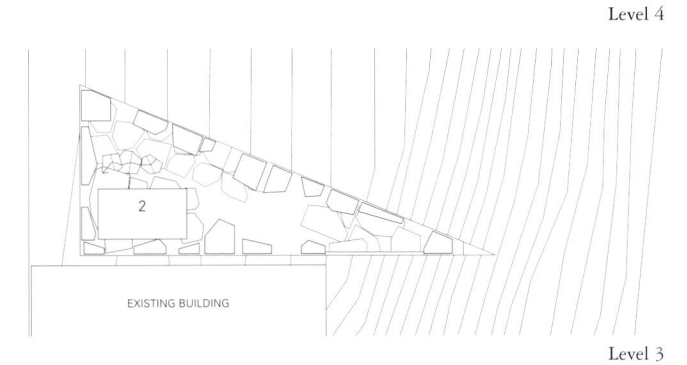

Level 3
EXISTING BUILDING

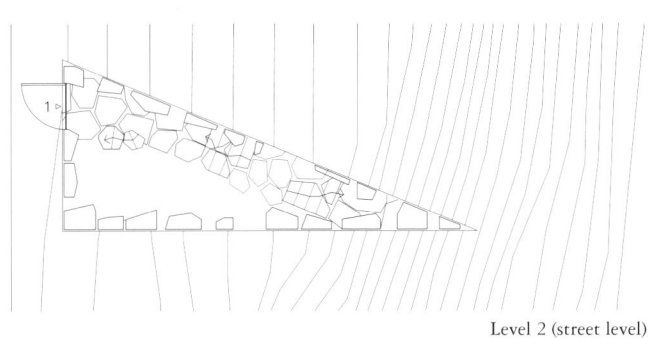

Level 2 (street level)

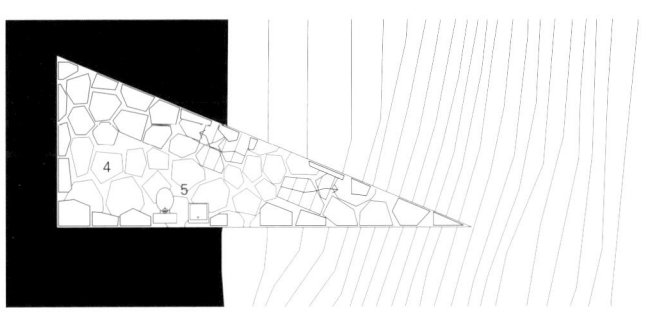

Level 1 S=1:150

1 ENTRANCE
2 SLEEPING SPACE
3 VIEWING AREA
4 SHOWER ROOM
5 WC

On the hillside of a residential area in Los Angeles, there is a simple Modern style house. The project consists of building a guestroom annex in a small plot left vacant beside the house.

What is proposed here is a new network-type structural form using fieldstone and steel rods.

A place where sparse stones appear to be floating in the air—if the prototype of architecture were the act of 'bringing sparsity to the place' and if the human body were to respond to that sparsity of place, this architecture is a direct embodiment of such 'place of density' as a prototype.

The network of rods and stones is, like a space truss, a structure in itself that integrates spaces, and for that reason, is also a set of furniture, a visual shield that blocks sunlight where density is high, as well as an open, translucent wall where density is sparse. It is an artificial, 21st-century rocky mountain or a futuristic cave where nature and the man-made intersect.

Glass supported on stone wraps the building's periphery. Various building restrictions pertaining to this sloped site defined the triangular crystal shape.

Interrelation between structure, space and function was sublimated to an architectural form. There is no doubt that such network type of form will develop on different scales, from the human body to architecture and to the city.

ロサンゼルスの斜面地の住宅地にシンプルなモダニズムスタイルの住宅が建っている。その住宅の横にわずかに空いた敷地に、ゲストルームを別棟で建てることを依頼された。

ここでは自然石とスティールロッドによるネットワーク的な新しい構造形式を提案している。

あたかも石が粗密をもって空中に浮遊しているような場所。建築の原型が「場に粗密をもたらす」ことだとするなら、そしてその場の粗密に人間の身体が応答していくものだとするなら、この建築はその原型としての「密度の場所」をダイレクトに実現する。

ロッドと石のネットワークは、あたかも立体トラスのようにそれ自体が空間を含みこんだ構造体であり、それゆえ同時に家具でもあり、また密な部分は日射や視線を遮り、疎な部分は開放的な半透明の壁となる。空間の抑揚が身体に働きかける。人工的につくられた21世紀の岩山、あるいは未来の洞窟のような、自然と人工が交錯する場所である。

建物の外周は石から支持したガラスで覆われている。斜面地の高さ制限や斜線制限から三角形状のクリスタルのような形状となった。

構造と空間と機能が相互に関係をもちあい、一つの建築的な形式に純化した。このネットワーク状の形式は、このような身体から建築、そして都市まで、スケールを変えて展開していくに違いない。

Interior

Longitudinal section S=1:150

Cross section

1 ENTRANCE
2 SLEEPING SPACE
3 VIEWING AREA
4 SHOWER ROOM
5 WC

NUBE ARENA

Las Torres de Cotillas, Spain, 2010 -
AUDITORIUM / PUBLIC SPACE

NEW PUBLIC SPACE
We believe that in the act of developing the new city of Las Torres de Cotillas, it is pertinent to, through the scope of the project for the new Auditorium of the city to offer to the citizens and visitors more than just a solitary building to house a music hall. Rather than a cultural building only used by a minority of the population, the project envisages to be a place for the people.

The project seeks to embrace a positive fusion of the Auditorium program and the Public space. The public space, is three-dimensionally interlaced in a continuum providing a platform for people to gather, meet and exchange, all over and around the building.

RE-INTERPRETING THE TYPOLOGY; FROM TRADITIONAL TO NEW
The new auditorium for Las Torres de Cotillas pays homage to the classical Theatre form of Carthagena arena, which is a symbolic idea for congregation and gathering. The design is initiated from this base reference in pursuit of a new typology, which will allow the performance chamber for a myriad of different application and uses.

NEW URBAN ICON
The new Auditorium for Las Torres de Cotillas is open towards the city on all directions. The ambiguous yet prominent public interface, and people's activity itself becomes a New Icon of the city, set in the center of the new city development. It combines and fuses together dissimilar programs and becomes a new interface between the commercial-business park, the natural reserve, and the future city development.

Beyond its primary functions of auditorium and school, the project defines new qualities of civic-ness; to be connected with the larger community. The new urban icon becomes a new landscape in constant evolution, setting a tempo for growth and life of the new city, which in turn affects its inhabitants.

FLEXIBILITY
Unlike the typical theatre formation, the spiral with the performance chamber in the center sets a strong focal point and an unique engagement to the city around it. The traditional front-and-back is replaced with an open-ness which enables a flexible theatre experience, and can accommodate diverse uses and configurations; from grande three-dimensional amphitheatre, typical proscenium theatre to flat-floor open-air convention.

Movable panel system allows enclosure and optimises the extent of space used for the auditorium, depending on the act, or program, spaces can be configured to suit. When the entire panels are stripped open, one will see the world's first open-air, naturally ventilated auditorium.

FUNCTION COMPOSITION/FORMATION
The programs are interlaced around the spiral, it is dispersed, not distant to one another but all sharing the same spiral and being able to co-exist and feel one another.

CIRCULATION
There are two grand approaches to the spiral; one being the public access which will lead you to the main cafe and to the exhibition space, and the other being the Auditorium entrance which leads you to the lobby space for the theatre functions. Moving into the spiral, the routes overlap and crosses at many intersections allowing one to traverse onto the other spirals. Lift access points are located at every half spiral to make the access to the upper and lower levels efficiently.

Level 1

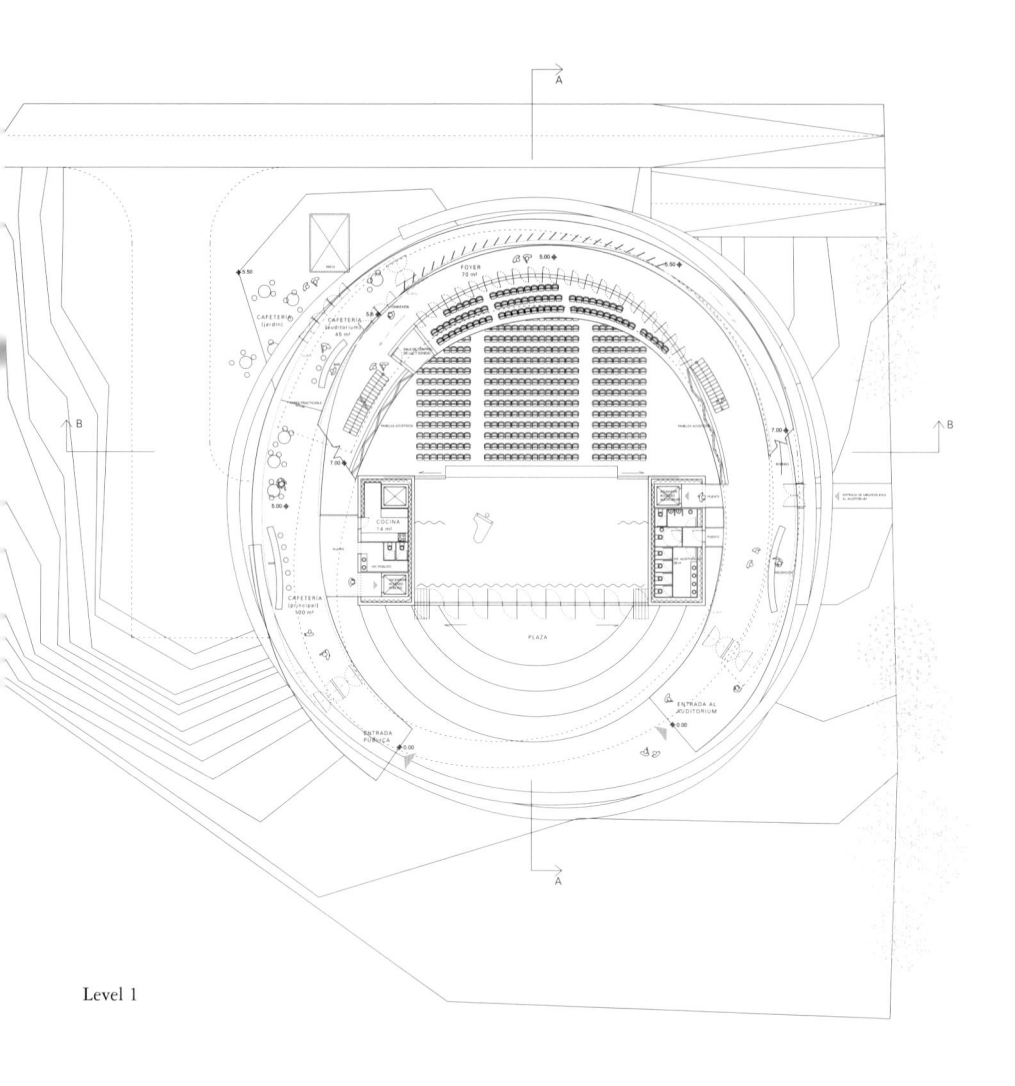

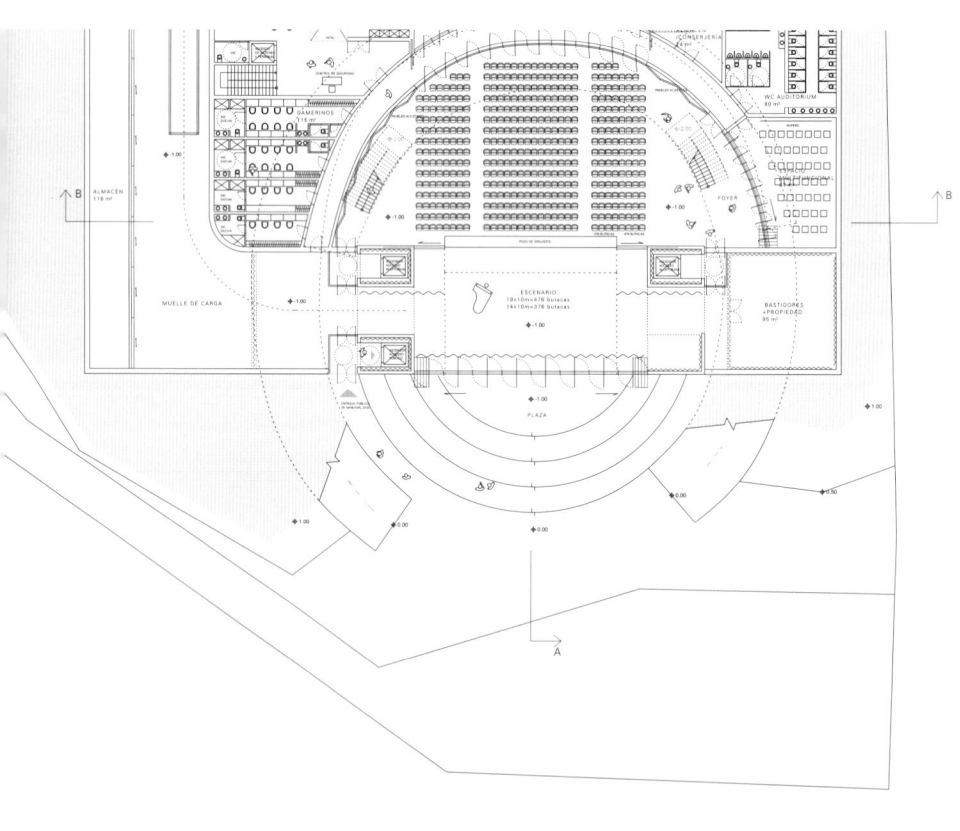

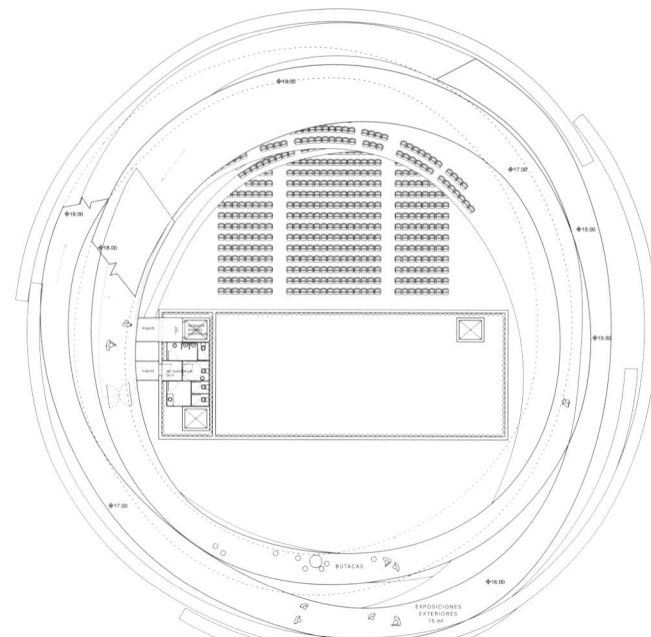

Basement

Level 4

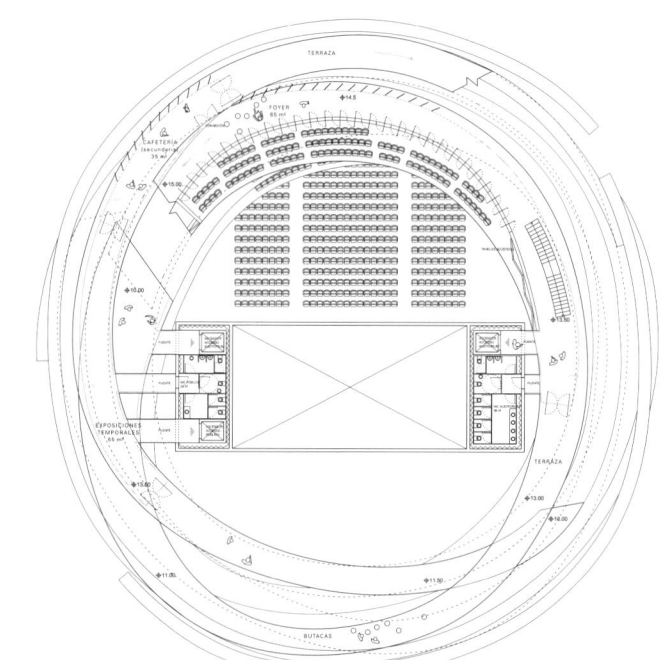

Level 3

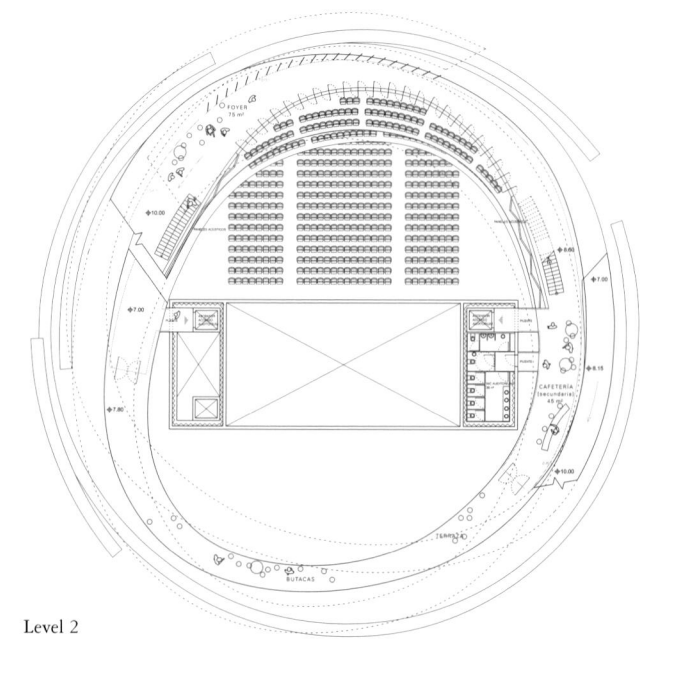

Level 2

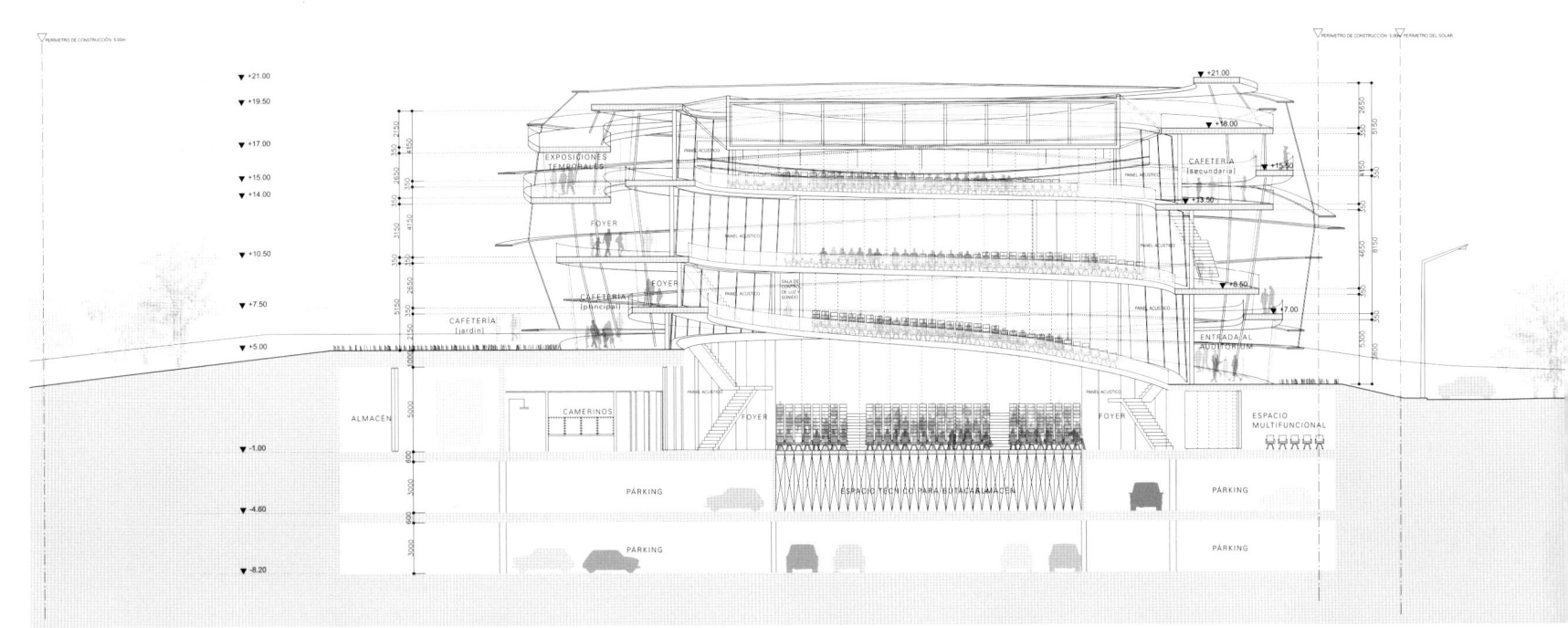

Section BB

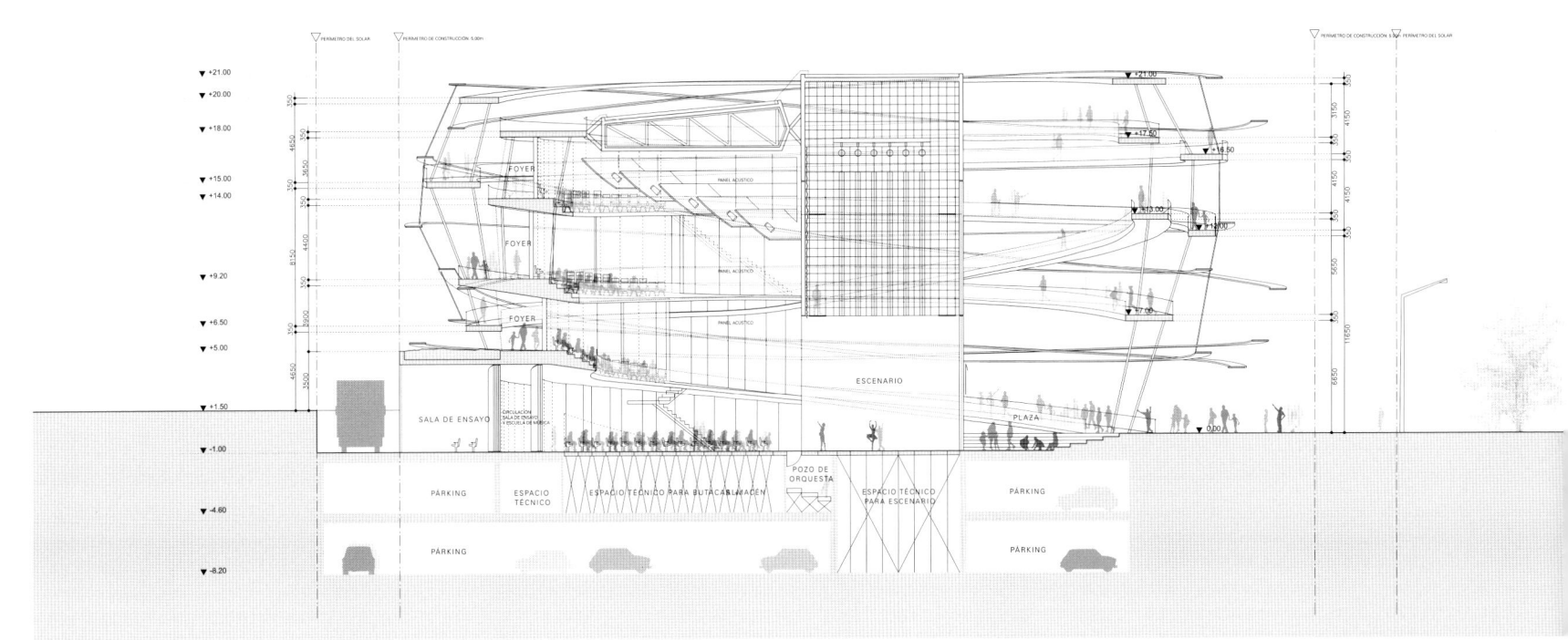

Section AA S=1:400

Nube Arena

Diagram

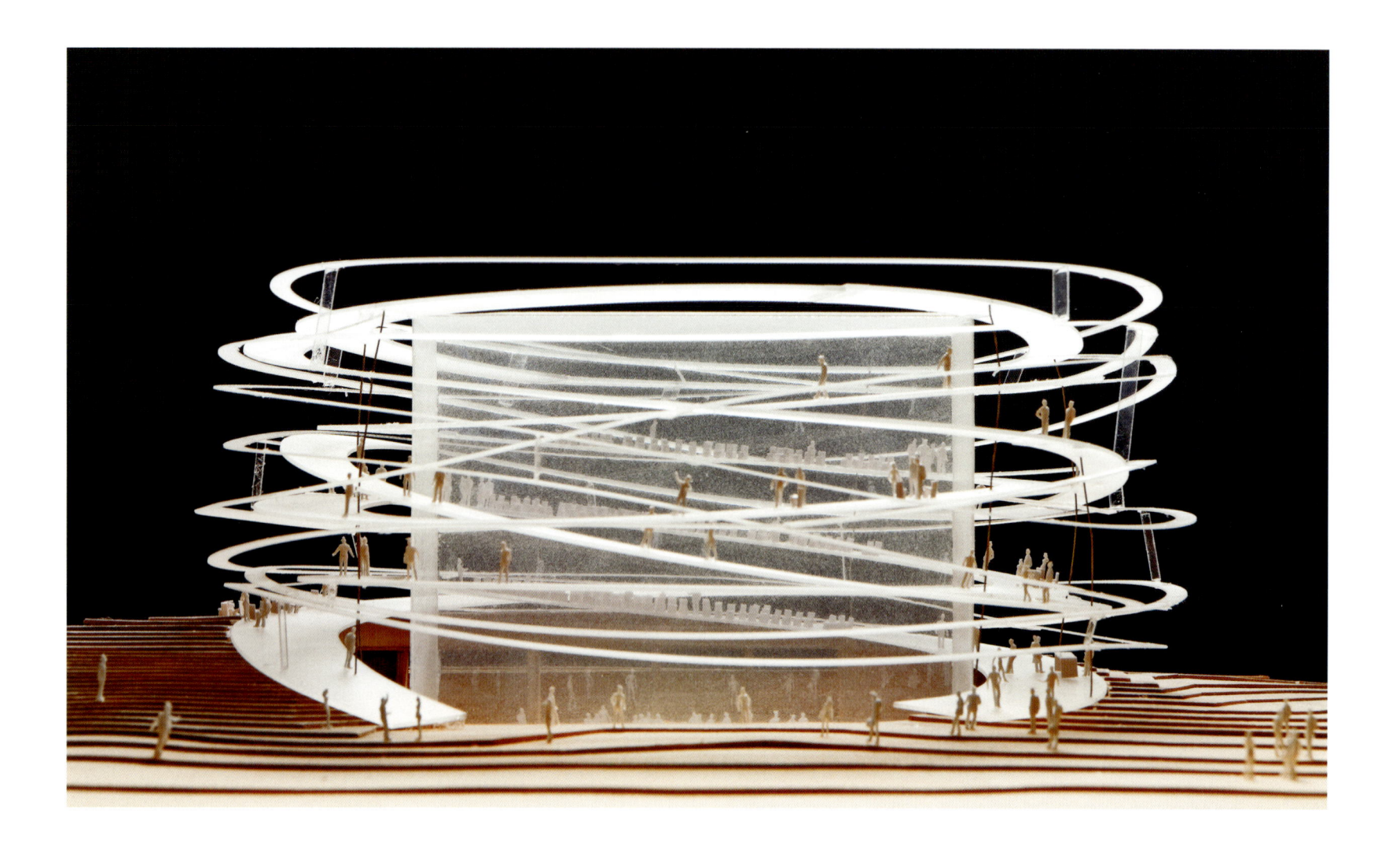

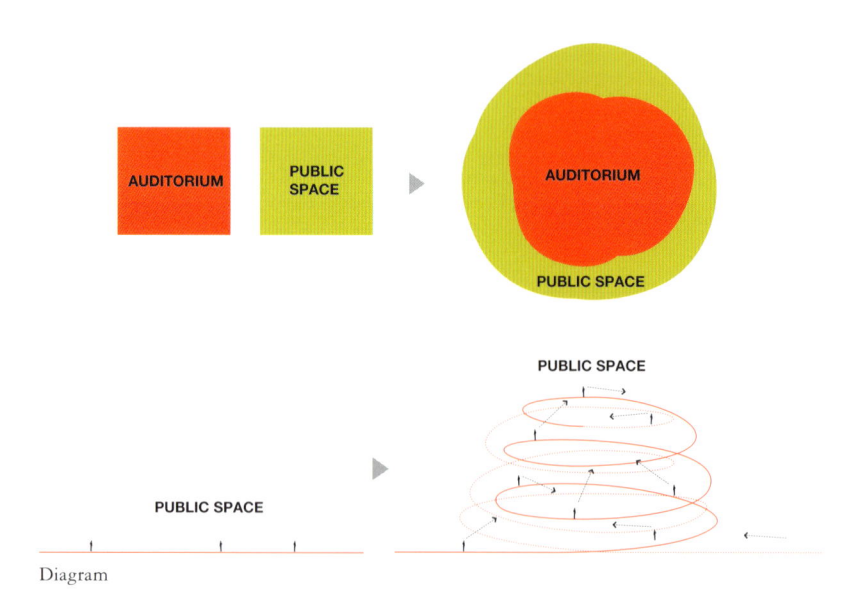

スペインのムルシアという街に800人のシアターを設計する国際コンペの2等案。

ここでは，人が集まる場所というものの原型的な，それでいて新しい形式を生み出すことを考えた。

劇場とは，つまり人が集まる場所である。でもその集まり方は，単に劇や音楽を聞くということを超えて，もっと多様であっていいのではないか，と考えることから設計が始まった。

この建築の骨格は，二つの渦を巻くスパイラル状のフロアが絡み合うことによってつくられる。それは古典的なアリーナの現代的な再構築とでも言える強い求心性を持つと同時に，雲のようなあいまいな領域によって緩やかに人の集まる場所をつくり出すとも言える。強い形式とあいまいさが同居している。閉じた求心性ではなく，開いた場である。このアリーナの中央にステージとフライタワーを配置することによって，半分は内部のシアターとして通常の劇場空間をつくり出し，残りの半分は外部のシアターとして，都市に開いた公共空間を生み出す。中央のステージは，状況によって内外それぞれのステージとして機能し，またステージの前後を開くことで内外を一体的に利用する大きなアリーナともなる。

中央の空間を取り巻く渦巻状のフロアは，エントランスであり，動線であり，ホワイエであり，またバルコニー型の客席の一部でもあり，カフェでもあり，展望スペースでもあり，小さな展示スペースも備えている。渦巻をめぐるパブリックな動線を備えていて，観劇を目的としない人々にとっても，気軽に集まることができる立体的な街路空間となることを意図した。ホワイエと劇場を隔てる防音壁は開閉式とし，劇場を使用していないときには開放され，またイベントによっては，ホワイエも含みこんだ全体を一体的に使うことも可能となる。

劇場という複雑なプログラムのすべてをこの中に内包したうえで，さらに都市的な機能を取り

Plaza

Plaza

込むことで，都市に開いた新しい劇場の在り方をとてもシンプルな形式として提示している。

大きなイベントのときに熱狂的に人が集まる場所であると同時に，イベントがないときにも，日常の生活の中で気軽に人々が集まり，時間を過ごし，ときにその両方が混在することで，新しい都市生活が生まれる。日常から非日常の間をグラデーションでつないでいくこと。都市的なスケール，インフラ的なスケールから建築のスケールを通り抜けて，家具的な身体スケールまでをつないでいくこと。

人が集まるという，とてもぼんやりとした，それでいてすべての日常のよりどころとなるような，そんなあいまいな状況に，「形」を与えるということ。その「形」は，現代においては，鮮やかな形式でありながら，どこまでもあいまいな，雲のような存在となるであろう。

Auditorium

Exhibition

Nube Arena

KULTUR PROJEKTE BERLIN

Berlin, Germany, 2010 -
EXHIBITION SPACE

Site

Clouds as a landmark in the city

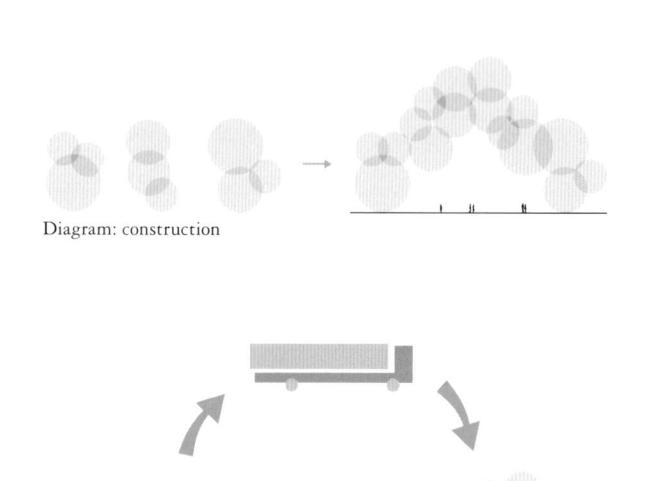

Diagram: construction

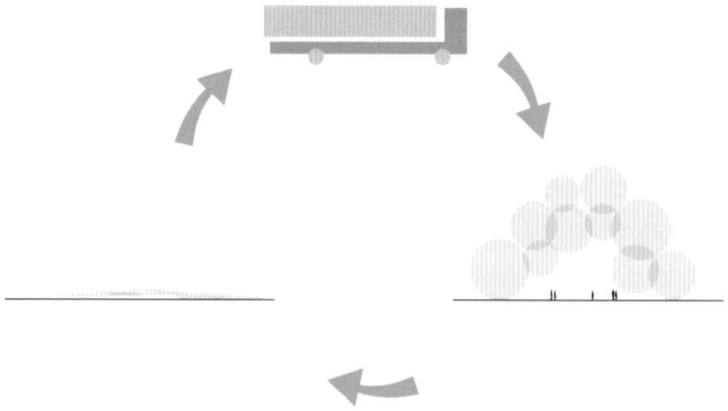

Diagram: re-use

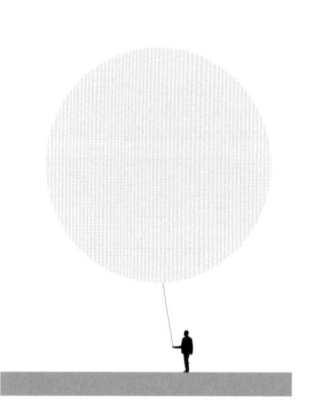

LIGHTNESS

Inside of each balloon, is a bi-mixture of Helium gas and air. Simple calculation of its ratio enables a buoyancy level to be lighter than that of its own dead-load (mass), in effect achieving a balloon which does not rely on any conventional sub-structural support. By minimising the quantity of material mass used, a structure which is far economical than conventional architectural approach possible in its area coverage is realised.

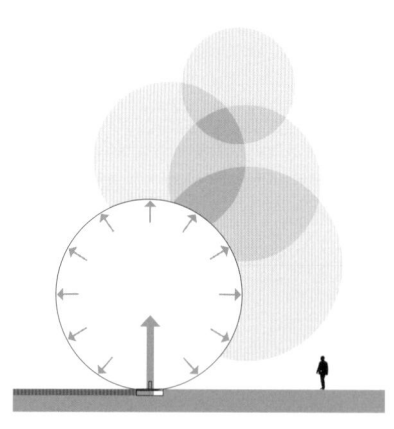

STRUCTUTURE

The convexo-concaved interior space covered by air and helium insulation creates a complex convection of heat, under the principle of a chimney-effect the heat can be stored or released through ventilation openings above to optimise the interior environment.

1. Grand space

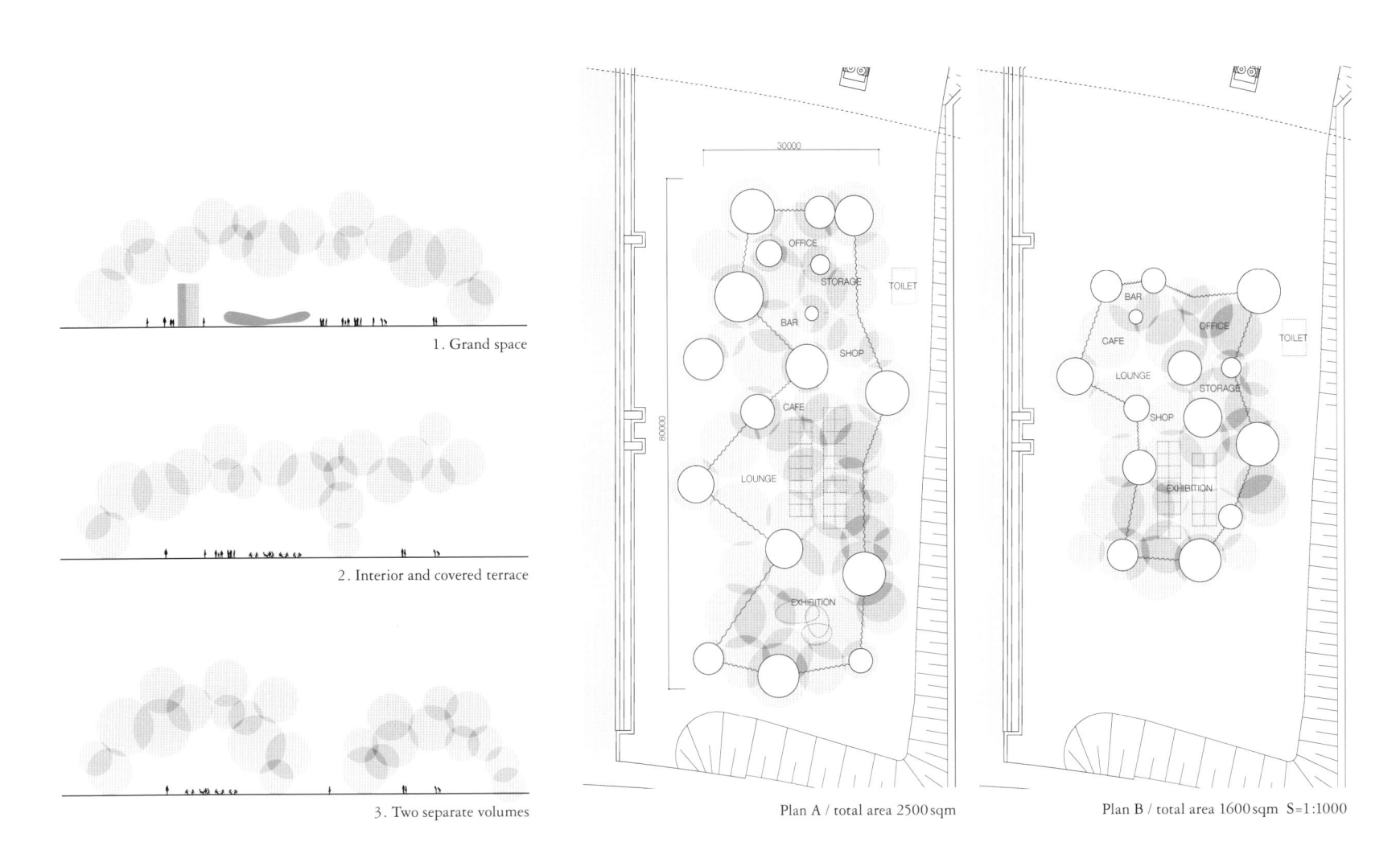

2. Interior and covered terrace

3. Two separate volumes

Plan A / total area 2500 sqm

Plan B / total area 1600 sqm S=1:1000

CONCEPT

The design specification for a Contemporary Art Exhibition set in Berlin, identifies a culmination of both innovation, economics and sustainability. Keeping this as its premise, we propose a space created by a lightweight, air-membrane structure.

This archipelago of balloons are all filled with a bi-mixture of helium and air. Being able to support its load solely by its buoyancy, the proposal envisages a new experiential roof form in a very moderate means.

The richly diverse space which emerges from this clouds offers much flexibility in its uses, which will foster dynamic engagement between the people.

Being both architecturally unique, the being which innately drift between the peripheral nature and the water of Spree river will endow a iconic existence which can clearly be seen from the surrounding.

CONSTRUCTING THE CLOUD

The cloud balloons are made from lightweight membrane skin, which is inflated upon the erection of the event.

The balloons, when deflated can be folded and compacted to fit into a conventional shipping container. The fabrication can either be undertaken off-site or on-site, and the inflation at any desired location. It can simply be fixed to a train, or a tugboat to be transported to the site.

And its attachment to one another can be procured in numerous levels, not necessarily requiring a highly trained trade.

The lightweight property of the membrane structure also allow the structure to be reallocated and inflated over and over again for continued re-uses.

FURTHER POSSIBILITIES

The cloud-like structure inflated prior to the opening, erected off-site and being transported by a mobile means. If budget allows, this entire course of process itself can become a promotion for the event.

The balloons when not in direct use, can be posited, floating on the Spree river; as another island beside the Museum Island.

This balloon becomes the icon for the Kultur Projekte Berlin.

DIVERSITY AND FLEXIBILITY

Resulting from dramatic budgetary reasons or a change in site, the scheme can accommodate radical changes in spatial requirements, form or size, and equally the plan of how the space will be segmented and used.

1. The size and scale of the cloud can be adjusted to suit the reduction in quantity of balloons.

2. The scheme is able to accommodate significant spatial requirements, i.e.; high ceiling space, long continuous space, etc...

3. The scheme can be cross-matched to facilitate smaller compartmentalized partitions.

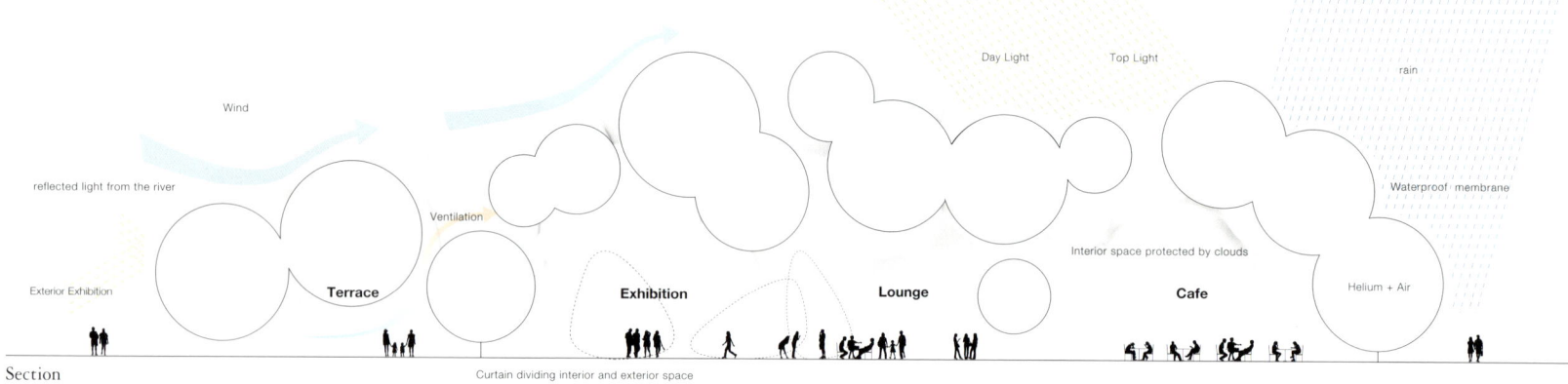

Section

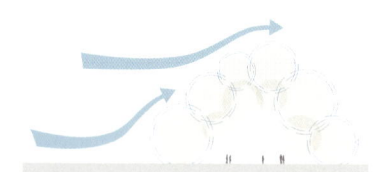

Wind • reflected light from the river • Exterior Exhibition • Terrace • Ventilation • Exhibition • Lounge • Day Light • Top Light • Cafe • rain • Waterproof membrane • Interior space protected by clouds • Helium + Air

Curtain dividing interior and exterior space

FORM
The non-solid and elastic qualities of the material is suited to distributing external loads throughout the entire structure avoiding structural stress to subsist on specific locations.

WATERPROOF
As the entire structure is composed of surfaces, it is also possible to fabricate the surfaces so as to achieve full waterproofing membrane above the exhibition where waterproofing is a pertinent task.

VENTILATION
The convexo-concaved interior space covered by air and helium insulation creates a complex convection of heat, under the principle of a chimney-effect the heat can be stored or released through ventilation openings above to optimise the interior environment.

DAY LIGHT
The convexo-concaved interior space covered by air and helium insulation creates a complex convection of heat, under the principle of a chimney-effect the heat can be stored or released through ventilation openings above to optimise the interior environment.

1. Change in size and scale

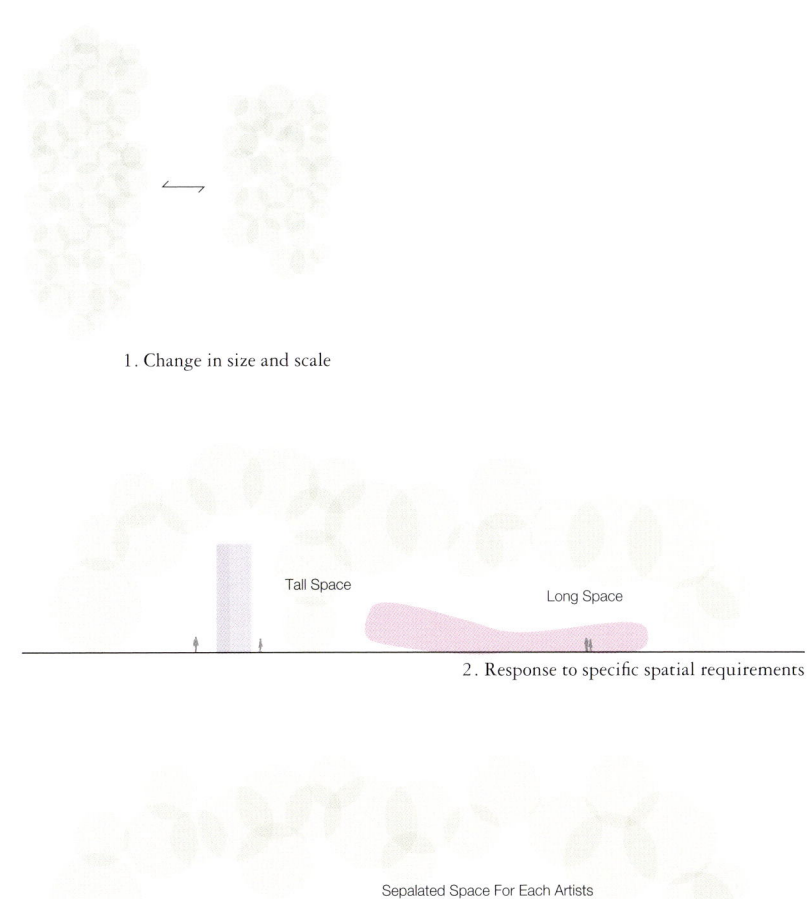

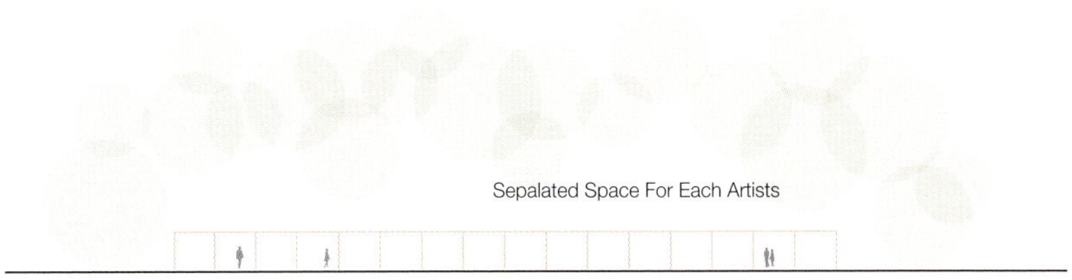

2. Response to specific spatial requirements

Tall Space　　Long Space

Sepalated Space For Each Artists

3. In conjunction with diverse space altering devices or systems

ARTIFICIAL LIGHT
The convexo-concaved interior space covered by air and helium insulation creates a complex convection of heat, under the principle of a chimney-effect the heat can be stored or released through ventilation openings above to optimise the interior environment.

コンセプト

ベルリン現代美術展の構成計画に求められたのは，イノベーション，経済性，サステイナビリティの極致を表現することにある。この計画はそのような前提条件の下で行われた軽量のメンブレイン構造による空間の提案である。

群島のように連なるバルーンには，ヘリウムと空気の混合気体が注入されている。浮力というごくありふれた方法によって自重を支えると共に，新しく実験的な屋根形状を構想することが今回の提案である。

クラウドが生み出す豊かな多様性は，一層多くの利用可能性を空間に付与するのと共に，人と人とのダイナミックな相互の交流を促している。

建築としての独創性と，周囲の自然とシュプレー川の水面を在るがまま漂う様は，周囲の環境から容易に識別できるアイコンとしての存在感をクラウドに与えている。

クラウドの建設

クラウド・バルーンは軽量のメンブレイン膜で構成される。イベント会場では上空で膨らませて使用する。

バルーンは空気を抜くと，通常の貨物コンテナのサイズへとコンパクトに折りたたまれる。敷地の内外で組み立て，あるいは必要とあれば場所を選ばず膨張させることができる。また，単純に列車へと固定し，あるいはタグボートで敷地まで運搬することも可能である。

バルーンは高度に熟練した技術を必要とすることもなく，様々なレベルで相互に連結させることができる。

何回も再利用するために構造を再配置して膨張させることができるのは，軽量なメンブレイン膜構造の特徴である。

更なる可能性

クラウド構造はオープニングに先立ち予め膨張させることで，敷地の外で組み立ててから移動して搬入することができる。予算に見合えば全体の生成プロセスもイベントのプロモーションとすることができる。

バルーンは使わない際，博物館島に浮かぶもうひとつの島として，シュプレー川に係留される。

このバルーンはベルリン文化プロジェクトのアイコンである。

多様性とフレキシビリティ

予算の大胆な削減や敷地の変更の結果，基本構成は空間的必要条件，形態や規模，あるいは空間のセグメント化と利用計画の決定に至るまで，ラディカルな変更にも適応可能なものとなった。

1. バルーンの数を減らし，クラウドの規模とスケールを最適化することが可能である。
2. 例えば天井のある空間，あるいは長く連続した空間といったように，基本構成は必要とされる空間条件へと適応することができる。
3. 基本構成は異なるものを組み合わせることで，小パーティションとして区画を構成することができる。

PUBLIC TOILET IN ICHIHARA

Ichihara, Chiba, Japan, 2011-12
PUBLIC LAVATORY

This is a public lavatory standing next to the Itabu station, of the local line "Kominato Railway" that passes through north to south of Ichihara city of the Chiba prefecture. It is consisted from two toilets; one is for a unisex including disabled and for female only. The Itabu station has such beautiful scenery that many people visit there, when Japanese cherries and field mustards are in full blossoms, and the leisurely atmosphere from the surrounding wooded near village is an attracted. We planned to design a public lavatory that suits the unique and beautiful environment.

In one way, this smallest public facility has opposit concept, i.e. publicness and privateness. As for that, close and protect from the surroundings will be a basic premise. However building in such a beautiful environment, how to not merely close but to keep closing and open to the surroundings at the same time was the subject. This concurrent subject is namely to question the primitive form of architecture. Furthermore due to surrounding beautiful nature, the question arises how to approach and architecturize the nature. Additionally how do we transform this tininess into a new value? This project stands at crossing point where all sorts of standards, i.e. public and private, opening and closing, nature and architecture and smallness and bigness.

The wall consisted by the 2 m high log-piles surround the approximately 200 square meter area with trees and flowers growing in. This isolated garden enclosed by the wall, we placed a glass box toilet. The whole natural garden that is closed from the sight of the people around is the area for the toilet. Cause of the simple boundary of the inside/outside and multiple layers of the meaning, following senses will always be ambiguous in a away but blend in to each other: public and private, openness and a sense of protection, nature and architecture, inside and outside, bigness and smallness. This is a proposal of a primitive form of architecture.

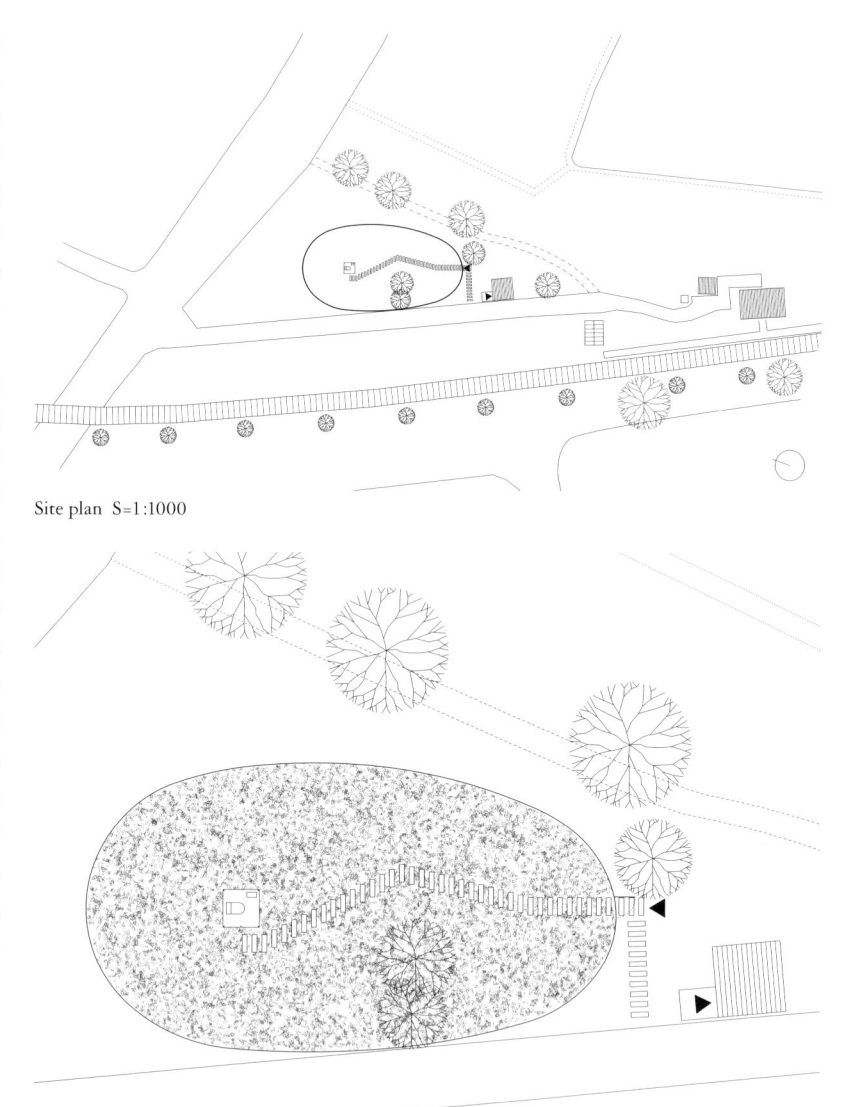

Site plan S=1:1000

Plan S=1:300

Section S=1:150

千葉県市原市を南北に通過するローカル線「小湊鉄道」の飯給駅に隣接して建つ小さな公衆トイレ。男女兼身障者用と女性専用の計二つのトイレからなる。飯給駅は桜や菜の花のシーズンには大勢の写真家が訪れるほどの美しい景観を誇る駅であり，周囲の里山のゆったりとした雰囲気が魅力的である。そのような美しい環境ならではの公衆トイレをつくることを考えた。

公衆トイレとは，ある意味で，最も小さな公共施設である。そして公共の場所でありながら，同時にとてもプライベートな場所である。それゆえ，周囲から閉ざし守るということが大前提となるが，このような美しい環境の中では，単に閉ざすのではなく，閉ざしながらいかに開くかということが問われる。そしてこの閉ざしながら開くということは，すなわち建築の原型を問い直すことである。また周囲が美しい自然であるゆえに，その自然をどう取り込み，建築化するのかという問いも生じる。さらにこの小ささをどう新しい価値に変換するか。公共とプライベート，開くと閉じる，自然と建築，そして小さいことと大きいこと，そのようなさまざまな尺度が交わる場所に，この公衆トイレのプロジェクトは位置しているのだ。

高さ2メートルの丸太杭による壁が，木々や草花の生い茂る約200平米の領域を取り囲む。その壁で囲われた庭の中に，ガラスボックスのトイレを配置した。周囲の視線から閉ざされたこの自然の庭全体がトイレの領域である。このシンプルな内外の境界の乖離と多層化によって，公共とプライベート，開放性と守られた感覚，自然と建築，内部と外部，大きなことと小さなことが常に両義性を持ちながら溶け合っていく。原型的な建築の提案である。

Aerial view

View toward a glass box toilet

Public Toilet in Ichihara

NORMANDY RENOVATION PROJECT

Normandy, France, 2011-
RESIDENCE

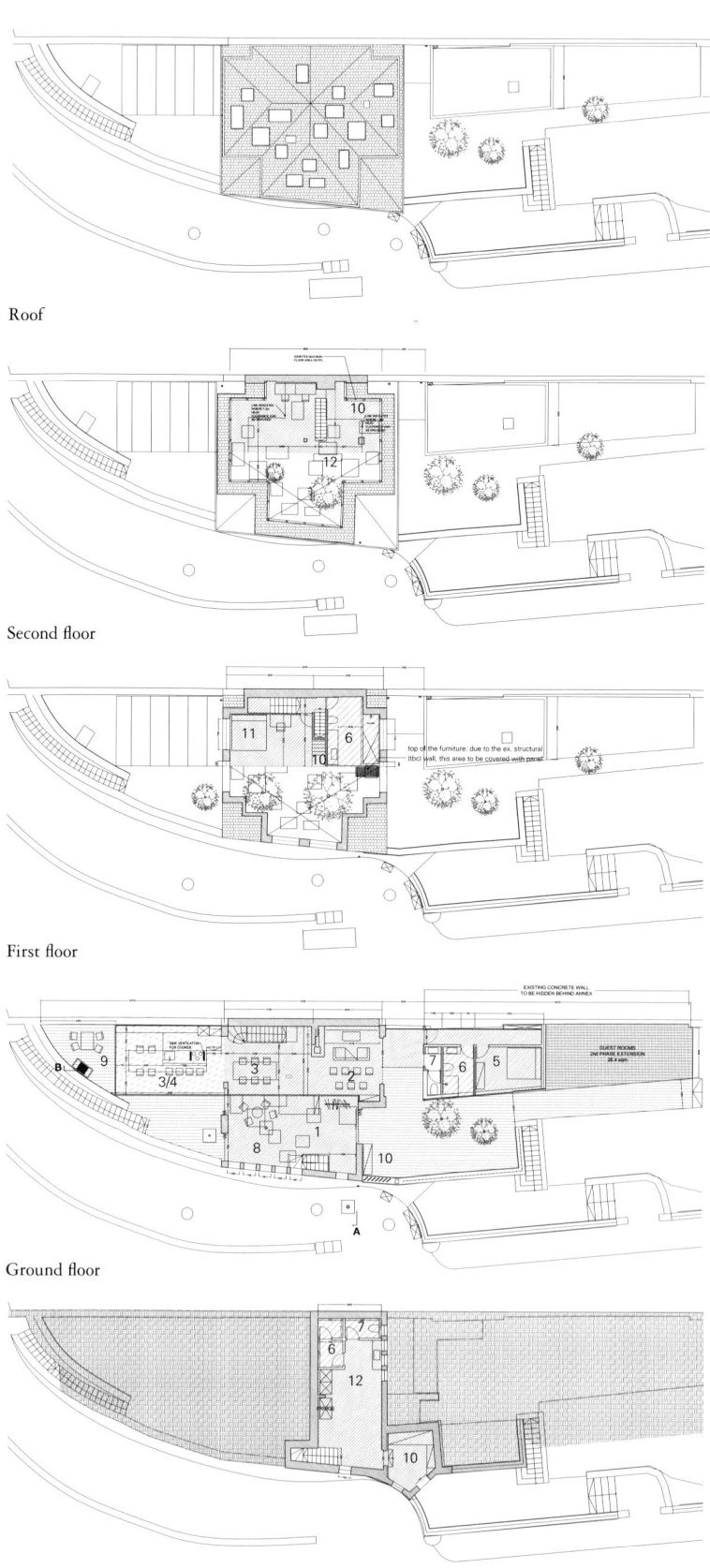

Roof

Second floor

First floor

Ground floor

Basement S=1:400

1. ENTRANCE LOBBY
2. LIVING ROOM
3. DINING ROOM
4. KITCHEN
5. GUEST ROOM
6. BATHROOM
7. TOILET
8. ROOFED GARDEN
9. TERRACE
10. STORAGE
11. MASTER BEDROOM
12. LAUNDRY
13. CHILDREN'S ROOM
14. BARBECUE AREA

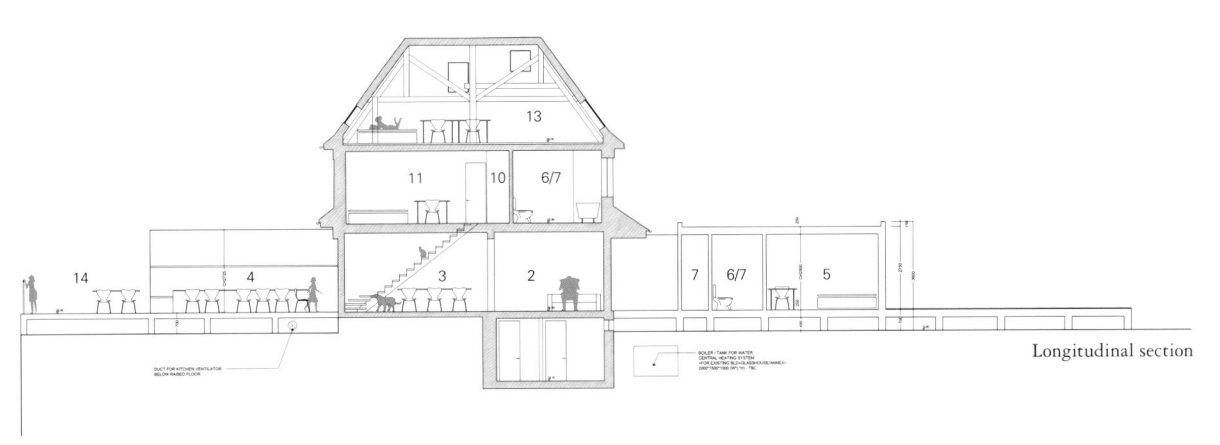

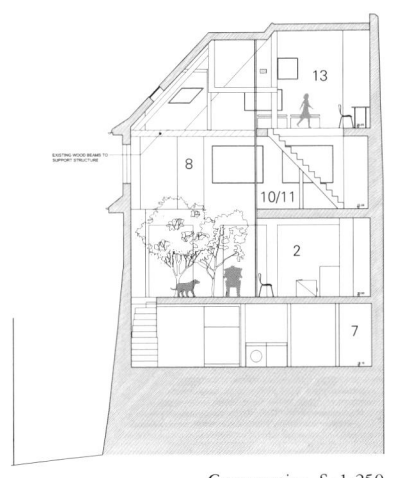

Elevation S=1:250

Longitudinal section

Cross section S=1:250

The project is a renovate plan of a 50-year-old house built facing Strait of Dover in the Normandy region. Rather than to renovate a building, the design was go-ahead with a sense to take the existing building as a clue and to reconstitute the living space. Because of the regulation of scenery treaty, the appearance of the existing building was preserved as it was. On the contrary, the inside was emptied as if curving the space out and it was made into an inner garden. Living space and family bedrooms were constituting just like to install a glass box in the inner garden. Multiplicity of the outside space was created by placing the inner garden between a terrace on the sea side and a garden on the land side. In addition, low-rise bedrooms on the land side will be arranged as an annex.

ノルマンディー地方，ドーバー海峡に面して建つ築50年の住宅の改修計画。建物を改修するというよりも，既存の建物を手がかりにして，生活空間を再構成するという感覚で設計を進めていった。景観条例の規制ゆえに，既存建物の外観はそのまま保存し，逆に内部をくり抜くように空っぽにし，そこをインナー・ガーデンとする。生活空間と家族の寝室などは，そのインナー・ガーデンにガラスの箱を設置するように再構成した。海側のテラスと陸側の庭の間にインナー・ガーデンを位置づけることで外部空間の多様性をつくり出す。また陸側には別棟で低層の寝室を配置する。

Normandy Renovation Project

BETON HALA WATERFRONT CENTER
Belgrade, Serbia, 2011-
COMMERCIAL BUILDING COMPLEX

Plan: 7-12 m S=1:1000

Concept

Beton Hala Waterfront Center

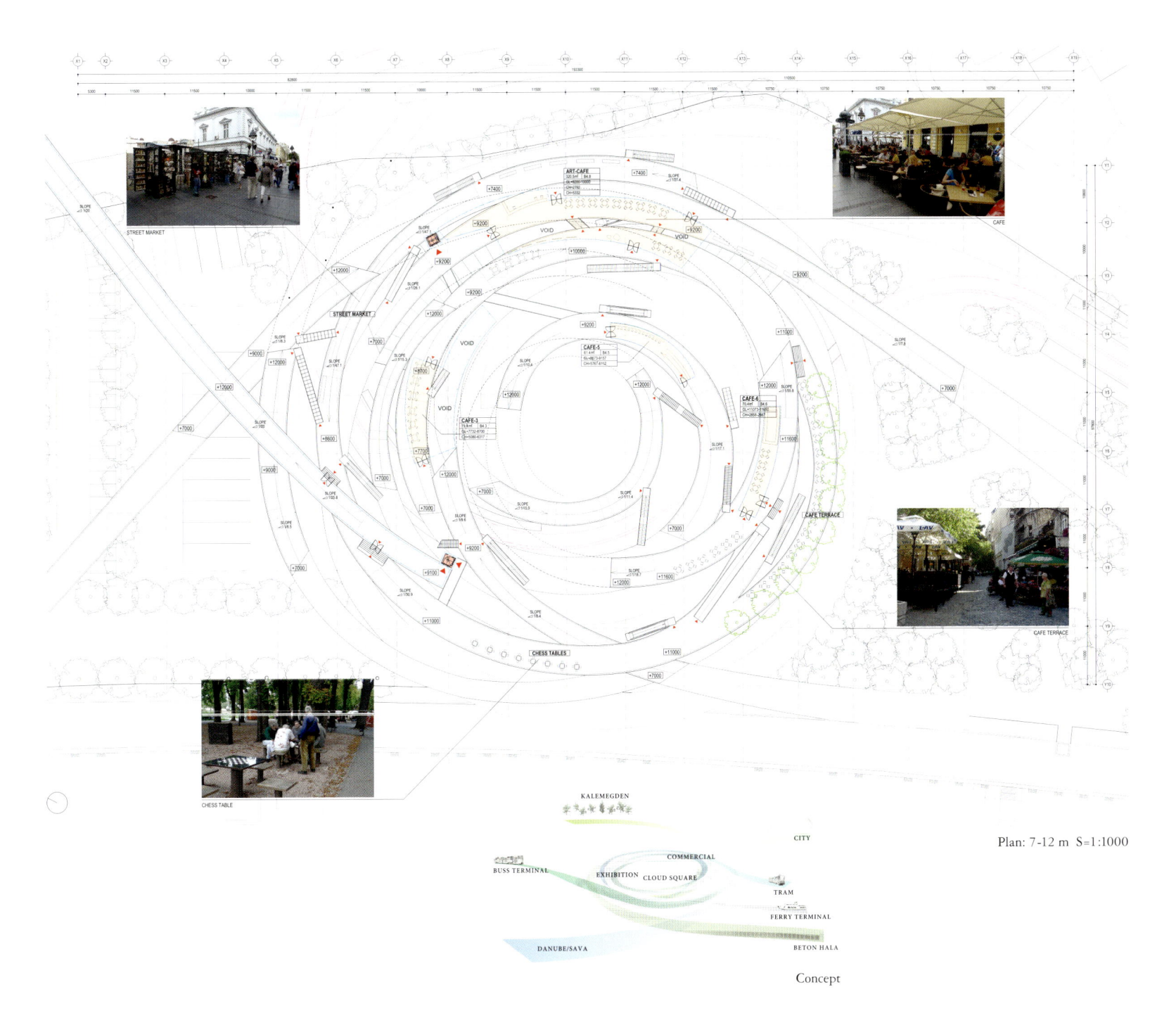

The project was aimed at creating a new urban base on a site adjacent to an old district in Serbia's capital, Belgrade. An international open competition was held in 2011 and Sou Fujimoto Architects was awarded the first prize.

The site is a triangle zone of Belgrade's old city district, a historical inherited fortress and Belgrade's lifeline, Sava River, which is connected to the Danube. Additionally, renovating and revitalizing Beton Hala, warehouses built facing the river, is included in the project.

The site that is surrounded by the old district, the fortress and the river is assumed to serve as a hub of touring, which people destine from different directions and disperse from to their goals. As a harbor of Danube cruise is adjoining, many tourists flow in and trams run through the site. Further, water taxis and bus stations are planned. Many visitors come from the fortress on a hill and from the old district and migrate towards their objectives. So to speak, the site might be 'flux' itself, or it might be a place of 'the center of whirl of various flows'. The idea of realizing the recognition of the situation into architecture formed the bone structure of the group of whirling slopes.

The whirl of overlapping slopes does not hinder the view of the backdrop fortress just like a moderate hill on appearance, but the spiral assembly of flow produces an overwhelming centripetal force as an urban open space where many people gather. Various inside space dot between spiral's interstice and functions such as cafes and galleries are allocated. It might be that the whole architecture, as it were, function as an infrastructure to generate people's density. A sense of denseness made by crowd, rather than the shape of buildings, makes the place special and a new shaped three-dimensional urban open space is formed.

This is a gigantic architectural open space weaved with many small paths. Small and big scale connectedly coexists. We formulated a new figure of architecture and city that crosses body, architecture, city, infrastructure and landscape.

このプロジェクトは，セルビアの首都ベオグラード旧市街に隣接する敷地に新しい都市の拠点をつくり出すものである。2011年に国際オープンコンペが行われ，藤本壮介建築設計事務所案が一等に選ばれた。

敷地はベオグラード旧市街と歴史遺産である城塞，そしてベオグラードの生命線であるサバ川—ドナウ川に挟まれた三角地帯であり，また川に面して建てられた倉庫群（ベトンハラと呼ばれる）を改修し再生することが計画に含まれている。

旧市街・城塞・川に囲まれたこの敷地は，人々がさまざまな方向からこの場所を目指して集まり，そしてまたそれぞれの目的地に向かって散っていくような，観光の拠点となることが想定されていた。ドナウ川クルーズの船着き場が隣接してそこから大勢の観光客が流れ込み，トラムが敷地内を通り抜け，水上タクシーやバスステーションが設置される。丘の上に位置する城塞や旧市街からも多くの観光客が流れてきて，それぞれの目的地に向かって移動していく。この敷地は，いわばそのような「流れ」そのものなのではないか，あるいは「さまざまな流れが合流する渦の中心」のような場所だと言えるのではないだろうか？ そしてそのような状況の認識をそのまま建築にすることは出来ないだろうか？ という発想から，この渦巻くスロープの群れという骨格が生まれてきた。

幾重にも重なるスロープの渦は，外観は控えめな丘のように背後の城塞への視線を妨げない佇まいを見せながらも，そのスパイラル状の動線の集合は人々が集まる場所としての都市広場としての圧倒的な求心性をつくり出す。スパイラルの隙間にはいくつもの内部空間が点在し，カフェやギャラリーなどの機能は割り当てられる。この建築全体は，いわば人の密度をつくり出すためのインフラとして機能していると言えるのではないだろうか。建物の形自体というよりも，人々の集合する密度感がこの場所を特別なものとし，新しい形の立体的な都市広場が生まれる。

それはいくつもの小道で編み上げられた巨大な建築的な広場である。小さなスケールと大きなスケールが連続的に共存する。身体と建築と都市，インフラストラクチャー，そしてランドスケープを横断していく新しい建築／都市の姿を構想した。

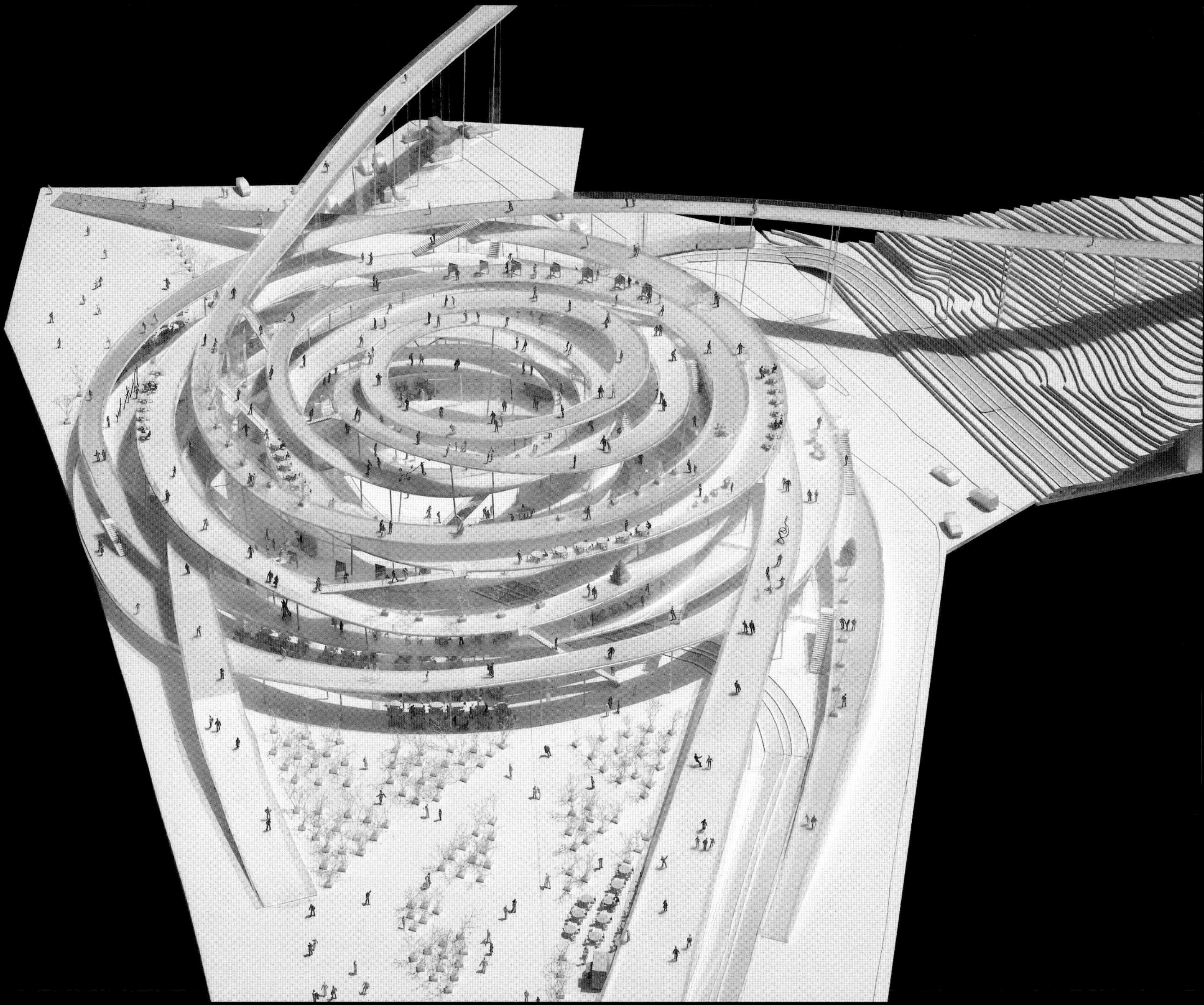

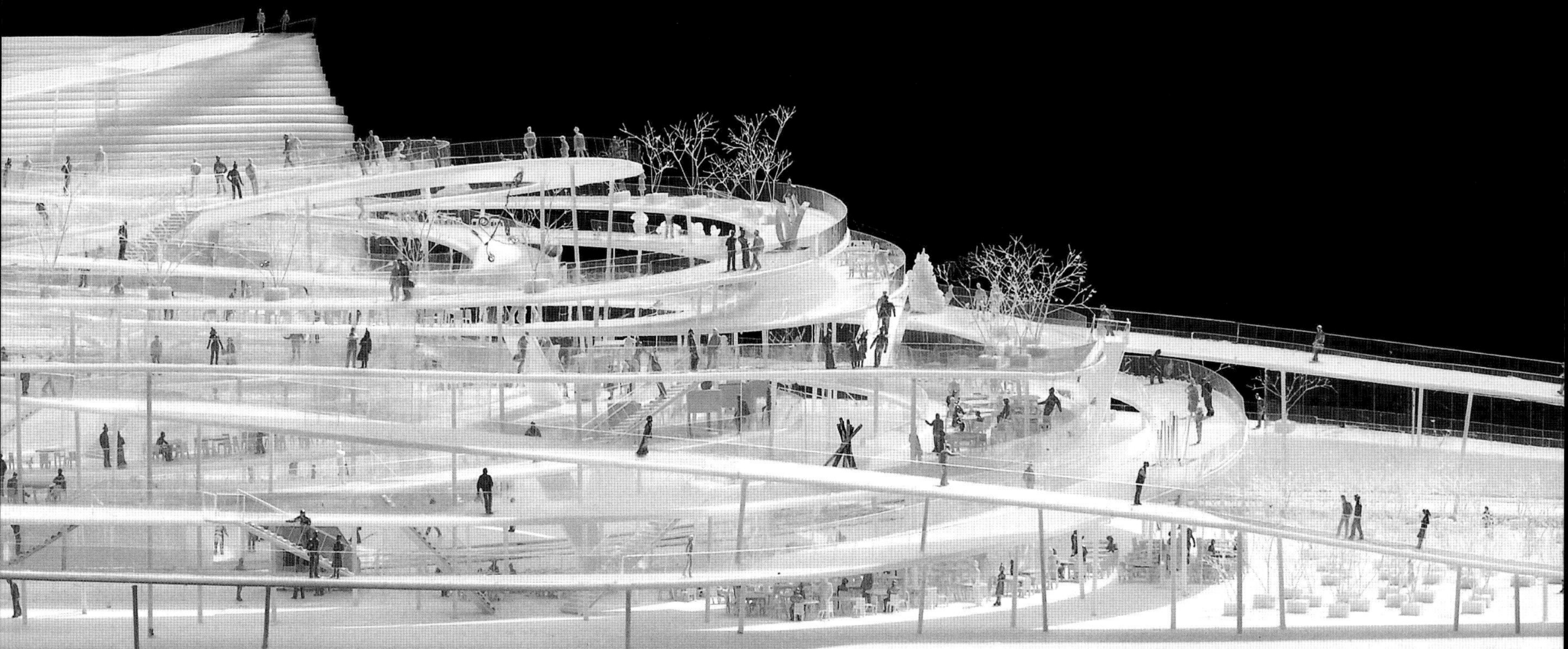

East elevation

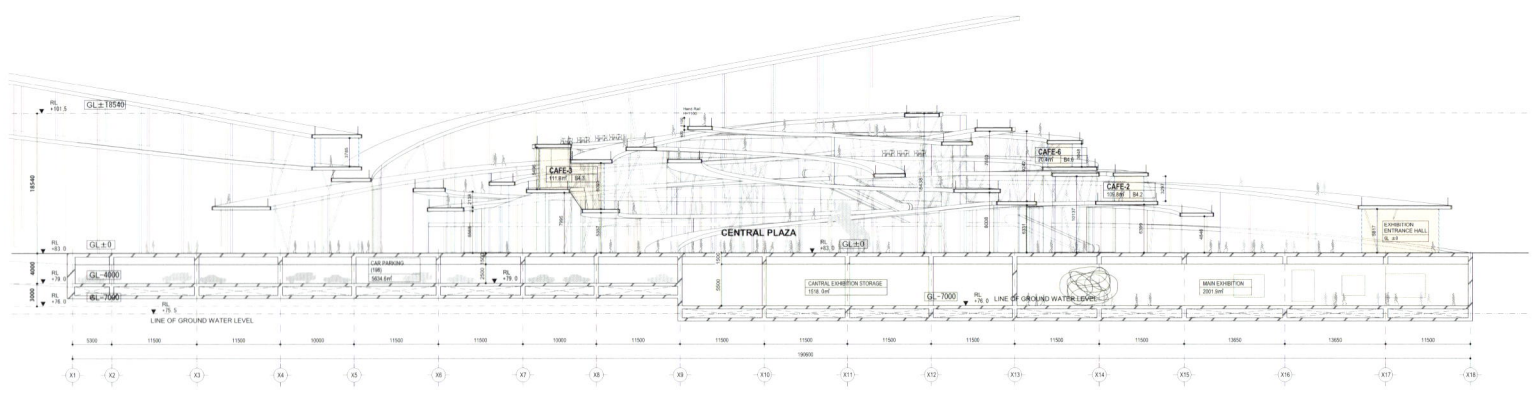

Section

South elevation S=1:1000

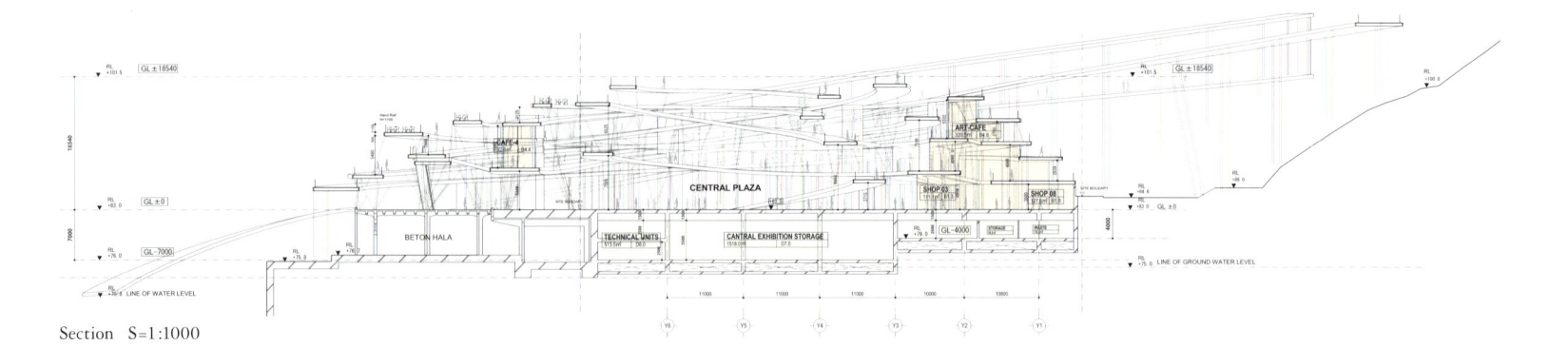

Section S=1:1000

Plaza

Middle level

Beton Hala Waterfront Center

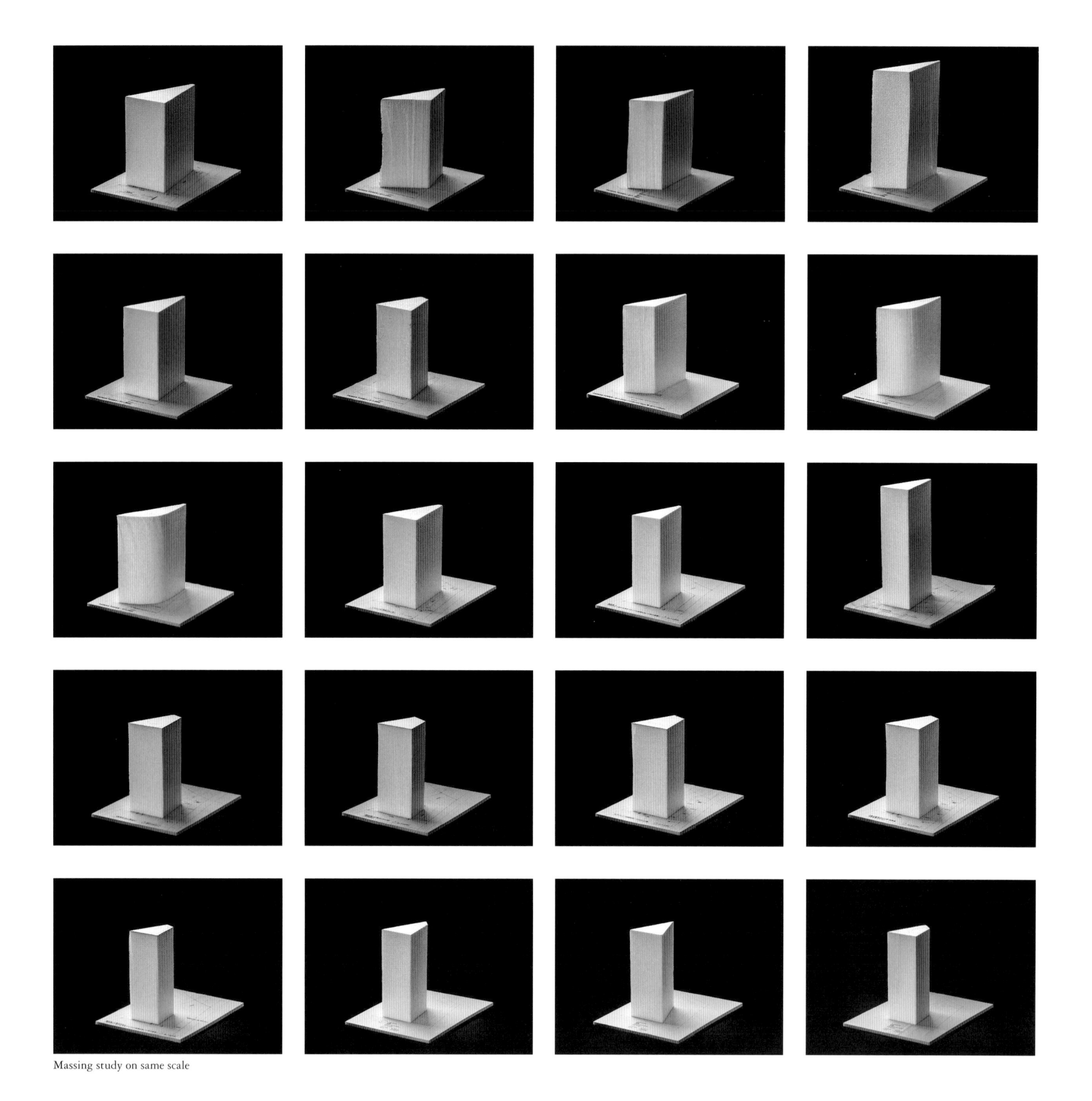

Massing study on same scale

TAIWAN TOWER

Taichung, Taiwan, 2011-
OBSERVATORY / MUSEUM

fig.1

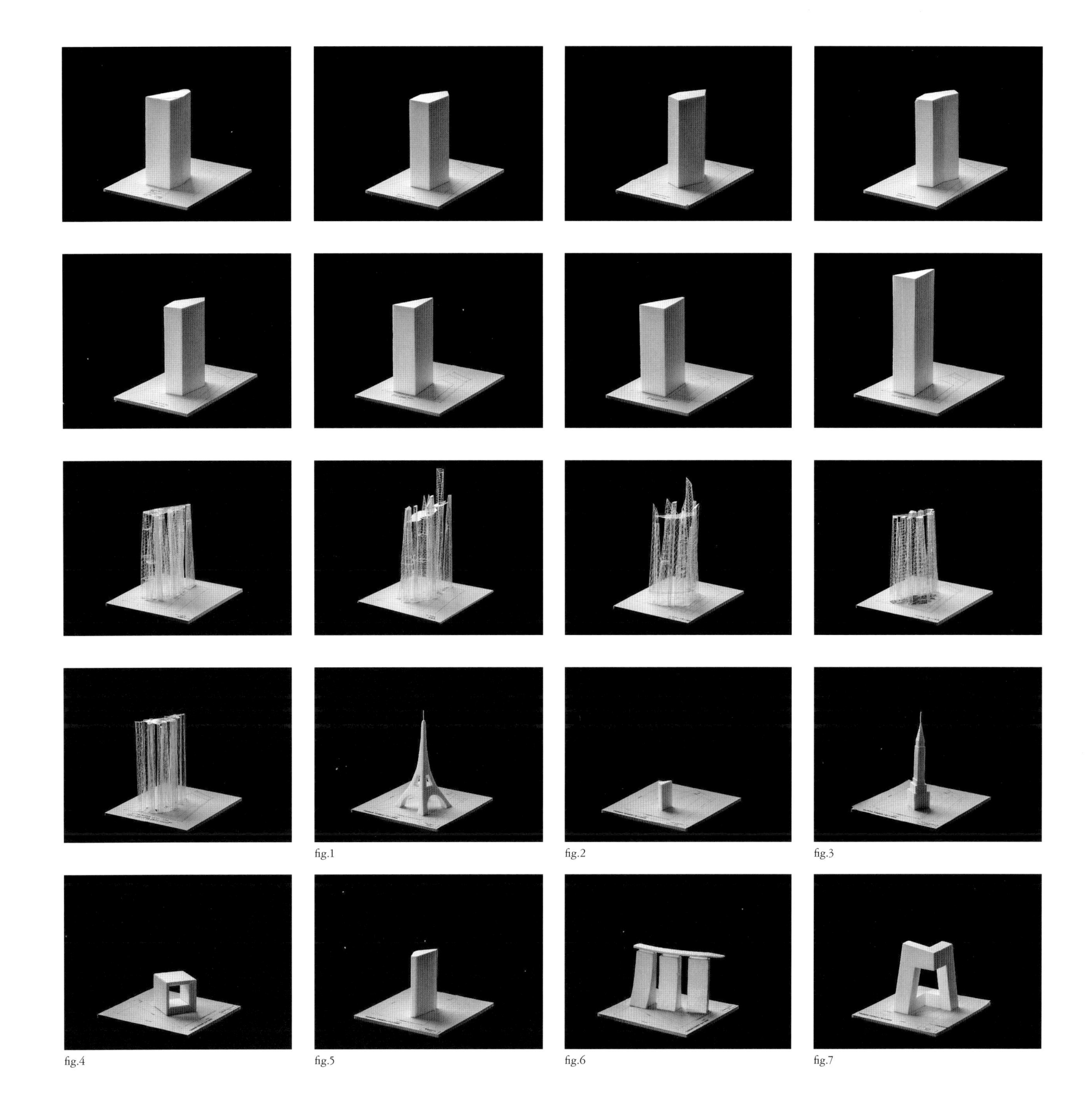

fig.2

fig.3

fig.4

fig.5

fig.6

fig.7

fig.1: Eiffel Tower / Gustave Eiffel (1889)
fig.2: Flatiron Building / Daniel Burnham (1902)
fig.3: Chrysler Building / William van Alen (1930)
fig.4: Grande Arche / Johann Otto von Spreckelsen and Erik Reitzel (1989)
fig.5: Dentsu Headquarters / Jean Nouvel and Obayashi Corporation (2002)
fig.6: Marina Bay Sands Singapore / Moshe Safdie (2010)
fig.7: CCTV/China Central Television / OMA (2012)

Taiwan Tower

BANYAN TREE

FORMOSA

Diagram

Our proposal for the taiwan tower, and the model for the green-architecture of the new generation, is the '21st Century Oasis'.

This tower proposes a new typology of a tower akin to transparent cloud, mist and alike, which is unlike any other towers in the past.

The two main sources of Inspiration comes from Taiwan itself;
BANYAN TREE—Inspired by the Banyan trees, creating a comforting urban plaza like space under a tree, this place will be a beautifully pleasant public space for the people of Taichung, formed by transparent delicate structural frame.
FORMOSA—Divine Taiwan island, in Portuguese—Inspired by FORMOSA, the proposal presents a floating roof-top garden soaring 300 m above ground, as a symbol of the divine island.

From nature and culture of taiwan itself, to the innovative design of the tower for the new era.

This tower will symbolize not only taiwan, but the environmental era of the 21st century.

Roof-top garden suspended 300 m above ground level in the sky provides the people of Taichung with an oasis in the city. This green-filled garden will be visible from everywhere and will be a symbolic landmark and existence.

NEW TYPOLOGY OF THE TOWER
The Eiffel Tower when it was conceived in Paris marked the age of 20th century, and became a role-model for many towers to follow. The tower proposed here is a tower as an origin of 21st century. We see the Taiwan Tower undertak-

Roof garden

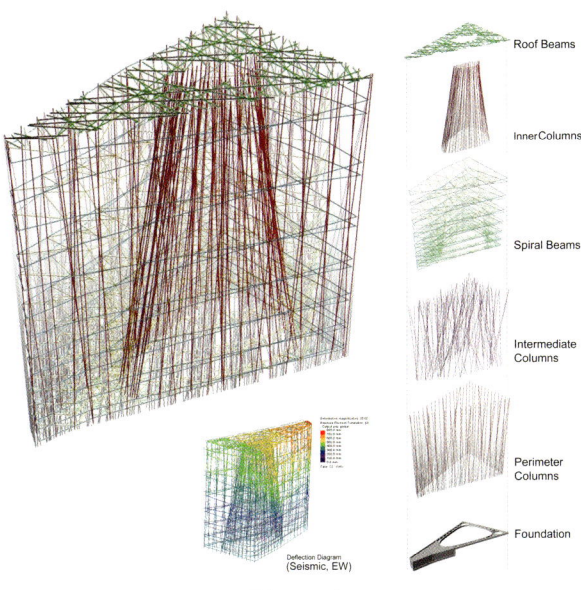

Diagram: frame

Roof Beams
Inner Columns
Spiral Beams
Intermediate Columns
Perimeter Columns
Foundation

Deflection Diagram (Seismic, EW)

ing the role that Eiffel Tower had undertook in modernity for the 21st century and beyond. This is a typology of tower that has never before existed.

Sited within the Taichung Gateways Green-belt, the tower exist as a comforting resting place for the surrounding campus and the adjacent cultural zones, the tower will provide a plaza-like space in direct continuation to the green-belt.

And by the green extended above in the roof-top garden, the formation brings a three-dimensional continuation of the greenery and garden.

This tower will create an URBAN OASIS in the Taichung Gateway, in the intersection of where transport/education/culture/nature converge.

The Tower has within it, a public observatory function with public services such as shops and cafe, and Museum of Taichung City Development, as well as large exterior spaces which allows for diverse uses and functions.

The primary structure is made from steel frame with generous space for attaching various renewable energy systems and lighting fixtures, making the tower itself a large energy-producing device and landmark which is visible from all over Taichung.

Atrium

Taiwan Tower

20c

Eiffel Tower	Chrysler	Empire State	Tokyo Tower	Petronas Towers	Taipei 101	Burj Khalifa	Kingdom Tower
Paris	New York	New York	Tokyo	Kuala Lumpur	Taipei	Dubai	Jeddah
1889	1930	1931	1968	1998	2004	2010	Proposal
324 m	318 m	443 m	333 m	452 m	508 m	828 m	1,100 m

↓ **ORIGIN**   **FOLLOWER**

21c

Taiwan Tower	XXX Tower	XXX Tower	XXX Tower
Taiwan	XXXX	XXXX	XXXX
2016	XXXX	XXXX	XXXX
300 m	XXXX	XXXX	XXXX

↓ **ORIGIN**   **FOLLOWER**

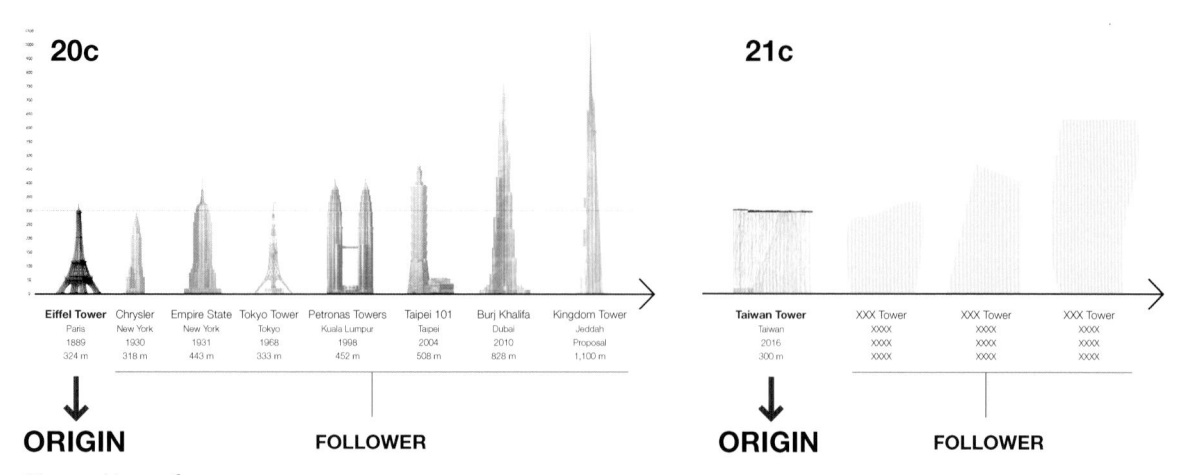

Diagram: history of tower.

Taiwan tower is expected to be a tower as an origin of 21st century

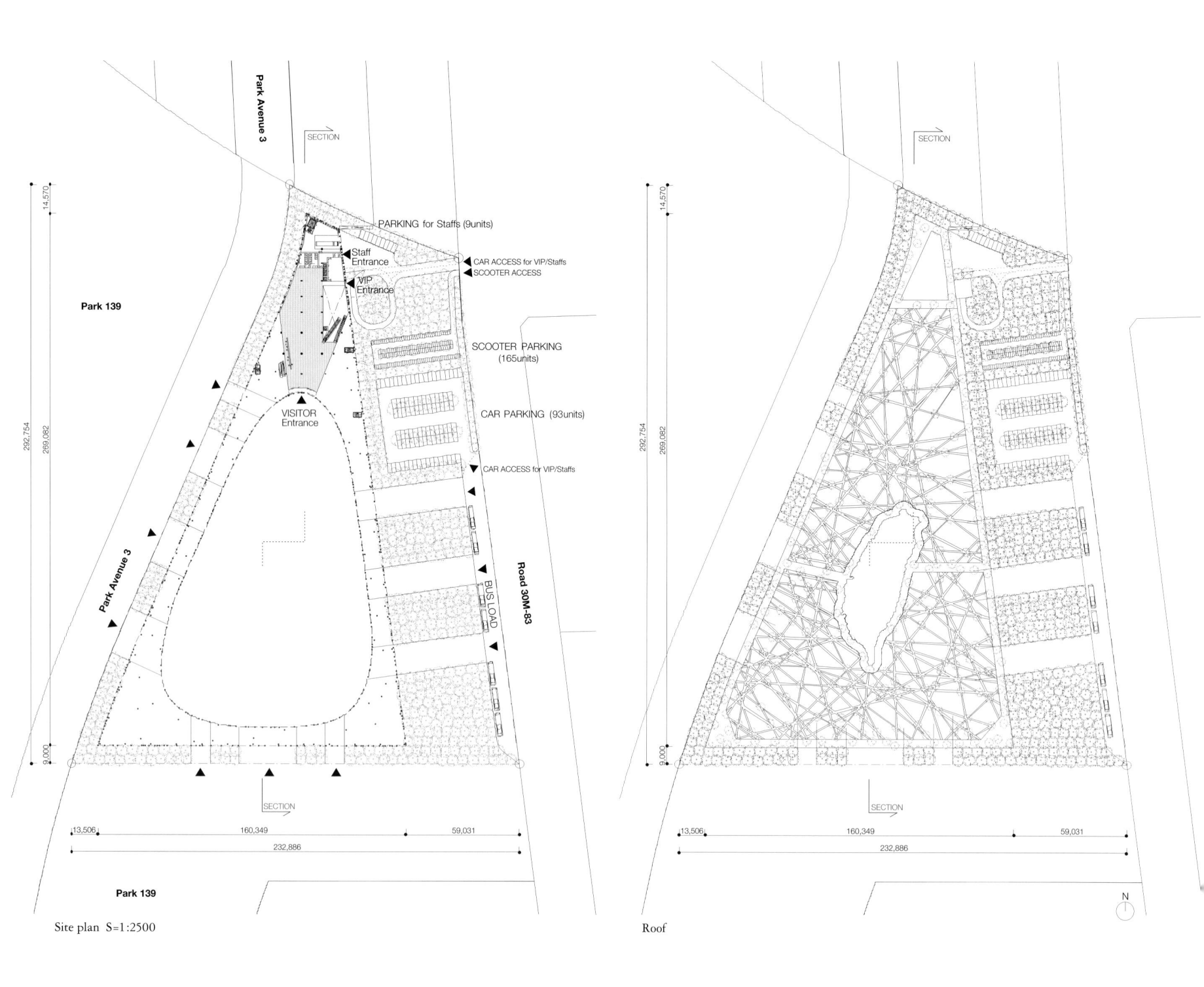

Site plan S=1:2500

Roof

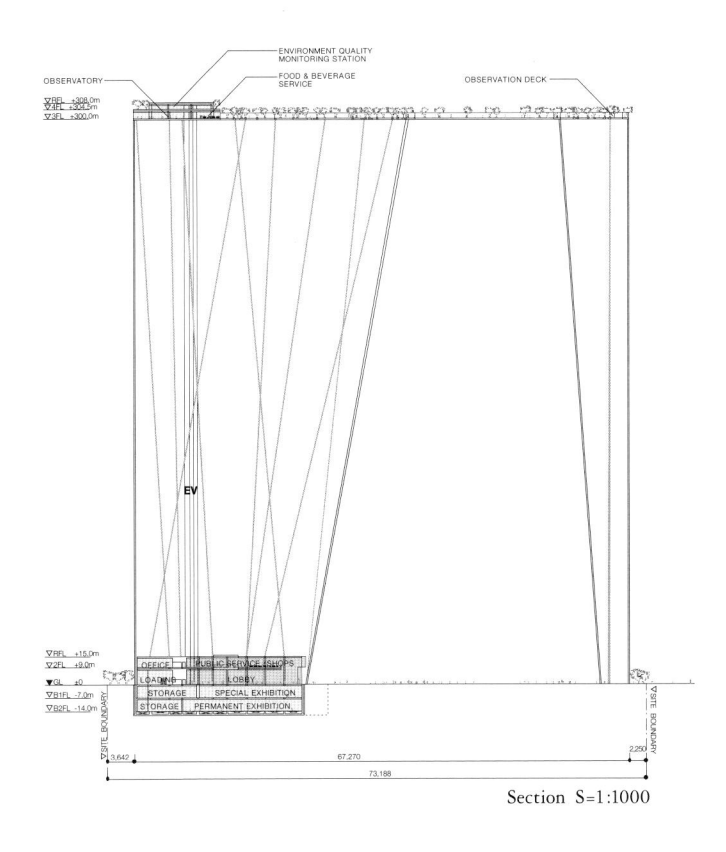

ぼくたちが提案するのは，これからの時代の建築のモデルとなるような新しいタワーである。それを「21世紀のオアシス」と名付ける。

このタワーは，今までの物体としてのタワーとは全く対極の，いわば領域的な，あるいは霞のようにゆらゆらと揺らいでいるような存在のタワーだ。300メートルの高さをもつ巨大なタワーが，とても弱いかすかな存在で都市の上空に揺らいでいる。そんなイメージである。それは人工物と自然物の「あいだ」のような新しい建築物のあり方を示唆するのではないだろうか？

このタワーを発想するにあたり，台湾という場所から出発して，二つのインスピレーションを受けた。

一つは，台湾の樹木「ガジュマル」。台湾でよく見かける，気根が蔓となって降り注ぐようなこの樹木の存在感と人々が木々の下に集まって過ごす情景から発想して，この繊細な構造体でつくられる領域性をもったタワーを構想した。都市の中に1本の巨大な樹木が立っている，というイメージである。この透明感のある美しい構造体は，木陰のような快適な都市広場をつくり出す。この場所は市民にとってのすばらしい公共空間となるだろう。

もう一つのインスピレーションは，麗しの島を意味する台湾島の別名「FORMOSA」だ。300メートル上空に美しい島を象徴する空中庭園をつくった。

こうして発想されたこのタワーは，台湾のシンボルであると同時に，自然と人工の融合する21世紀の環境時代の新しいシンボルとなることを意図している。

エッフェル塔は，20世紀の文化の中心であったパリにおいて，時代を象徴するタワーであり，その後，世界の様々なタワーがフォローするオリジンとしてあり続けている。私たちの提案するこの台湾タワーは，21世紀を象徴するオリジンとしてのタワーである。20世紀にエッフェル塔のあったパリが担っていた役割を，21世紀では台中が担っていくようなタワーとなればと考えている。世界に類のない全く新しいタワーの提案である。

このタワーは周辺のキャンパスや文化ゾーンの拠り所となるよう，グリーンベルトと連続する広場のような場所となる。また，タワーの屋上にグリーンが展開することで，視覚的にもグリーンが立体的に連続していく。そして流通／教育／文化／自然といった様々なものが集積する台中のGateway CityにURBAN OASISをつくり出す。

地上から300メートル上空のタワーの最上階には展望機能，地下階には台中市歴史美術館，地上階・2階にはロビーの他，ショップやカフェなどの開かれたパブリックな機能が入る。また，巨大な半屋外空間は様々な用途に対応することが可能である。

鉄骨造からなる巨大なフレームは，照明や様々なエネルギーシステムが取り付けられ，タワー自体が大きなエネルギーを生み出す装置として機能することを考えている。

台湾タワーは2017年に一般オープン予定だ。

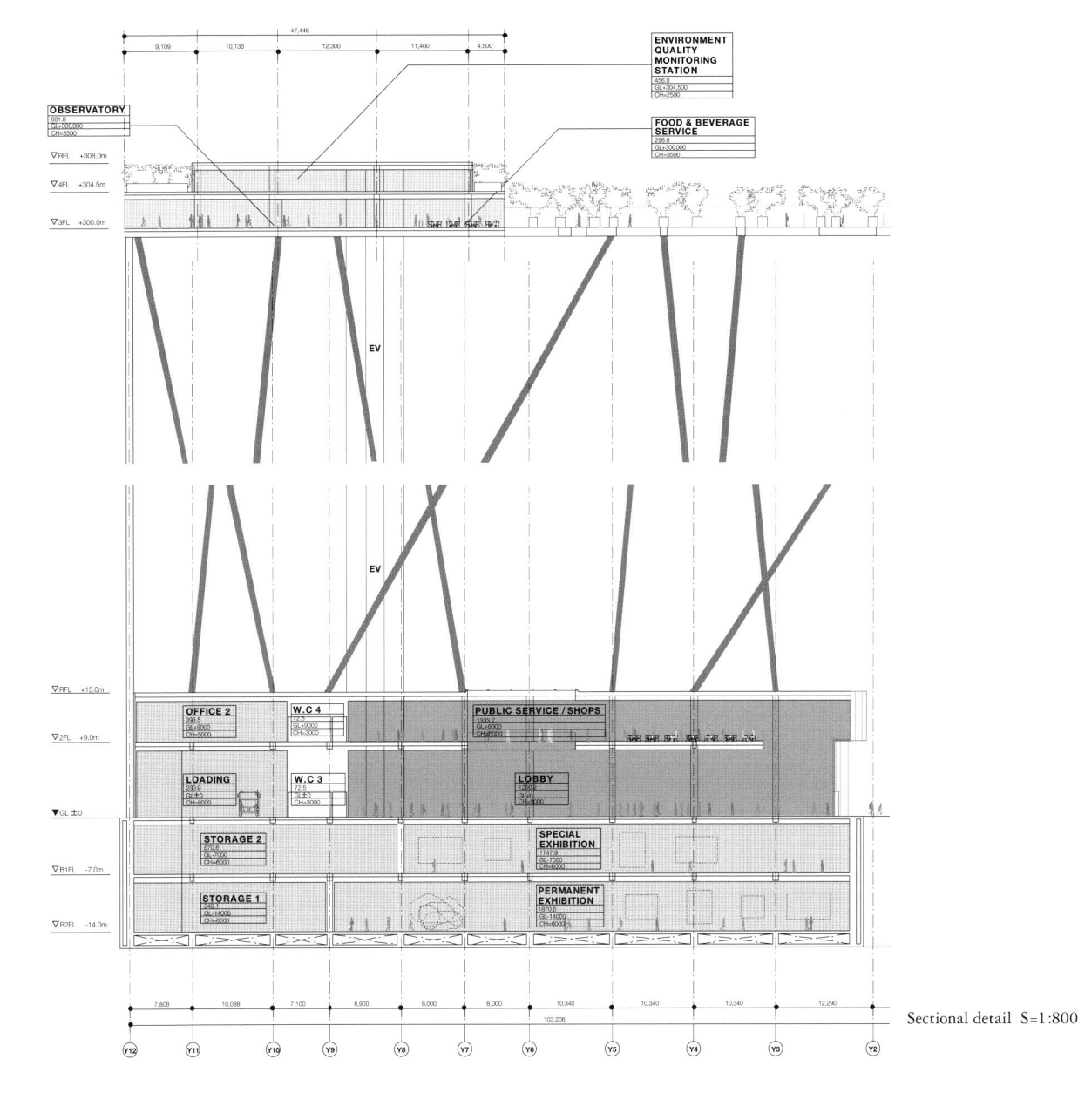

RIZHAO CITY CLUB CHINA

Rizhao, Shandong, China, 2011-
CLUBHOUSE

This architecture is a symbol of the environmental era, fusions the natural and artifact elements of the "forest" and "waterfall" in an innovative way.

The project uses the entire site as a forest and places the different functions inside. In this plan, we intend to create various landscapes leading to the rivers, ponds and forests of the surrounding environment, as well as circulations and spaces for strolling through the forest.

A great number of trees are planted surrounding area of the site and buildings, even internal space of the building. The water front across both indoors and outdoors to generate a new landscape, blending exterior and interior spaces into one vibrant environment.

The waterfall and the trees keep protect privacy, and create dynamic views marked with glimpses of the river.

The project places all of its functional elements with views of the garden, allowing each room to retain unique characteristics while still being connected under a large roof in a continuous one-room layout.

Integrated architecture by waterfall and forest with surrounding river environment, we intend to create a public space that connect with surrounding nature.

Courtyard

Corridor

「森」,「滝」という自然と人工物が今までにない新しい形で融合した,環境時代を象徴する建築。

本計画は敷地全体を森とし,各機能を森の中に配置することにより,川,池,森(周辺環境)へのさまざまな風景と森林の中を散策するような多様な動線や空間をつくることを目指している。

敷地周辺や建物外部のみではなく,建物内部にまでたくさんの木々が植えられ,水辺空間が内部空間と外部空間を横断することによって内部と外部が混じり合う豊かな環境と新しい風景が生まれる。

滝と木々によってプライバシーを確保しながらも,垣間見える川へのダイナミックなビューをつくり出す。

全ての機能が庭に面する良質な眺望を備える計画とし,それぞれが特徴的な場所をつくりながらも,巨大な屋根の下でひと繋がりになっているワンルーム空間となっている。

広大な川を含めた周辺環境と滝と森によってつくられる建築が融合することで,周囲と連続した豊かなパブリックスペースをつくることを意図した。

Rizhao City Club China

Plan S=1:600

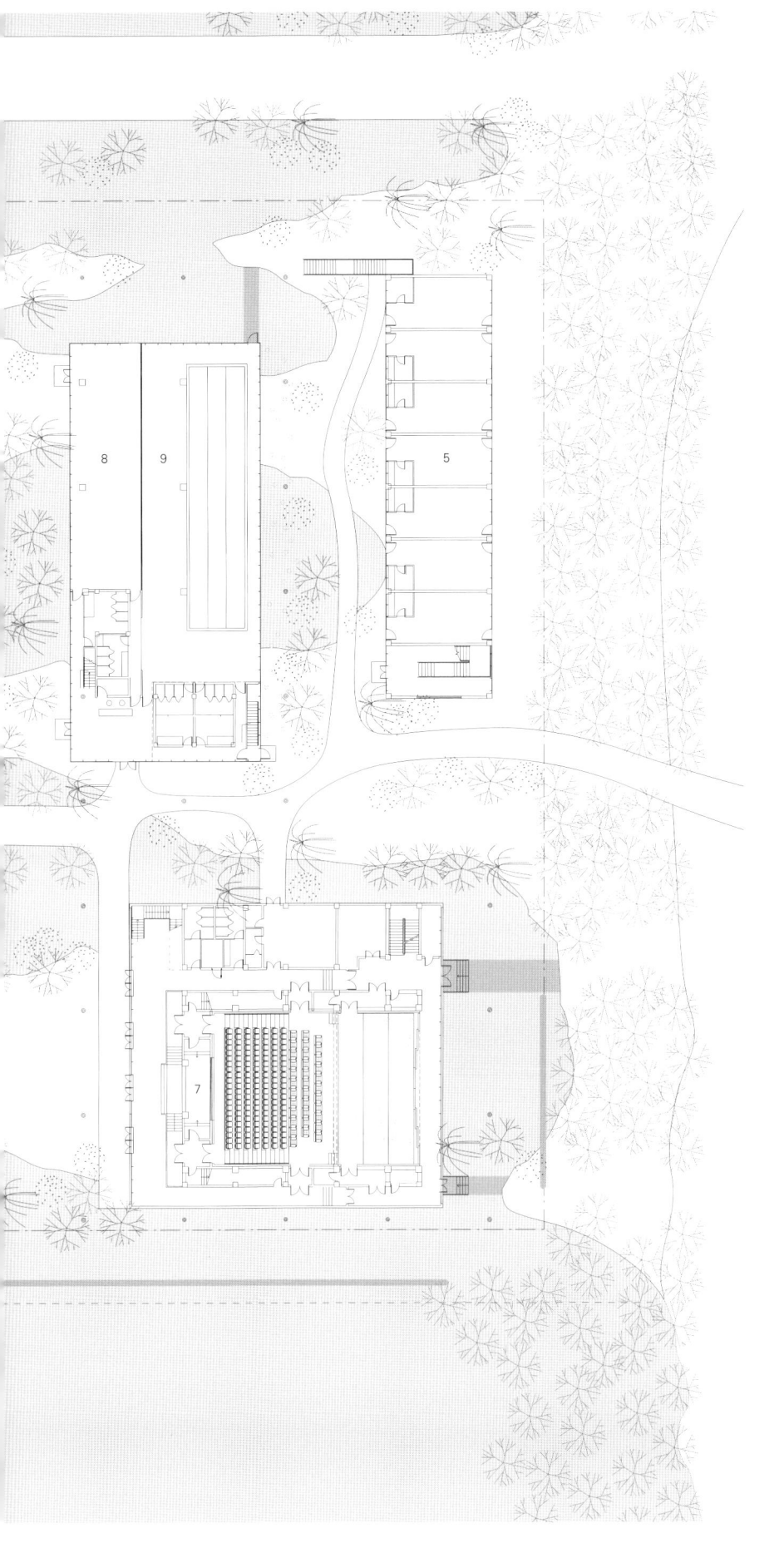

1 ENTRANCE HALL
2 MUSEUM
3 RESTAURANT
4 KITCHEN
5 GUEST ROOM
6 OFFICE
7 THEATRE
8 GYM
9 SWIMMING POOL

Under construction

Rizhao City Club China

SMALLEST/LARGEST ART MUSEUM

Château La Coste, Aix-en-Provence, France, 2011-
MUSEUM

This is a proposal for a new typology of an art museum. Each painting has a small box of minimum dimensions, for rainwater and light protection. The museum experience starts outside where one is connected to nature, and set amidst the forest. While walking in the forest each painting will be introduced individually. The artwork is seen in a new light, with the nature as its backdrop. The visitors' perception thus vary, depending on the time of the day, season and weather. The space embodies new types of space for viewing art, opening up spatial potential for expansion, a new typology for an art museum.

Latest scheme: each box facing various direction
最新案：キューブの外装が鏡面の模型：自然の中に溶け込むようなイメージ。絵は様々な方位を向き，見え隠れする

PHASE 1-1: CLOUD
Covered floating cloud-formed structure, cave-like space stands up. It was planned modular structural system of steel or acrylic tube like 'Serpentine Gallery Pavilion 2013'

—

雲状の架構を浮かべる。その下は、洞窟状のスペースとなる。提案時は、サーペンタイン・ギャラリー・パヴィリオンのように、モジュール化した鉄かアクリルによるチューブを連結させてつくるイメージだった

PHASE 1-2: GRADIENT GALLERY
Spiral composition with curved glass. Layering glass screens generate a gradual relationship between inside and outside space and will give sense of the depth to the facade

—

曲面ガラスによりスパイラル状の構成をつくる。中と外が緩やかにつながり、外観としても不思議な奥行きを醸し出す

PHASE 1-3: BETWEEN THE HORIZON
The interior space emerges between undulating roof and floor. By layering horizontal planes with openings, space for human and art works is conceived together with the earth and the sky

—

湾曲した水平面に挟まれたスペース。湾曲面には孔があり、環境的なレイヤーとして働く。空と大地、アートと人が一体化する無限遠の空間のイメージ

PHASE 1-4: RING
Ring-shaped roof with landscape scale. Beneath artificial roof, small interior space and undulating land will make three-dimensional relationship

—

非常に広い領域にリング状の屋根を掛ける。その下の一部が屋内化される。地形を利用して、地上面との立体的な関係が意識されていた

PHASE 1-5: GLASS CLOUD
Glass house with mountain-like roof. Transparent area is enclosed in the natural forest with natural light

—

地形がそのまま透明な領域になったようなイメージ。森の中にそのままいるような、光に溢れたスペース

PHASE 1-6: GARDEN GALLERY
Open-sky pavilion in the forest enclosed by double-height wall with openings. A part of wall houses interior space

—

森の一部を孔の開いた壁で囲い取った案。インテリアのようで、屋外そのままがつながっている。一部に完全な室内をつくることにしていた

PHASE 1-7: FLOATING FOREST
Piled-up glass boxes pavilion. It is an image that spaces emerge around trees according to various programs. Generating small cubic 'architecture' around objects is linked with latest scheme

—

森が立体化したようなイメージ。いろいろなプログラムごとに、木の周りにスペースが発生する。オブジェクトを手掛かりに周囲に場を発生させ、それを小さいキュービックな「建築」で囲うという意味で、最新案につながるとも言える

PHASE 2: FLOATING STONE PAVILION
Eliptic cylindrical pavilion with piling up stones. Inspired by the traditional stone architecture of Aix-en-Provence, it's intended to update primitive 'wall' vocabulary of architecture

—

内法で6.5×4mというワンルームのパヴィリオン。エクサンプロヴァンスの伝統的石造建築のイメージも重ねながら、原初的な「壁」の建築をアップデートするアイディア

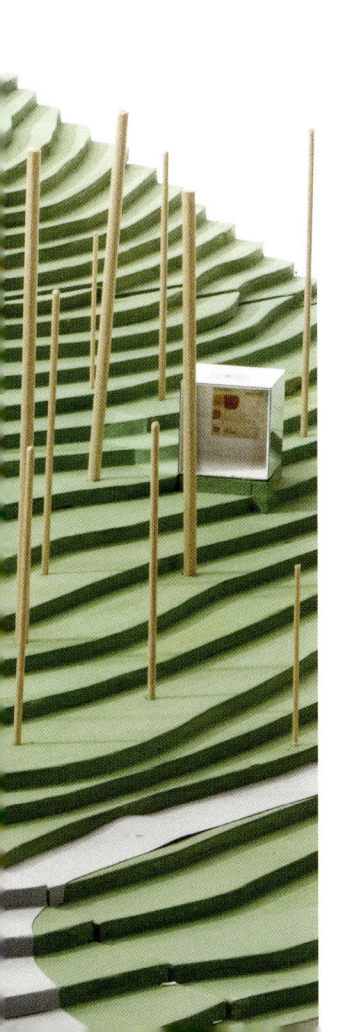

Smallest/Largest Art Museum

Site plan S=1:400

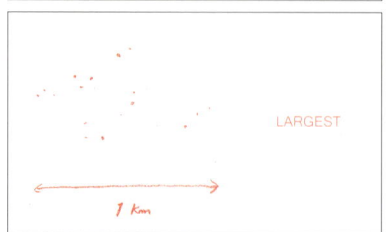

Sketch: One cube would be a smallest museum for a painting, but despersed it in the large site, it would be become a largest museum as a whole
キューブひとつなら，絵画1点に対応する最小の美術館。ランドスケープの中に点在すれば，全体で大きな領域の美術館とも言える

Massing study on site

Latest model: exterior walls made of stones. Inspired by ruin and landscape of Aix-en-Provence
最新案：キューブの外装が石張りの模型。エクサンプロヴァンスの風景や廃墟のようなイメージを持っている案

美術館のタイポロジーへの新しい提案。各々の絵画にはそれに見合う小さな箱が与えられ，雨水と日射から保護されている。美術館の体験は，森に囲まれ，自然と触れ合う屋外の空間から始まる。森の中を歩いてゆくと，絵画が一つひとつ目前に現れる。芸術作品は新たな光の状態で，背景の自然と一体に鑑賞される。そのため一日の時間のなかで，あるいは季節や気候によって，来館者の受ける印象は変化する。これは美術を見るための新しい空間であり，空間の拡張可能性を切り開く，新しいタイポロジーの美術館である。

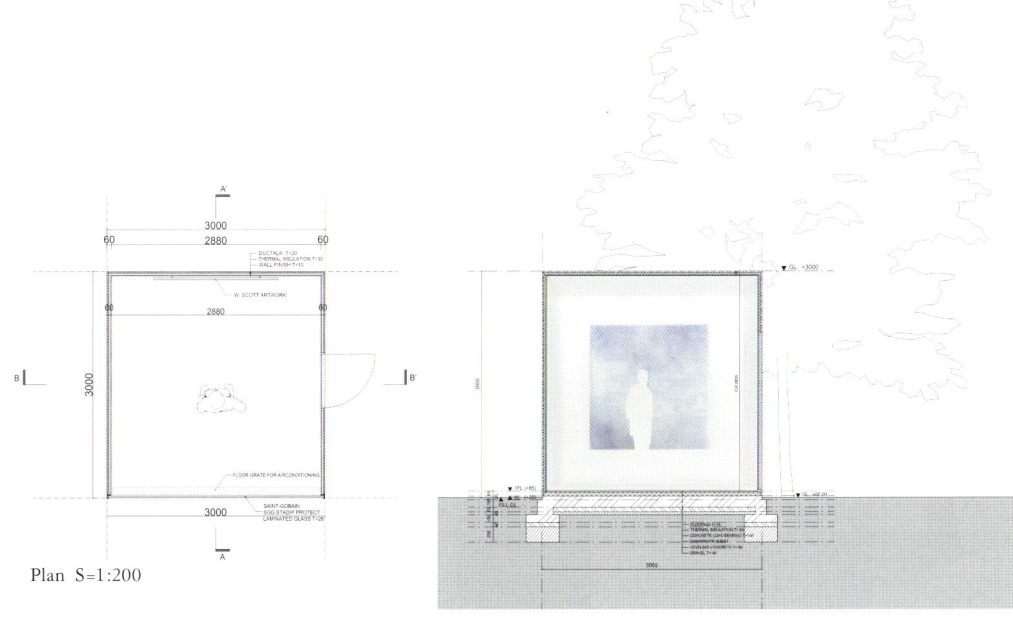

Plan S=1:200

Section S=1:200

Smallest/Largest Art Museum

VITAMIN SPACE ART GALLERY

Guangzhou, China, 2011-
ART GALLERY

Plans for an Art Gallery near Guangzhou.

The site is a part of a redeveloping area within a rural landscape of rice paddy fields, where restaurants, residences and other cultural facilities are being constructed.

The project spans over approximately 4,600 m² to include an exhibition space, storage, office, mini-library, bookshop and outdoor cafe that continue with the flow landscape. Because of the client demand to build a place with a sense of community, where visitors can experience art among artists and gallerists even in outstate, therefore I plan to create a space like a small city.

My original plan was repairing and containing all the programs into the existing buildings to propose some advantage with the landscape. Although the idea continued to develop, incorporating the requests and proposals suggested by the client, we had to restart to think about the old buildings which must required re-construction. We then began to consider a concept from a different angle, to see if we can physicalize "fusion of architecture and landscape." After speaks with the client, we have been studying to built the architecture looks way "natural," like the clustering small villages standing around the site. We are keep continue to visit a site with client to develope our design more.

Site

Latest scheme: units are connected with stairs
最新案：階段で各ユニットが繋がっている

Site plan S=1:1000

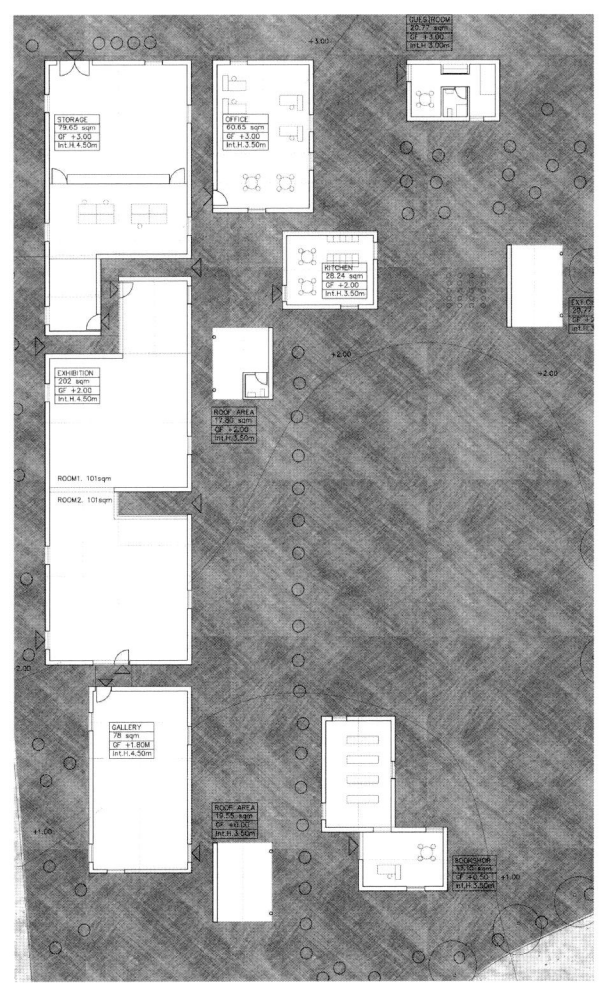

Plan S=1:500

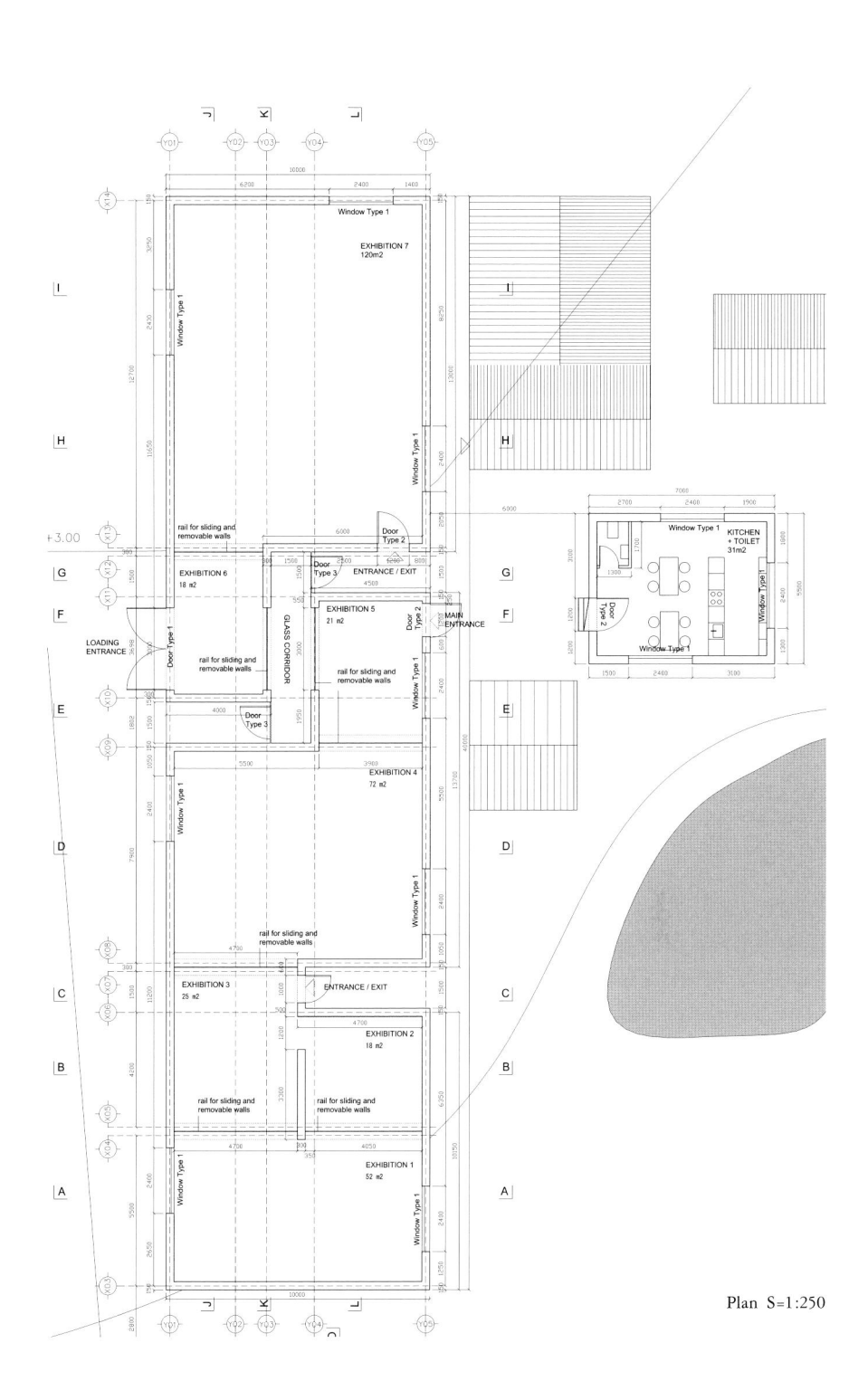

Plan S=1:250

Vitamin Space Art Gallery 69

1 PHASE 1: LOUVER

Proposal covering entire building site by a roof with louver. This structure seemed to be too large for budget

—

敷地全体をルーバーで覆う案。予算を考慮した結果、ルーバーの採用は難しいことがわかった

2 PHASE 2: PERGOLA

Existing buildings house galleries, library, cafe and office in flexible plan with partition. For new part, sun shading pergola made of fabric for agricultural use cover palm tree garden accommodating multi-purpose use including art exhibition. Proposal of orchard-like space

—

既存棟を残すことを前提に、幾つかの機能を敷地に配置し、強い日差しを遮る為に敷地全体をパーゴラで覆う案。

既存棟に収まるライブラリーやカフェ、オフィスなどの機能は、時にはギャラリーとしても使えるように、間仕切りによるフレキシブルな構成となっている。予算の関係上、ルーバーからパーゴラへと素材を変え、最終的には農業用のファブリックをヤシの木にかけ、その下に必要な機能を配置し、ネットが掛けられた果樹園の様なスペースを提案した

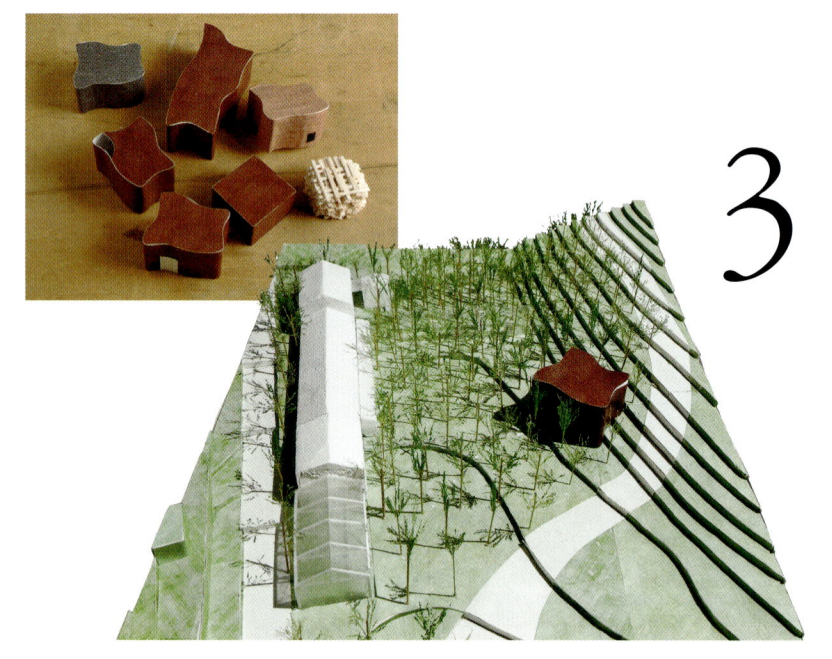

3 PHASE 3: PALM TREE

Planting more palm trees to existing palm grove, two pavilions are set. One is narrow glass box housing library and cafe, and another is gallery space with iconic form. The form of the gallery was examined, being conscious of not understanding when it was built

—

ヤシの木が生えている敷地に、更にヤシの木を植えて林のグラデーションをつくり、密度の濃い日陰部分にガラスボックスのカフェ/ライブラリーを配置した案。

ヤシの木で日差しを遮ることでガラスボックスを外部空間に溶け込ませ、ヤシの木の間から本棚が見える風景をつくりだすことを意図している。展示室も庭に配置している。展示室の形は、いつの時代に建ったかわからない遺跡の様な形、意味がないようでありそうな形をイメージしてスタディを重ねている。

クライアントの提案により、新棟は開発エリアのオーナーが所有している廃材(舟板)を利用してつくることを考えた

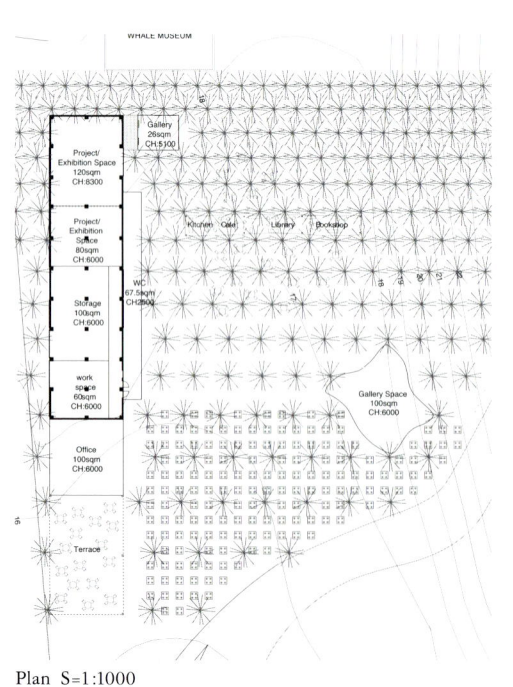

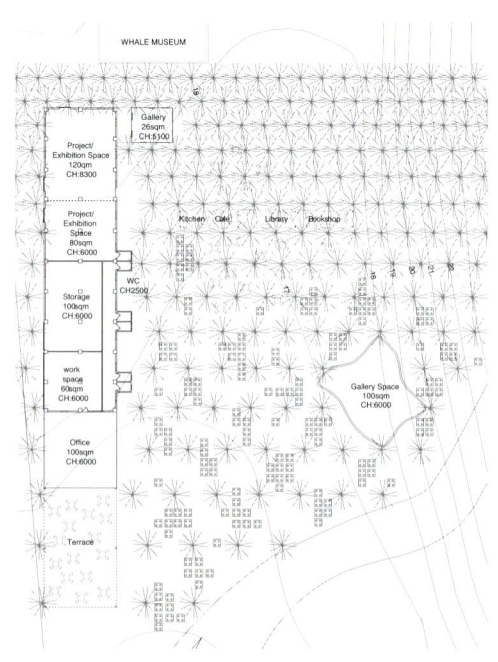

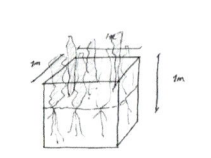

Plan S=1:1000

Mobile farm

4 PHASE 4: FARM

Accommodating to new request from the client to integrate 'art' and 'agriculture', 'mobile farms (movable planting pot)' was set on palm forest. Intensive layout (left) and dispersed layout (right)

—

クライアントからの「農業とアートを融合させたい」という新たな要求と、「モバイルファーム」(持ち運び可能な農地)という提案を受け、ヤシ林案にモバイルファームのプログラムを統合した案。1坪農地がビットマップ状に配置されている

左：集約した配置 (2012年5月15日)

右：散在した配置へ変更する (2012年6月13日)

5

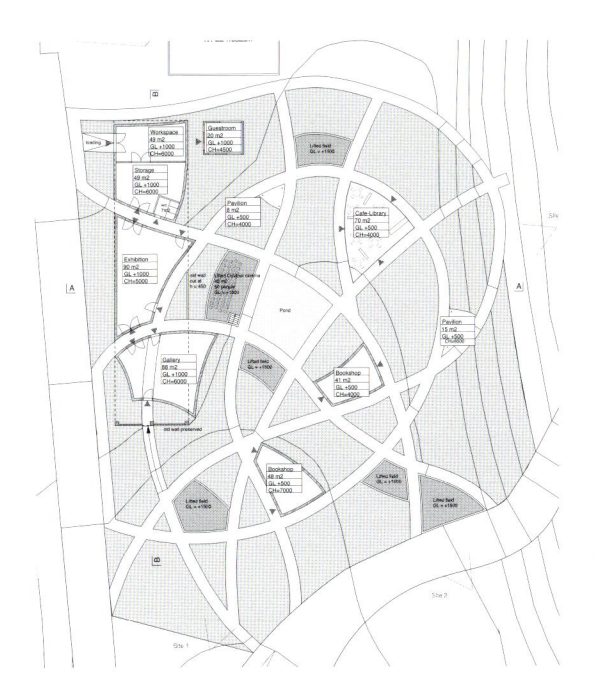

PHASE 5: UNPAVED FOOTPATH 1
According to growing the importance of 'farm-land' concept, site was divided into many lots by unpaved footpath. Some lots was used as farm, rice field and the others were for buildings. Form of buildings and pattern of path, lots are studied at the same time

—

クライアントにとって農業がより重要になってきたことから、「農地」というコンセプトに絞り、あぜ道パターンによって切り分けられた間を建築や農地、水田とした案。道によって切り取られる建築と、建築によってつくられる道の形を並行してスタディした

6

PHASE 6: UNPAVED FOOTPATH 2
To make more natural pattern of path, it was fitted to the topography

—

動線をより自然な形にする為、動線を地形に合わせて繋いでいき、その間にヴォリュームを配置した案。自然と建築がより絡み合う様に、道とヴォリュームのスタディを重ねている

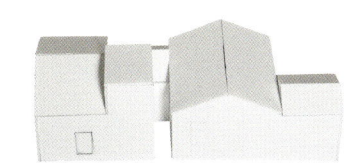

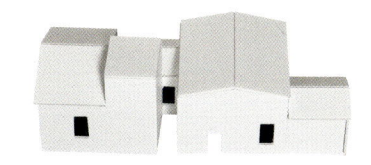

7

PHASE 7: VILLAGE
Proposal of arrange the buildings with gabled roof making an alley in-between, like the village around the site.

For natural randomness, refusing rigid functional relationship between building volume and program, two or three gabled-roof units houses multiple program and some programs cross over multiple units.

In the latest proposal, study on interior space with material and outside staircase on the roof is ongoing

—

周辺の集落のように都市的に路地をつくりつつ、切妻屋根のイエ型の建築を組み合わせた案。

ランダムさを持った「自然さ」が出るようにヴォリュームスタディを行った。プログラムと切妻ヴォリュームは一対一対応ではなく、ヴォリューム3つで1つの展示室、ヴォリューム1つの中に倉庫とワークスペース、という構成としている。現在、内部空間や素材等を検討中。今後、クライアントのアート活動によってこの案が敷地全体に展開していくことも視野に入れた計画としている。

最新案では、この集落の至る所に階段が付加されている

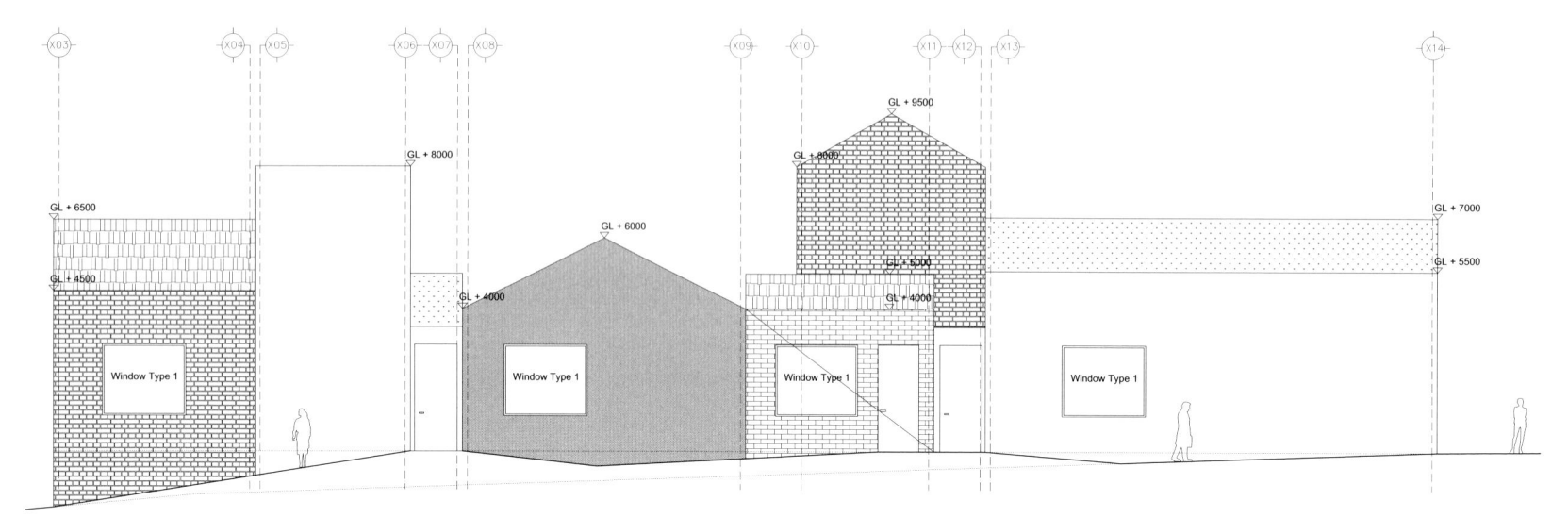

Elevation S=1:200

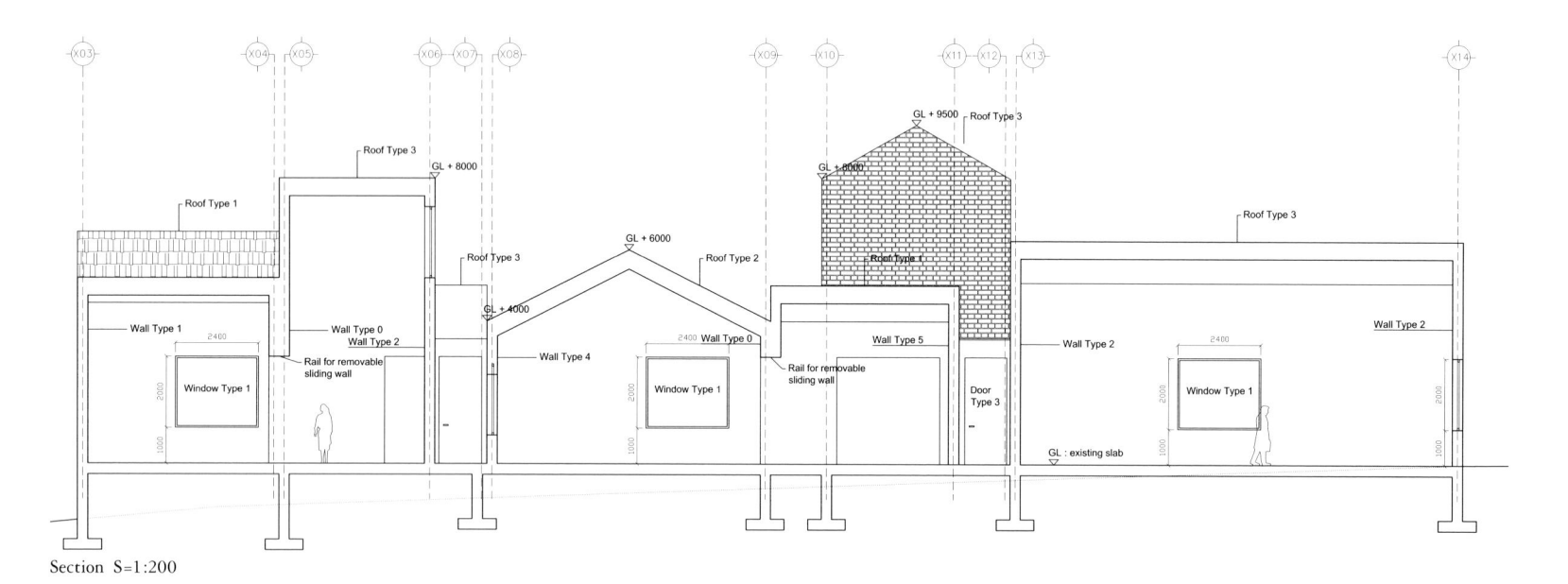

Section S=1:200

　広州郊外に建設予定のアートギャラリー。

　敷地は田園地帯の中のレストランや文化施設, 住宅などの再開発が進んでいるエリアの一角に位置している。

　約4,600平方メートルの敷地に展示室, 倉庫, オフィス, ミニライブラリー, ブックショップ, 屋外カフェがランドスケープと一体となって敷地全体に広がる計画としている。小規模ながらも都市のようなコミュニティをつくり, アーティスト, ギャラリスト, 来場者が一体となってアートを体験する場所をつくりたいというクライアントの要望があったことから, 小さな都市のような場所をつくることを考えた。

　当初既存建物を改修し, そこに全てのプログラムを収めることを前提に, ランドスケープで何かを提案することを考えていた。その後, クライアントの要望・提案や諸条件により案を展開していったが, 途中で既存建物の老朽化により建て替える必要があることが判明した為, 一度リセットし, 「建築とランドスケープの融合」という観点からコンセプトを形にすることを検討し始めた。その後クライアントとの対話を通して敷地周辺の集落のような, 建築の「自然な建ち方」のスタディを重ね, 現在に至っている。今後クライアントと現場を一緒に廻りながら設計を進めていく予定。

INTERVIEW
ALL IS ONE, ONE IS ALL
すべては一つであり，一つはすべてである

SIGNIFICANCE OF THE STAIRS

GA I've asked you to pick up themes that are common among your ongoing projects and show them on a correlation diagram (p.83): City, Nature, Network, Landscape..... Now let's talk about some of these keywords. A quick overview of your projects reveals a surprisingly great number of stairs.

Sou Fujimoto (SF) We've gradually amassed a variety of keywords during the past 10 years or so since we managed to get our studio on the right track. Architecture/City, Interior/Exterior, Small Scale/Big Scale, Simple/Complex, Private/Public, Nature/Architecture..... By merging or connecting concepts that are in a sense extreme opposites, I wished to make them my driving force in creating new architectures. Each of these keywords is typical and ordinary, and therefore primordial and fundamental as a topic. In reality, each pair of opposing elements will never merge together, nor will the interior and exterior will form a continuum. Nor will the city will blend with architecture. But raising a series of such impossible questions will trigger discoveries and reinventions in architecture. I believe that new forms, nested styles, and my own way of differentiating and recombining in a network have all been derived from such attempts. But it's true that recently I'm having more and more stairs in my work (laughs). Many of them are tiered connections and winding lines of circulation. For me, stairs are a clue to expanding the architecture that's inside myself, rather than a mere feature of architectural forms. Not that I've always been obsessed with stairs, though.

GA Isn't there a common ground between the stairs and expressing something through the differential?

SF Well, let's say that in the case of Primitive Future House (2001) the tiered style surfaced as part of our differential approach. But at that time, I was thinking about something undifferentiated, that looks like the stairs but that doesn't quite fit the stairs. Something that contains a variety of elements because it's undifferentiated.

GA I have a feeling that more possibilities were open back then. In recent projects it seems as though you are using stairs when you need to reconcile with real situations. Just like the fundamentals being transformed into something else when they are popularized. Doesn't it mean that the root of your thinking is being achieved in a different form?

階段の意味

GA 現在進行しているプロジェクトについて，共通するテーマをピックアップして相関図をつくっていただきました（p.83）。「都市」「自然」「ネットワーク」「ランドスケープ」……，いくつかのキーワードについて話していきましょう。それにしてもプロジェクトを俯瞰すると，階段が多く出てきますね。

藤本 事務所が軌道に乗り始めてからのこの10年くらいの間に，徐々にいろいろなキーワードが蓄積してきました。「建築/都市」「内部/外部」「小さなスケール/大きなスケール」「単純/複雑」「プライベート/パブリック」「自然/建築」など，ある意味では対極にあるような概念を融合したり連続させたりすることで，新しい建築を生み出す原動力にしていこう，という思いがありました。それぞれはとても当たり前のキーワードですが，それ故に根源的なトピックだとも言える。それぞれの対立項は，実際には決して融合しないし，内部と外部は連続はしない。都市と建築も溶け合わない。でもそのような不可能の問いを立てることで，建築の発見や再発明のきっかけになる気がするんです。新しい形や，入れ子のような形式，微分してネットワーク的に再結合するといったぼくなりの方法は，そういう試みから生まれてきたのだと思います。ただここ最近は，たしかに階段的なるものが増えてきている気がする（笑）。段状のものでつながっていたり，くねくねした動線が多いですね。階段は，単なる建築造形的な興味というよりは，自分の中の建築というものが広がっていく手がかりとして考えているような気がします。昔から階段が好きだったわけではないのですが。

GA 何かを微分化して表現するという思考と階段は，共通しているところがあるんじゃないですか？

藤本 「Primitive Future House」（2001年）の時は，そうですね，微分化の思考の一つとして，段々状の形式が浮上してきた。ただ当時は，階段のようでもあるけど階段に収まらない，未分化である何かを考えていました。未分化ゆえに，いろいろなものを含み込んでいるような。

GA あの時は，もう少し可能性が開かれていたと思うのですが，最近のプロジェクトでは，リアルな状況で折り合いを付ける際に階段を利用しているようにも見える。原理が大衆化される時に何かにすり替わっている，とでもいうような。思考の根っこみたいなものが，形は変わって達成されているということでは？

藤本 たとえば「サーペンタイン・ギャラリー・パヴィリオン」（2013年, p.86〜）で，段々のような，同時にストラクチャーでもあるようなもの究極の状態をつくり上げることで，その未分化の建築というもののある種の結晶化ができたと思うのです。一方で，「サー

Primitive Future House (2001)

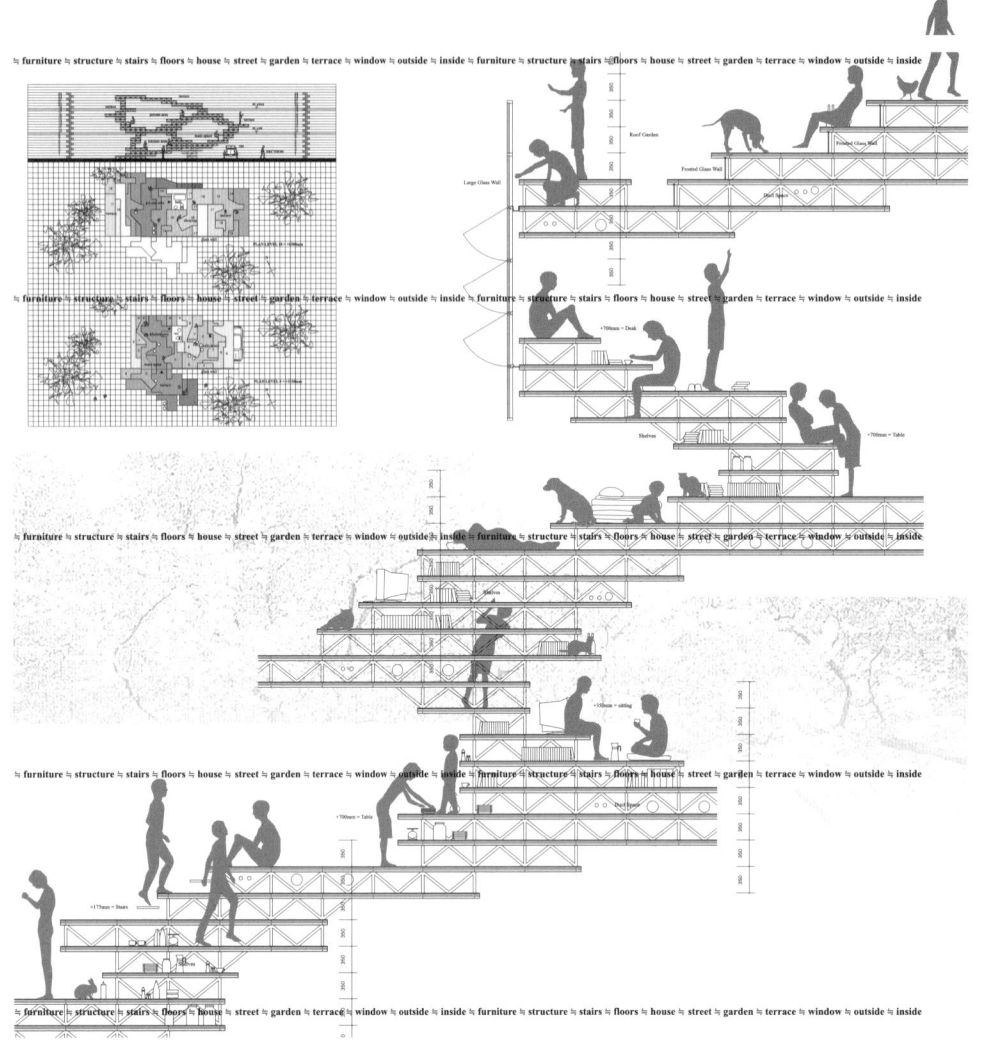

Primitive Future House: section S=1:100

SF For example in Serpentine Gallery Pavilion (2013, p.86-) I succeeded in crystallizing an undifferentiated architecture by creating an ultimate state of being both stairs and structure at the same time. While with Serpentine I saw a variety of potentials further along the way, I also noticed that eventually, it's a style that best shines within a quite limited scale and situation. Which I already knew back in the time of Primitive Future as a sort of foresight. There was this one project where I created a private mansion using the same method as Final Wooden House (2008), but the 35 cm module conceived for Final Wooden House didn't suit the 500 m² house, as it required a meaningless repetition of the same unit. We eventually doubled the scale and changed to a 70 cm module. From that I learned that the 35 cm scale is not universal to any type of situation, that it is only achieved

ペンタイン」はその先にさまざまな可能性が広がると同時に，実際は，あるかなり限定されたスケールと状況で一番輝く形式なのかなという気もしました。それは「プリミティブ・フューチャー」の時から予感としてありました。ある時「モクバン／くまもとアートポリス次世代木造バンガロー」(2008年)の方法を使って豪邸をつくるプロジェクトがあったのですが，500平米ぐらいの広さだと「モクバン」の35cmのモデュールは合わない。無意味に単位を繰り返さなくてはならなくなってくる。結局ダブル・スケールにしてモデュールを70cmに変更したんです。その時に35cmというスケールは決してどんな状況でも普遍的なのではなく，ある種の空間の大きさと建築的な状況において達成し得るものなんじゃないかなと感じたわけです。

「サーペンタイン」をやってみて，内部空間の大きさとか廻りの状況，人の密度や光の粒子の細かさなどの総体として，40cm，80cmという格子のあのスケール感が上手くいったとあらため

in a specific size of space and architectural situation.

In my experience with Serpentine I really felt that the sense of scale of that 40 cm x 80 cm grid was just perfect in terms of size of internal space, environmental situation, density of visitors and size of particles of light. As mentioned in the previous interview, in a Middle Eastern projects (Souk Mirage, p.176-, 2013- / Outlook Tower, p.182-, 2013-) right after Serpentine I worked on a commercial facility that looks like Serpentine from a distance, in which case I had to be practical and adopt a 5 m span. I felt that, when creating an urban facility with a totally different scale, forcing myself to use the same small scale would just sound false, that it would be an example of very wrong fundamentalism.

At first I was attracted to the multilayered aspect of the stairs which created a rich diversity of results in various projects, but when I try to capture it as a format in large it tends to rigidify. That might be why I am now beginning to see some interest in this method — the stairs — that's in a sense old and new at the same time. And I enjoy the freedom and the diversity of possibilities that expands from the fact that they are nothing more than the stairs, compared to the monotony of a prototype with the potential to transform into anything.

There's something that's been attracting my attention lately which is the stepwell in India. I've come across a picture of it on the Internet and was surprised that such thing existed in the world. A gigantic, monumental structure, a human scale, and a scale of community in between. I really liked to see these things forming a natural continuum. While it had a clear format, its experience would offer different meanings as it cuts across different scales. That's what fascinated me most. By the way, people told me that some of my works are reminiscent of Escher's.....

GA I agree with them. They really look Escheresque. With those stairs in a loop.

SF The moment you mention stairs there's a whole history of attempts that the stairs have gone through which accompanies the imagery and you feel like seeing a certain type of expanse and richness there. And expect fruitful results in proposing the addition of something new. So that's the type of things that I have in my mind, which makes me especially attracted to stairs lately.

GA I think that the well-organized linguistic aspect of the stairs can be observed in the nature as well as in the

Serpentine Gallery Pavillion (2013): model study

て実感しました。最初のインタヴューで話したように,「サーペンタイン」直後の中東のプロジェクト(『スーク・ミラージュ』p.176〜/『アウトルック・タワー』p.182〜,共に2013年〜)で,遠くからは概ね同じように見える商業施設を考えたわけですが,ここでは割り切って5mのスパンに変更しました。スケールのまったく違う都市的な施設をつくる時に,小さいスケールをそのまま使って無理矢理折り合いを付けるのはウソくさい,それこそ悪しき原理主義だと思ったわけです。

当初は,段々という方法が持つ意味の多層性のようなものに惹かれていて,個別のプロジェクトでは豊かな結果が生まれているけれども,でもそれを大きな形式として捉えようとするとどうも硬直化してしまう。そんなこともあって,階段,というある意味で古いと同時に新しい方法に,面白さを感じ始めているのかも知れません。何にでも変化し得る原型ゆえの単調さに対して,階段でしかないことから広がる可能性の多様さと自由さを楽しんでいる。

最近気になっているのが,インドの階段井戸。たまたまネットで写真を見て,こんなものが世の中にあるのかと驚きました。

man-made, the city or in architecture. The stepwell in India was about striking a balance between the drilled topography and the man-made, along with the community system and slavery that also come into the picture. Because you need manpower to carry water from there.

Viewed in this light, the stairs in Final Wooden House are what determines a space as well as a landscape. Looking at some of your ongoing projects there are stairs that look like networks. Stairs that link slabs that are found in different places in a network. Which is expressed quite differently from Final Wooden House. For instance, let's take Setonomori Houses (2013, p.156-). What's your view on it? A group of buildings are arranged taking advantage of level differences that, as an ensemble, makes up a landscape. Living units are connected in a network by means of stairs.

SF The initial plan had more stairs, featuring stepped corridors around the volume that surrounded the entirety. Although we had to be realistic and get rid of that idea to fit the budget.

The site is located in a town with lots of steep slopes and stairs that climb from the Seto Inland Sea up to the mountains, which became a great source of inspiration for me. Taking a walk in the vicinity you pass through a narrow, 1 m-wide path that branches from the road to go to a house below, or take the stairs and climb up 5 steps to get to the house above. Such network typical of a hillside village really intrigued me. I also find the same type of interest in Tokyo. There's plenty of slopes in Tokyo, as well as old small paths. That's the type of landscape that I find intriguing.

GA Is that because Hokkaido is flat?

SF Probably. Towns in Hokkaido are all flat. Where I grew up happened to be a wooded cliff-top area of a fluvial terrace, where I used to explore and play as a child. But when I went to town it was all flat so I used to have this imagery that "nature's fun, town's boring." But when I came to Tokyo I found a lot of slopes and steps and started to think that going out on town's fun, too. And when I visited the site by the Seto Inland Sea I found there my favorite landscape. I took it as an occasion for me to reconstruct a town and at the same time integrate the topography of the sloped site.

So I drew up a plan that features path-like stairs, or connecting corridors — that also serve as balconies —

巨大なモニュメンタルな構築物と，人間のスケールとその間のコミュニティのスケール。そういうものが自然と連続しているのがすごくいいなと思った。明確な形式性を持ちながらも，その体験はさまざまな意味を持ちながらスケールを横断していく。それがとても面白かった。それと，ぼくのやっていることのいくつかがエッシャーみたいだと言われたことがあるのですが……。

GA ぼくもそう思う。本当にエッシャーみたいですよね。階段がループになっていたりして。

藤本 階段と言った途端に，階段が試みてきたありとあらゆる歴史がそこに付随してきて，それだけで，ある種の広がりと豊かさが生まれて来るような気がします。そこにさらに新しいものを提案することの豊かさもありそうだなと。そういったことが自分の中では絡み合っていて，階段については特にここ最近，とても気になっているんです。

GA 階段が持っている整理された言語性は自然の造形にも通用するし，人工物，都市だったり建築にも通用しているところがあると思います。インドの井戸は，堀った地形に対してどう人工的なものと折り合いをつけていくかということだし，コミュニティの制度，奴隷制度みたいなことも関係してくる。人力でそこから水を運ぶわけですから。

そう考えると，階段は「モクバン」において，空間を規定するものでありランドスケープでもあった。今進行中のプロジェクトをいくつか見ると，それはネットワークとも言える。いろいろな場所にあるスラブをネットワークとしてつなぐ階段。それは「モクバン」と全然違う現れ方ですね。例えば今年完成した「せとの森住宅」(2013年, p.156~)は，どうですか？ 段差を利用して建物を配置し，それが群としての風景になる。階段で各住戸はネットワーク化されている。

藤本 最初の案は，もっと階段を多用していたんです。ヴォリュームの廻りに階段廊下が巡っていて，それで全体が覆われているような案でした。現実的に予算の問題で淘汰されましたが。

敷地周辺は，瀬戸内の海からすぐ山に上がっていく坂道や階段の町で，そこからのインスピレーションが大きかった。辺りを歩くと，道路から枝分かれしした幅1m程の小径を通って下の家に行ったり，5段ぐらいの階段で上の家に行ったりと，傾斜地の集落ならではのネットワークがすごく面白いと思いました。それはぼくが東京に感じている面白さでもあります。東京は坂が多くて，いまだに小さい道がたくさんある。そういう風景が面白いと感じてしまうんです。

GA 北海道が平らだから？

藤本 そうですね，北海道の町って平らなんですよ。たまたま

Setonomori Houses (2013): study model

that envelope the entire village to be used as a part of living space. There was an unbelievable amount of stairs. Perhaps it was my very first take on the stairs in the true sense. Path-like stairs, stairs as a place for living, and a place covered under a net of stairs each becomes a room of some kind. Instead of having the space between two houses surrounded in a two-dimensional manner, it is covered up to make that place an interesting three-dimensional space.

I am now working on a shop facade in Miami that faces a square. On my first proposal I tried to create a space that would have been a fusion between the square and the facade, just to be a little inventive. Since I was also working on Setonomori Houses, I thought that by extending the stairs they would make an interesting three-dimensional square. Because it was a two-story commercial facility, I thought that a multitiered network-like square would be fun, in which a person hanging around the square would be, without knowing, walking on the upper floor of the shop. The proposal itself was turned down, but I became more and more fascinated with the idea of a net-like structure percolating through the public space to be used not only as lines of circulation but also as a cover that provides a place to spend some time, creating places of various densities.

Looking back, maybe it was an imagery of a place that looks like the Indian stepwell suspended in the air. Then this monster of stairs started to expand, like a network. In the hope of creating something close to a town, nature or a place like a forest that I'd always been interested in..... I was excited that I might have found a tool that would help me better connect public spaces with other places from a different point of view.

ぼくが育った場所は，河岸段丘の崖の上で雑木林になっていて，小さい頃そこで探検ごっこをしていました。でも町に行くと平らで，だから「自然は楽しい，町はつまんない」とずっと思っていた。ところが東京に来たら，坂や段々がたくさんあって，町も意外と楽しいなと。瀬戸内の敷地に行ってみたらまさにぼくの好きな風景が広がっていたので，これは，町的なるものを再構築するチャンスだし，同時に敷地自体が傾斜しているので地形も融合できそうだと思ったわけです。

そこで，階段というか，渡り廊下でできた——渡り廊下はバルコニーも兼ねていますが——道的なものが，集落全体を包み込んで生活空間にもなっている案をつくってみました。あり得ないぐらい階段がたくさんあった。もしかしたら，本当の意味で階段をやり始めた最初だったのかもしれません。道的な階段と生活の場所としての階段と，階段的なる網目に覆われた下に広がる場所，それはある種のルームになります。家と家との間が二次元的に囲われている場所ではなくて，覆われた三次元的な空間になっていて，面白いのではないかと。

今マイアミで，広場に面したショップのファサードの設計をしているのですが，最初のプロポーザルの時，ただのファサードではつまらないので，広場とファサードが融合したような場所をつくれないかと考えました。ちょうど「せとの森住宅」をやっている頃だったので，階段が延びてそのまま立体的な広場になっていたら面白いと思ったわけです。二層分の商業施設だったので，広場をうろうろしているうちにいつのまにか上の階に行っているという複層化されたネットワーク的な広場。案としてはボツになったのですが，網目状のものが公共空間に滲み出して，単なる動線だけではなく覆いにもなるしそこで過ごす場所にもなる。場所の密度をいろいろにつくるというアイディアが，だんだん面白くなってきた。

それは今思うとインドの階段井戸を空中に引っ張り上げたよ

Interview: All is One, One is All

Now I am trying to deploy the stairs in various forms in my search for the reason why I am so interested in stairs. The very act of doing so would hopefully update different roles such as thinking in terms of landscape as a backdrop for the stairs, the differential approach in thinking as in Final Wooden House, and connecting elements in an ambiguous manner. But on the other hand, I don't like it when it's "so I end up with stairs, again" (laughs).

GA Anyway, you'd always start trying with stairs, right?

SF Let's put it this way: I always find a proposal of stairs tucked somewhere in the pile (laughs). Next thing I do is pick it up and think "what am I gonna do with this?" This the way I usually work.

NETWORK-TYPE THINKING TAKES SHAPE

GA To sum up, the stairs are cutting across various functions. They relate to us on a scale that is closest to the body as a path, or a network, and sometimes as an accumulation of steps. In this way they make it possible for us to cross over an enormous urban space as well as a tiny space, the perfect example being the Indian stepwell. And what's more, they serve as a roof. Although originally they don't come with vacant space underneath, sometimes the space below becomes the main subject. I'm really impressed with such demonstration of optimism (laughs).

SF I'd rather explore my environment rather than focus on a single matter (laughs). I love seeking out the primordial, but don't necessarily think that everything in the world should be like that, fundamentally. As soon as I come up with something interesting, I'd imagine that it would lead to another interesting thing and would want to continue my exploration. That's the way I always feel. Then, talking about a certain keyword will lead to every other keywords, and talking about a project will cover every other projects.

Maybe I have a train of thought that's network-like, in the natural sense of word, in that whenever I talk about one thing I also talk about everything at the same time. When I come up with 10 ideas, these 10 would loosely connect with each other to become the 11th idea. Or else, telling one story instantly gives a new meaning to the other story that's over there..... I'm intrigued to such kind of situations.

GA That's exactly like Escher's drawings.

SF Recently, as I was talking about Serpentine, it

うな場所のイメージだったかもしれません。だんだん階段のおばけみたいなものがネットワーク的に広がっていった。ぼくが興味を持っていた，町とか自然的なもの，森のような場所に近づけるのではないか……。公共空間とそうでない場所を違う視点で上手く結びつけるような役割を果たしてくれる道具を発見したな，と盛り上がったんです。

今は階段をいろいろな形で展開してみて，自分が階段に興味があるのは何故なのか探っているところです。その行為自体が，階段のバックグラウンドにあったランドスケープ的な考えとか，「モクバン」的な微分の考え方とか，曖昧につなげるといった様々な役割をアップデートしているはずです。ただ，一方で「また階段になっちゃったよ」というのはちょっと嫌で(笑)。

GA でも，階段をやってみようとまずは考えるわけですね。

藤本 というか，気がついたら階段の案が必ず紛れ込んでる(笑)。それで，「その先をどうしようね？」と考え始める。そんなやり方をしています。

ネットワーク的な思考が形になる

GA 階段が機能を横断しているということですね。道やネットワーク，時には一つひとつの段の集積として身体に一番身近なスケールで関係してくる。それによって，巨大な都市スペースでも小さな空間でも渡って行ける。インドの階段井戸がまさにそうですね。おまけに屋根にもなる。従来は下に空間がないものなのに，その空間が主だったりする。そういう楽天性は，すごいと思うんです(笑)。

藤本 一つの物事を突き詰めるより，周囲を探索したい性格なのかもしれません(笑)。根源的な何かを見つけるのはすごく好きですが，世界のすべてが原理的にそうじゃなきゃいけないという感じはあまりない。面白いものを一つ思いついたら，もう一つ別の面白いものにつながるんじゃないか，と感じて次々と切り開いていきたい。そんな風にいつも思っています。すると，どのキーワードを語り始めても全部のキーワードに繋がってくるし，あるプロジェクトの話が全てのプロジェクトに被ってくる。

本来的な意味でネットワーク的な思考をしているのかもしれません。ある一つのことを語った瞬間に全部を同時に語っているみたいな。10個のアイディアを思いついた時にその10個が緩やかにつながっていって11個目のアイディアとなっていく，あるいは，一つの話をしたら，同時に向こうにある別の話が新しい意味を帯びてくる……。そういう状況に惹かれるところがあります。

GA まさしくエッシャーの絵ですね。

藤本 最近，「サーペンタイン」の話をしていて，「ジョン・ソーン美

reminded me of the time when I first saw John Soane's Museum. The museum is a residence-like space packed with art collections. After a while spent in the museum, I couldn' help but notice that the space behind the collections was beginning to surface. Then I began to see not only art collections but also the spaces in between that presented themselves as being equally valuable as the art collections. Moreover, I felt as if objects, space and various scales in which they relate to one another began to pile up in layers, and had this feeling that the entirety of the space that enclose them became visible all of a sudden. The experience left a strong impression in me. It was as if the object of my interest has appeared before my eyes in a radical form, which took me by surprise.

 Serpentine consists of 80 cm x 40 cm grids, and the way these small spaces overlap in many layers is like a transparent John Soane Museum, as if all the collections have disappeared and all that remain are the layers of spaces. People can't walk inside a 40 cm-grid space, but they can access to the spaces beyond by reaching out their arm. Dogs can easily pass through. While the superposition of such small spaces creates a sense of continuum that gives an illusion that half of our body might sink into it, it also creates a multilayered feeling that a number of rooms and countless different worlds are adjacent and interrelated. Something that may be described as a space in which bubble-like layers of scales merge together. So the grid is at the same time the frame as well as a cluster of differently-scaled square bubbles. What mattered was not only the grid's smallness, but also the spaces in between and the totality — every aspect was important.

 A "forest-like" place that I often refer to is a perfect example of a place with such multilayered scale that offers multilayered experiences one after another. Very small things that can be held in the palm of our hand and small spaces that surround them overlap with things with different scales such as leaves and branches and trees, and the spaces that surround them further overlap. From the clusters of trees and the distribution of fluctuations of their densities to the endless expanse of the forest, a variety of scales emerge one after another and form relationships, and sway. A place where scales and resolutions of what is visible change according to time, season, and those who see them. I've come to realize that what I meant by 'forest-like' was in fact my interest in such aspects.

術館」を見た時のことを思い出しました。住宅のような空間に美術品がぎっしり置いてある美術館ですが，しばらくいるうちに，置いてあるものの背後の空間が必然的に浮かび上がってくるのです。すると，美術品だけではなく，間のスペースそれ自体が美術品と等価な存在として見えてくる。さらに言うと，モノと空間とそれらが関係し合うさまざまなスケールが重層してきて，それらをまとめている空間全体が一挙に見えてくる感じがして，とても強烈な印象でした。自分が興味を持っているものが過激な状態で現れたようですごく驚いた。

 「サーペンタイン」は80cmと40cmのグリッドですが，その小さな空間が幾重にも重なっていく感じが，まるで美術品が消え去って，重層する空間だけが残った，透明な「ジョン・ソーン美術館」のような様相なのかもしれません。40cmグリッドの空間は歩いては入れないけど手を伸ばせばその向こうの空間にアクセスできるし，犬だったらそのまま通り抜けてしまう。そのような小さな空間の重なりは，身体が半分入ってしまうような連続感があると同時に，幾つもの部屋や無数の別世界が隣接して関係し合っているような多層的な感覚でもある。泡のように幾重にも折り重なって湧き上がる多層的なスケールが溶け合った空間，とでも言うのでしょうか。だからグリッドは，フレームであると同時に，いろいろなスケールの四角い泡の集合だとも言える。グリッドの小ささだけが重要だったのではなく，その間のスペースや総体，その全部に意識があった。

 ぼくがよく言う「森のような」場所というのは，まさにそのような多層的なスケールの場所で，多層的な経験が折り重なっていく感覚です。手のひらに載るようなとても小さなモノたちとその周囲を取り巻く小さな空間に，葉や枝や木々という異なるスケールが重なり合い，それらを取り巻く空間がさらに重なり合う。さらに言うと木々の群れやその密度の揺らぎの分布から，終わりが見えない森の広大さまで，幾つものスケールがさまざまに顕われては関係を取り結び，揺れ動く。人によって，時間や季節によって，見えてくるもののスケールや解像度が変化していく場所。「森のような」と言っていたのもそういう興味だったんだなあと，あらためて気づきました。

 その話に関係してくるか判りませんが，この前，中国のクライアントが禅の庭を見たいということで，京都へ一緒に行きました。ぼくは仏教には詳しくないし，禅寺でどういう生活が行われているかも判りませんが，彼がしきりに「あらゆることがインテグレートされている」と言うのです。確かにそうだなと。単にカッコいいとか建物と自然が調和しているという話でもない。何百年続いてきた結果，ちょっとずつ変わりながらいろいろな

Though I'm not sure if it has anything to do with that, I had a Chinese client who wished to see a real Zen garden and we went to Kyoto together the other day. I am personally not that familiar with Buddhism, nor do I know what's it like to live in a Zen temple. But the client kept telling me that "everything is integrated" and I felt the same way too. It's not about looking simply cool or buildings being in harmony with nature. As a result of enduring hundreds of years, a variety of things have been slowly and slightly changing and been integrated to form a beautiful synthesis. Everything is perfectly interlocking, from the mechanism of society to the way architecture is created and the way it is used. I felt that having everything in perfect harmony is a strength. Interactions are so thickly layered that you can no longer tell what is the original starting point. No one knows if human living was derived from the form, if space was derived from human living, if human living sprung up from culture, or if culture emerged from layers of human living. Cause and effect are so intermingled that it's hard to tell one from the other, and yet so in harmony with one another. I was deeply impressed by architecture as that something that looks like a network, as a complete integration that transcends the design of objects.

On the other hand, Ryoanji Temple was very special — there was something unusual about it, as if it were a

ものが融合されて，美しい統合体になっているのです。社会の仕組みと建築のつくられ方，その使い方と，どこまでも全部かみ合っている。あらゆるものが調和しているというのは強いなと感じました。なにから始まったのかがもはや判然としないくらいに，相互作用が何度も重なり合っているような感覚です。形から暮らしが出てきたのか，暮らしから空間が生まれたのか，文化から生活が湧き出たのか，生活の重なりの中から文化がにじみ出てきたのか，もはや判らない。判らないくらいに原因と結果が入り交じって，ただひたすらに調和しているとしか言いようが無い。建築というモノのデザインを超えた徹底的な統合，ネットワークのようなものに深く感銘を受けました。

その一方で，龍安寺だけは，一種異様な感じで，そこだけ別の時間が流れているというか，別の宇宙が横たわっているような気がしました。観光客が手前にズラッと並んでいてその向こうにはもちろん誰もいませんが，その間には無限の隔たりを感じました。

GA　それは確かにそうですね。距離感がない。何キロも先にあるような風景が目の前にあるという。とても素晴らしい人に会った時とか，風景を見た時と同じことが起こっている。昔よくあったのですが，磯崎新さんと話していると，面と向かっているのに5キロ先にいるように感じるんです。気が遠くなるような。

藤本　人間龍安寺ですか，恐ろしいですね(笑)。

GA　そう，似ている感じがする。言われていることはすごく

Ryoanji Temple, Kyoto

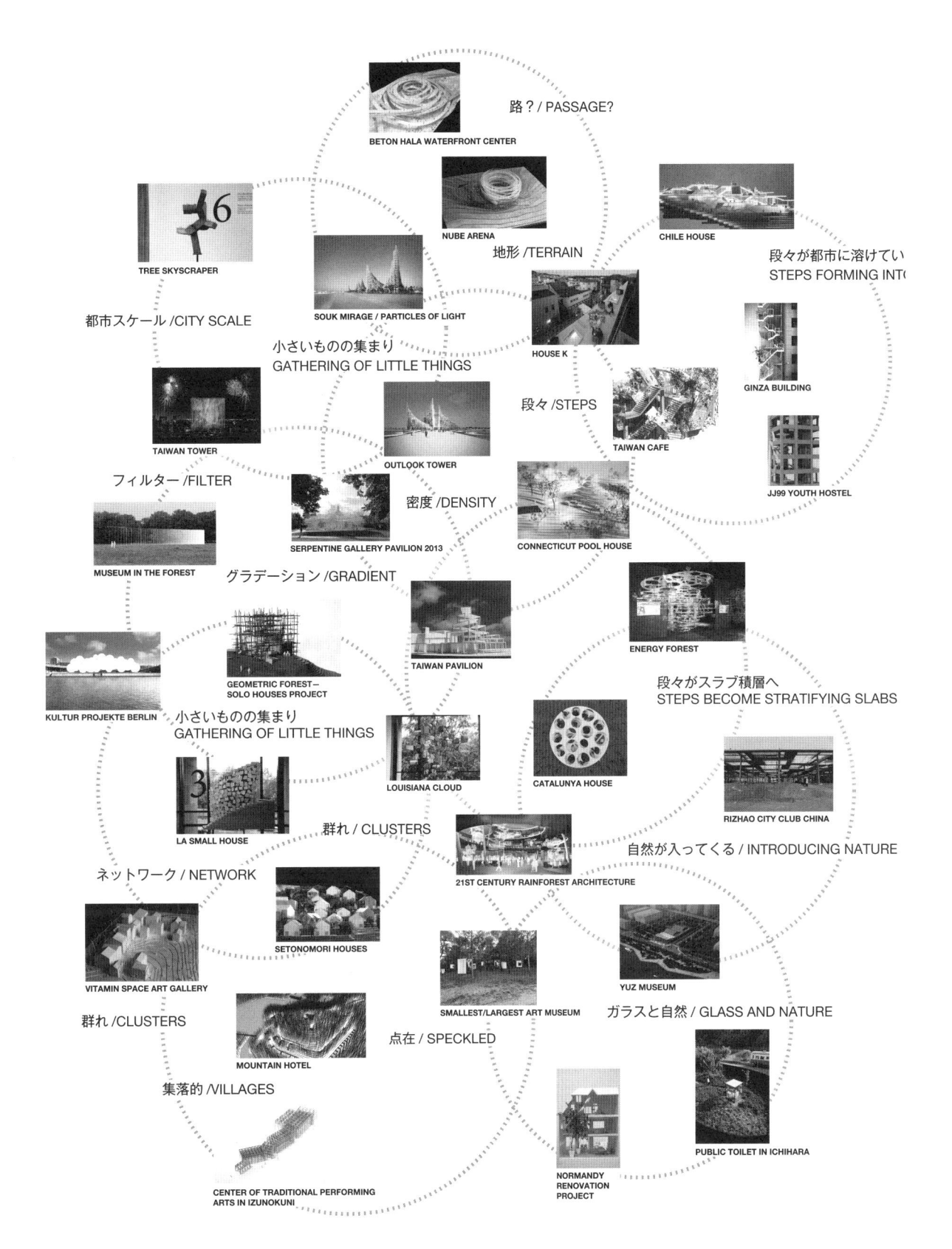

路？/ PASSAGE?
BETON HALA WATERFRONT CENTER

NUBE ARENA

地形 /TERRAIN

CHILE HOUSE

段々が都市に溶けてい
STEPS FORMING INTO

TREE SKYSCRAPER

SOUK MIRAGE / PARTICLES OF LIGHT

都市スケール /CITY SCALE

小さいものの集まり
GATHERING OF LITTLE THINGS

HOUSE K

GINZA BUILDING

段々 /STEPS

TAIWAN TOWER

OUTLOOK TOWER

TAIWAN CAFE

JJ99 YOUTH HOSTEL

フィルター /FILTER

SERPENTINE GALLERY PAVILION 2013

密度 /DENSITY

CONNECTICUT POOL HOUSE

MUSEUM IN THE FOREST

グラデーション /GRADIENT

ENERGY FOREST

KULTUR PROJEKTE BERLIN

GEOMETRIC FOREST –
SOLO HOUSES PROJECT

TAIWAN PAVILION

段々がスラブ積層へ
STEPS BECOME STRATIFYING SLABS

小さいものの集まり
GATHERING OF LITTLE THINGS

LOUISIANA CLOUD

CATALUNYA HOUSE

RIZHAO CITY CLUB CHINA

LA SMALL HOUSE

群れ / CLUSTERS

自然が入ってくる / INTRODUCING NATURE

ネットワーク / NETWORK

21ST CENTURY RAINFOREST ARCHITECTURE

SETONOMORI HOUSES

VITAMIN SPACE ART GALLERY

YUZ MUSEUM

群れ /CLUSTERS

MOUNTAIN HOTEL

点在 / SPECKLED

SMALLEST/LARGEST ART MUSEUM

ガラスと自然 / GLASS AND NATURE

集落的 /VILLAGES

PUBLIC TOILET IN ICHIHARA

NORMANDY RENOVATION PROJECT

CENTER OF TRADITIONAL PERFORMING ARTS IN IZUNOKUNI

Projects diagram

Interview: All is One, One is All

different universe in another time that filled the space. Tourists were sitting in a line in front of us, and of course no one was behind them, but I felt an infinite distance in between.

GA Exactly. You lose your sense of distance. Right in front of you is a landscape that looks like it's several kilometers away. Same thing happens when you meet a truly extraordinary person or see a truly extraordinary view. I used to experience that a long time ago when I talked with Arata Isozaki. I stood face to face with him but felt as if we were 5 km apart — such an endless, mind-boggling feeling.

SF A Talking Ryoanji Temple — that's scary (laughs).

GA Yes, there's something similar to it. I understand what you mean very well.

SF Leaving something extraordinary to posterity. I realized that, other than the accumulation of day-to-day efforts, some things linger on forever because they are unusual. I lost my words for a few hours after visiting Ryoanji Temple. There it felt as if time that flows in front of my eyes had a great span that covers the whole width of history, as if an infinite distance and depth were within an arm's reach. As if all were one and one were all.....

GA Now that sounded like it had something in common with your story about stairs (laughs). Our original plan was to have you elaborate on certain keywords, but now that's no longer necessary. A story about stairs are not about stairs. Just like the many aspects that are expressed in various forms in your design.

SF I love Borges and Borges' writings are like that. The kind of feeling that, within the circular ring of time, this very instant and eternity emerge with equal values while my own smallness and the greatness of being part and whole of history overlap.....

That sort of mood might be close to that of my ongoing project. When I mention a thing it instantly shows everything. When I talk about a thing everything is exposed. I have no choice but to explore the future of architecture in a mixture of such powerlessness and omnipotence. This is something that I haven't been much aware of, but through our talk today, I was able to get a clear picture of it.

August 7, 2013, Sou Fujimoto Architects
Inteview by Yoshio Futagawa

よく判ります。

藤本 ひたすらにすごいものを後世に残す。日々の積み重ねだけでない、異様さゆえにずっと残るようなものもあるんだなと実感した。龍安寺を見た後は、その後何時間か言葉が出なくなりました。そこでは目の前に流れている時間が同時に全歴史を横断する長大な時間であるような感覚でもあり、またすぐ手の届くところに無限の距離と深淵を感じるものでもある。すべては一つであり、一つはすべてである、とでもいうような……。

GA それは、藤本さんの階段の話と通じますね（笑）。当初の予定では、いくつかのキーワードについて話していただくつもりでしたが、必要なくなってしまった。階段の話であって階段ではない。藤本さんの設計に様々な形で現れる様相のようなものですね。

藤本 ぼくはボルヘスが好きで、ボルヘスの文章はそういう感じなんです。円環をなす時間の中で、今この瞬間と永遠が等価に立ち現れて、自分の小ささと歴史の一部であり全部であるという巨大さが重なる感覚というか……。

その雰囲気が、今進めているプロジェクトにも近いのかもしれません。一つのことを言った瞬間にそれがすべてのことを表している。一つのことを話したのに、全部につながってしまう。そういう無力感と全能感が重なり合う中で、建築の未来を切り拓いていくしかない。自分としてははっきり気づいていなかったことですが、今日、お話ししたことで浮かび上がってきたような気がします。

2013年8月7日、藤本壮介建築設計事務所にて
聞き手：二川由夫

SOU FUJIMOTO
RECENT PROJECT
2012-/2013-

SERPENTINE GALLERY PAVILION 2013
Kensington Gardens, London, U.K., 2012-13
PAVILION

Overall view from main wing on northwest
北西側本館より見る

Site plan S=1:2500

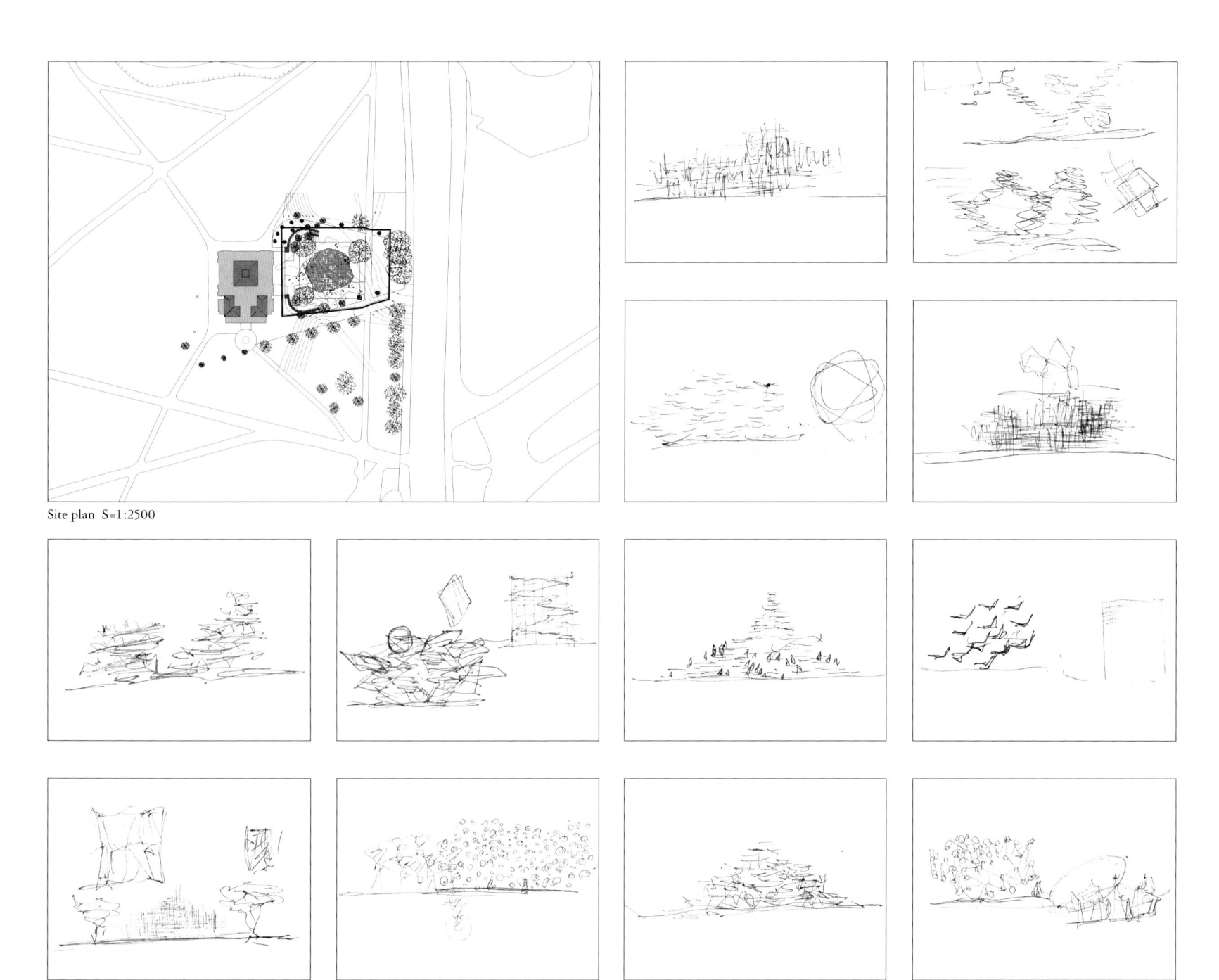

Sketches

THE INTERMEDIATE PAVILION BETWEEN NATURE AND ARTIFACTS

Every year since 2000, various architects have designed a summer pavilion in the open space in front of Serpentine Gallery. Not only there is an aspect for people to relax, spend their time and sometimes create places to enjoy many event programs in a luxurious park, but also there is another important aspect that forefront architects suggest a way of future buildings, and people enjoy them.

What we propose here as the thirteenth Serpentine Pavilion for 2013 is a building-like landscape similar to cloud, where people can diversely occupy the place, or a transparent spatial topography.

The pavilion is composed of delicate three-dimensional lattices of 400 mm cubes and 800 mm cubes, each made of steel rods in 20 mm square section. The whole building is in the shape of a deformed ring, which can be entered inside from two entrances. Those lattices enclose space like walls at certain locations, and at another location they cover space like a roof and prevent rain. In addition, they become a topographical form, which offers a step where people can sit, climb and listen to lectures. In other words, this ring-shaped structural body and its steps become an artificial geography and function as a place to stay for people visiting here.

Transparent polycarbonate discs are installed in the gaps of the three-dimensional lattices like fish scales and they serve as a shelter from wind and rain. Non-slip-processed glass is placed at the steps as a sitting surface.

Because of the sensitive structure, the whole pavilion must be felt like geometric haze. It is intended to create a new nature and man-made environment where in a beautiful landscape and a non-natural geometry are mutually knitted in the context of this picturesque Kensington Gardens. It is not just a building and also not mere greenery, and it is something intermediate between nature and artifacts.

Owing to its transparency, people on the street can see the building of Serpentine Gallery through the pavilion, overflowing three-dimensionally with many relaxing visitors. It will become symbolic scenery of a blend of the history-inheriting building and the new pavilion.

自然と人工物の間のようなパヴィリオン

2000年以来毎年，ここサーペンタイン・ギャラリーの正面のオープンスペースに夏のパヴィリオンがさまざまな建築家たちによってデザインされてきた。それらはこの豊かな公園の中で人々がくつろぎ，時間を過ごし，時にさまざまなイベントプログラムを楽しむ場所をつくり出すだけではなく，最先端の現代建築家が未来の建築のあり方を示唆し，それを人々が楽しむという側面も大きい。

2013年，13回目のサーペンタイン・パヴィリオンとして我々がここに提案するのは，人々がこの場所で様々に過ごすことができるような，雲のような建築的なランドスケープ，あるいは透明な空間的地形である。

パヴィリオンは20ミリメートル角のスティール棒による400ミリメートル角と800ミリメートル角の繊細な立体格子でできている。建物全体は揺らいだリング状をしており，二つの入り口から内部に入ることができる。それらの格子はある部分では壁のように空間を囲い込み，ある部分では屋根のように空間を覆って雨を防ぐ。また別の場所では段々状の地形となって，人が腰掛けたり登ったりレクチャーを聞いたりする斜面になる。つまりこのリング状の構造体とその段々が人工的な地形となって，ここを訪れる人々にとってのさまざまな居場所として機能する。

立体格子の隙間にはポリカーボネート製の透明なディスクが鱗のように設置されて，雨風をしのぐためのシェルターとなる。段々部分にはノンスリップ加工のガラスが座面として設置される。

その繊細な構造ゆえに，パヴィリオン全体が幾何学的な霞のように感じられるにちがいない。この美しいケンジントン・ガーデンというコンテクストの中で，美しい自然と人工的な幾何学が相互に編み込まれたような，新しい自然＋人工環境をつくり出すことを意図している。単なる建築でもなく，また単なる自然でもない，自然と人工物の中間的な存在である。

この透明性ゆえに，通りからは，立体的にくつろぐ多くの訪問者であふれるパヴィリオンを通してサーペンタイン・ギャラリーの建物を見ることができる。それは歴史遺産的な建物と新しいパヴィリオンとが融合する象徴的な風景となるであろう。

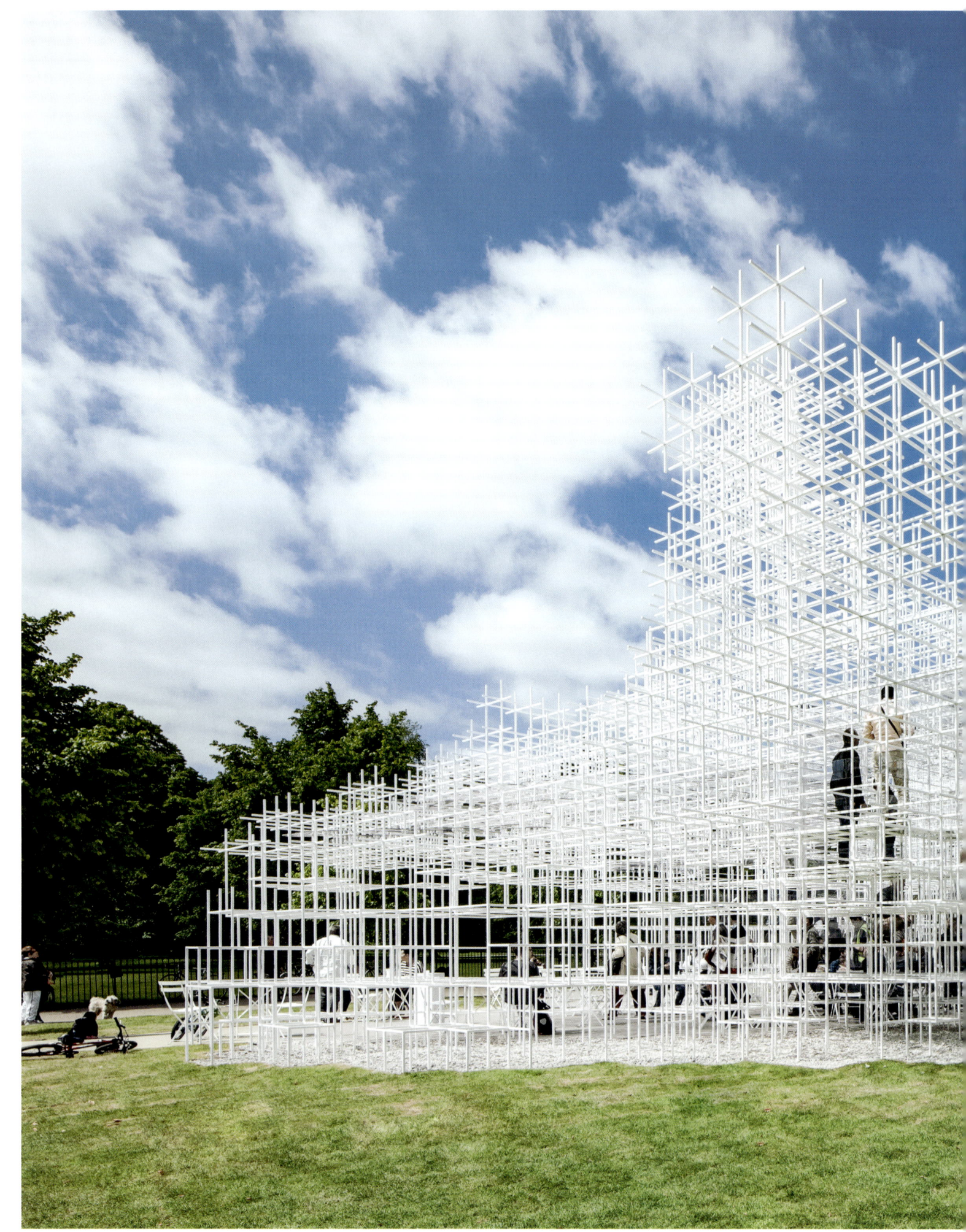

Overall view from south 南側全景

Serpentine Gallery Pavilion 2013

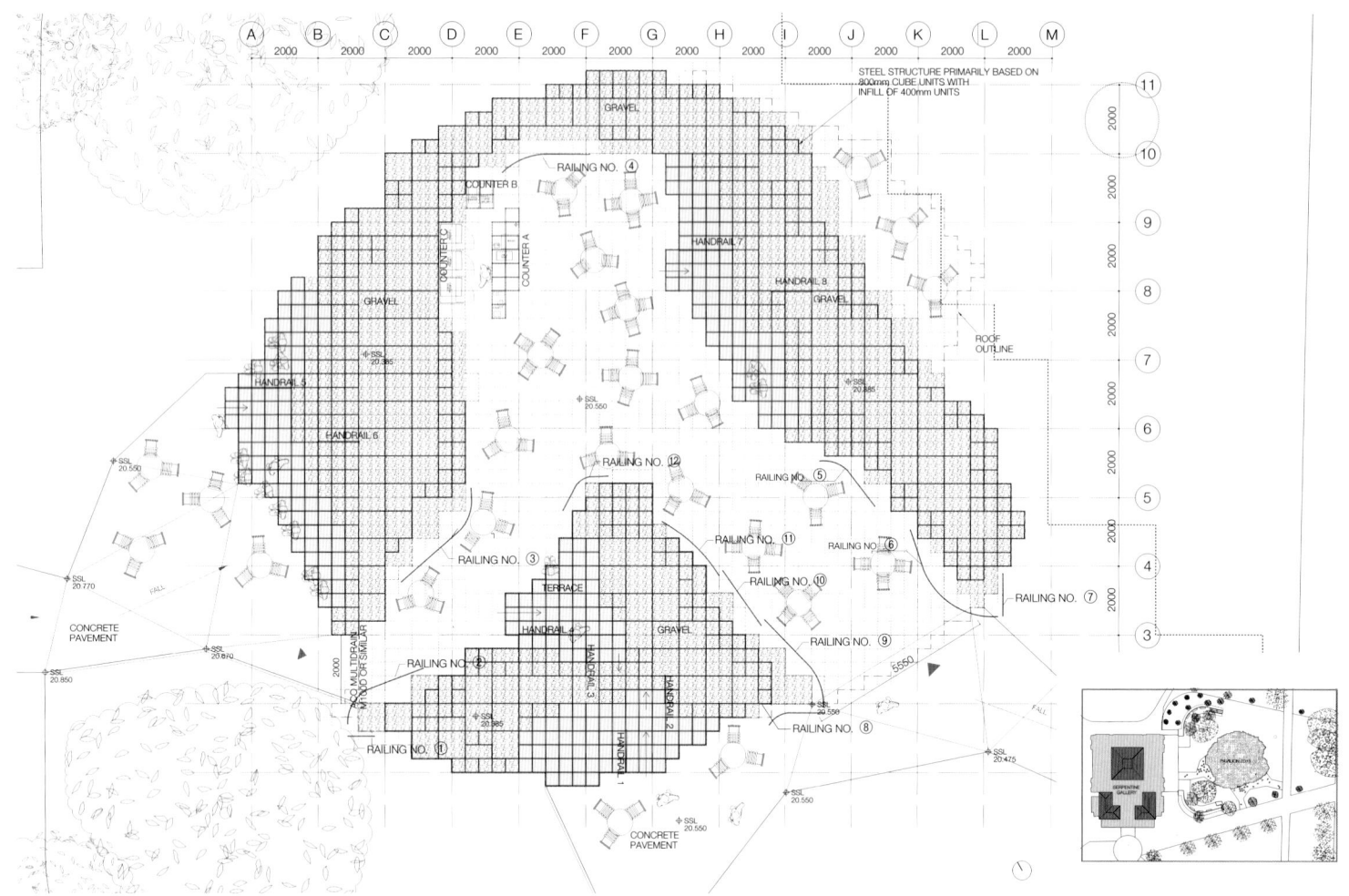

Plan S=1:200

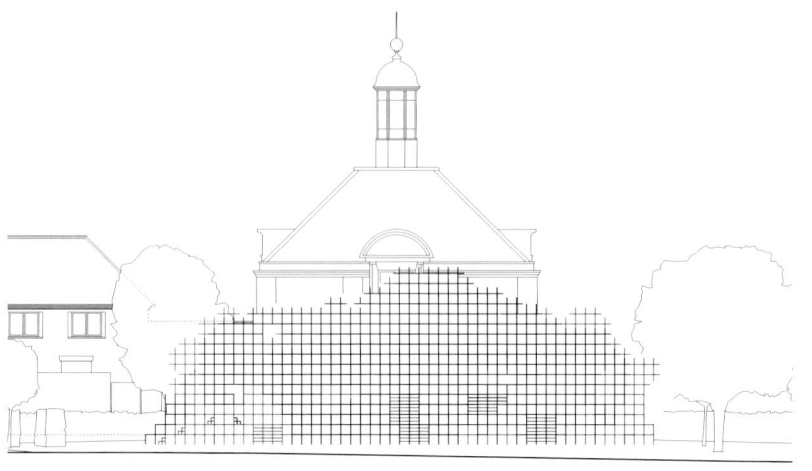

East elevation

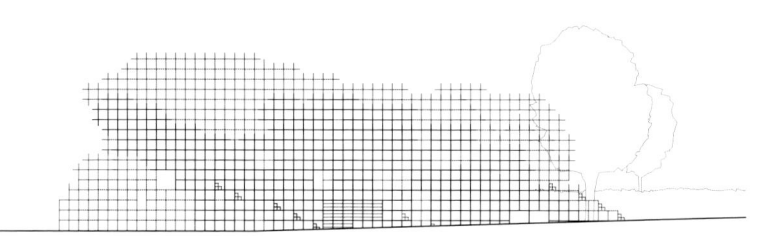

North elevation

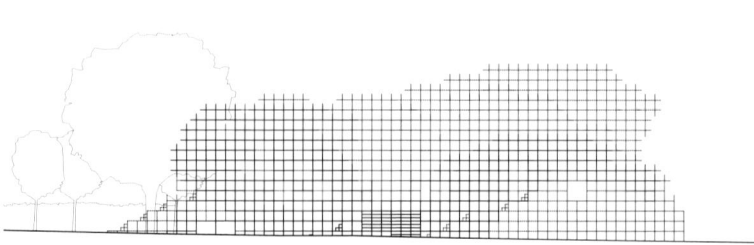

South elevation S=1:300

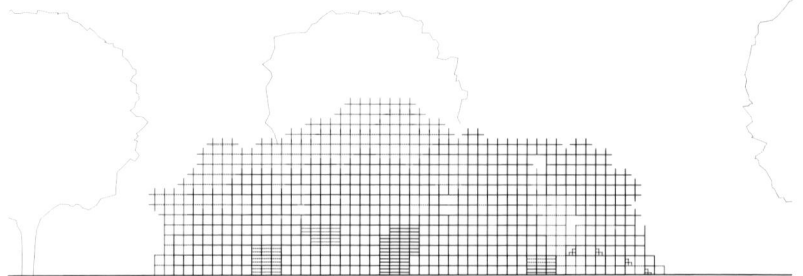

West elevation

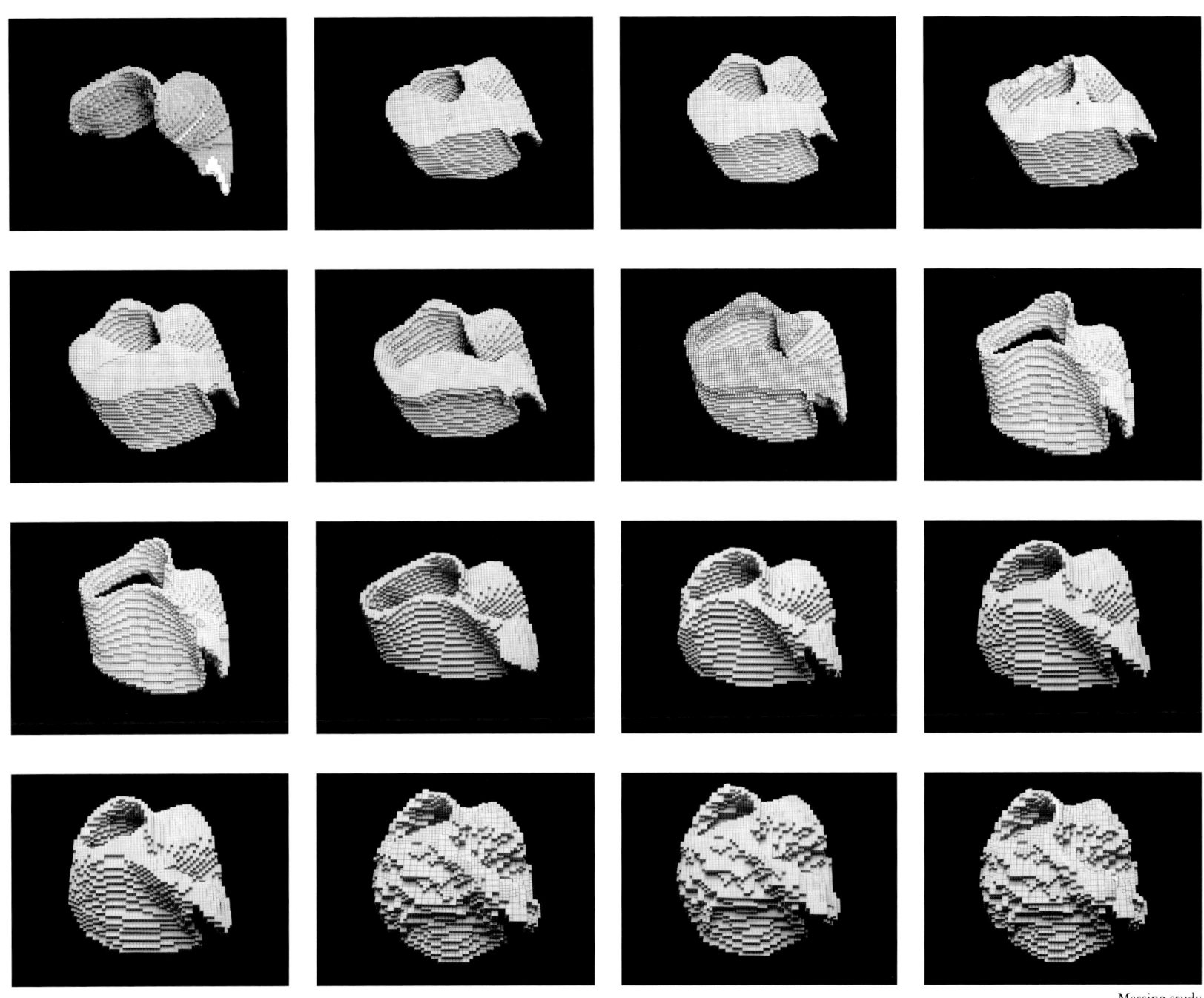

Massing study

Serpentine Gallery Pavilion 2013

South view. Lattices are covered with glasses partly and used as stairs / seats on lecture. Cafe on left.
Polycarbonate discs are set on top and side to keep out rain
南から見る。グリッドフレームは部分的に客席や階段になる。左にカフェ。
雨を防ぐためのポリカーボネイトのディスクが、角度を変えて上面、側面に付けられている

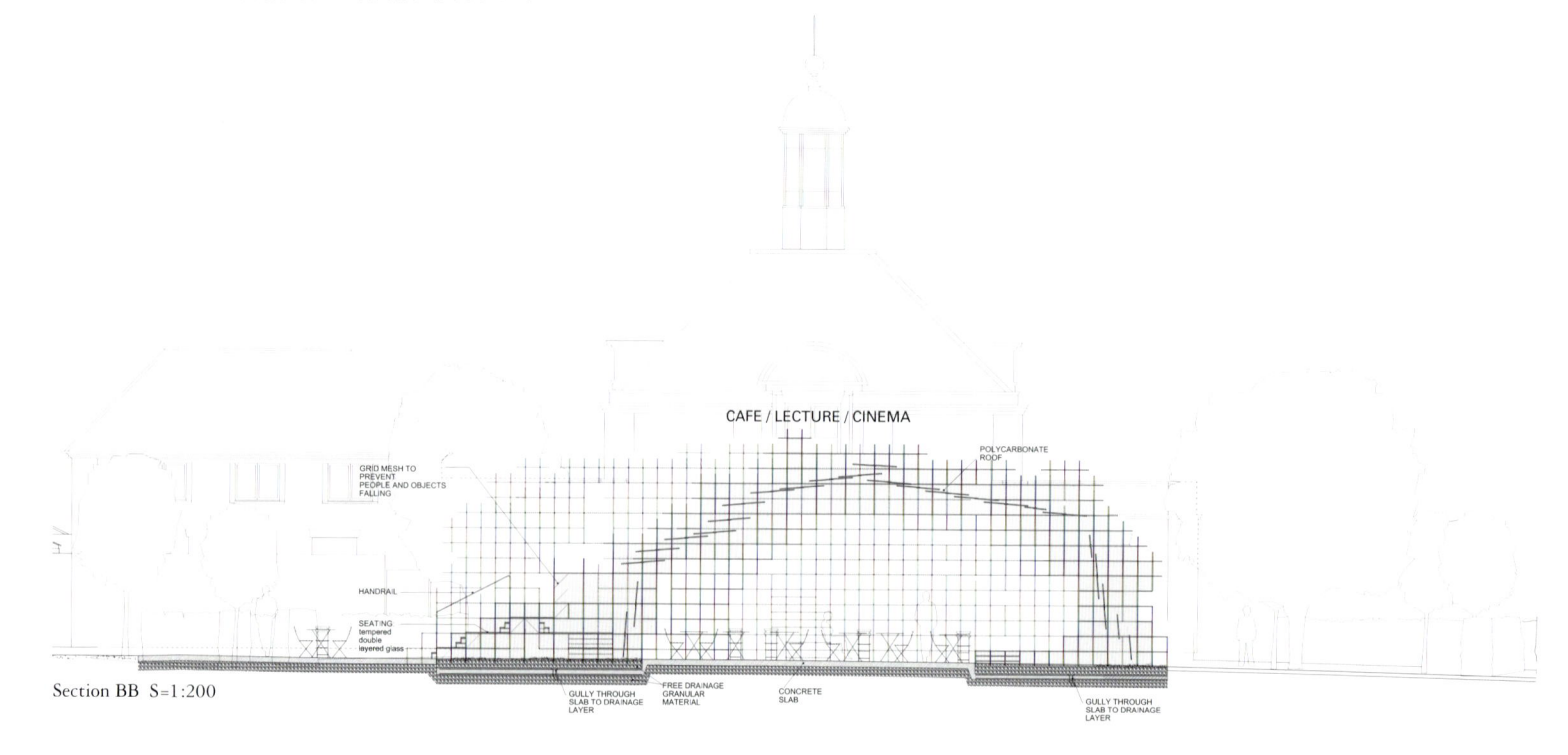

Section BB S=1:200

Evening view from cafe counter 夜景。カフェ・カウンターより見る

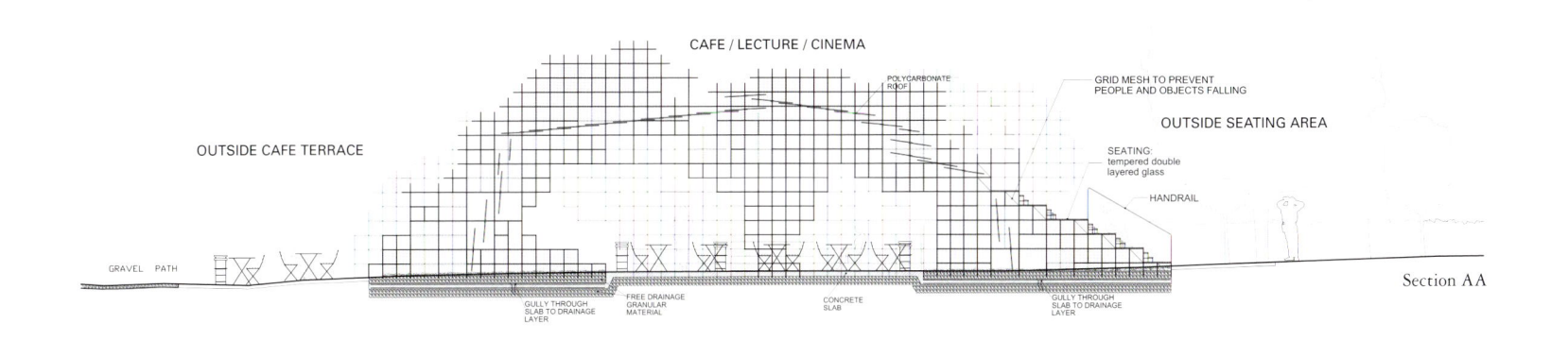

CAFE / LECTURE / CINEMA
POLYCARBONATE ROOF
GRID MESH TO PREVENT PEOPLE AND OBJECTS FALLING
OUTSIDE CAFE TERRACE
OUTSIDE SEATING AREA
SEATING: tempered double layered glass
HANDRAIL
GRAVEL PATH
GULLY THROUGH SLAB TO DRAINAGE LAYER
FREE DRAINAGE GRANULAR MATERIAL
CONCRETE SLAB
GULLY THROUGH SLAB TO DRAINAGE LAYER
Section AA

Serpentine Gallery Pavilion 2013

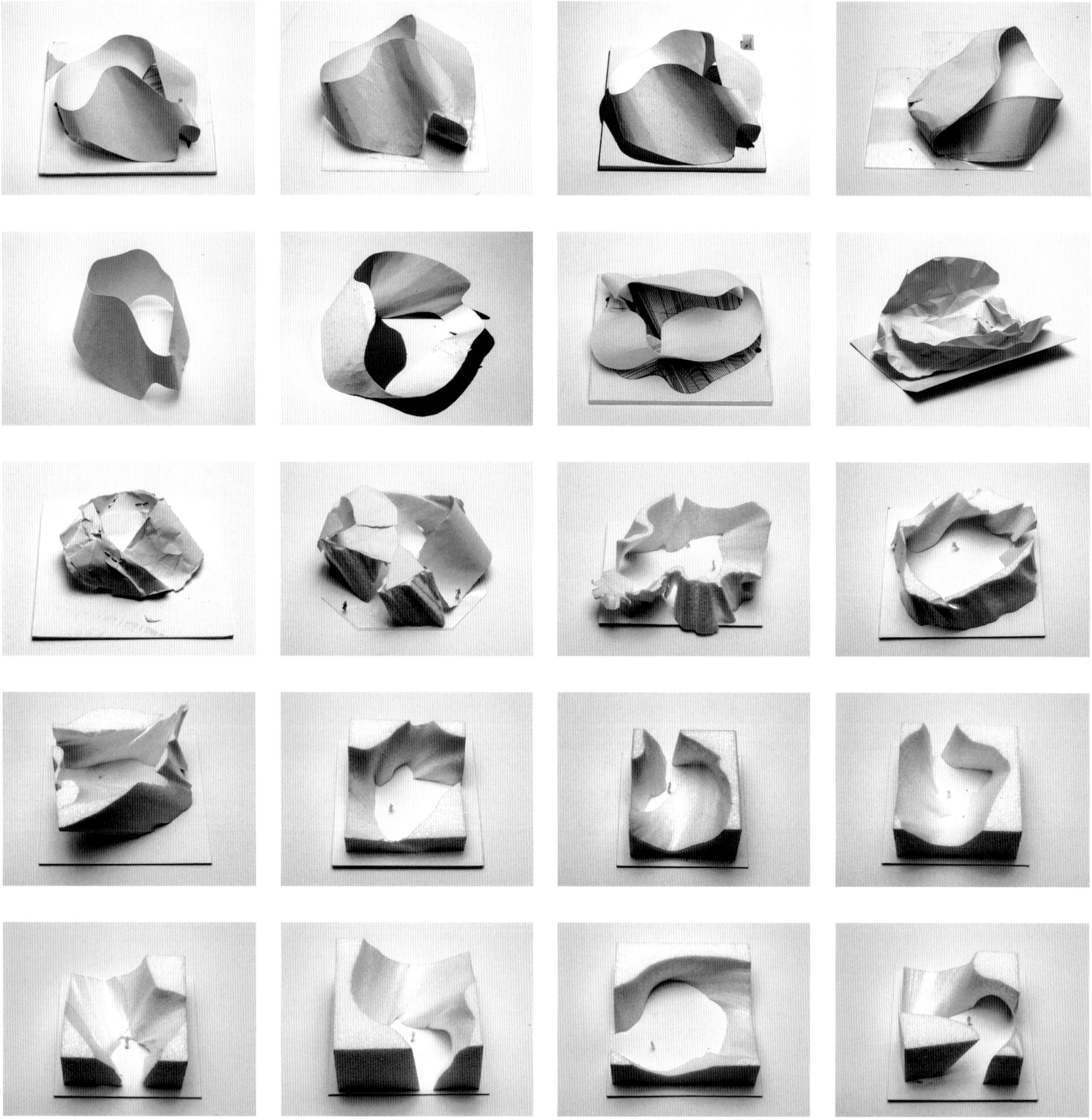

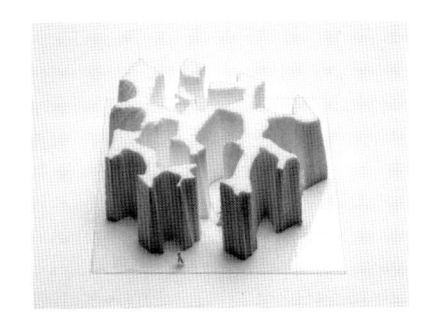

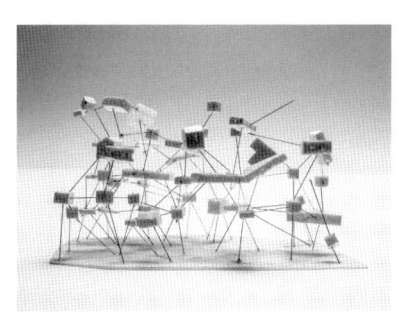

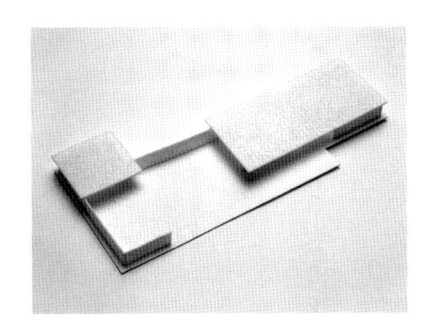

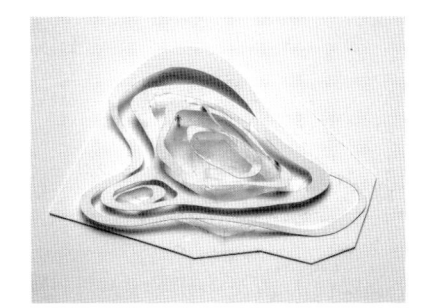

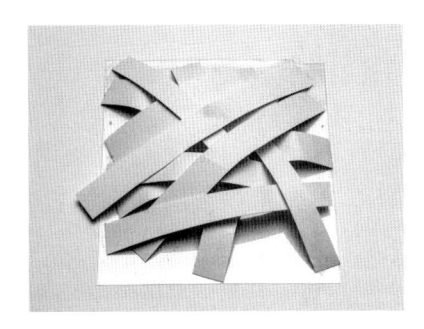

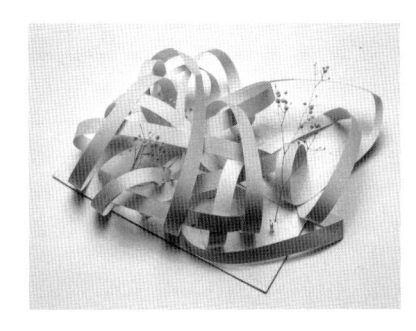

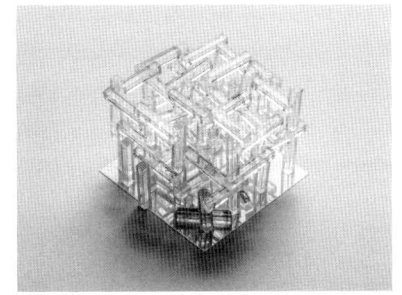

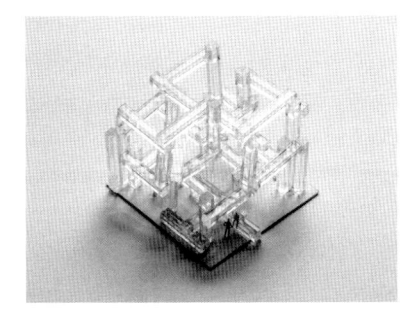

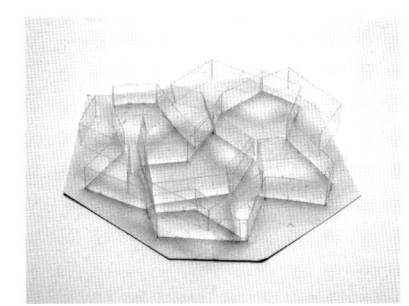

Study

Serpentine Gallery Pavilion 2013

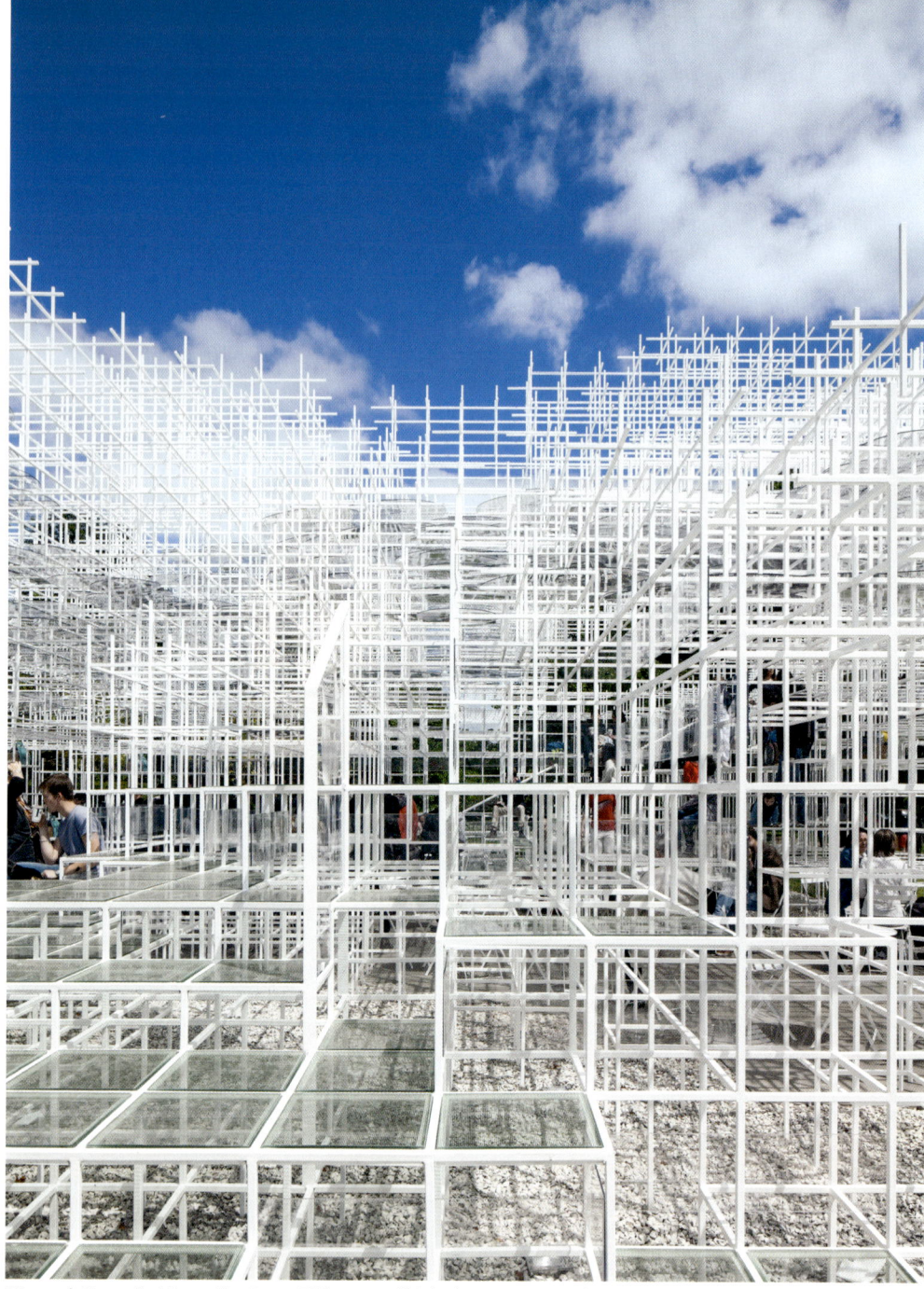

West end. Covered with nonslip glasses 西側のテラス。滑り止め加工されたガラスの床が埋められている

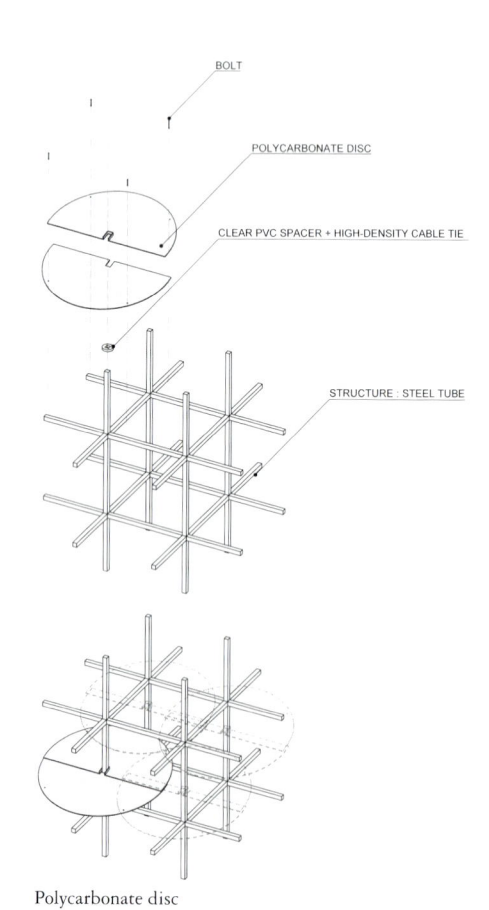

Polycarbonate disc

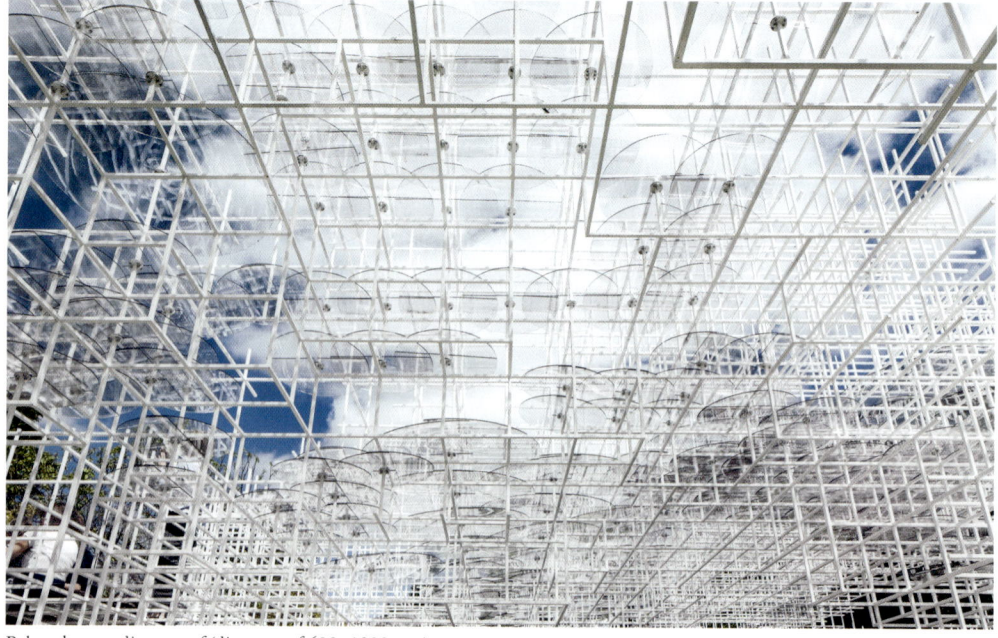

Polycarbonate disc as roof (diameter of 600, 1200mm)
「屋根」の見上げ。直径600mmと1,200mmの2種類のポリカーボネイトのディスクが差し込まれている

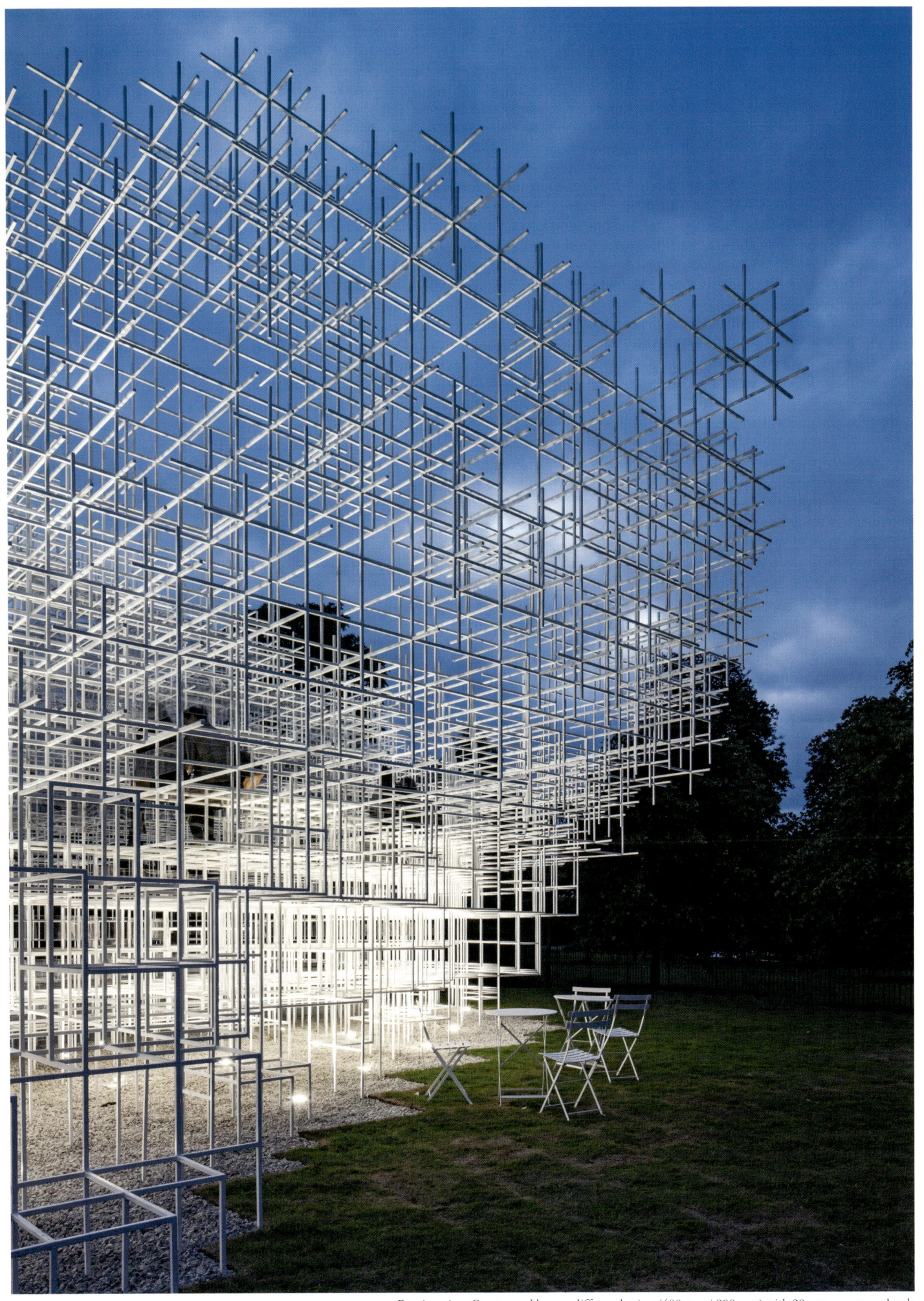

Evening view. Constructed by two different lattices (400 mm / 800 mm) with 20 mm-square steel rods
夜景。20mm角のスティールを、400mmと800mmのグリッドで組んだストラクチャー。2種類のグリッドが不思議な疎密感を生み出している

Serpentine Gallery Pavilion 2013

GEOMETRIC FOREST – SOLO HOUSES PROJECT

Cretas, Spain, 2012-
RESIDENCE

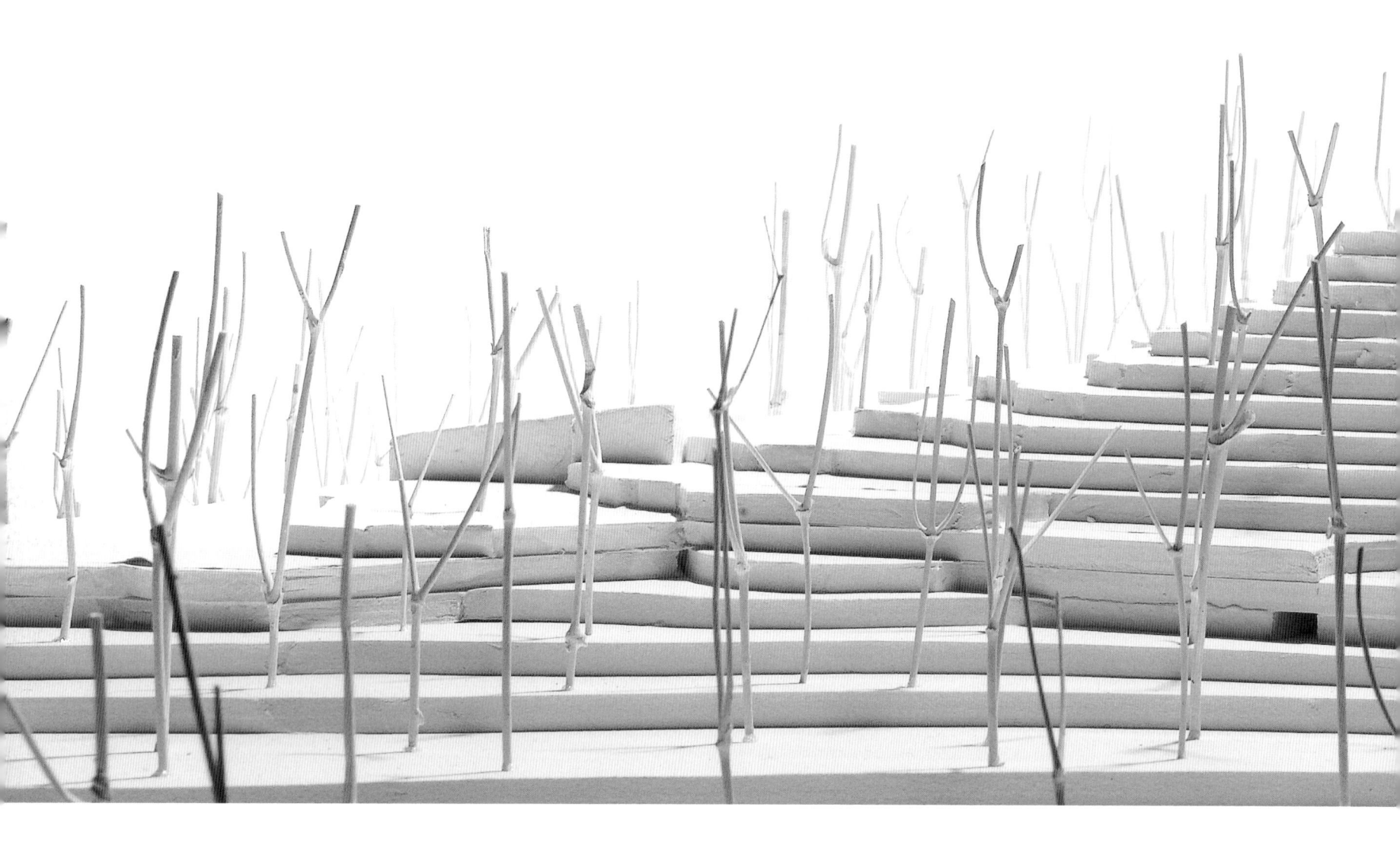

Site plan S=1:1000

1 MECHANICAL
2 LIVING ROOM AND KITCHEN
3 BEDROOM
4 BATHROOM
5 STORAGE
6 SWIMMING POOL
7 GUEST ROOM
8 TERRACE

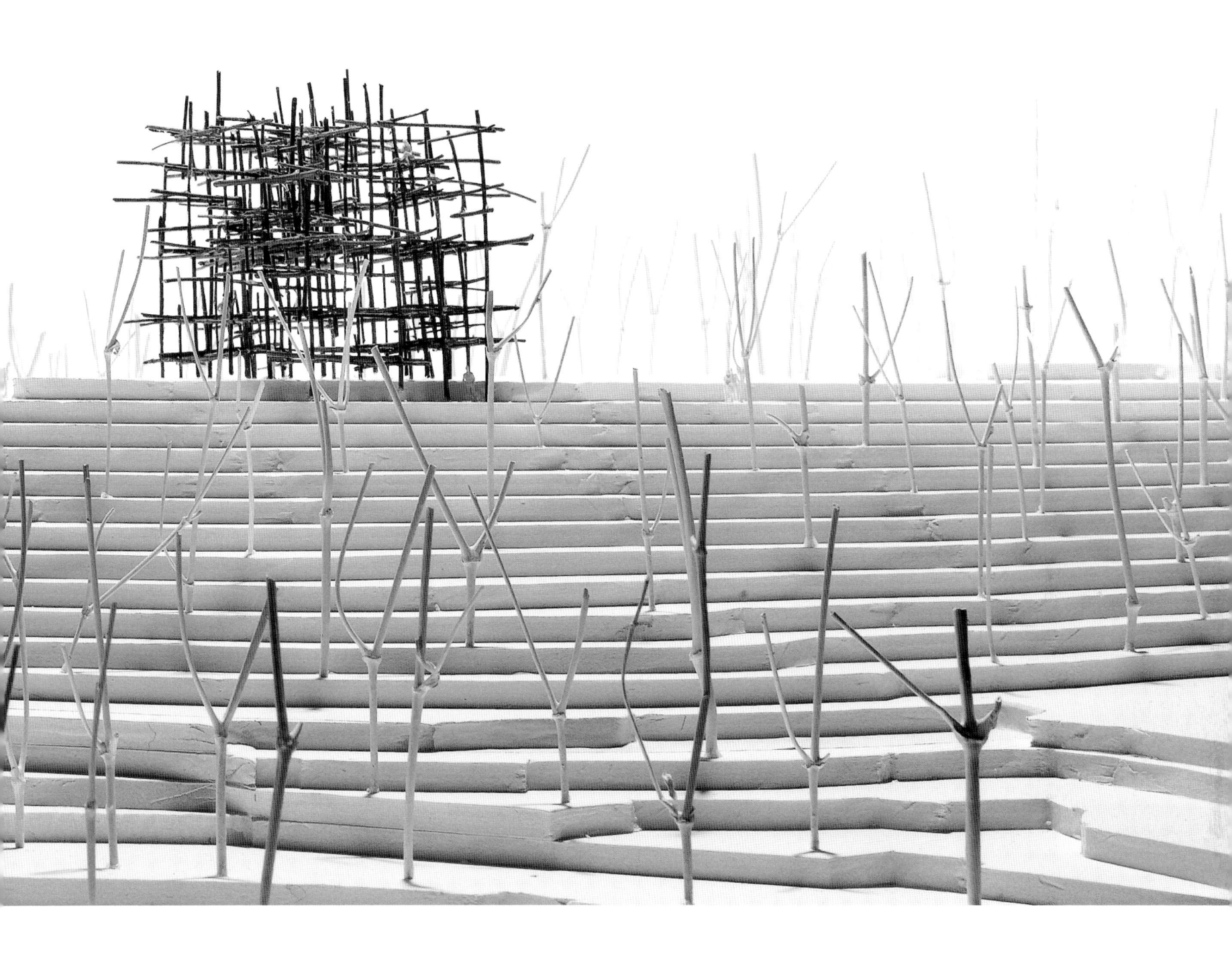

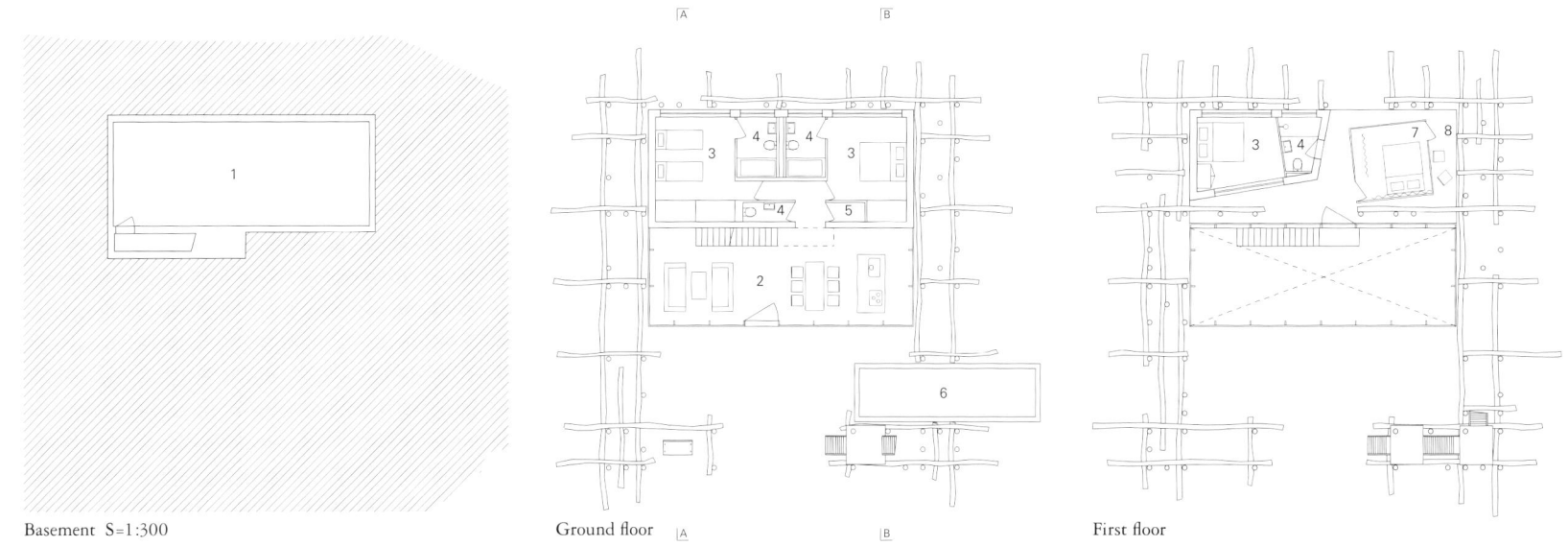

Basement S=1:300

Ground floor

First floor

Geometric Forest – Solo Houses Project

The weekend house on a hill that is two hours drive away from Barcelona. There are four bedrooms, a living-dining room and a large open-air terrace. Around the site a wonderful view of great nature extends.

The residence is, so to speak, like a place of a geometrical forest.

Log that is raw and in natural shape is assembled into three-dimensional porous lattice and creates a loose territory. Refreshing wind pass through the half natural and half artificial structure. While blocking off strong summer sunshine, it takes in foliage-filtering sunlight. The place is protected moderately, but is endlessly open.

People can clamber up the three-dimensional lattice using their body. As there is a space where a person can stay for a while at the upper part of the structure like an air terrace, people can move freely in the artificial forest, as if climbing a tree. Additionally, at the space between the lattices, places that can be used to put a potted plant or used as a shelf are interspersed.

A place to live is filled with chances for people to get involved in a variety of activities and also is to generously enclose a fairly comfortable domain with wind and sunlight. The three-dimensional forest should become a new and yet fundamental place for people to live.

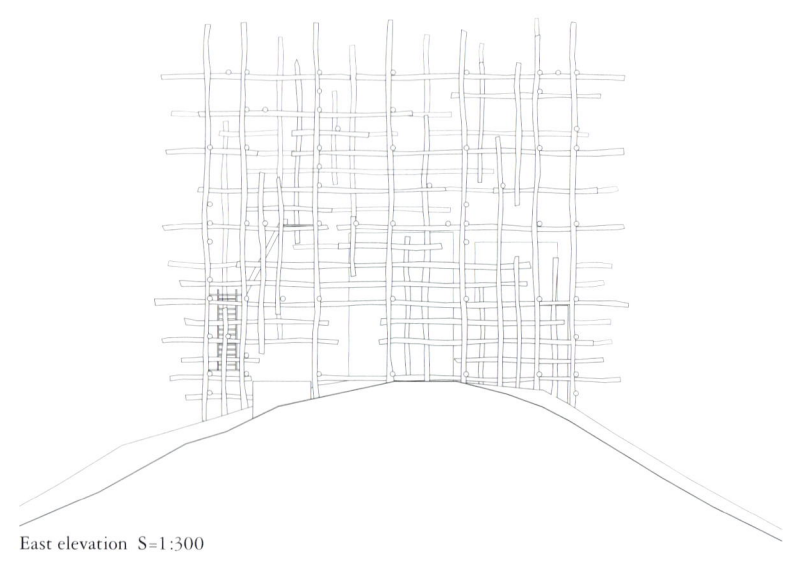

East elevation S=1:300

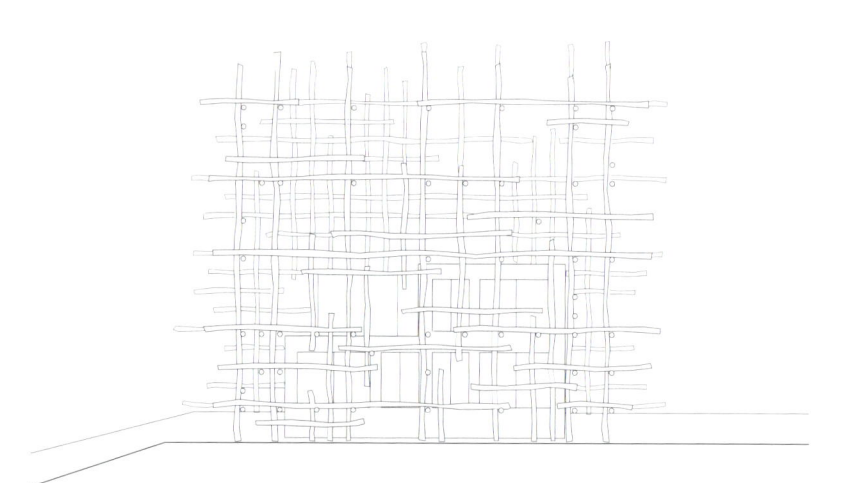

North elevation

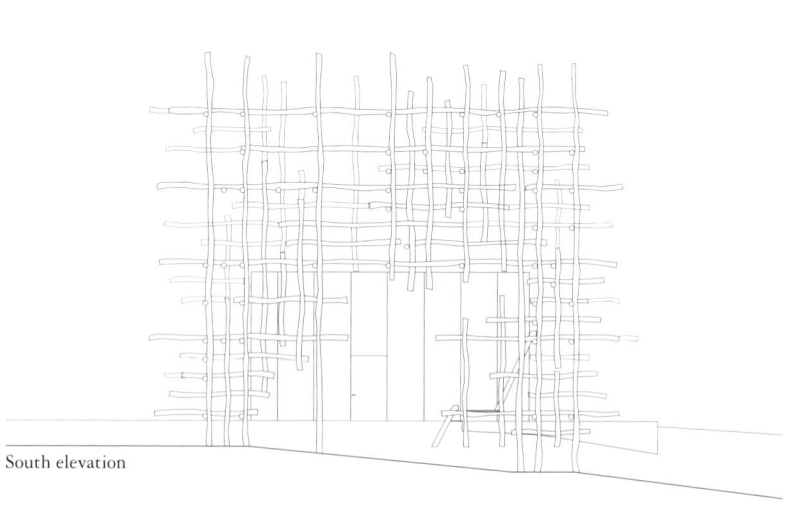

South elevation

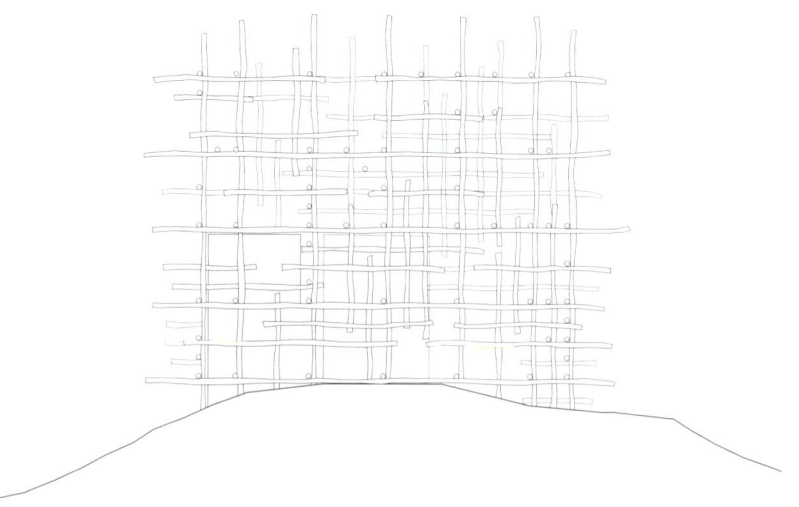

West elevation

バルセロナから車で2時間の丘陵地に建つ週末住宅。四つのベッドルームとリビングダイニング、大きな外部テラスを持つ。周辺には大自然のすばらしい眺望が広がる。

この家は、言ってみれば幾何学的な森のような場所である。

製材されていない自然の形状の木材を疎密のある立体格子状に組み合わせて緩やかな領域をつくりだす。この自然と人工の間のような構造体の隙間にはさわやかな風が吹き抜け、夏の強い日差しを遮りながら、木漏れ日のような光を取り込む。緩やかに守られていながらどこまでも開放的な場所。

人はこの立体格子の中を、自分の身体を使ってよじ上っていくことができる。構造体の上の方には空中テラスのように身を寄せることができる場所が用意されているので、木登りをするようにこの人工的な森の中を縦横無尽に動き回ることができるだろう。またこの格子の隙間には、例えば鉢植えを置いたり、棚として使うことができるような場所が散在している。

住むための場所とは、人がさまざまに関わることができるきっかけに満ちた場所であり、また風や日差しなど適度に快適な領域を緩やかに囲い取ることである。この立体格子の森は、人が住むための新しくも原初的な場所となるにちがいない。

1 MECHANICAL
2 LIVING ROOM AND KITCHEN
3 BEDROOM
4 BATHROOM
5 STORAGE
6 SWIMMING POOL
7 GUEST ROOM
8 TERRACE

Section BB

Section AA S=1:300

Geometric Forest – Solo Houses Project

TAIWAN PAVILION

Tainan, Taiwan, 2012-
PAVILION / SHOWROOM

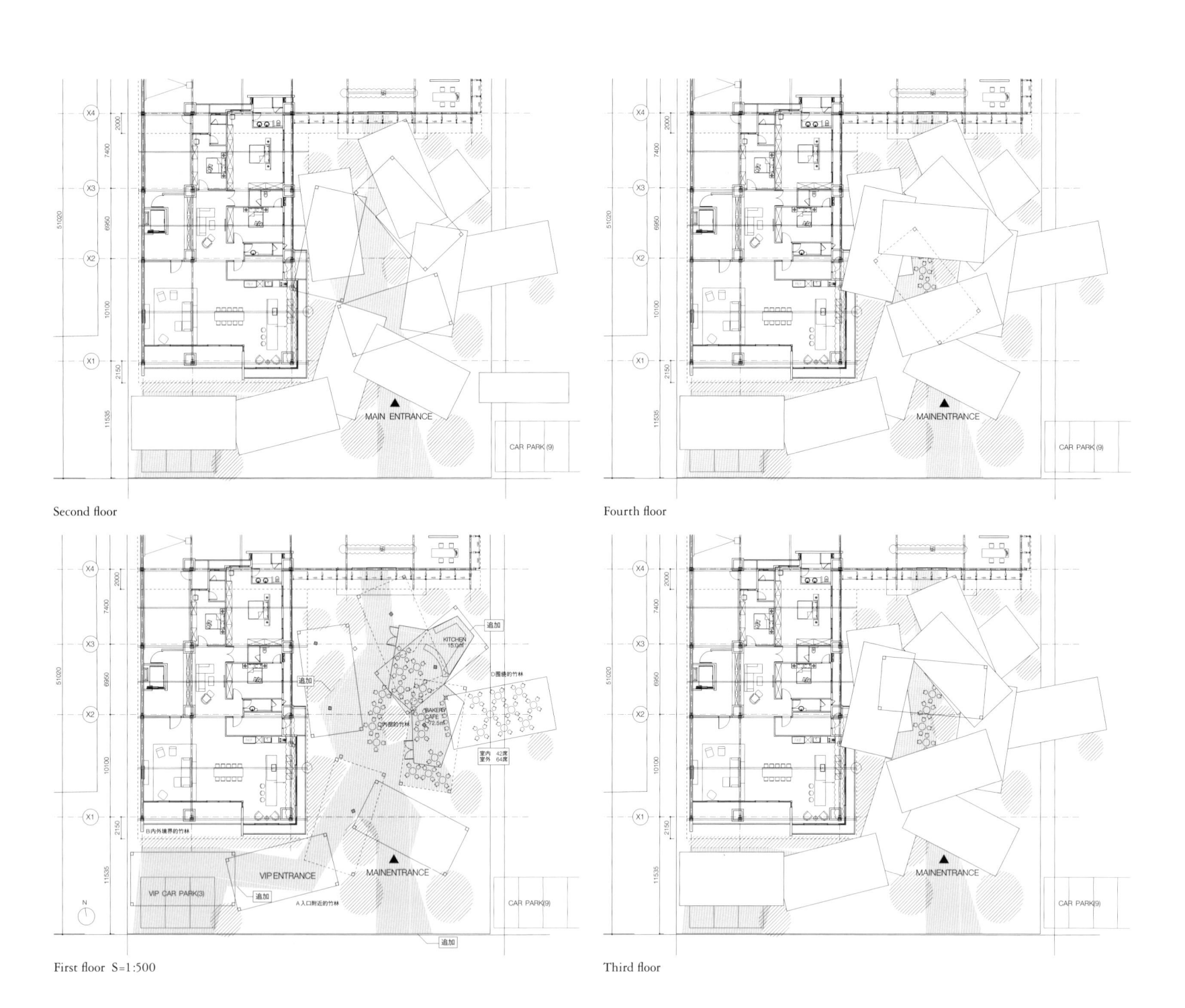

Second floor

Fourth floor

First floor S=1:500

Third floor

Overall view

Roof

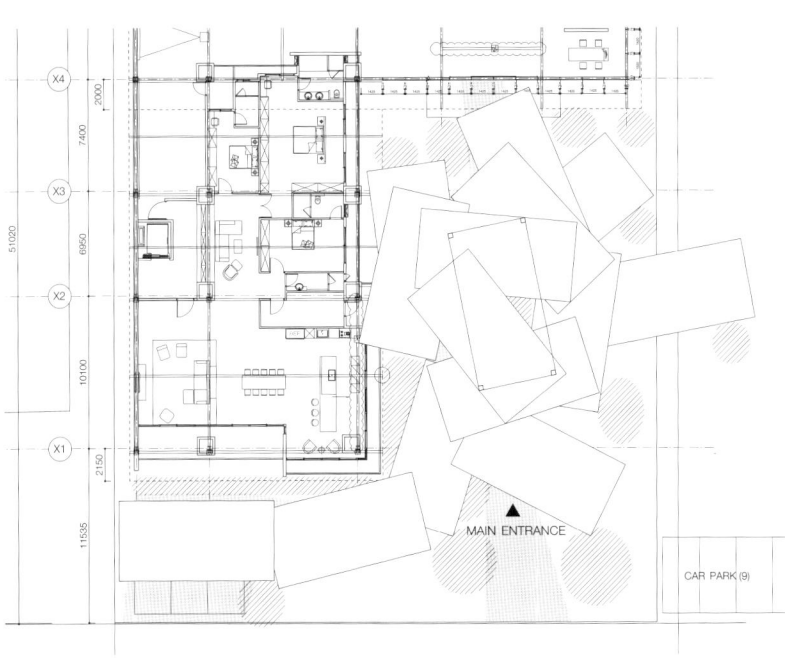

Fifth floor

The pavilion was planned on a front yard of the sales space of an apartment under construction in Tainan City. Since the site is Taiwan, it was intended to create an archetypal structure that will become a model of architecture built in the area where has a lot of rain and strong sunlight. That is the reason why the plan is something that gives new form in what is called roof. The gigantic tabular structural body is, so to speak, a model of roof. Piling the tables on top of each other, a roofed space with full of gaps is built. It is open to sky and outer space in various ways while keep sun out and drains rain water like a waterfall. Additionally, it can directly become three-dimensional architecture with plural floors, as there are many floor-like places in those gaps. Moreover, this table is considered as also ground level. It may be possible to build up a multi-layered garden or a forest by providing plants on each level. It is a prototypical proposal that is very simple and at the same time has potentials for diverse advancement.

YH Pavilion

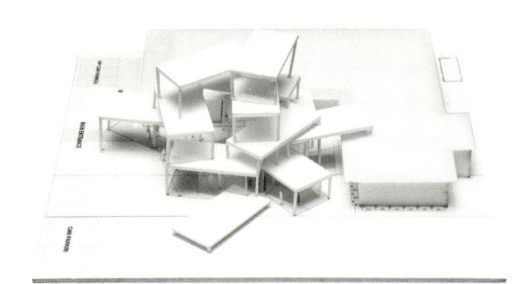

Study

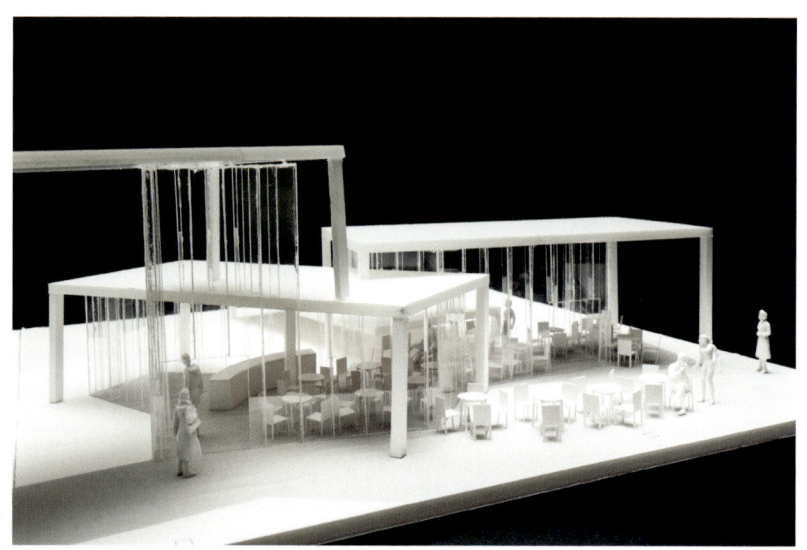

Bakery cafe

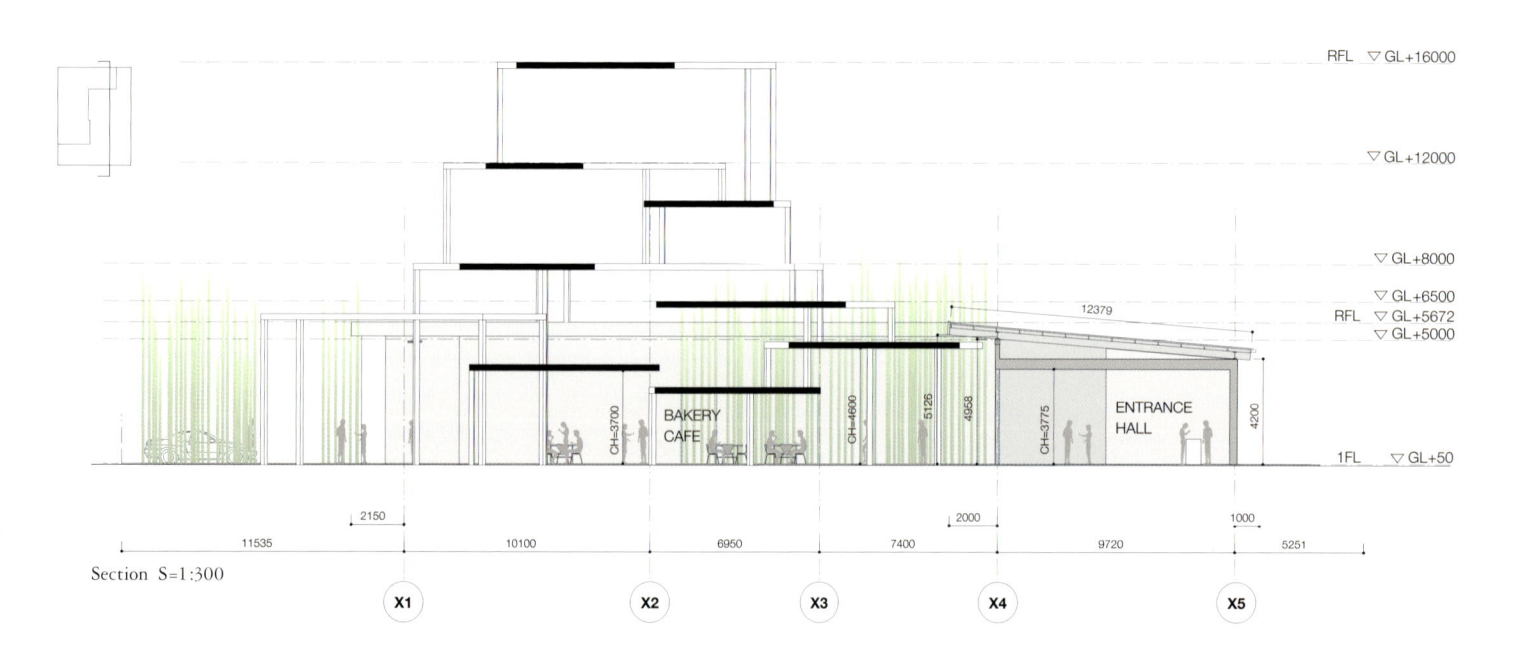

台南市で建設中のマンションの販売スペースの前庭に計画されたパヴィリオン。台湾ということから，雨が多く日射しが強い地域における建築のモデルになるような原型的な構造体をつくることを意図した。それゆえ，屋根というものに新しい形を与える案となっている。巨大なテーブル状の構造体は，いわば屋根の原型である。そのテーブルを幾重にも重ねていくことで，大きな隙間だらけの屋根空間が出来上がる。日射しを遮りながらも様々に空と外部に開かれ，また幾重にも連なる滝のように雨を受け流していく。またそれらの隙間には床のような場所が幾つもつくられるので，そのまま複数階をもった立体的な建築ともなり得る。またこのテーブルは地盤面でもある。それぞれのレベルに植栽を展開することで，複層的な庭，または森をつくり上げることも出来るだろう。とてもシンプルで同時に多様な展開があり得る原型的な提案である。

Section S=1:300

CONNECTICUT POOL HOUSE
LAYERED ROOF / FLOATING STONE HOUSE

Connecticut, U.S.A., 2012-
POOL HOUSE

Layered Roof

Floating Stone House

LAYERED ROOF

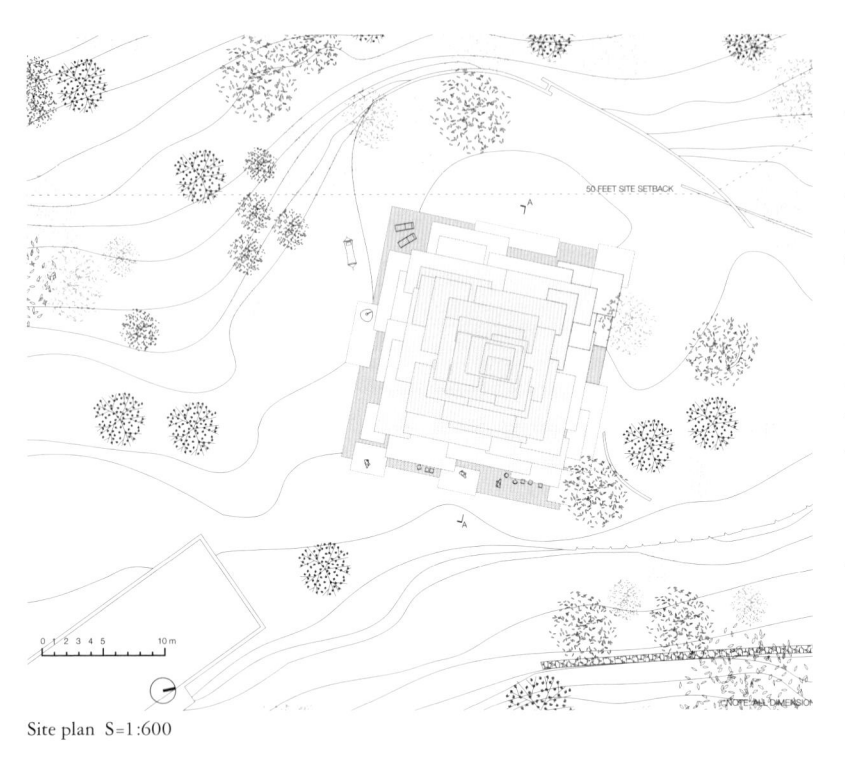

Site plan S=1:600

Regarding to the given task, an open like house on one level, we propose to redefine roof as architecture. With the silhouette of a mountain shape, Layered Roof is a series of light and thin horizontal slabs overlapping each other without touching. The house rises up and culminates 12 m (40 feet) above ground. Playing with the sunlight, creating unexpected patterns of shadows, the interior is a rich experience where the border between the sky and the house, between the garden and the indoor space vanishes.

Under this generous play of heights, the indoor space contrasts by its simplicity and flexibility.

Divided by sliding walls, the interior space allows a complete openness as well as privacy.

More than only a roof, Layered Roof becomes the house itself, as a whole, acting as shelter, as walls, terraces and furniture ...

FLOATING STONE HOUSE

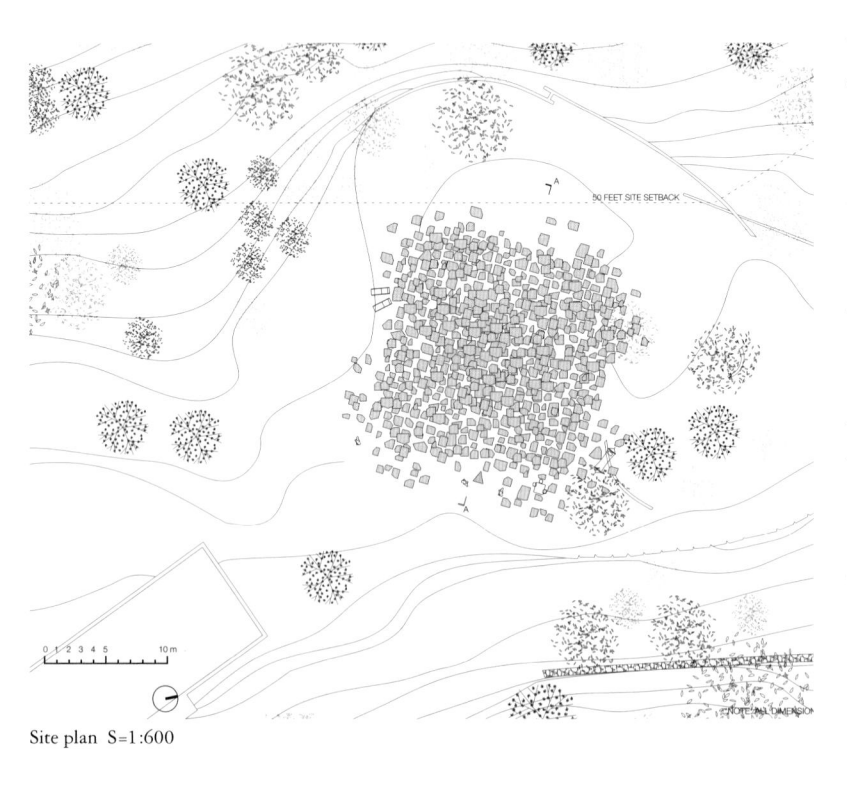

Site plan S=1:600

This proposal introduces a new architectural intervention: floating stones being used as a construction component. The pool house consists purely of stones, acting as joints for the space-frame-type structure. The outdoor shell acts as the main structure of the house, from which the glass roof is suspended while the indoor structure is independant.

Floating in the air, the stones diffuses the borders of the roof with the sky and the garden. It creates a unique play of light, shadows and colors, always changing, in accordance with seasons, time of day or weather.

The ambiguity between the massiveness and the weightlessness of the stones is reinforced by the openness of the indoor space. Acting as a roof, walls and as furniture, the different rooms find their place naturally among them, largely open to each other or easily enclosed with sliding doors if wished.

The Floating Stone House rises up lightly in the garden among the trees, interacting and changing with the weather and the sun light, as a roof of many experiences.

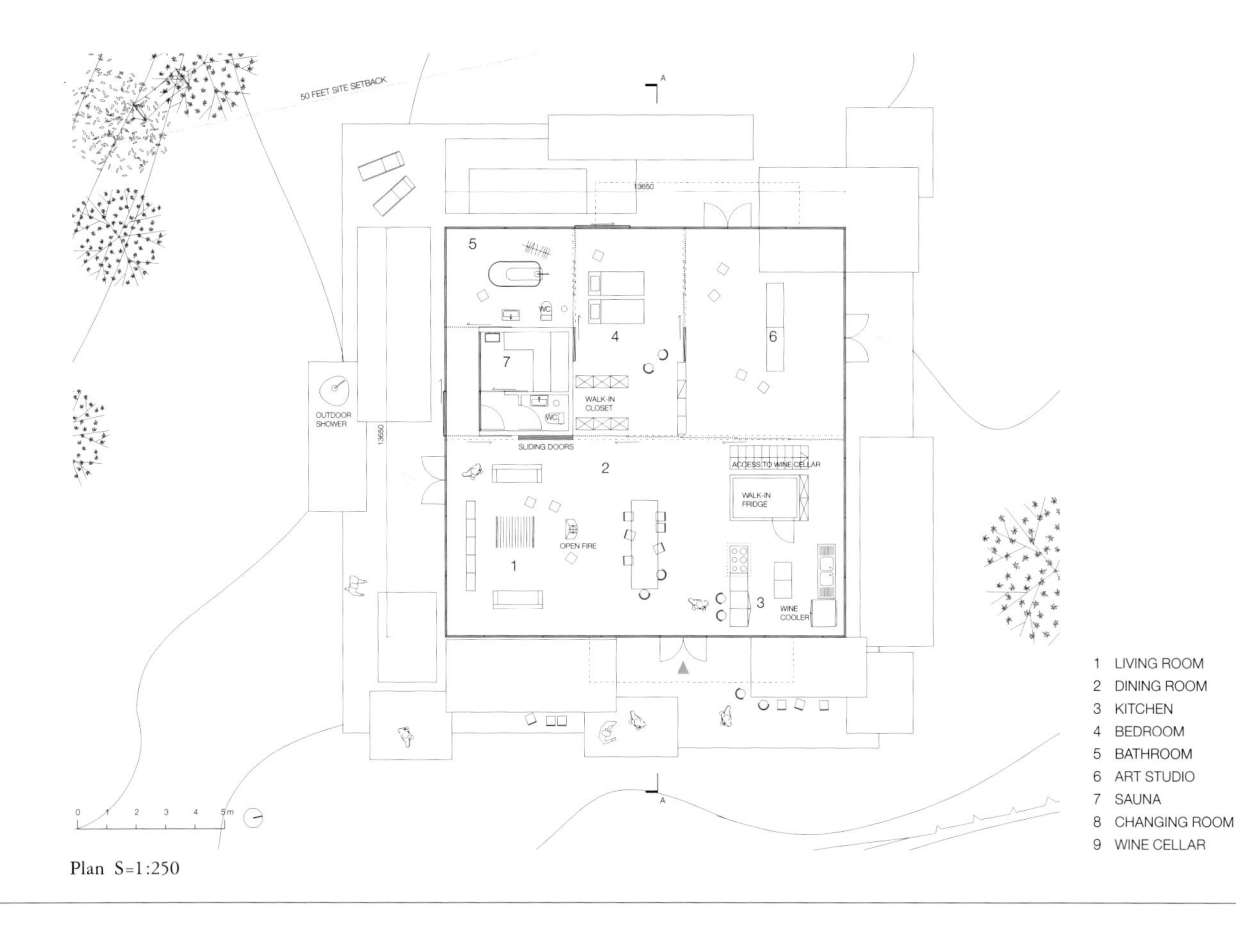

平屋のような開放性のある住宅が求められていたので，私たちは屋根を建築として再定義し提案したい。積層する屋根は薄く軽い水平なスラブが連続して重なりあい，12メートルの高さまで立ち上がる山型のシルエットをつくり出す。陽の光と戯れ，思いがけない影のパターンをつくり出し，家の中はまるで空と家の境界線上に置かれたかのようである。庭と室内の境目は消え去り豊かな空間体験が生み出される。

この多様な高さの操作により，対照的にインテリアのシンプルさとフレキシビリティが際立つ。

可動壁で室内を仕切ることで，プライバシーに配慮しつつ徹底的な開放感を両立させている。

単なる屋根というものを超えて，積層する屋根は家そのものになり，また時に家全体がシェルターや壁やテラスや家具としても機能する。

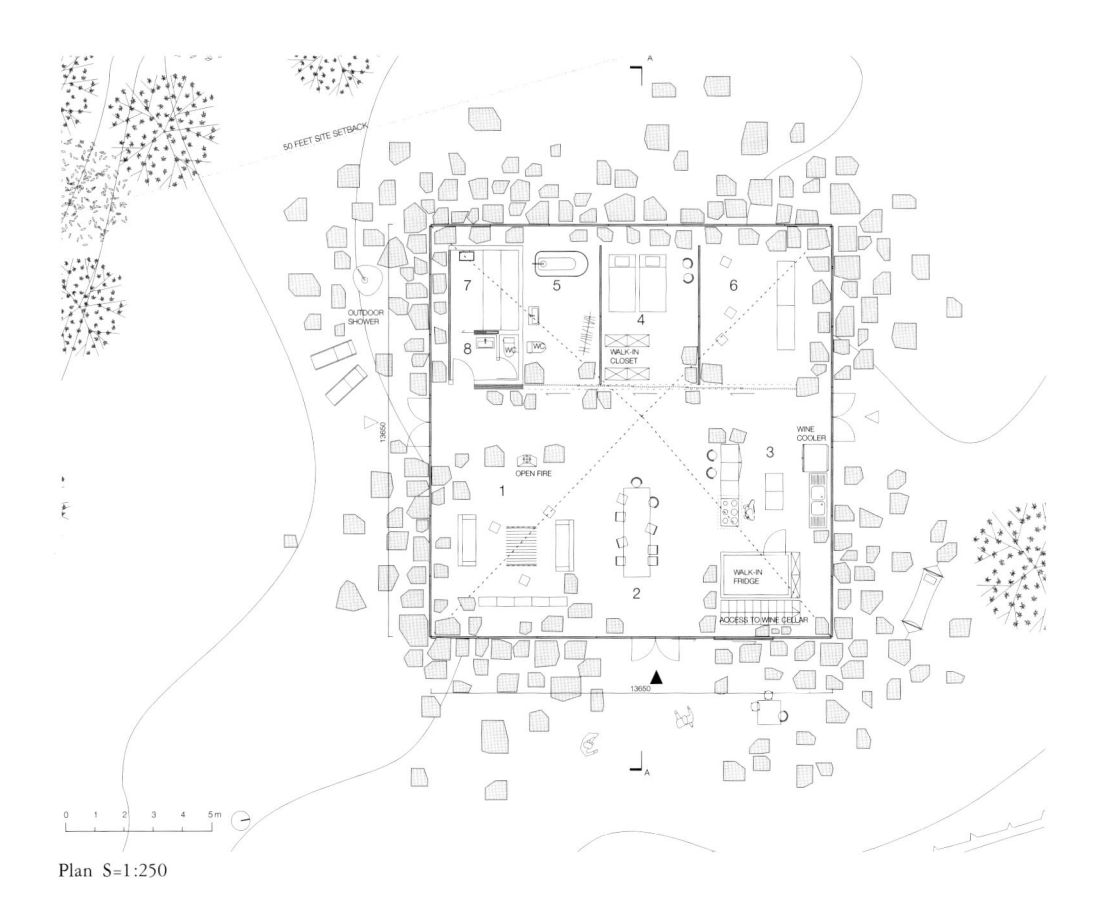

1 LIVING ROOM
2 DINING ROOM
3 KITCHEN
4 BEDROOM
5 BATHROOM
6 ART STUDIO
7 SAUNA
8 CHANGING ROOM
9 WINE CELLAR

Plan S=1:250

この提案では新たな建築的介入の仕方を提案する。宙に浮いた石は建物を構成する部品として使われている。スペースフレーム型の構造の接合部は純粋に石のみで接合されプールハウスを構成している。外側の外殻は主構造として働き，そこから屋根が吊られ，室内の構造は自立している。

空中に漂う石が空と庭の境界線を曖昧にし，日の移り変わりや気候，季節によって常に変化する光と影，様々な色をユニークに演出する。また開放的な内部空間が石の重さと浮遊感の両義性を強調する。

互いに大きく開いたり，また必要に応じ可動壁で容易に閉じられることで，屋根や壁や家具として機能しながらそれぞれの部屋に自然と居場所ができあがっていく。

宙に浮く石の家は木々に囲まれた庭の中に軽やかに立ち上がり，多様な体験に満ちた屋根として天気や日の光とともに変化し影響しあう。

Plan S=1:250

Connecticut Pool House – Layered Roof / Floating Stone House

LAYERED ROOF

FLOATING STONE HOUSE

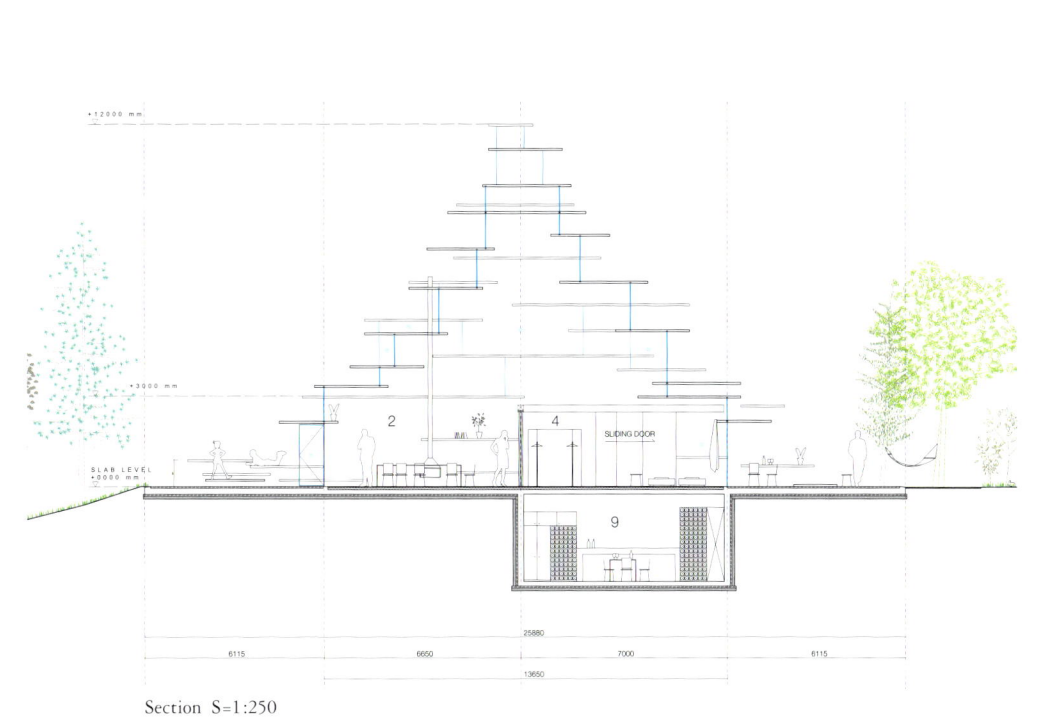

Section S=1:250

1 LIVING ROOM
2 DINING ROOM
3 KITCHEN
4 BEDROOM
5 BATHROOM
6 ART STUDIO
7 SAUNA
8 CHANGING ROOM
9 WINE CELLAR

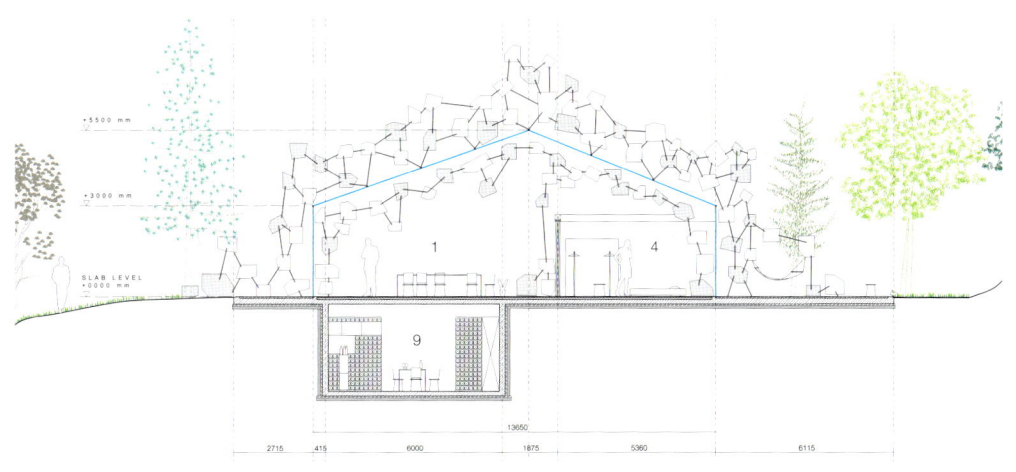

Section S=1:250

Connecticut Pool House – Layered Roof / Floating Stone House

CATALUNYA HOUSE
Caldes de Malavella, Spain, 2012-
RESIDENCE

Circle/Square schemes are both studied currently
現在, "丸"案と"四角"案を同時にスタディしている

CIRCLE

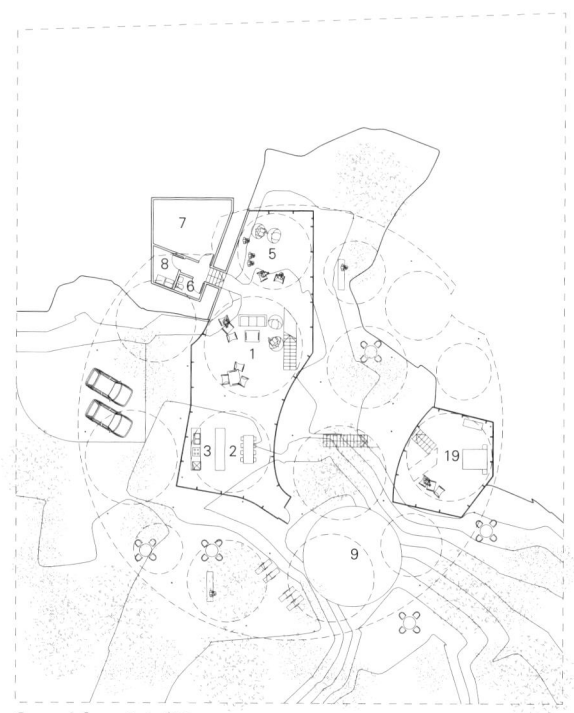

Site plan S=1:1000

Ground floor S=1:600

SQUARE

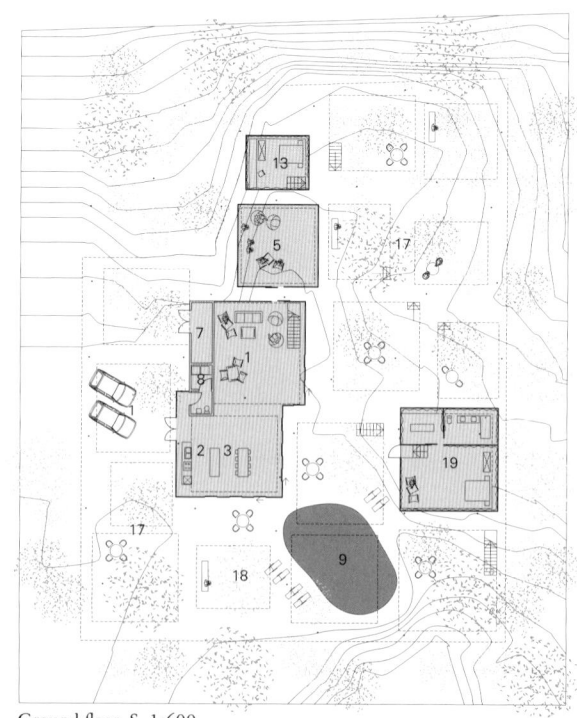

1 LIVING ROOM
2 DINIG ROOM
3 KITCHEN
4 BEDROOM
5 AUDIO-VISUAL
6 BATHROOM
7 STORAGE
8 LAUNDRY
9 POOL
10 ENTRANCE
11 OFFICE
12 LIBRARY
13 GUEST ROOM
14 DRESSING ROOM
15 LOFT
16 CARPORT
17 GARDEN
18 CABANA
19 MATER BEDROOM

Site plan S=1:1000

Ground floor S=1:600

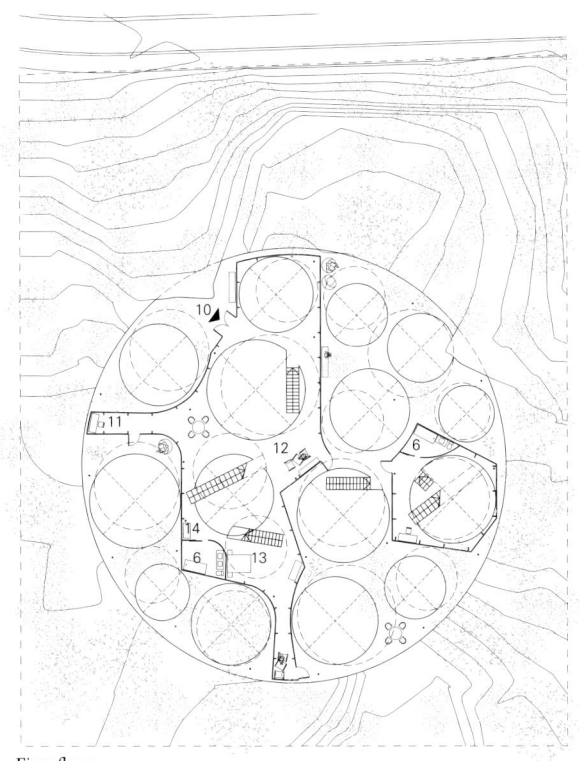

First floor

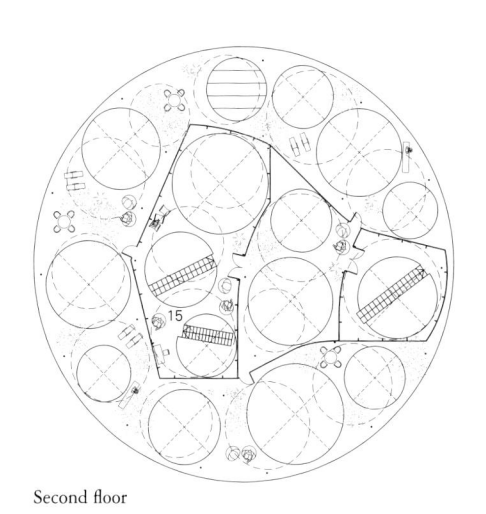

Second floor

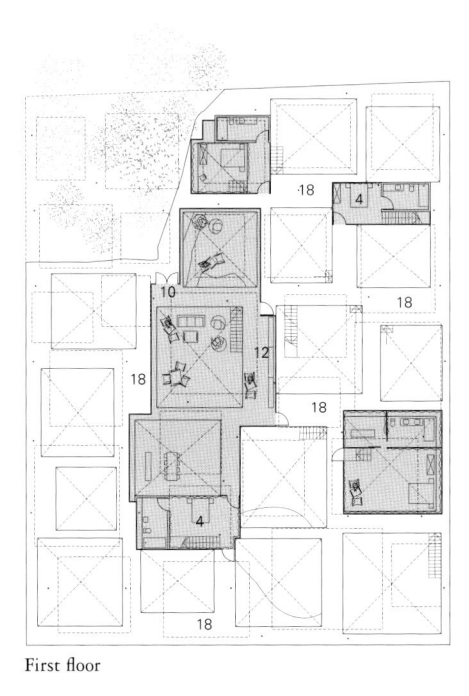

First floor

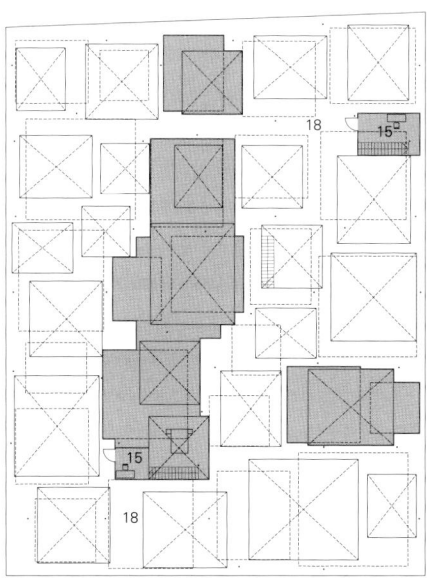

Second floor

A villa planned in a resort community facing a golf course 70 km northeast of Barcelona, Spain. The site's terrain is rolling and surrounded by a vast expanse of forest.

What we propose here is an architecture as a 'multi-layered forest.' Set in a rich natural environment, not only the interior spaces but also the exterior terrace that floats in the air are certain to be a place for living a rich life. Slabs with many apertures are piled up and trees are arranged in between in order to create a three-dimensional terrace space or a three-dimensional forest. In other words, this layering of slabs is a reinvention of natural terrain by means of artificial framework. We were focused on building a rich, habitable environment instead of constructing a house.

The interior space is defined by simply partitioning the three-dimensional terrace with glass. In this manner, the entire house becomes a multi-layered place encompassing a complex combination of interior and exterior. Round / square apertures are misaligned as they overlap, generating a sense of forest-like spatial ensemble. On the undulating ground level, these laminated slabs will be felt as a porous roof. The in-between floors are reminiscent of a three-dimensional city or a hanging terrace afloat in the forest. As the floor goes up there is a growing sense of opening toward the sky. Diversification of indoor/outdoor spaces is the consequence of void layering.

Fusion between indoor and outdoor spaces and multi-layered landscape are the key concepts of this residence, that are bound to become important subject themes in architecture in the years to come.

Circle

Square

CIRCLE

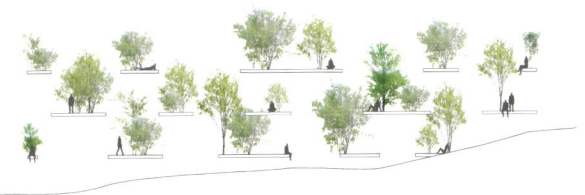

Diagram

SQUARE

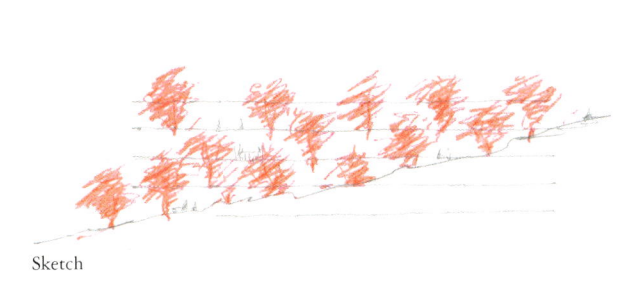

Sketch

Catalunya House

スペイン，バルセロナの北東70キロに位置する，ゴルフコースに面した別荘地に計画されている別荘住宅。敷地には起伏があり，周囲は豊かな林が広がっている。

ここに提案するのは「多層的な森」としての建築である。

このような豊かな自然環境の中では，内部空間だけではなく，空中に浮かぶ外部テラスも豊かな生活の場所となるはずだ。ここではたくさんの開口を空けたスラブを積み上げ，そこに樹木を配置することで，立体的なテラス空間，あるいは立体的な森をつくり出す。このスラブの積層は，自然の敷地を人工的な構造体によって再発明したものだと言えるのではないだろうか。家を造るのではなく，人が住むことができる豊かな環境を構築することを考えた。

内部空間はこの立体テラスをシンプルにガラスで区切ることで囲い取る。家全体が内部と外部を複雑に内包した多層的な場所となる。幾つもの丸い／四角い開口は各層でズレながら重なるので，森のような空間の重層感が生まれる。起伏した地上レベルではこれらの積層スラブは多孔質の屋根として感じられるであろう。また中間階では森の中に浮かぶ空中テラスか立体都市のようでもあり，上階に行くに従って空に開けた開放感が生まれる。ヴォイドの積層によって多様な内部／外部空間が生まれる。

内外の融合と多層的なランドスケープというこの住宅のコンセプトは，これからの建築の重要なテーマとなるに違いない。

CIRCLE

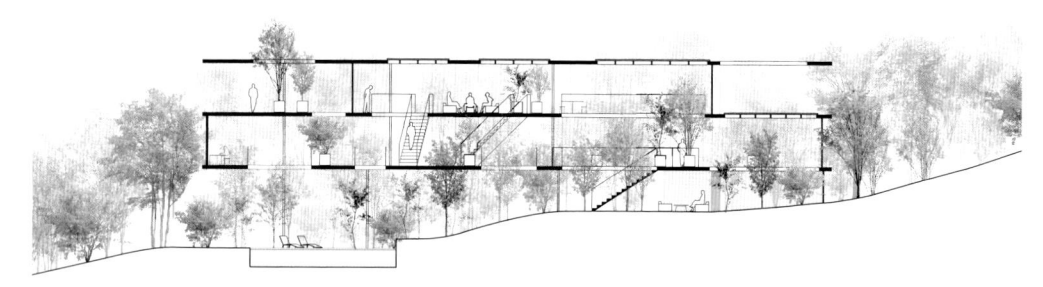

Section S=1:400

SQUARE

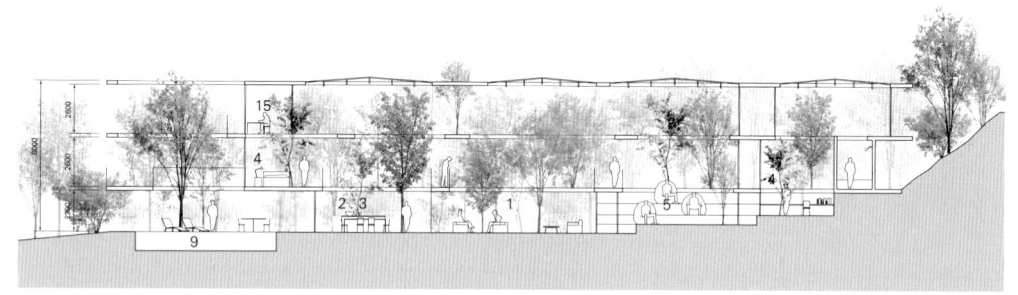

Longitudinal section

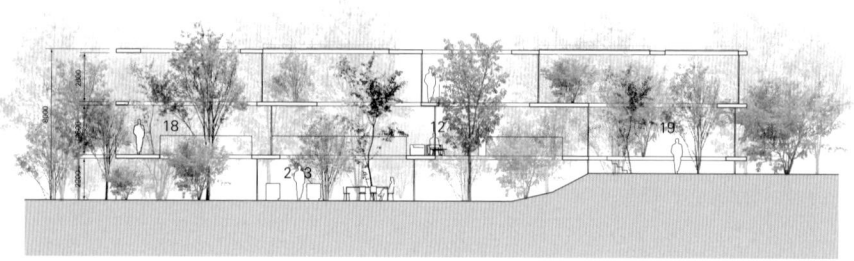

Cross section S=1:400

21ST CENTURY RAINFOREST ARCHITECTURE
Libreville, Gabon, 2012
CONFERENCE CENTER

Site plan S=1:6000

Our proposal is for a new conference center inspired by the rainforest, expressing the nature, service and industry of an emerging Gabon. Gabon has an abundance of rich rainforest of which its people can be proud of.

The rainforest, structured according to its ecosystem, form, height, and variety of vegetation, forms a rich natural environment. Our proposal is to form such an environment for the new conference center. A variety of circular slabs with large holes are layered and shifted creating a complex and diverse environment akin to the stratification of the rainforest. By placing trees in the voids of the stacked slabs, the three dimensionality of rainforest-like vegetation can be created. In taking a cue from the rainforest, we are proposing a conference center unlike any other in the world, which embodies Gabon's unique identity as well as its comfortable and diverse exterior environment. This new form of the rich union of nature and artificiality is the architectural embodiment of Gabon emergent's 'GREEN / SERVICE / INDUSTRY'.

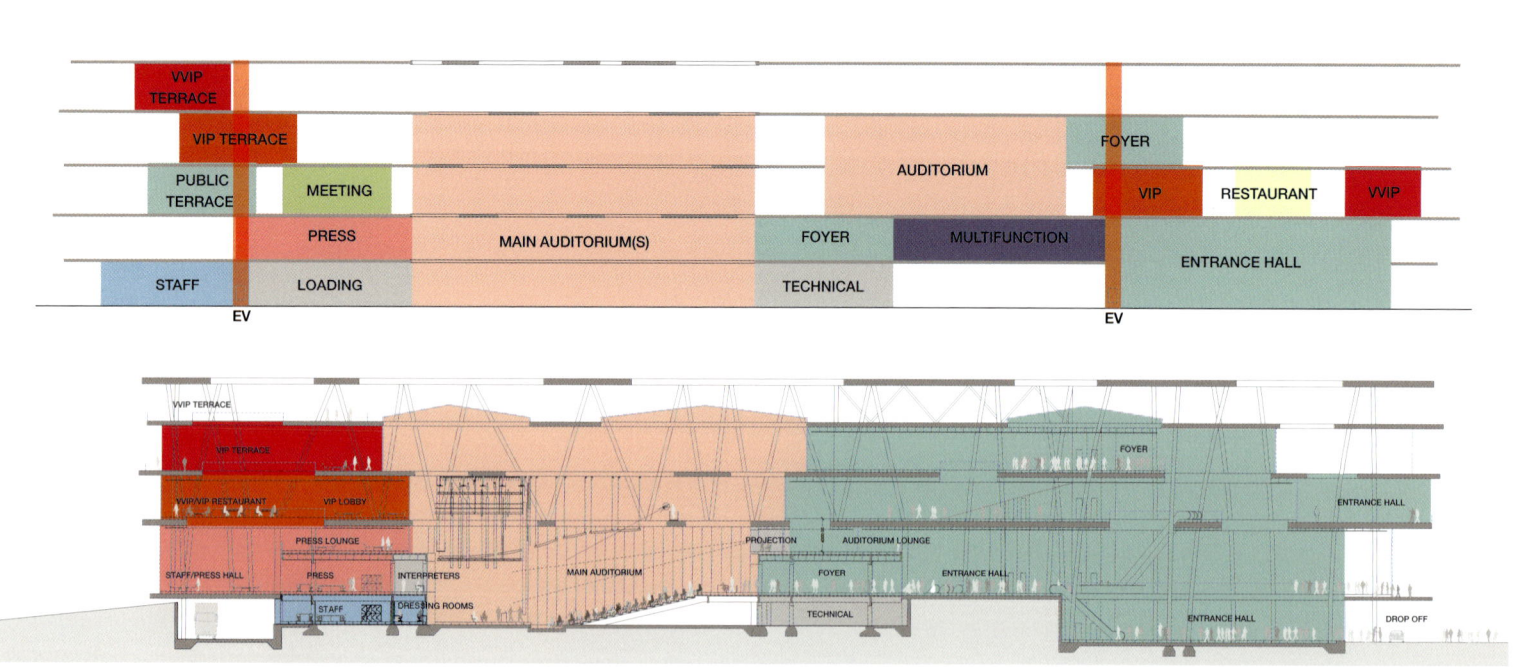

Zoning diagram

Garden

Auditorium

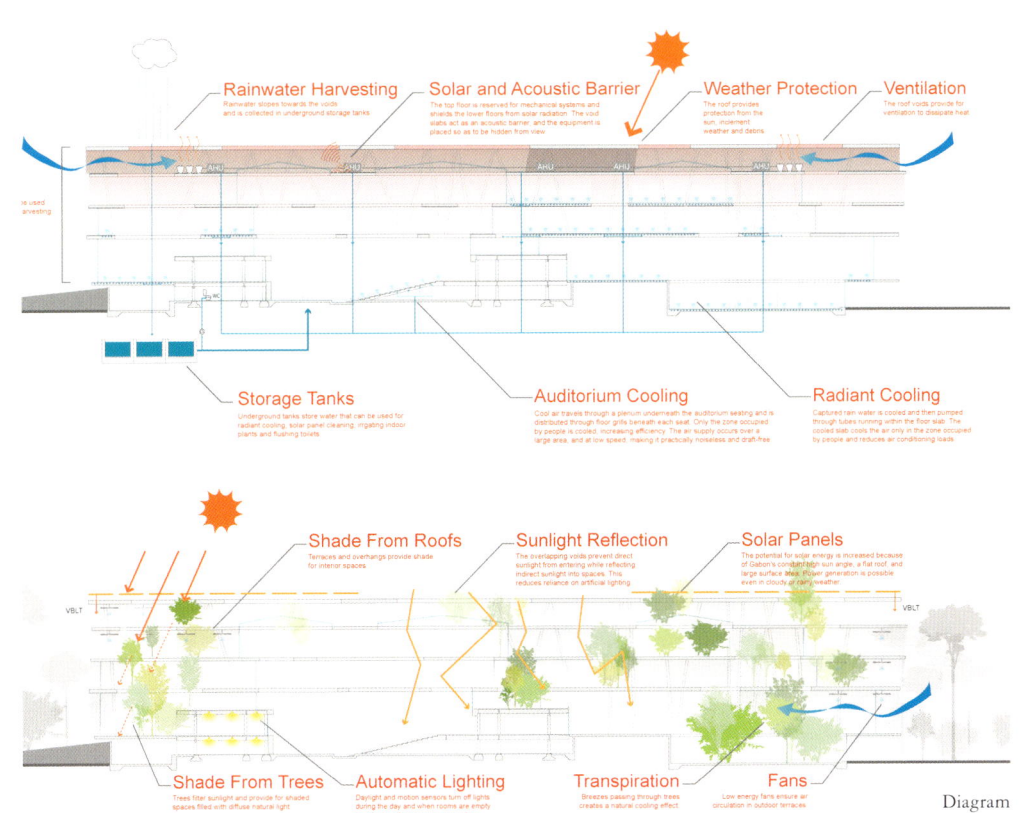

Diagram

ガボンには人々が誇る豊かな熱帯雨林がある。この提案は、そのガボンの熱帯雨林に着想を得たコンファレンスセンターの提案であり、成長するガボンの自然やサービス、産業を表現している。

熱帯雨林はその生態系や高さ、形状、また多様な植生によって自らを構成し豊かな自然環境を生み出している。私達の提案は新たなコンファレンスセンターにそのような環境をつくりだそうとするものである。大きなヴォイドを持った様々なスラブがずれながら積み重なり、複雑で熱帯雨林の重なりのような多様な環境をつくり出す。また積層するスラブのヴォイド内に木々を配置することで、熱帯雨林のような植栽が立体的に広がる。熱帯雨林をアイディアのきっかけにして、私たちはガボンの独特なアイデンティティを体現する独創的なコンファレンスセンターと、快適かつ多様な外部環境を提案する。自然と人工物が豊かに融合したこのコンファレンスセンターの形はガボンの新たな緑とサービス、産業を建築的に表現している。

21st Century Rainforest Architecture

Second floor

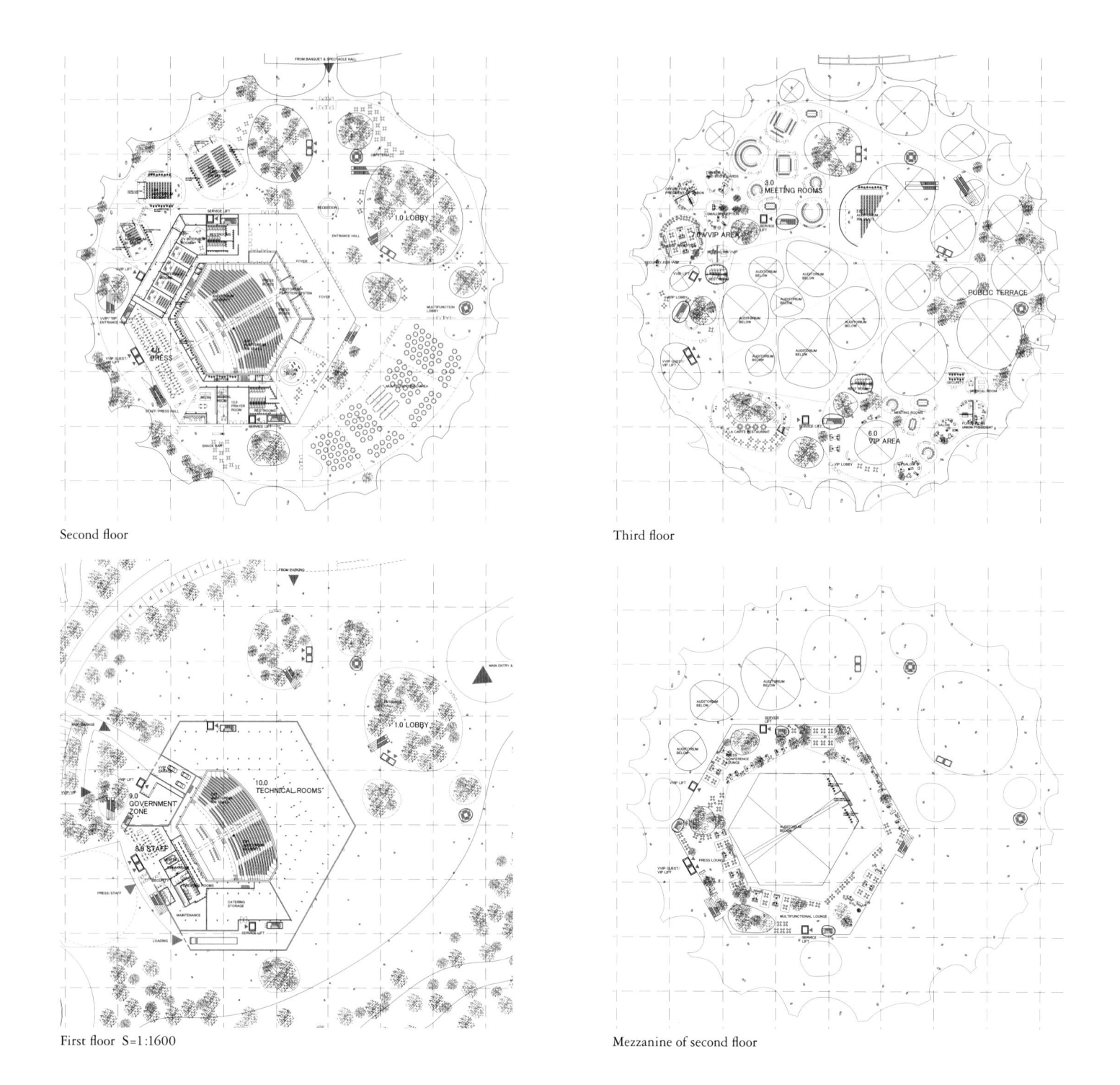

Third floor

First floor S=1:1600

Mezzanine of second floor

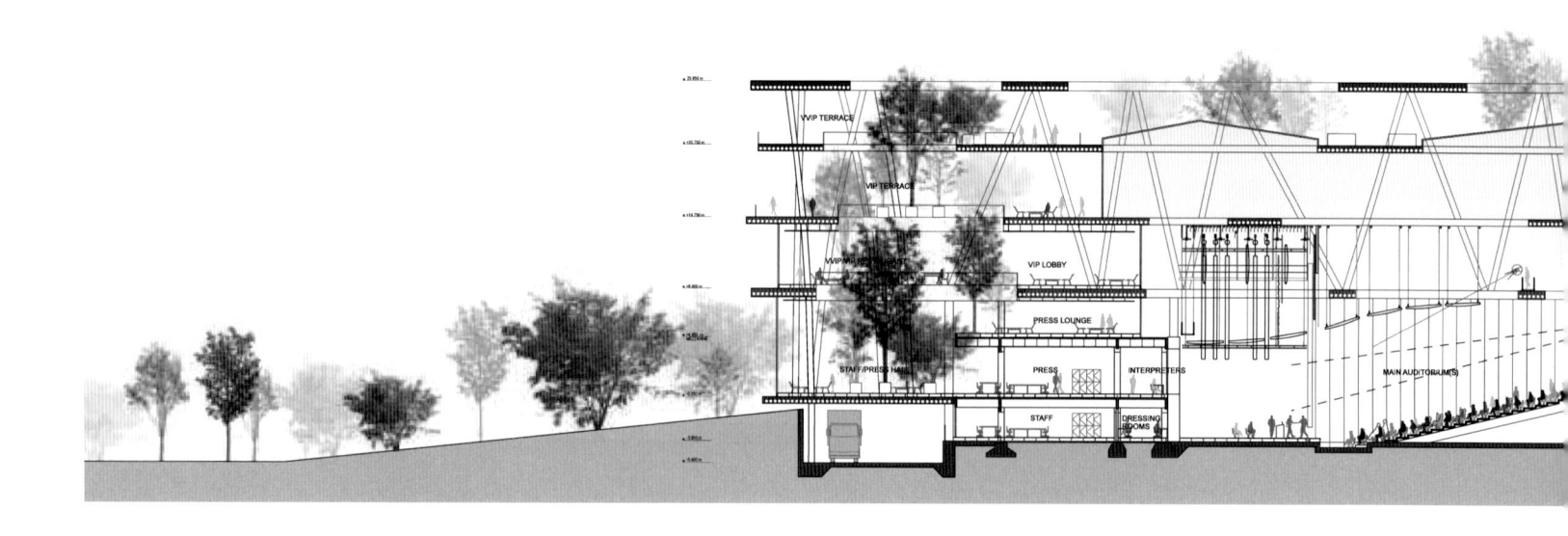

Fifth floor

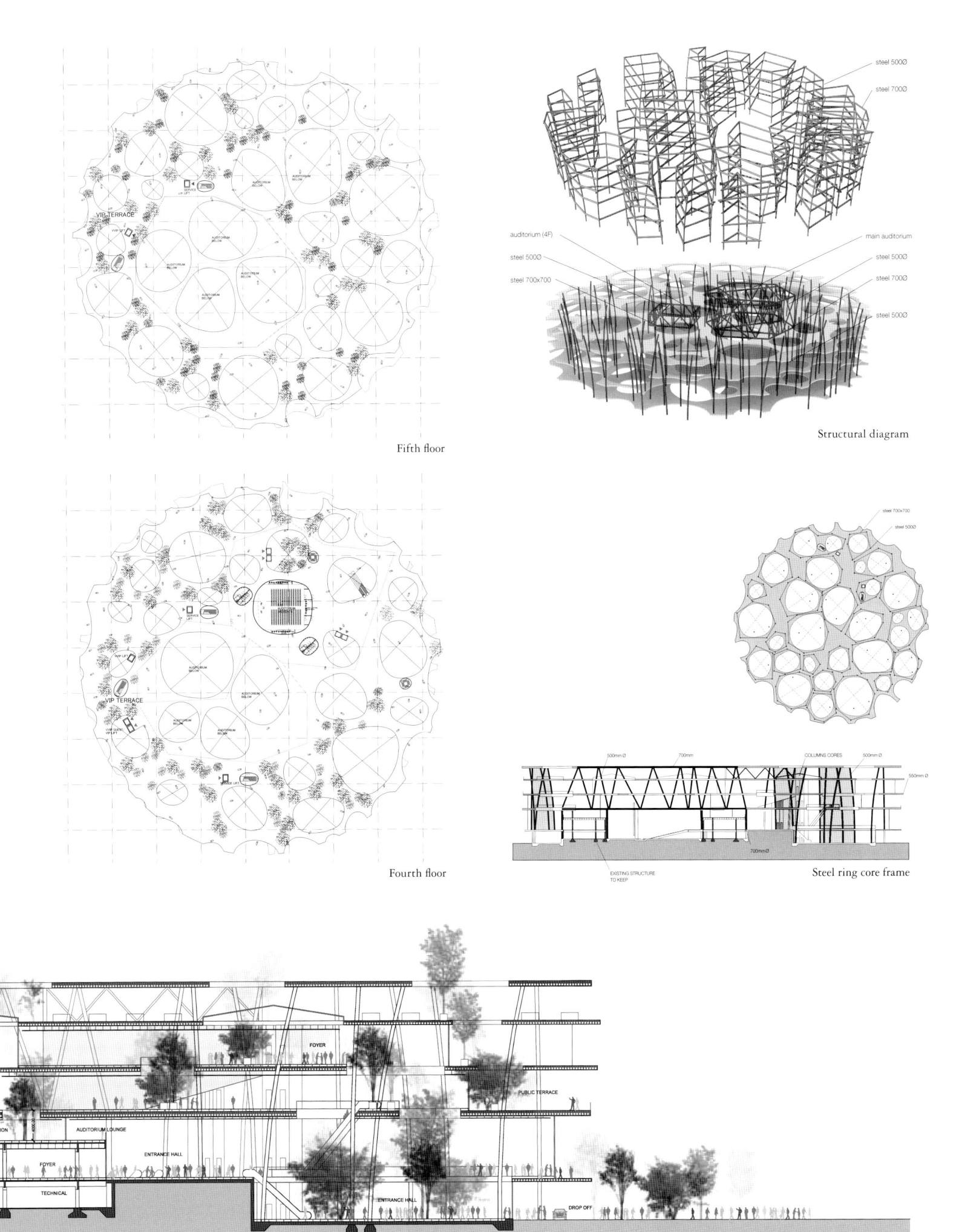

Structural diagram

Fourth floor

Steel ring core frame

Section S=1:600

21st Century Rainforest Architecture

ENERGY FOREST

2012-
URBAN PLANNING

Energy forest in Tokyo

Tokyo

HISTORY OF THE ENERGY STATION

In previous eras, the 'energy station' was a place of rich communication between people. At 'Chand Baori', the 9th Century water-well in India, people seeking water gathered and shared in communication. Entering the 20th Century, as forms of energy and types of fuel were rationalized, the 'energy station' was shaped by the considerations of speed and convenience. As a result of this shift, the energy station has lost its function as a communication place, instead becoming a place of transience; a 'drive through' point, a place people pass by on the road. Our proposal is for an 'energy station' like a single tree. Much like the energy station of the past, it is overflowing with various kinds of activity and communication. Nature, energy and people mix together in this 'energy station' for the 21st Century.

ENERGY FOREST

Our proposal is for an Energy Station like a large tree. Like the way a tree brings together many different living things, this place brings together many people and other creatures. In this place, light, wind, and rich vegetation mix with the activity of many different people, vehicles, insects and animals, forming the complexity of the 21st Century Energy Station.

Cloud

Multi Layers

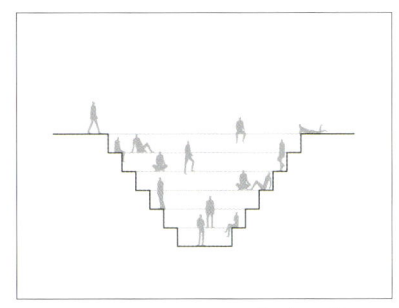

21ST CENTURY MOTION

If we think of the form of energy in the future, the consideration of how people and things flow and move is of great importance. The concept of movement in the Modern era has been a study in functionality and rationality. This kind of motion is formed by the basic assumption of the importance of efficiency: 'the shortest distance / shortest time'. The future motion that we are thinking of is more like Brownian movement, a form of movement filled with complexity. This new rich form of movement is motion based on the valuation of 'variable routes / comfortable time'.

RELATION TO THE CITY: ROME

We create an Energy Forest in Rome, a city with many historical buildings. With a scale similar to communication places such as the Coliseum or the Roman Forum, the energy station can be seen as a contemporary space. Combining the qualities of 'road' and 'place', our proposal creates a new flow for the streets of Rome, enlivening the various activities of its people.

RELATION TO THE CITY: TOKYO

We deploy Energy Forest in the sky above a giant pedestrian junction in Shibuya, Tokyo. The Energy Forest intertwines shops, station, road, vehicles and people, creating a spiral of activity. Inviting the various flows of people, it creates a comfortable resting environment and a refueling space filled with vegetation.

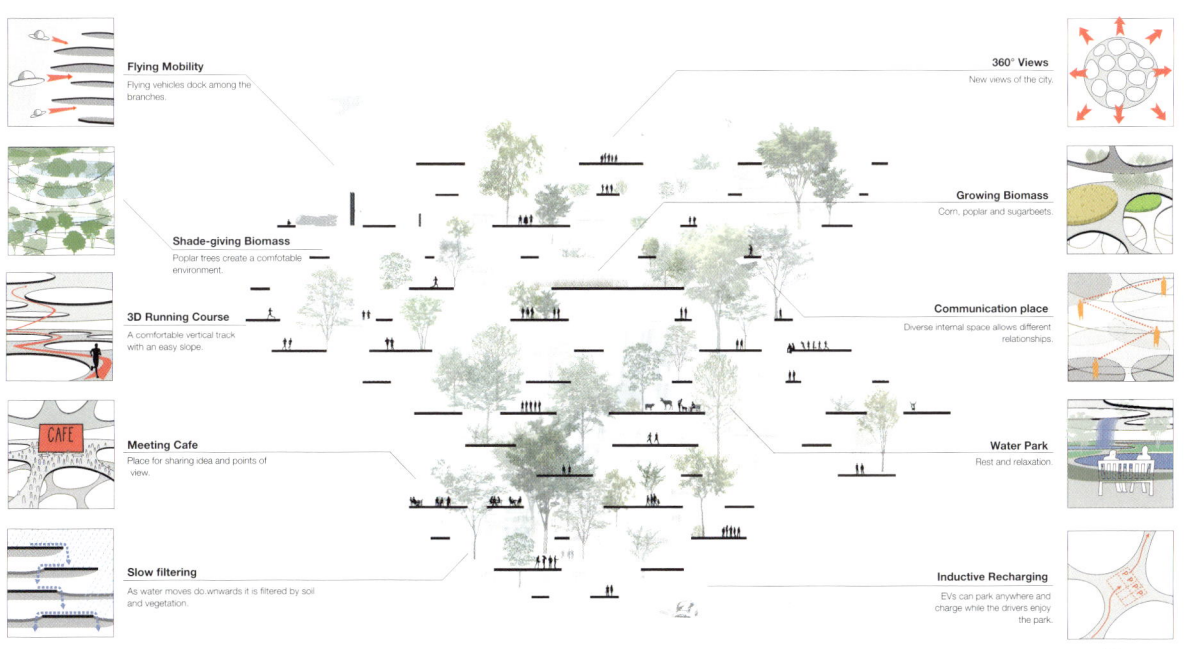

Ancient: Communication by Gathering

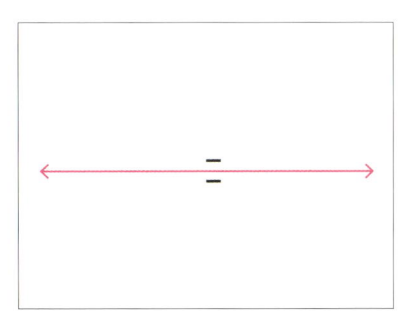

Modern: Functionality by Transience

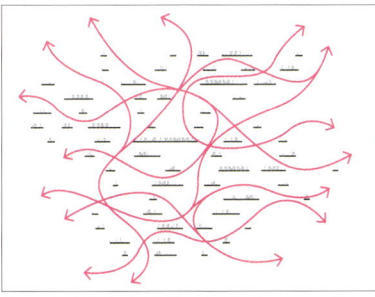

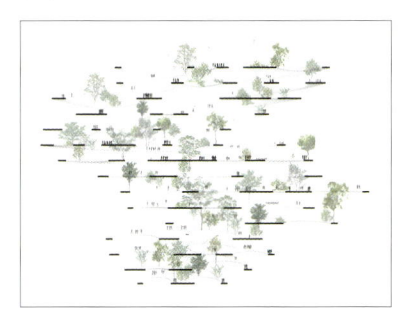

Future: Communication and Functionality

Diagram

Energy Forest

ENERGY FOREST: the installation was realized for the "*ENERGY. Oil and Post-oil Architecture and Grids*"
Architettura e reti del petrolio e del post-petrolio exhibition at MAXXI — National Museum of XXI Century Arts, Rome

MAXXI Architettura Collections, Courtesy of Fondazione MAXXI. Photo by Sebastiano Luciano

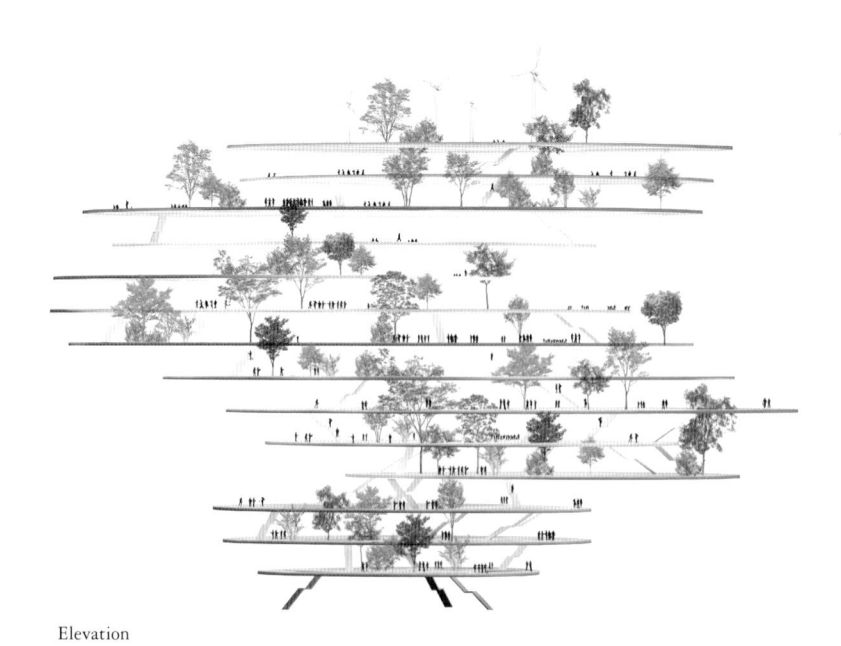

Downward view

Elevation

124

Rome

エネルギー・ステーションの歴史

かつて、エネルギー・ステーションは豊かなコミュニケーションの場所であった。9世紀にインドで建設された「チャンド・バオリ」の井戸には水を求める人々が集まり、コミュニケーションを共有していた。20世紀に入り、エネルギー形態や燃料の種類が合理化されるにつれて、エネルギー・ステーションには速さと利便性が求められるようになった。そのような追求の結果、エネルギー・ステーションはコミュニケーションの場としての機能性を失い、一時的な場所、「ドライブ・スルー」するポイント、車道を走り、通り過ぎるだけの場となってしまっている。それらを考慮して、1本の木のようなエネルギー・ステーションが私たちの提案である。これは様々な活動やコミュニケーションが溢れる、かつてのエネルギー・ステーションさながらの計画である。自然、エネルギー、そして人間が、この21世紀のエネルギー・ステーションでは混じり合うように存在している。

エネルギー・フォレスト

私たちは大樹のようなエネルギー・ステーションの計画を行った。木が多くの生命を運ぶのと同様に、この場所には多くの人々や生物が集まってくる。この場所は、光、風、そして豊かな自然の存在が、人間や自動車、昆虫、動物の様々な活動と混じり合い、21世紀のエネルギー・ステーションに相応しい複雑性を形成している。

21世紀のモーション

未来のエネルギーの形について考えるならば、人々や物事がどう流れ、どう動くのかを考えることが何よりも重要である。近代にとって、運動の概念は機能性と合理性への追求であり続けた。これらのモーションは、「より近く／より速く」といった効率性への追求を重視する基本的仮説によって構成されている。私たちの考える未来のモーションは、ブラウン運動により近い、複雑性によって満たされた運動形態である。このように新しく豊かな運動形態は、「複数のルート／快適な時間」といった価値判断に基づくモーションである。

都市との関係性：ローマ

我々は歴史的建築物が数多く残るローマにエネルギー・フォレストをつくろうとしている。コロッセオやフォロ・ロマーノといったコミュニケーションの場所と同様のスケールを備えてはいるが、エネルギー・ステーションは現代の空間である。「道」と「場」の本質を組み合わせることによって、ローマにおける新しい道の流れを生み出し、人々の活動に様々な刺激が与えられる。

都市との関係性：東京

エネルギー・フォレストは東京・渋谷の巨大なスクランブル交差点の上空に展開される。エネルギー・フォレストにはショップや駅舎、道路や自動車、人々が編み込まれ、らせん状のアクティビティが生成される。そこでは様々な人々の流れを引き込むことで、快適に休める環境と、自然に満たされた燃料の補充スペースが生み出される。

Energy forest in Rome

MAXXI Architettura Collections, Courtesy of Fondazione MAXXI. Photo by Sebastiano Luciano

TREE SKYSCRAPER

2012-
URBAN PLANNING

This is an imaginary super-skyscraper project. Through taking an arboroid form as the shape of the skyscraper, each floor can have a stepped terrace even though it is a super high rising building, intend to make the diverse living environment of a skyscraper. It would be a super-skyscraper as landscape. Intend to be for not only offices but also a complex with complicated functions including housing, hotels and etc. Moreover when we imagine a city with the arboroid forms super-skyscrapers standing in crowds, it is possible to build up the holizontal connection with the each towers and a more complexed multistory urban-space could be produced in the shape forest.

架空の超高層の計画。樹状の形態を採ることによって，超高層でありながら各階に段々状のテラスを設けることができ，高層ビルの生活環境を多様化することを意図している。ランドスケープ的な超高層ビルといえる。オフィスだけではなく，集合住宅やホテルをはじめ，複雑な機能が複合した建築を想定している。またこのような樹状の超高層が群れをなして林立する都市を想像するとき，横方向のネットワーク的な連結が可能となり，より複雑な森状の高層都市空間が生まれるであろう。

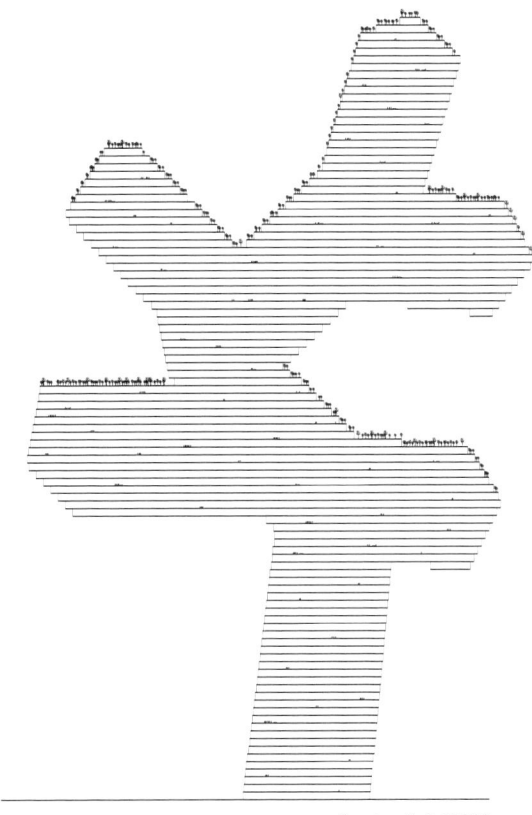

Section S=1:10000

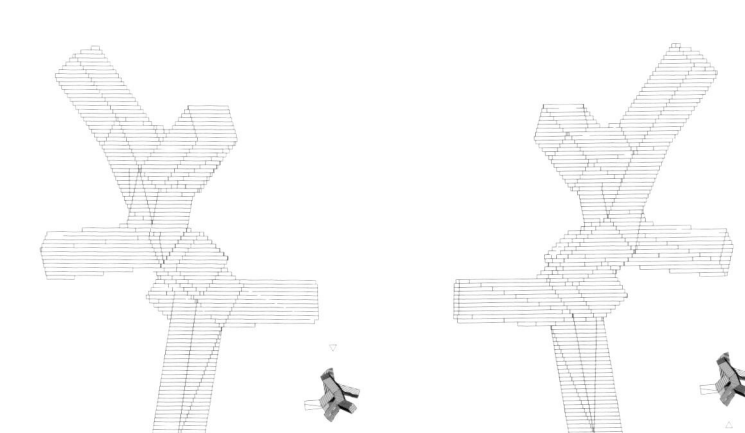

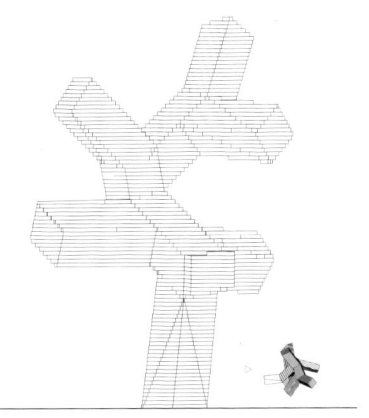

Elevations S=1:20000

Tree Skyscraper　　127

LOUISIANA CLOUD

2012-
URBAN PLANNING

Concept image

This is an imaginary high rising urban planning project. The three-dimentional connection in between the floating volumes provide a new type of architecture that is different from the conventional skyscrapers. Each volume has a rooftop garden formed as wooded forest. Due to this sky garden whole high rising urban city appears to be like a sterically-modified and the artificial forest. We have took into consideration of the possibilities of various scales; from 30 m high, 100 m high skyscraper or over 600 m high super-skyscraper.

Section S=10000

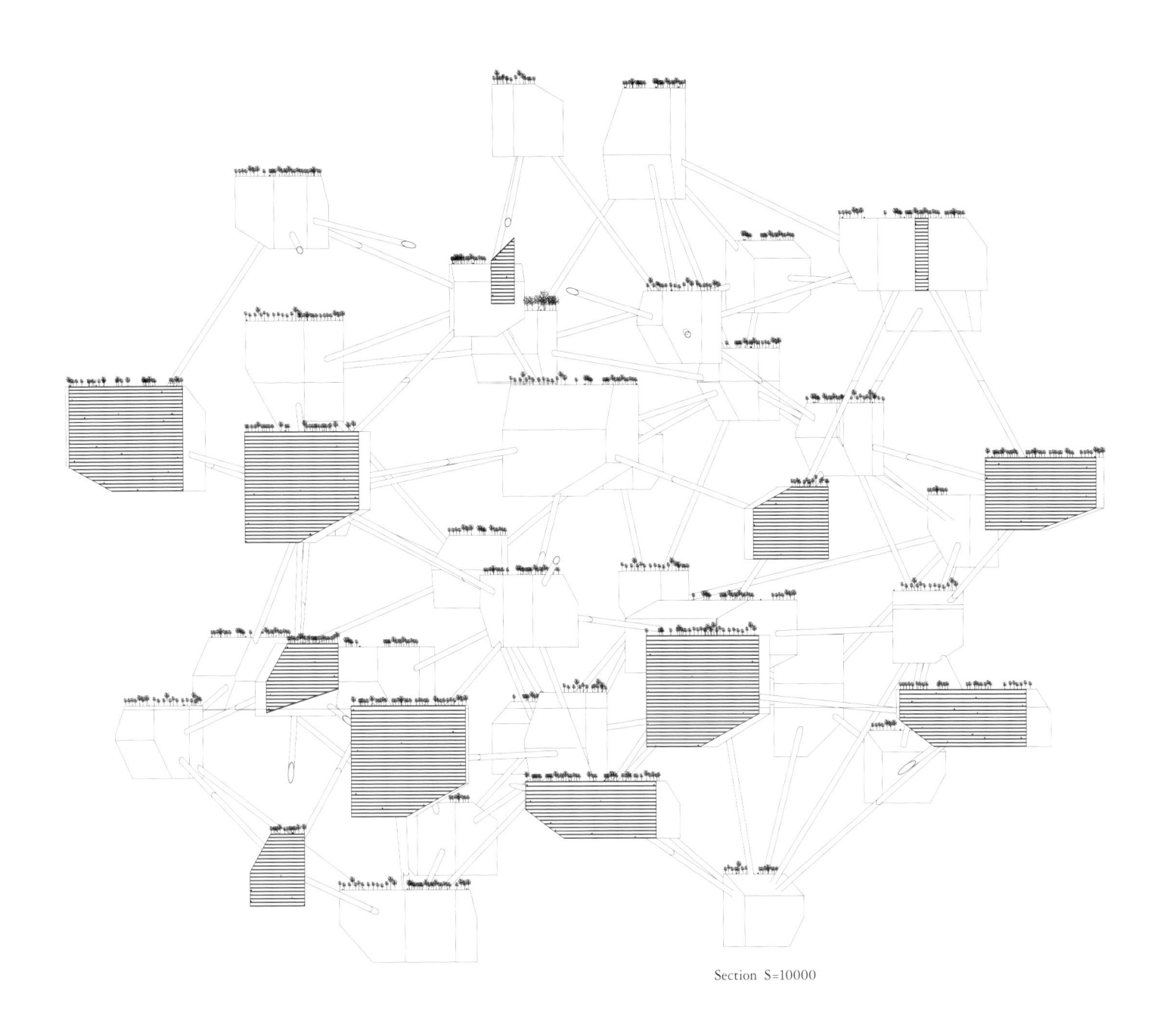

架空の高層都市建築のプロジェクト。3次元的に浮かぶ島状ヴォリュームの立体的なネットワークによって、従来の高層ビルとは異なる立体的な建築をつくり出す。各ヴォリュームの屋上は木々で覆われた森のような屋上庭園となっており、それゆえにこの高層都市建築全体が、立体的で人工的な森の様相をなす。高さ30メートルの建築から100メートル以上の高層建築、そして600メートル超の超高層立体都市まで、さまざまなスケールでの可能性を視野に入れている。

Louisiana Cloud

MUSEUM IN THE FOREST

Taoyuan County, Taiwan, 2012-
MUSEUM

The site is located in a forest where people can admire a beautiful lake in the Taoyuan suburbs. A museum to hold various art exhibitions and events was required. Projects of diverse facilities such as restaurants and cottages are also concurrently progressing in the vicinity of the site.

Roof and wall, gradually changing from transparent to white, gently connect the forest and exhibition rooms.

The interior space is slowly altered from a bright exhibition room that is covered by surrounding trees to opaque and protected one, enclosed by white walls. We conceived a museum that makes people to enter the deep forest while sensing the buzz of swaying trees.

敷地は桃園郊外の美しい湖を眺めることができる森の中。様々なアートの展示や催しを行う美術館が求められた。この敷地周辺にはレストランやコテージなど様々な施設の計画も同時に進んでいる。

透明から白へと徐々に変化する壁と屋根は展示室と森を緩やかに繋ぐ。

周辺の木々に覆われ透明で明るい展示室から、白い壁で覆われ不透明で守られた展示室へと徐々に変化していく。揺れ動く木々のざわめきを感じつつ森の奥へと入っていくような美術館を考えた。

Site plan S=1:2000

Early scheme: glazed wall with gradation of transparency by film

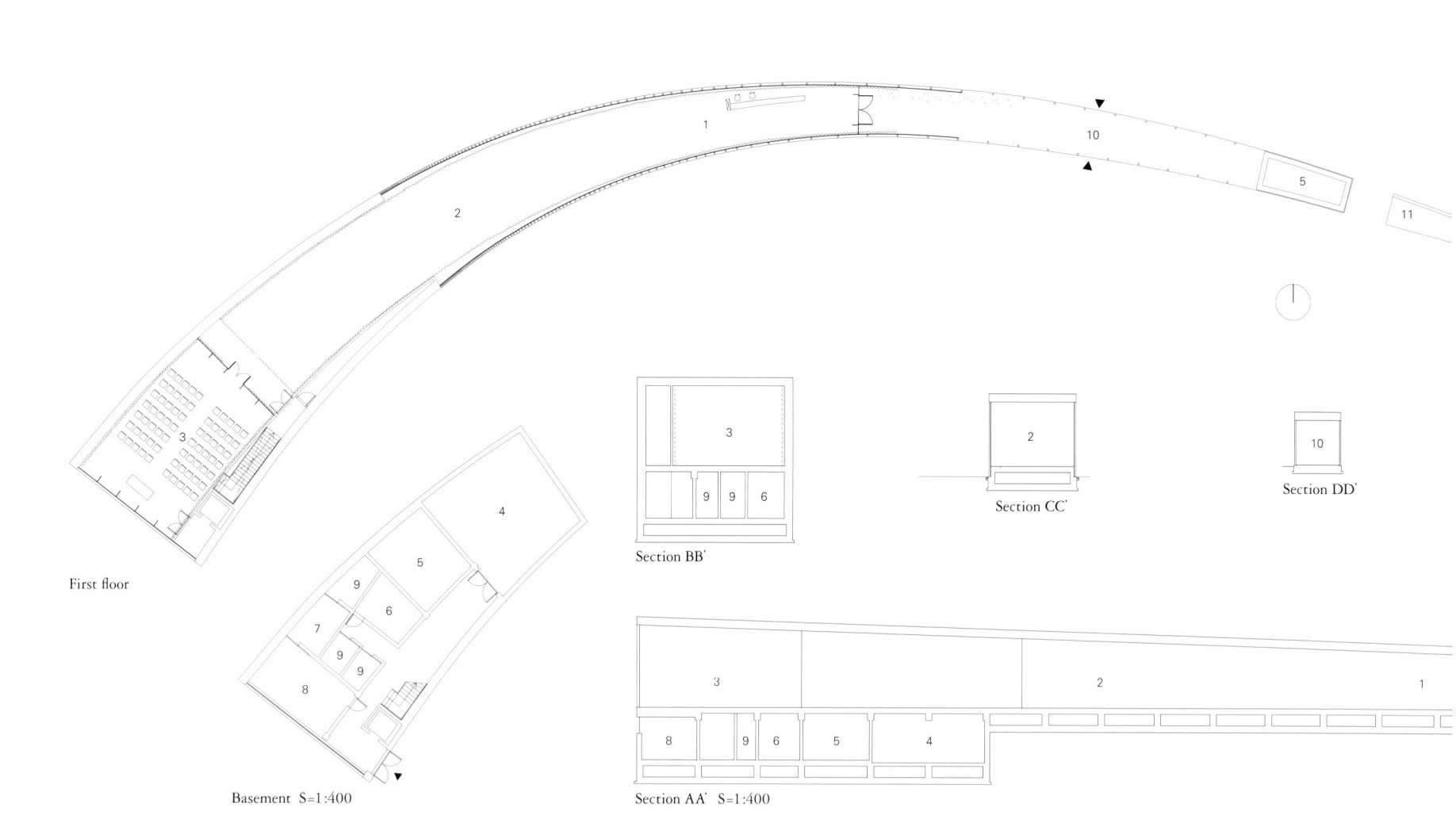

First floor

Basement S=1:400

Section BB'

Section CC'

Section DD'

Section AA' S=1:400

Concept

View toward side wall

1 ENTRANCE HALL
2 EXHIBITION SPACE
3 MULTIPURPOSE SPACE
4 MECHANICAL
5 STORAGE
6 SPARE ROOM
7 POWDER ROOM
8 WATING ROOM
9 WC
10 CANOPY
11 BENCH

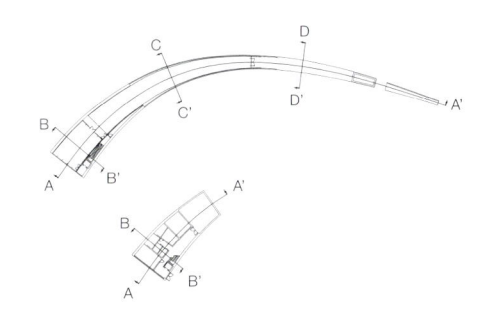

Interior

Museum in the Forest

CENTER OF TRADITIONAL PERFORMING ARTS IN IZUNOKUNI

Izunokuni, Shizuoka, Japan, 2012-
AUDITORIUM

This project, which is a motif of open theater from the Noh period, joins nature from the Genji-yama Mountain, and creates a square in which architecture and landscape fuses, and becomes a hub for the area. Intended to create a festive area where tradition is inherited and connects with the future.

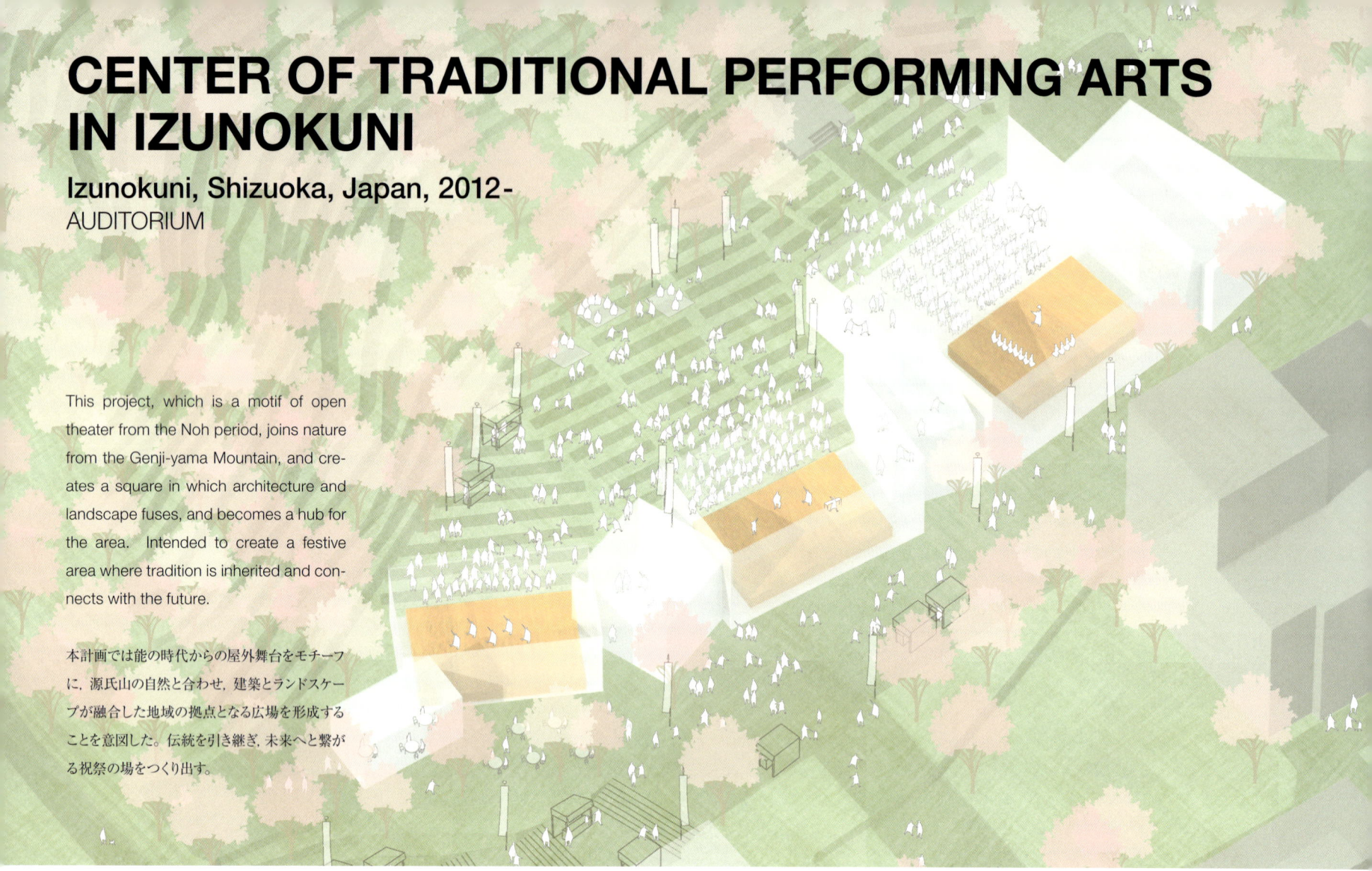

本計画では能の時代からの屋外舞台をモチーフに，源氏山の自然と合わせ，建築とランドスケープが融合した地域の拠点となる広場を形成することを意図した。伝統を引き継ぎ，未来へと繋がる祝祭の場をつくり出す。

Site plan and program

Section (stage)

A STAGE IN THE TOWN / A STAGE IN NATURE

3 STAGES
The open-air stage in the center, the 100 seats theater, and the training studios will each open up to the square when events are held. The stages will become an open-air theater by fusing with the landscape, and a hub for the area bringing prosperity to the town through festivals and events.

A MULTI-PURPOSE STAGE
The open-air stage in the center is normally utilized as sightseeing information booths and small galleries. In addition the training studios could be used as not only for training, but also for experiment stages, exhibitions and events.

街の中の舞台／自然の中の舞台

3つの舞台
中央の屋外舞台，100席の劇場，練習スタジオ，それぞれがイベント時には広場に向かって開かれる。ランドスケープと融合して屋外劇場となり，祭りや行事などを通して地域に賑わいをもたらす地域の拠点となる。

多目的に使うことが出来る舞台
中央の屋外舞台は普段は，観光情報コーナー／ミニギャラリーとして使用され，練習スタジオは，練習だけではなく，実験劇場や展示，イベントにも使うことができる。

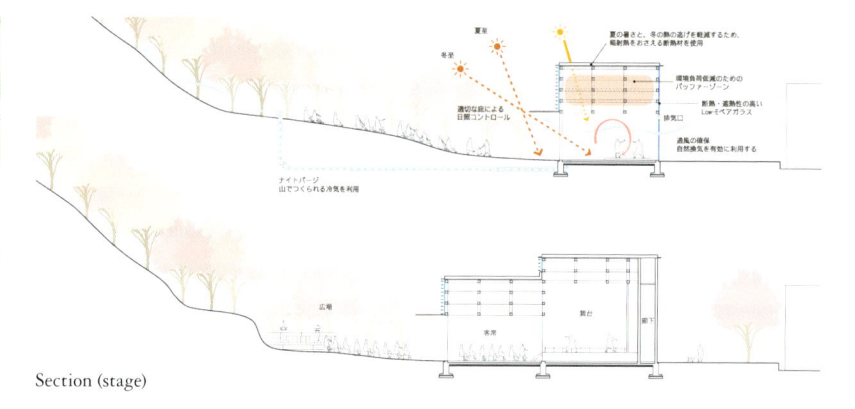

ENVIRONMENTAL PLANNING UTILIZING THE LANDFORM AND INHERITING TRADITIONAL WOODEN ARCHITECTURE
Columns and beams are sterically assembled into grids as in folk dwellings serving as a huge air space. During summer-time, the heat is reduced by this void. In addition, at winter-time by spreading the gathered heat in the ceiling, the interior is heated.
- By utilizing the Night-Purge Ventilation, the cold air coming down from Genji-yama Mountain can be taken inside.
- The eaves set up on the square, control the sunlight during summer and winter.
- We apply insulations that moderate the radiation heat in order to reduce the summer heat and the heat loss in winter.
- Plan to ensure overdraft and effectively apply natural ventilation.

地形を生かし，伝統を継承する木造建築による環境計画
民家のように立体的に組まれた柱，梁の格子は，大きな空気層の役割を担う。夏は熱射を軽減し，さらに，冬は天井に溜まった熱だまりを拡散することで室内を温める。
- ナイトパージを利用し，源氏山から降りてくる冷気を室内に取り込む。
- 広場側に設けた庇によって夏場，冬場の日差しをコントロールする。
- 夏場の暑さと，冬場の熱の逃げを軽減するために輻射熱を抑える断熱材を使用する。
- 通風を確保し，自然換気を有効的に利用する計画とした。

First floor S=1:600

Scond floor

Elevation S=1:800

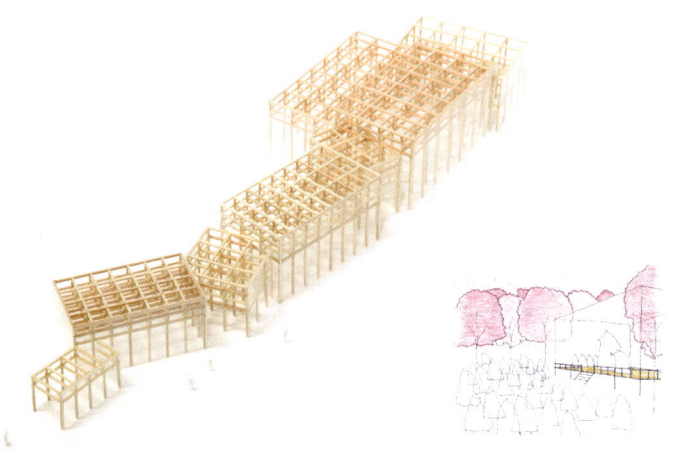

THE TIMBER FRAME THAT FUSES THE TRADITIONAL AND MODERN AGE

Propose a new type of wooden architectural space create by overlaying beam frames, which resemble folk dwellings and modern sophistication. The light drops on the frame, which is sterically assembled into grids, inheriting the beauty of the wooden architecture that the Japanese folk dwellings once had.

THE RURAL KABUKI THEATER LIKE FRAME FORM BY THE EBISU COLUMN NETWORK

The huge column standing between the border of the earth floor and the hall is generally called the Central Pillar (Daikoku Bashira column), however, the Smaller Pillar (Shokoku Bashira column a.k.a. Ebisu Bashira column) which is the column standing between the hall, parlor and storage could be seen in the folk houses as the Ueno House and the Egawa House in the Izunokuni district. In this proposal, not using a Central Pillar, but a successive colonnade with Smaller Pillars, gridded frame structure with quake resisting walls by semi-rigid jointing of each of the capitals are set. The roof structure has a rural Kabuki theater like multi-layered rigid cubic gridded roof truss, being able to not only set up a pillar in a long-span but also hanging objects for events.

伝統と現代を融合する木架構

民家のような梁組みの重なりと、現代的な洗練によって新しい木造建築の空間を提案する。立体的な格子に組まれた架構に光が落ち、日本民家が持っていた美しい木造建築を現代に継承する。

恵比寿柱ネットワークによる農村舞台のような架構形式

土間と広間の境にある大きな柱を一般的に大黒柱と呼ぶが、旧上野家住宅や江川邸など、伊豆の国市地域の民家では、広間と座敷、納戸の境にある柱を小黒柱(恵比寿)と呼ぶ架構形式が見られる。今回の提案では、1本の中心性を持った大黒柱ではなく、分節された屋内・屋外空間の境界に現れた連続する列柱を恵比寿柱群と見立て、この柱頭を複数階レベルで半剛接合することで、耐震壁付き面格子ラーメン構造とした。屋根構造は農村舞台のような複数段の剛強な立体格子状の小屋組みを持ち、大スパンを飛ばすのみならず、イベント用の吊り物も可能となっている。

Timber frame

Center of Traditional Performing Arts in Izunokuni

YUZ MUSEUM

Shanghai, China, 2012-
MUSEUM

Before (below) and after (above)

136

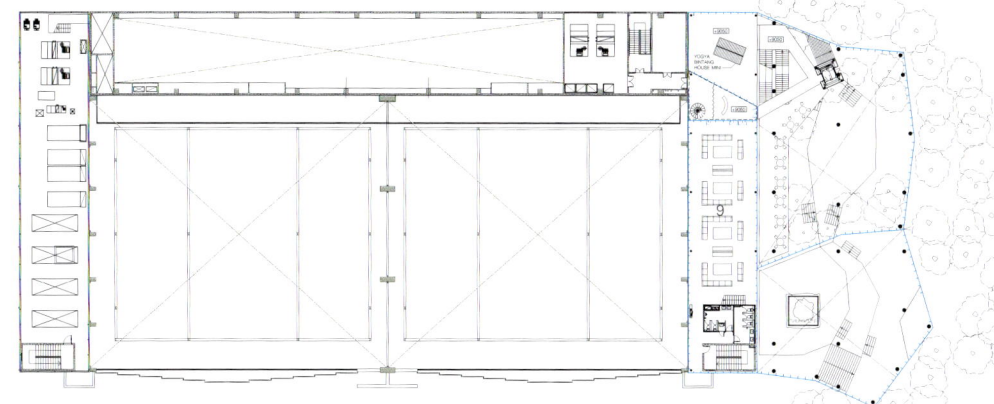

The project is a contemporary art museum, planned in the Xuhui district of Shanghai. The existing warehouse of several decades old is to be renovated. The existing large space, which is characterized by a beautiful truss structure, is renovated as exhibition space of the contemporary art and it was intended to maintain the presence of the building in the cityscapes as much as possible including the silhouette of the roof. A glass box is installed as if covering the space in front of the existing building and it serves as entrance space of the whole new art museum. The entrance hall is large space with ceiling height of approximately 15 m, and a lot of trees are planted inside, which appears to continue from outer space. It feels like to build the indoor entrance garden just before the existing building. A cafe, restaurant, shop and special exhibition room are three-dimensionally located in the glass void space. The floor level of the entrance changes into a stepping form along the topography, and it can be used as an auditorium. It may be said that it is the plan that attempted continuation and inversion of inside and outside on a city scale.

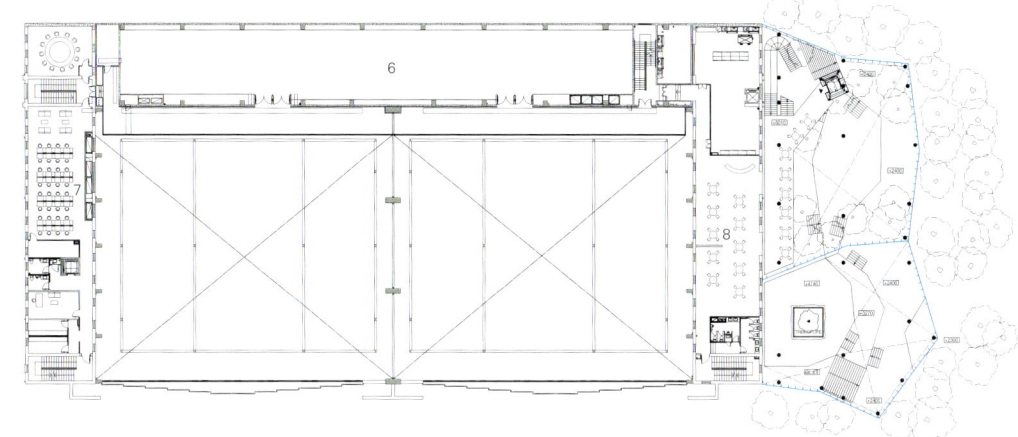

1 MAIN ENTRANCE
2 TICKET BOX OFFICE & CLOAK
3 ENTRANCE HALL
4 PERFORMANCE STAGE
5 MUSEUM SHOP
6 EXHIBITION
7 ADMINISTRATION
8 CAFE
9 VIP LOUNGE

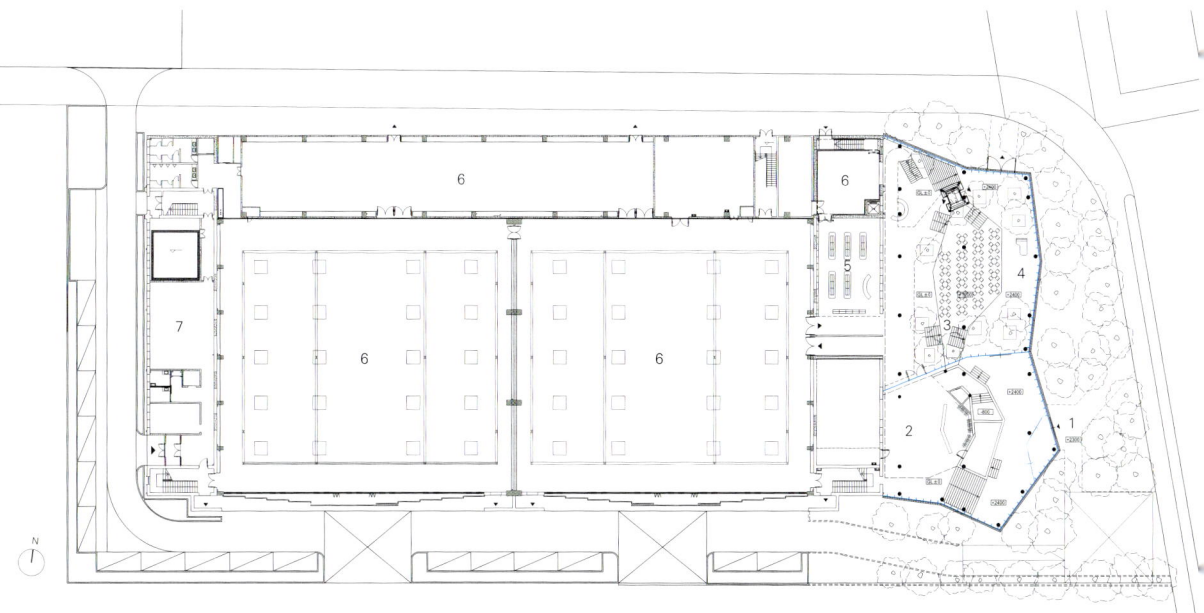

Third floor

Second floor

First floor S=1:1000

YUZ Museum

Southeast view

Entrance hall

Performance stage

1 MAIN ENTRANCE
2 TICKET BOX OFFICE & CLOAK
3 ENTRANCE HALL
4 PERFORMANCE STAGE
5 MUSEUM SHOP
6 EXHIBITION
7 ADMINISTRATION
8 CAFE
9 VIP LOUNGE

Section S=1:600

上海の徐匯区エリアに計画している現代美術館。築数10年の既存倉庫をリノベーションする。美しいトラス構造が特徴的な既存の大空間はそのまま現代美術の展示空間として改修し、屋根のシルエットを含めた都市景観の中での建物の存在感をなるべく維持することを意図した。既存建物の手前にガラスボックスをかぶせるように設置して、新しい美術館全体のエントランススペースとする。エントランス空間は天井高さ約15メートルの巨大空間で、内部には外構から連続するように多数の樹木が植えられる。あたかも既存建物の手前に屋内のエントランス庭園を設けるような感覚である。そのガラスの吹抜け空間には、カフェやレストラン、ショップや特別展示室が立体的に配置される。エントランスの床レベルは地形に合わせて段々状に変化しており、オーディトリアムとしても使うことが出来る仕様となっている。内外の連続と反転を都市的なスケールで試みた計画であるといえる。

Staircase / elevator

Exhibition space

Under construction

FUTUROSPEKTIVE ARCHITEKTUR
Kunsthalle Bielefeld, Bielefeld, Germany, 2012
EXHIBITION

ARCHITECTURE AS FOREST
SICLI Pavilion, Geneva, Switzerland, 2012-13
EXHIBITION

FUTUROSPEKTIVE ARCHITEKTUR

ARCHITECTURE AS FOREST

I believe the Architecture of the future lay within some being akin to a Forest.

Within a forest, from leaves and insects and the seeds it carries, to the grand scale of the tree trunks, myriad of truly diverse matters interrelate and coexist. It is this diversity that I am strongly attracted to. Richness born from space between order and chaos. Thus if Architecture akin to a Forest can be created, it will be a place of complexity, rich in diversity far beyond preexisting architecture and cities of today. And its inhabitants will organically be a part of this diversity.

The projects exhibited here are attempts to create new notion of nature and man-made environments — Three-dimensional forest, Geometric forest, Urban forest, and so on. Some projects have been realized, some solely conceptual, and some of which are currently in development. Ranging from small/micro architecture to colossal buildings and urban facilities several-hundred meters tall. Architecture as Forest, presented here is the future of Nature and the future of Architecture.

The Forest as the origin shines light towards the future of Architecture.

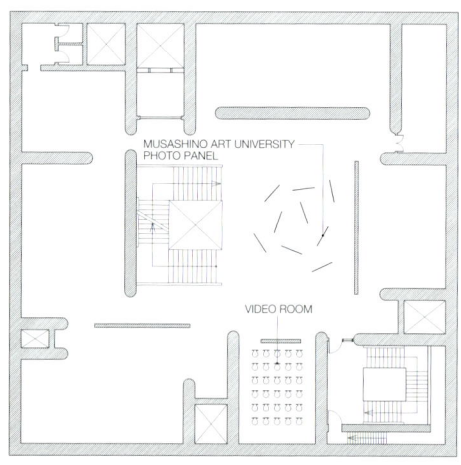

Third floor

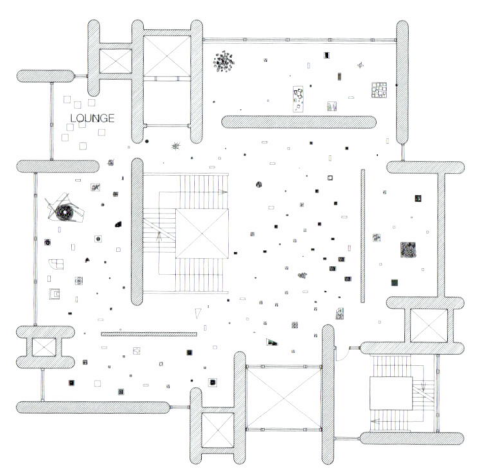

Second floor

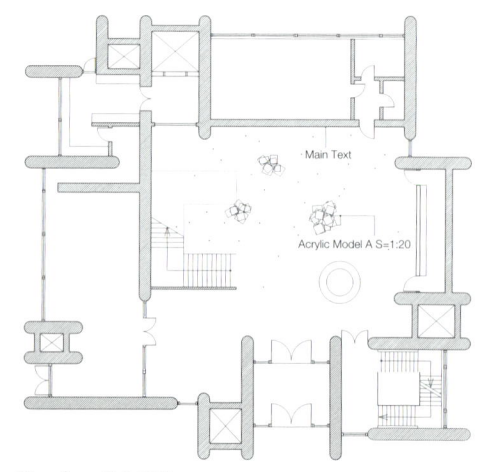

First floor S=1:500

ARCHITECTURE AS FOREST

森としての建築

ぼくは，これからの建築は，森のようなものになるのではないかと考えている。

　森とは，葉や虫や種などのとても小さなものから巨木のスケールに至るまで，実にさまざまなモノたちがお互いに関係し合いながら共存している。その多様性にぼくは惹かれる。秩序と無秩序の間が生み出す豊かさ。だから森のような建築をつくることができるとするなら，それは今までの建築や都市を超えた複雑で豊かな多様性の場所となるであろう。人間もその多様性の有機的な一部となる。

　ここに展示するさまざまなプロジェクトは，立体的な森，幾何学的な森，都市的な森など，いままで見たことのなかった新しい自然／人工環境をつくり出す試みである。実現したプロジェクトもあれば，コンセプチュアルな試みもあり，現在進行中の計画もある。とても小さな建築から，高さ数百メートルの巨大建築や都市施設までが含まれる。ここで提示する森としての建築は，未来の自然であり，未来の建築である。

　森という原初から，未来の建築を照らし出す。

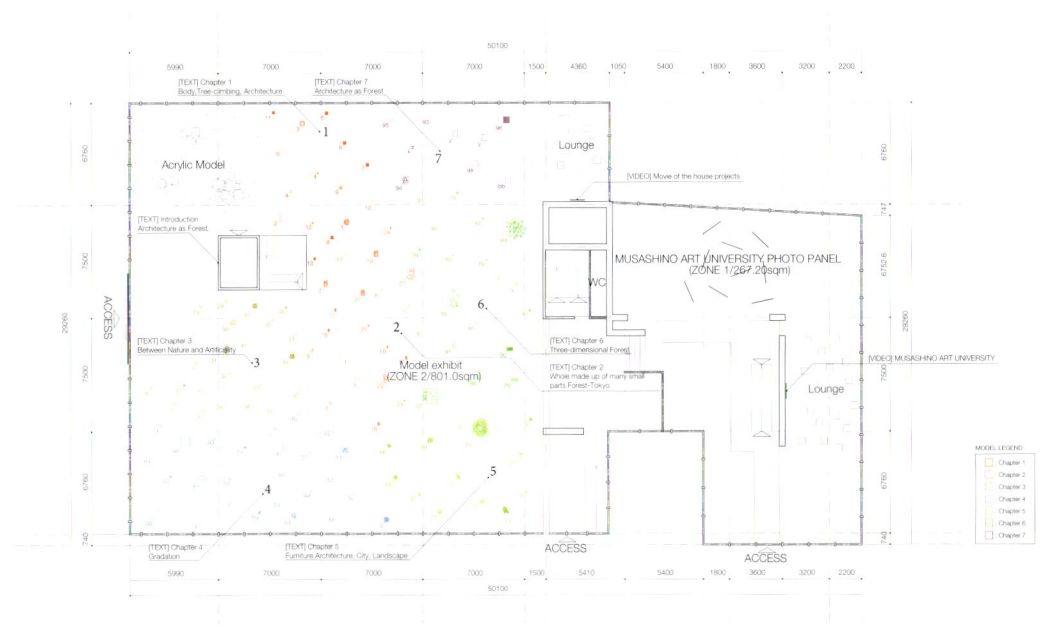

Plan S=1:500

MOUNTAIN HOTEL
China, 2012-
HOTEL

Our site is a small mountain in the countryside of China. This area is famous for its beautiful lakes and streams, and wild bamboo covering the valley's terrain. We plan to make a hotel inside and surrounding the mountain, to make mountain and hotel merge together and form a new nature/architecture.

The architecture of the entrance hall is hollowed out like a tunnel form in the mountain, providing space for functions such as a restaurant, bar, and lounge.

Guests can feel the change of nature through large floor to ceiling windows in each space while relaxing in the hall. Four types of guest rooms are located at the base of the mountain. Half-burried guest rooms, fading into the bamboo forest, create complete silence and privacy for guests. Each room has a big window open to the mountain scape.

Guest rooms and mountain merge together, creating new space for living.

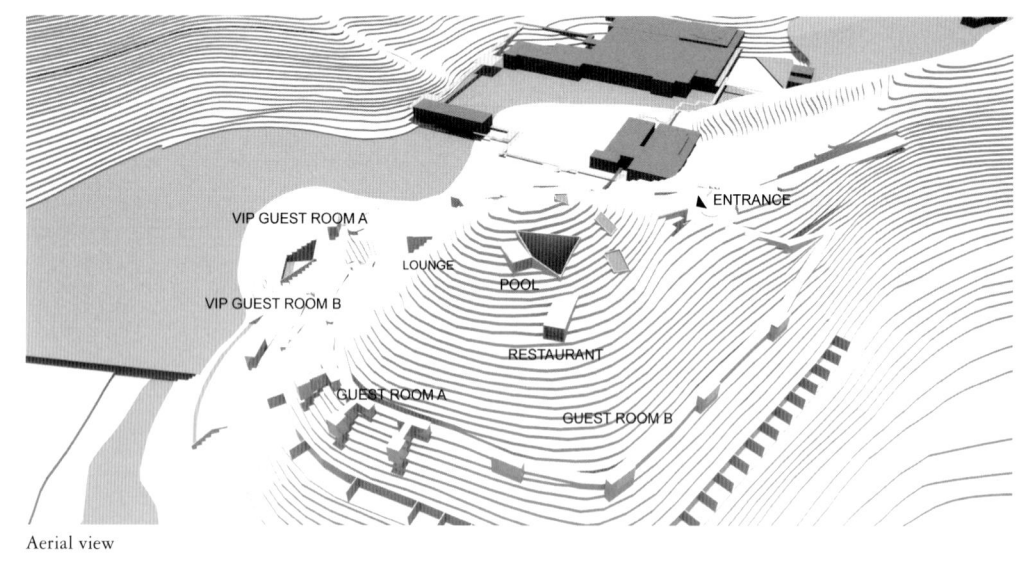

Aerial view

CAR ACCESS

ENTRANCE

CART PATH

EV

VIEW
VIEW

GUEST ROOM B

VIEW
VIEW

GUEST ROOM A

VIP GUEST ROOM B

VIP GUEST ROOM A

WATER AREA **BAMBOO AREA**

N

Site plan S=1:1000

Mountain Hotel

0

PHASE 0: INITIAL SKETCH
This is the initial sketch after visiting a site. Seems there are only windows show up on the mountains surface

—

敷地を見た後に描かれた最初期のスケッチ。山に窓が開いているだけのようなイメージ

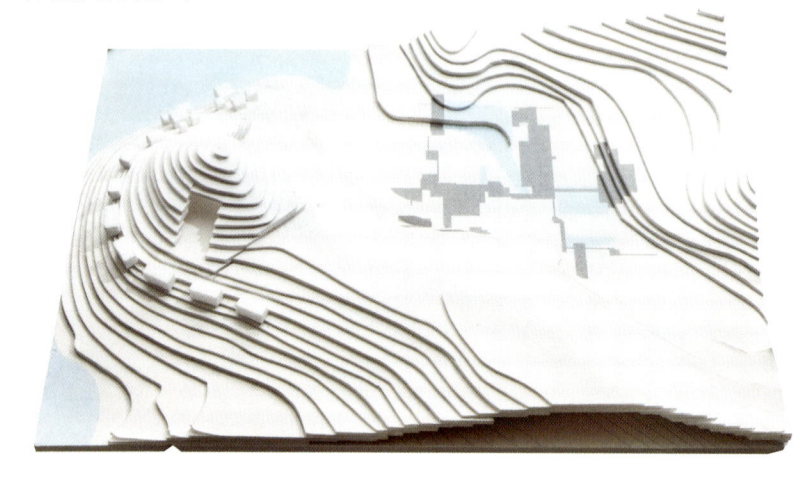

1-A

PHASE 1-A: MOUNTAIN
Site model: plot of hotel is at the mountain on left. This plan were came up with the 'mountain image' on a first presentation. Main building is sit on the waterfront, on right

—

敷地全体の模型。左側の山の部分が、藤本の設計するホテル棟。模型は1回目にプレゼンテーションした案の一つである「山」案。右側の水際に建つのが、本館

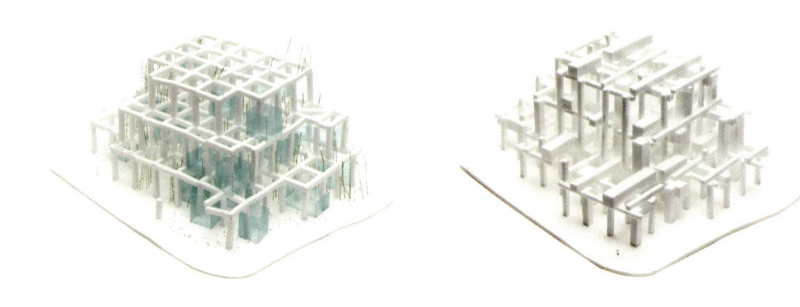

1-A

PHASE 1-A: MOUNTAIN
Considering to cut off top part of the mountain and put some new structures. Studied in some detail of the skeleton version as its structure. Imagine the mingle space such as inside a forest or cave

—

山の頂部を切り取りストラクチャーを載せる案のうち、スケルトンにする案を少し詳しくスタディ。森のような、洞窟のような、空間が輻輳するストラクチャーのイメージ

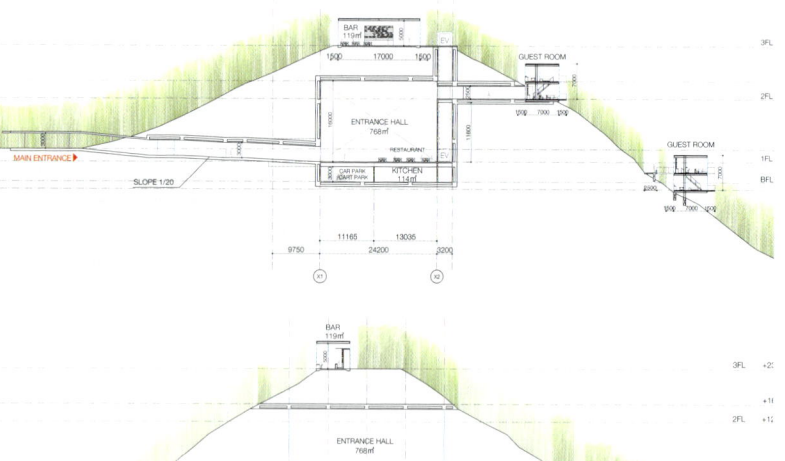

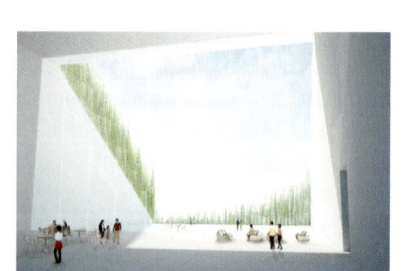

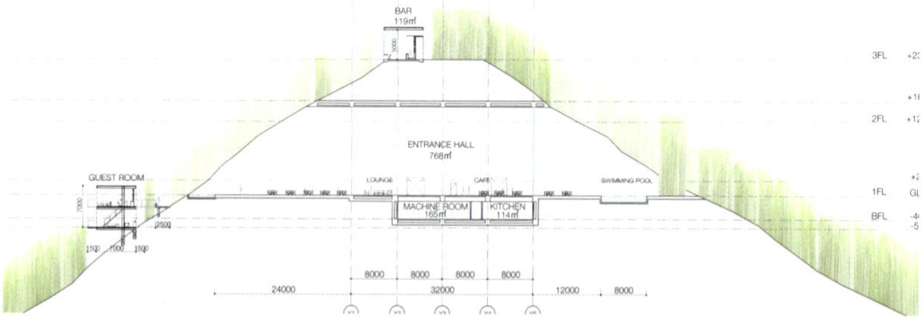

1-A

PHASE 1-A: MOUNTAIN
Tring to insert a simply large void in a mountain instead to make it artificial

—

山自体をあまりに人工化するのでなく、単純に大きなヴォイドを抜く

Sections S=1:1500

1-B

PHASE 1-B: LAYERED SLAB

This is the one of study that replaces top parts of the mountain with new structures. Layered floating slabs formed simple configuration and mingling both inside and outside. Concerned its getting too large structure

—

山の頂部を構造物に置き換える案のうち、浮いたスラブの積層による比較的単純な構成に、内部と外部が混ざり合う案。大きくなりすぎる点が懸念された

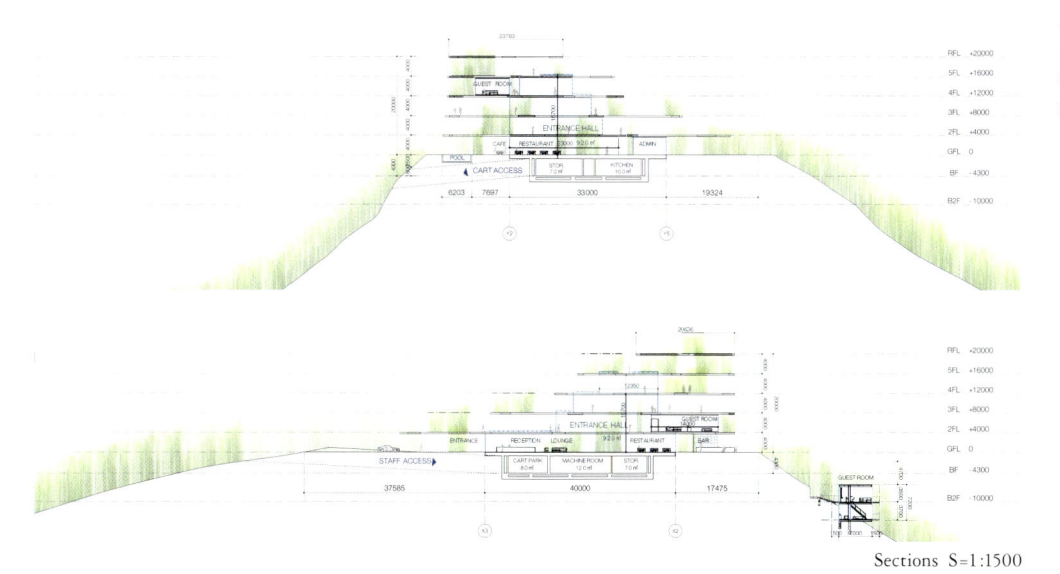

Sections S=1:1500

2

PHASE 2: COMPLEX - MOUNTAIN AND SLAB

'Complex' version proposed at second presentation which is merged phase 1-A with phase 1-B. Scale-down a lobby volume while partially cut out the mountain but pointed out as still too large. After all Fujimoto reconsider about the initial image

—

2回目にプレゼンテーションした、フェイズ1のA、Bを折衷したような「複合」案。ロビーのスケール感などを抑えつつ、山を部分的にカットした案だが、まだ大きすぎると指摘された。この後、最初のイメージに立ち戻って考え直すことになる

3

PHASE 3: SHAFT

In the process of rethinking the initial scheme, getting the idea to makes the 'shaft' into the mountain using depth difference caused by mountatin's figure. Each room could be three-dimensionally connected. During the rethinking, Fujimoto prepared a sketch and the model by himself (left). And design team make a organized model based on his images (right). You could see each room's connections clearly

—

案を最初から考え直す過程で、山の形による地中深さの違いを活かしたシャフト案が浮かび上がる。各スペースの関係も立体的になりそうだった。この考え直し段階では、藤本自身がスケッチを描き、模型もつくった［左］。
［右］は藤本のイメージを元に、整理した模型。各スペースの関係がよく判る

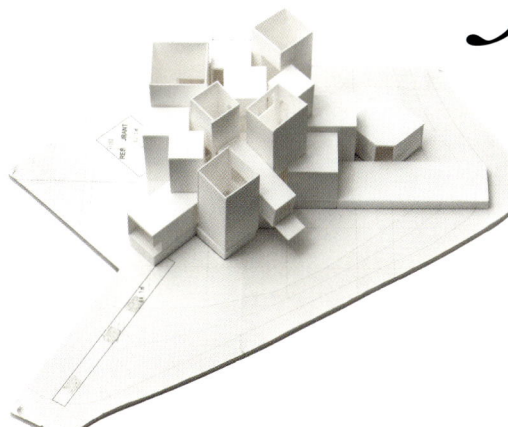

Mountain Hotel

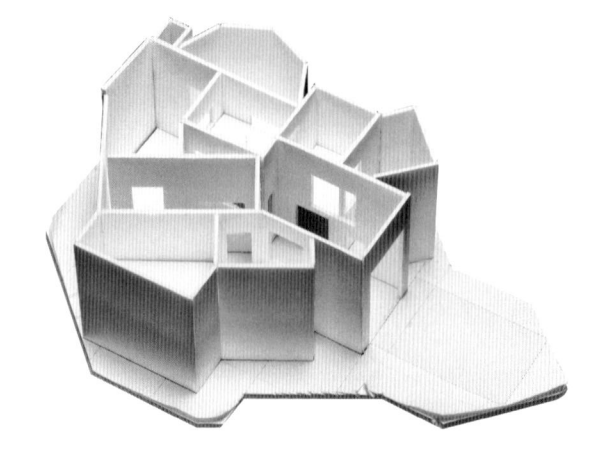

4   PHASE 4: ANCIENT MONUMENT

As 'shaft' scheme was seemed too complicated, tried to organize it more clearly in architectural shape. After all added a specific image something like ancient monument

—

「シャフト」案は複雑すぎるということで、外形がはっきりした建築的な案に整理。その時に、古代遺跡のような具体的なイメージが付加された

Study process of the 'shaft' scheme. Considering the program, how the form would be like? Team still continue study

—

「シャフト」案からの展開をスタディ。プログラムの内容も加味しながら、どのようなものがありえるか考えていくが、決め手に欠ける

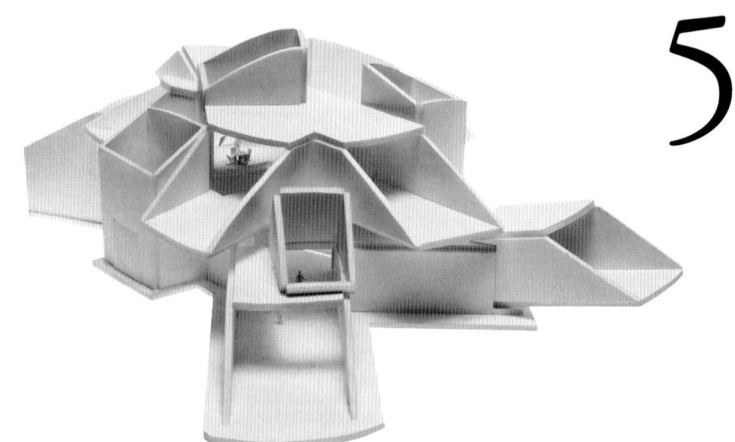

5   PHASE 5: DIAGONAL SHAFT

Left: model made by Fujimoto himself. He considered how to connect to the ground surface and tried to makes the diagonal shaft in the figure. Obviously his mind was move forward to the next phase.
Right: detail model based on Fujimoto's, made by staff. Still it looks complicated but connection of each room is now easily to understand. Because Fujimoto noticed hunging up about 'shaft' idea too much, tried to make more simple connection of the each program

—

［左］は、どこで地上に接するかを考えながら、藤本自身が作成した模型。「シャフト」案を斜めにしていった雰囲気だが、意識は確実に次のフェイズに向かっていた。
［右］は、藤本模型をベースに、スタッフがより詳細につくった模型。各空間の関係はよく判るが、やはり複雑すぎる。「シャフト」的なアイディアにとらわれていると感じ、プログラムをシンプルに関係づけることから考え直すことにする

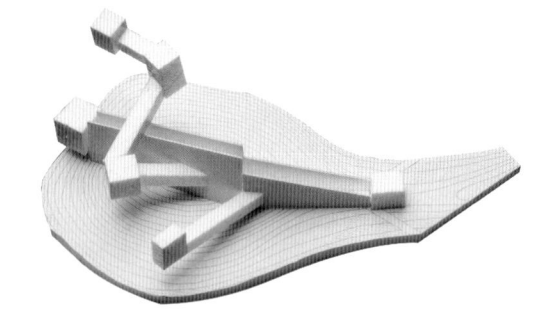

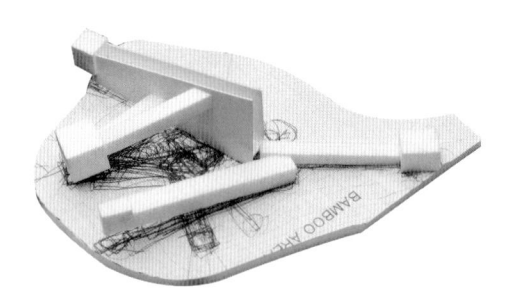

6   PHASE 6: CORRIDOR

Study of circulation: models showing connection of each program with corridor (=route). All of them are going to be built in under the ground. While considered the circulation, he also studied the connection with the landform of the mountain.

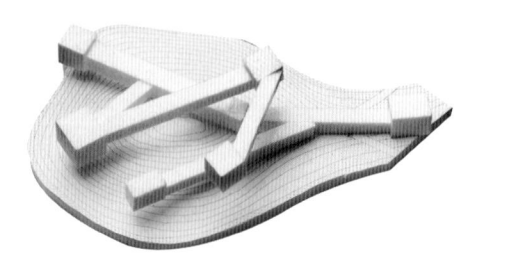

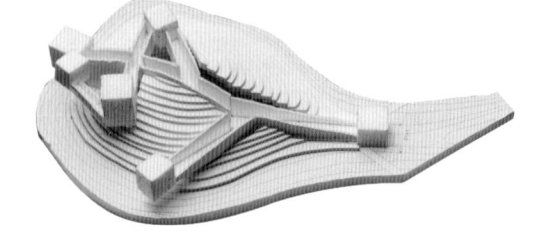

—

ホテルの各プログラムをどのように接続するか、単純に廊下＝ルートでつなぐスタディ。

地中のルートの構成をスタディしているが、ルートを検討しながら、地形との関係もスタディしていた。

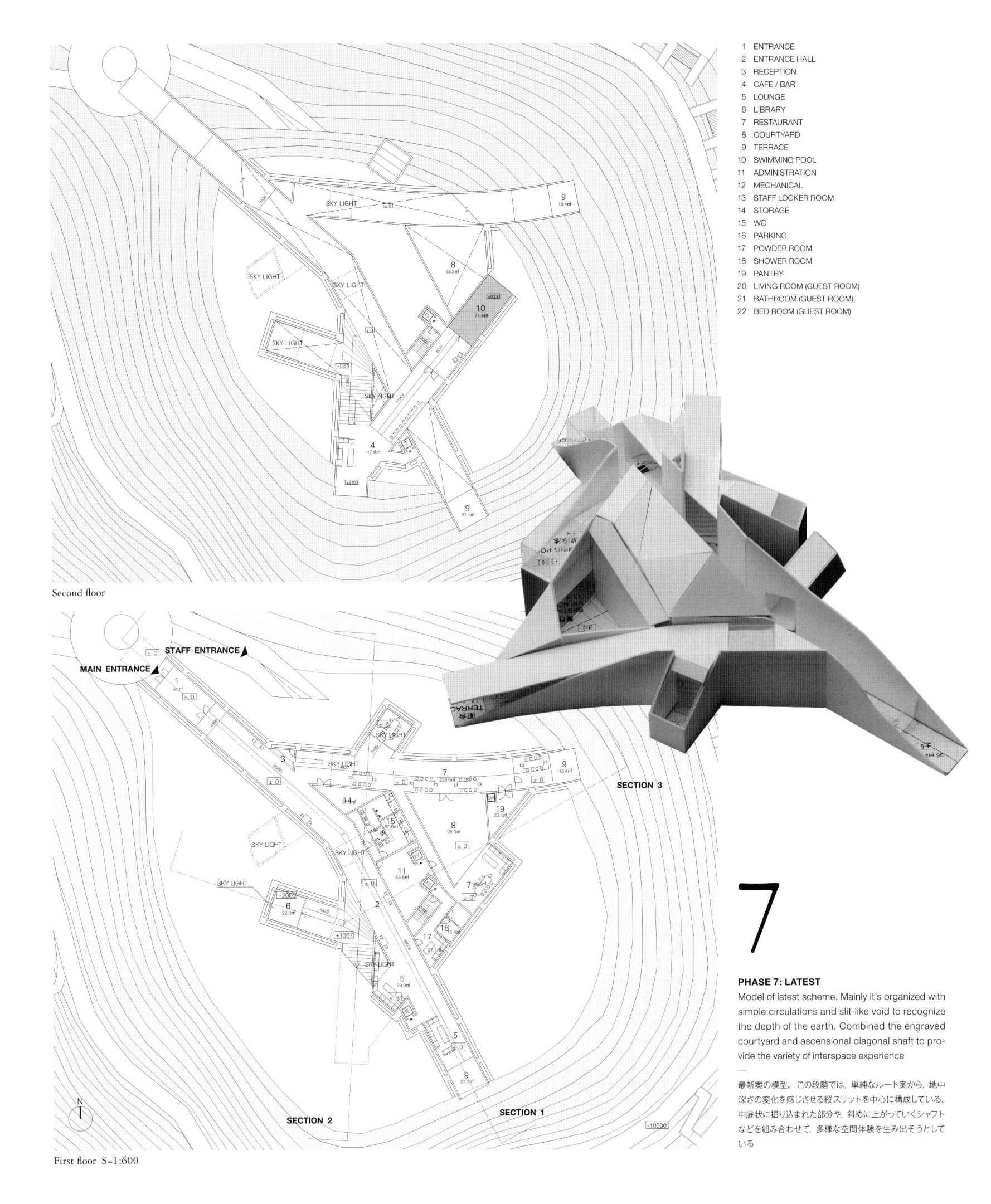

1	ENTRANCE
2	ENTRANCE HALL
3	RECEPTION
4	CAFE / BAR
5	LOUNGE
6	LIBRARY
7	RESTAURANT
8	COURTYARD
9	TERRACE
10	SWIMMING POOL
11	ADMINISTRATION
12	MECHANICAL
13	STAFF LOCKER ROOM
14	STORAGE
15	WC
16	PARKING
17	POWDER ROOM
18	SHOWER ROOM
19	PANTRY
20	LIVING ROOM (GUEST ROOM)
21	BATHROOM (GUEST ROOM)
22	BED ROOM (GUEST ROOM)

Second floor

First floor S=1:600

7

PHASE 7: LATEST

Model of latest scheme. Mainly it's organized with simple circulations and slit-like void to recognize the depth of the earth. Combined the engraved courtyard and ascensional diagonal shaft to provide the variety of interspace experience

—

最新案の模型。この段階では、単純なルート案から、地中深さの変化を感じさせる縦スリットを中心に構成している。中庭状に掘り込まれた部分や、斜めに上がっていくシャフトなどを組み合わせて、多様な空間体験を生み出そうとしている

Mountain Hotel

Section 1

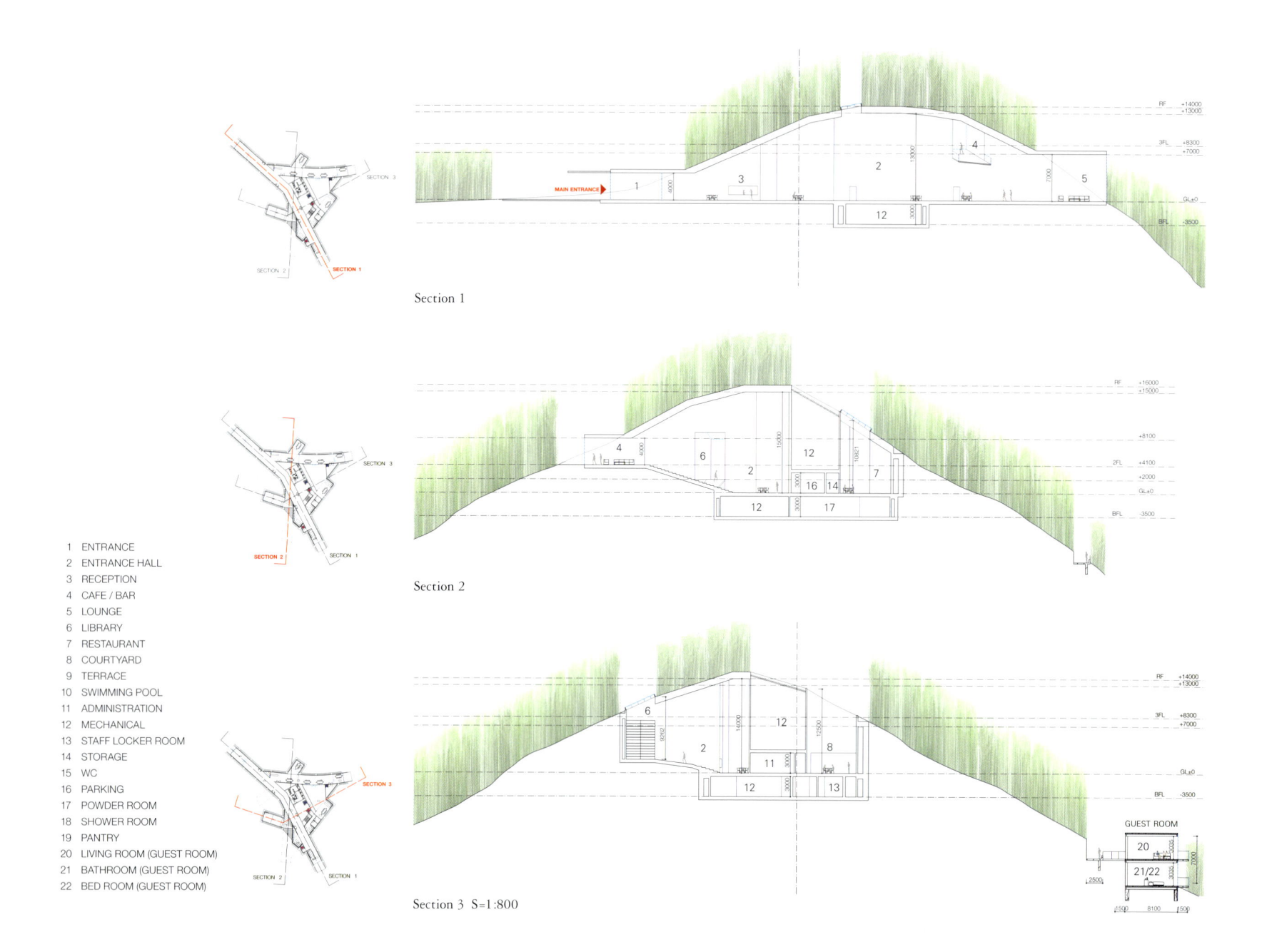

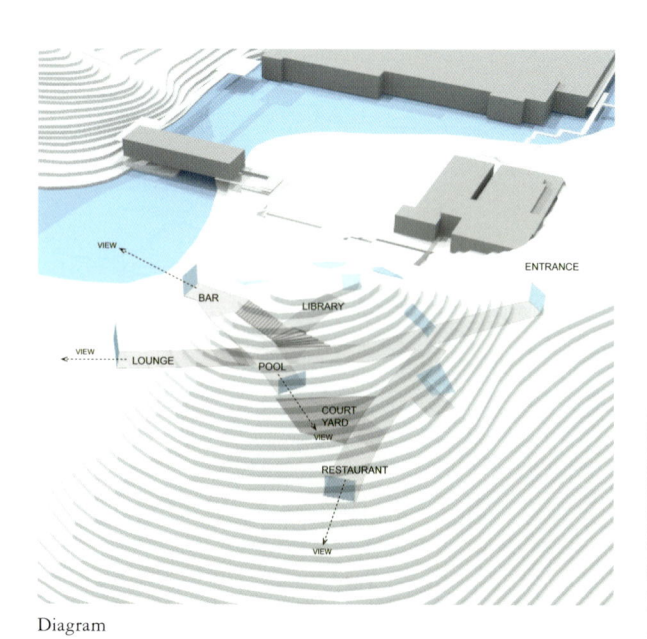

Section 2

Section 3 S=1:800

1 ENTRANCE
2 ENTRANCE HALL
3 RECEPTION
4 CAFE / BAR
5 LOUNGE
6 LIBRARY
7 RESTAURANT
8 COURTYARD
9 TERRACE
10 SWIMMING POOL
11 ADMINISTRATION
12 MECHANICAL
13 STAFF LOCKER ROOM
14 STORAGE
15 WC
16 PARKING
17 POWDER ROOM
18 SHOWER ROOM
19 PANTRY
20 LIVING ROOM (GUEST ROOM)
21 BATHROOM (GUEST ROOM)
22 BED ROOM (GUEST ROOM)

Diagram

Aerial view

Entrance

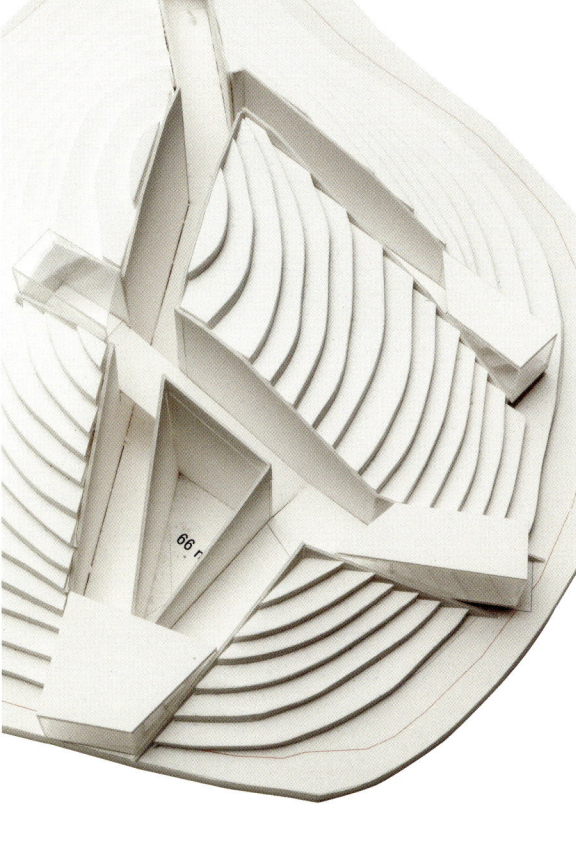

Restaurant

Library

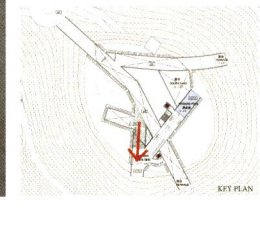

Cafe/bar

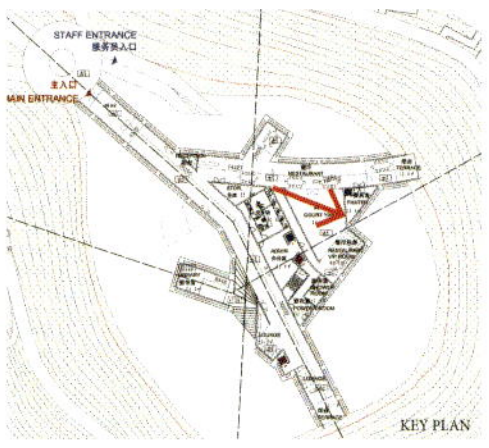

Courtyard

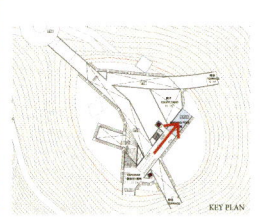

Swimming pool

敷地は中国の水源から湧き出る豊かな水が川となって流れ，池や沼沢が散在する穏やかな里山の風景が広がる場所である。私たちのホテルはそのうちの一つの小高い山の上に位置している。竹林が青々と茂る山の内部に，山の中腹に，そして山の麓の湖畔の近くに，ホテルの施設群は点在する。山とホテルとが融合し一体となった，山でありつつホテルでもあるような新しい自然/建築として，このホテルを設計した。

山の中をトンネル状にくり抜き，それがそのまま建築となったホテルのエントランスホール。レストランやバー，ラウンジなどの機能があり，ゲストはホール内でゆっくりくつろぎながら，各空間に設けられた大きなガラスの開口より自然の移ろいを感じることができる。

竹林に囲まれた山を半分くりぬいたかのようなゲストルーム群。四つの異なるタイプの住戸が，山のまわりにぐるっと配置されている。前面一面の大きなガラス窓による開放感を持ちつつも，山の中に半分埋まることによって，山と一体化してランドスケープにとけ込む。

各客室からは，竹林の隙間から湖畔やその向こう側に広がる山並みの風景が眺めることができる。

Mountain Hotel

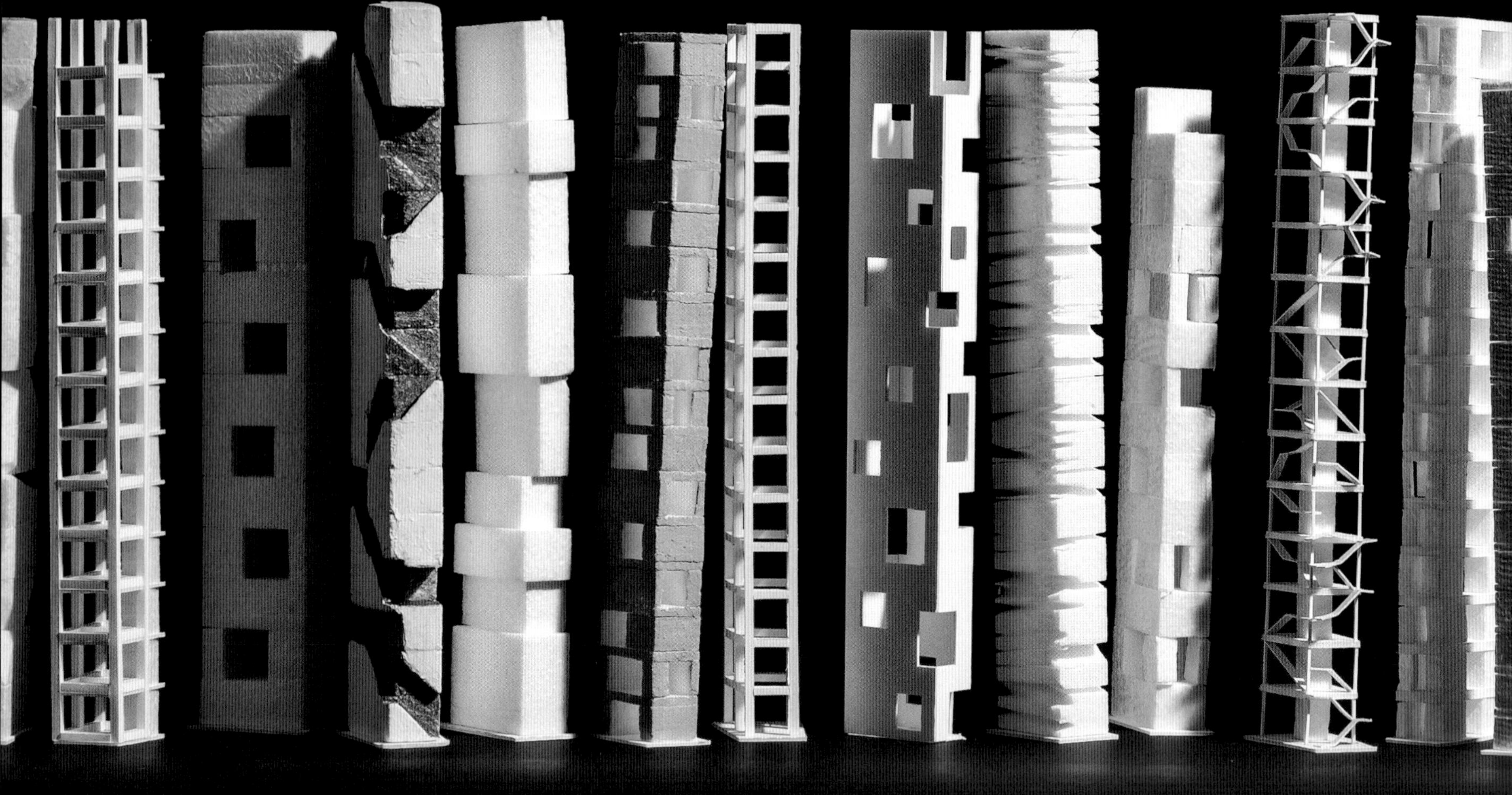

This is an office+residence project in a small site facing the main street of Ginza.

Various shapes of stairways will be installed on the surface of the tower building.

On the stairways, trees and chairs will be installed to provide people with a place to rest as it like a private terrace.

This outdoor space in a staircase pattern doesn't divide each floor, and becomes a three-dimentional alley like space that forms a community for the users.

Overflowing people's activities and properties appear on the surface to generate a flesh richness explession in the town of Ginza.

銀座の大通りに面する小さな敷地に計画中のオフィス+住居。

タワー状に佇む建物の表面にはさまざまな形の階段がとりつく。

その階段には木々が置かれたり，広い踊り場では椅子を置いて休んだりと，プライベートテラスとして利用することができる。

この階段状の外部空間は各階を分断することなく，利用者同士のコミュニティーを形成する立体的な路地のような場所となる。

人々の活動や，ものが表面にあふれ出すことで，銀座のまちに新しく豊かな表情をつくり出す。

Study model

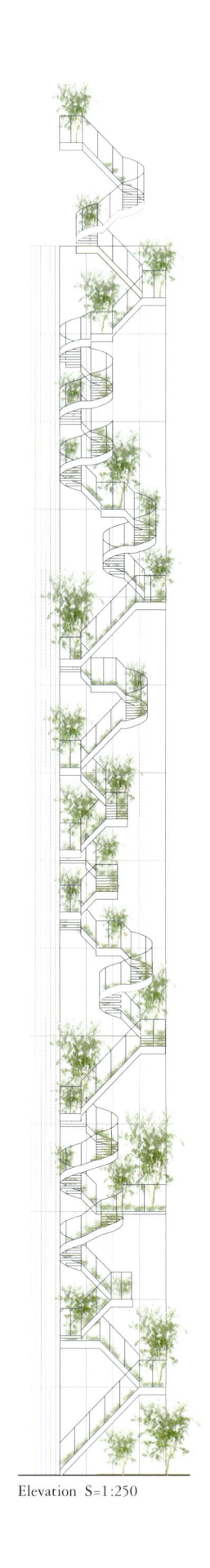

◁ View from main street

Elevation S=1:250

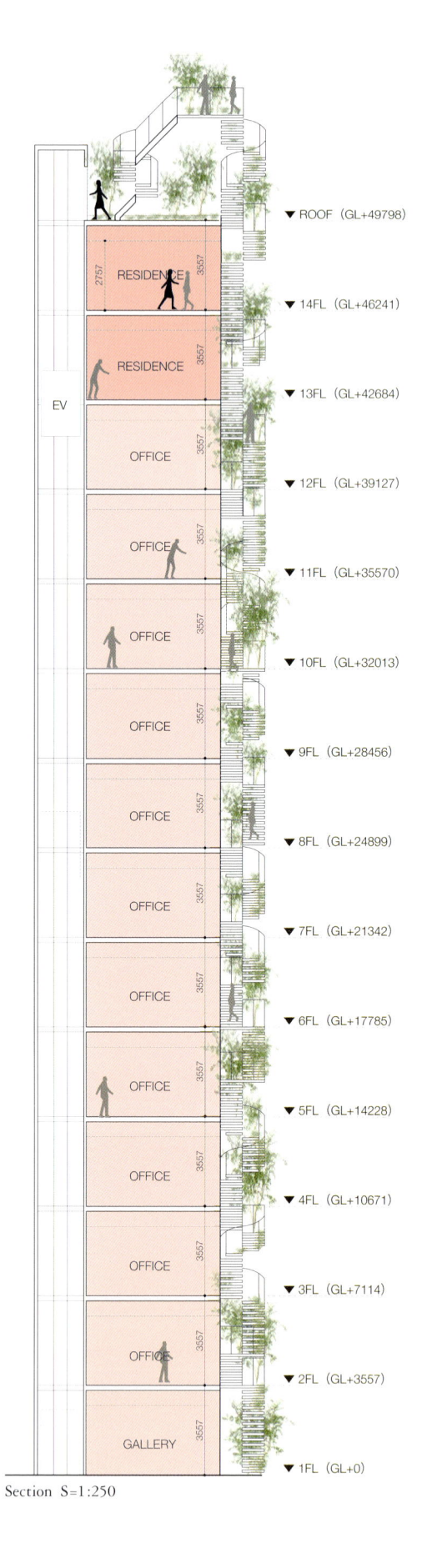

Section S=1:250

▼ ROOF (GL+49798)
▼ 14FL (GL+46241)
▼ 13FL (GL+42684)
▼ 12FL (GL+39127)
▼ 11FL (GL+35570)
▼ 10FL (GL+32013)
▼ 9FL (GL+28456)
▼ 8FL (GL+24899)
▼ 7FL (GL+21342)
▼ 6FL (GL+17785)
▼ 5FL (GL+14228)
▼ 4FL (GL+10671)
▼ 3FL (GL+7114)
▼ 2FL (GL+3557)
▼ 1FL (GL+0)

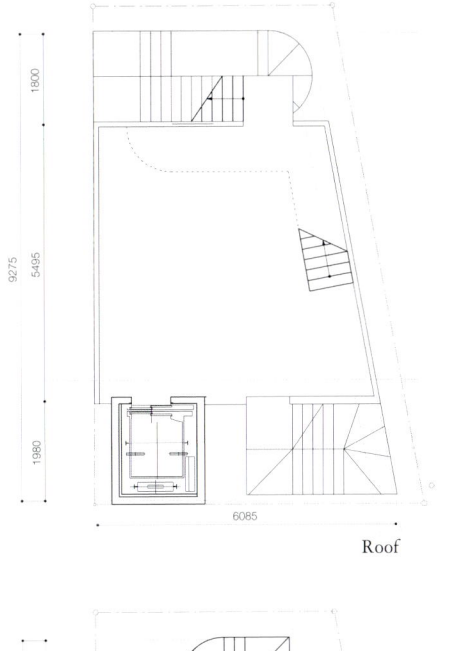

Roof

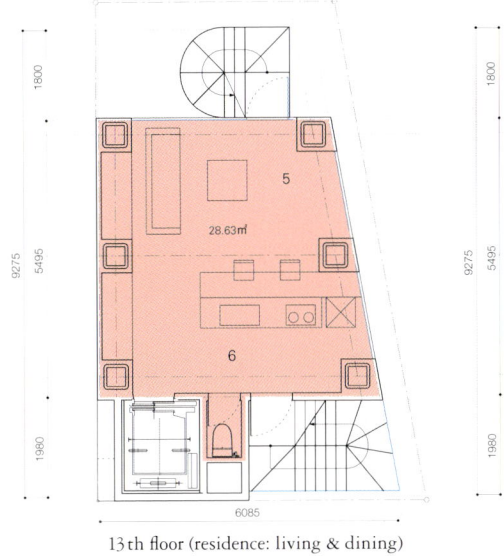

13th floor (residence: living & dining)

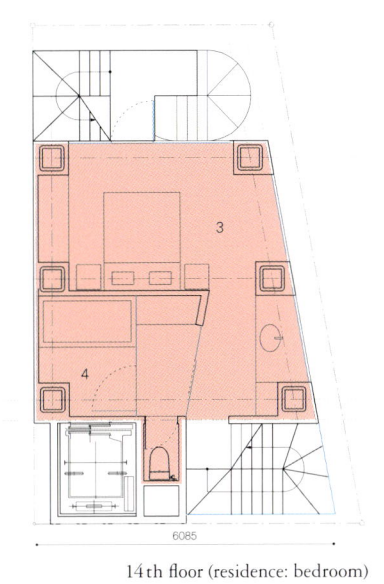

14th floor (residence: bedroom)

Staircase

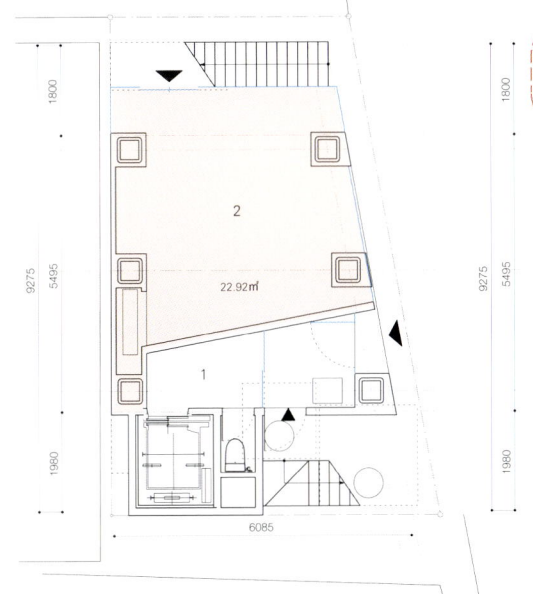

First floor (entrance) S=1:150

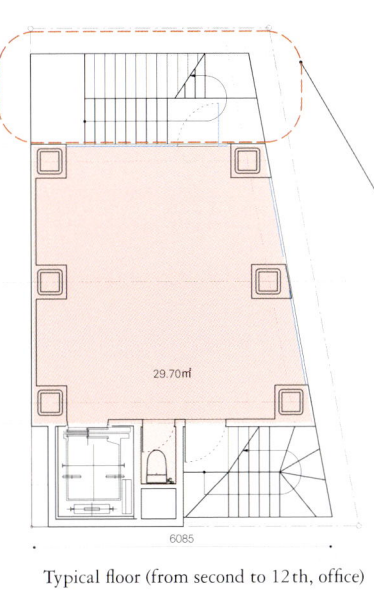

Typical floor (from second to 12th, office)

階段の形状は階によって異なります。
平均5㎡の占有バルコニーとして有効に
活用できます。

1. ENTRANCE HALL
2. GALLERY
3. BEDROOM
4. BATHROOM
5. LIVING ROOM
6. KITCHEN

Ginza Building

JJ99 YOUTH HOSTEL
Tainan, Taiwan, 2012-13
HOTEL

Whenever I am in a city of Taiwan, I am impressed by how open and attractive the spaces of various stores and restaurants are. Sometimes these stores are flowing into the sidewalks, which are also lined with trees, turning the streets into vibrant and richly abundant spaces.

We would like to incorporate this lively spirit of the Taiwanese streets into the project site. This hotel is an example of how the city seeps into the architecture, much like the way architecture melts into a city. It is as if we are morphing these streets themselves into three-dimensional spaces where the visitors can stay inside. Our plan is to generate a new spot where the city blends with the architecture, and the natural integrate with the man-made, to create the open and lively, vibrant urban spaces of Taiwan.

'Large Tree'—as it cities of Taiwan become three-dimensional, it supposed to looks like a big tree that houses many creatures inside.

台湾の街の中で感じるのは，さまざまな商店や飲食店の空間が，都市空間に対してとてもオープンで，また時には歩道にまではみ出していたりしていて，街路には街路樹も植えられていたりして，とてもにぎやかで豊かな街路空間となっていることである。

私たちは，そのような台湾の街路空間の豊かさを，この敷地の中にも立体的に取り込みたいと考えている。都市の中に建築がとけ出していくように，このホテルでは，建築の中に都市がとけ込んでいく。まるで台湾の街路が立体化して，その中にそのまま宿泊しているかのようなイメージである。台湾の都市空間のように開放的でにぎやかな，都市と建築，自然と人工とが融合した全く新しい場所にしたいと考えている。

「大きな樹」—台湾の街を立体化したら，それは様々な生き物の生息する大樹のようになるだろう。

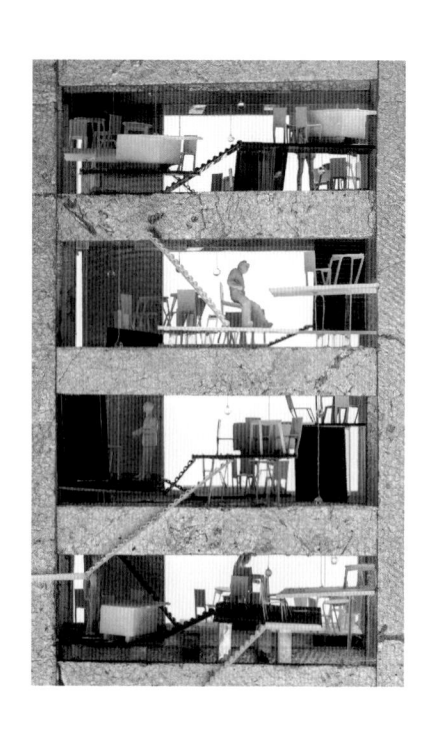

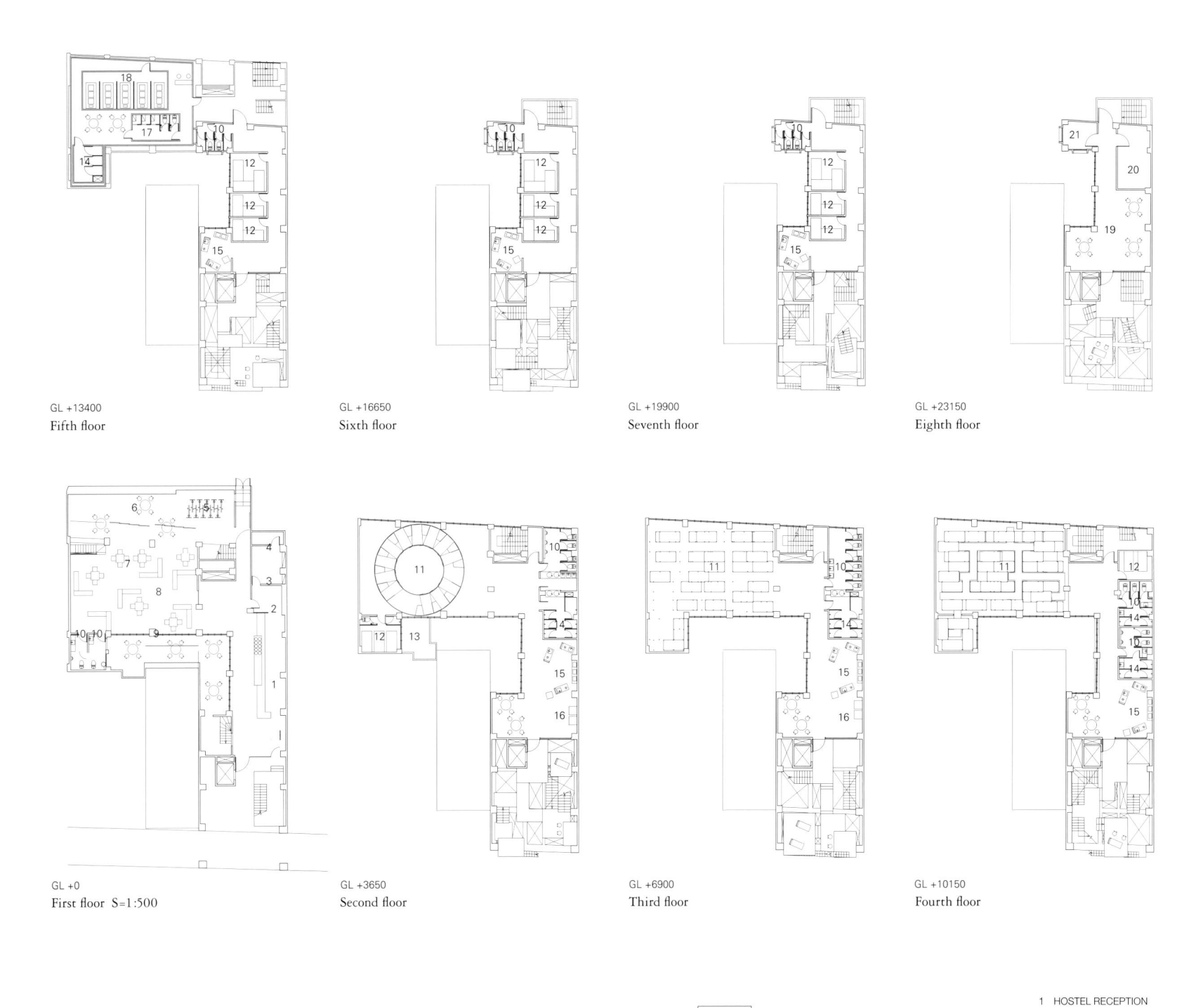

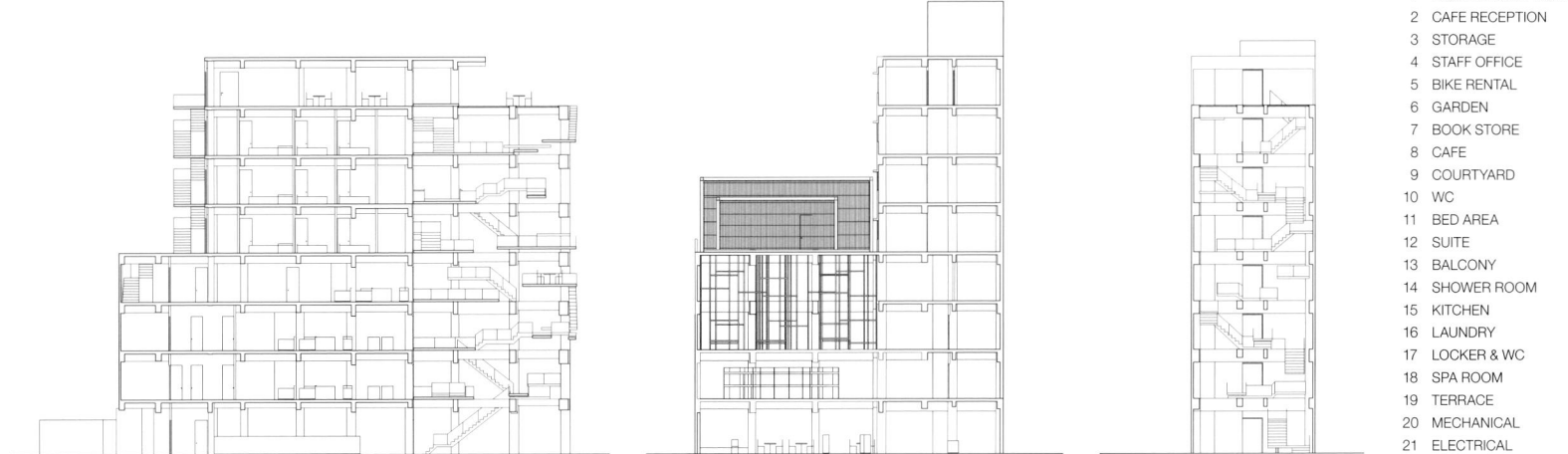

GL +13400
Fifth floor

GL +16650
Sixth floor

GL +19900
Seventh floor

GL +23150
Eighth floor

GL +0
First floor   S=1:500

GL +3650
Second floor

GL +6900
Third floor

GL +10150
Fourth floor

Sections   S=1:500

1 HOSTEL RECEPTION
2 CAFE RECEPTION
3 STORAGE
4 STAFF OFFICE
5 BIKE RENTAL
6 GARDEN
7 BOOK STORE
8 CAFE
9 COURTYARD
10 WC
11 BED AREA
12 SUITE
13 BALCONY
14 SHOWER ROOM
15 KITCHEN
16 LAUNDRY
17 LOCKER & WC
18 SPA ROOM
19 TERRACE
20 MECHANICAL
21 ELECTRICAL

JJ99 YOUTH HOSTEL

SETONOMORI HOUSES

Coastal Area of the Seto Inland Sea, Japan, 2012-13
TOWNHOUSE

Overall view from east 東より見る全景

The project is a housing complex of 26 units, located between the mountains near the Seto Inland Sea. The site is on a sloping terrain where traces of the old tiered platforms still remain. When I visited the site, I felt a strong impression of the local scenery, a landscape of houses scattered in front of the mountain range. I also found the steps and the steep paths that run between these houses very attractive. Taking all of this into account, I plan to build a "new scenery" which will become a link into the future.

To match the scale of the local houses nearby, each building will have 2 units built into one, and the project will include 13 of these simple gable-roofed buildings. The layout takes the entire landscape into consideration, including

Site plan S=1:500

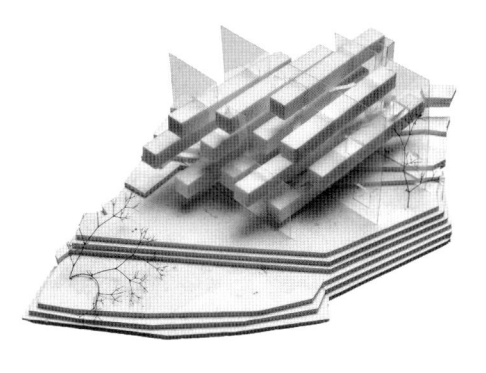

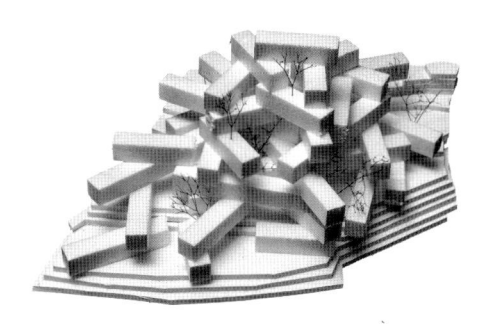

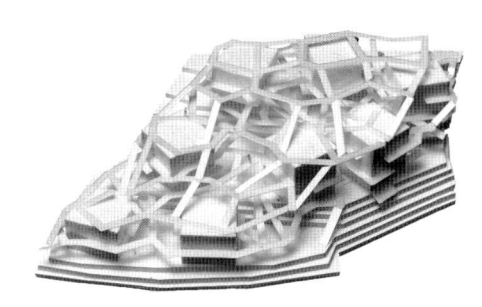

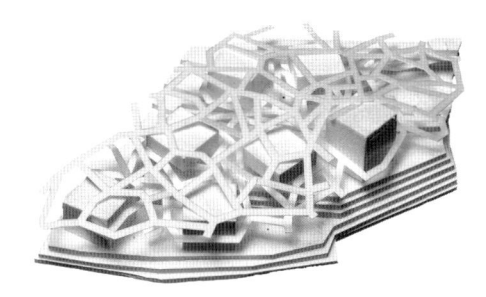

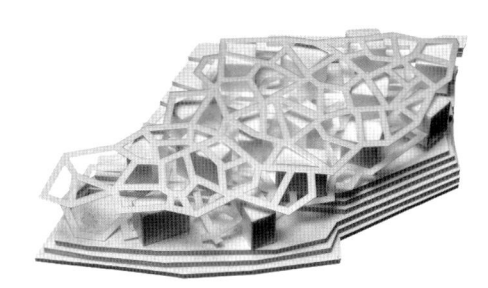

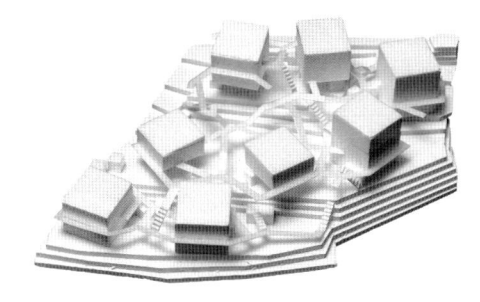

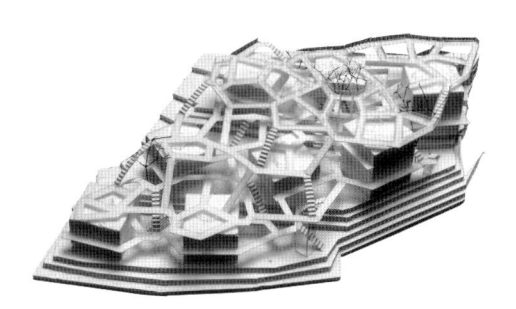

the relationships between landform and access points, as well as the view and the paths. Over 100 trees are planted between the buildings so that the project does not obstruct the mountainous landscape in the background. The trees also act as a flexible boundary line that protects the privacy between in each unit.

Paths, stairs, handrails, outdoors storages, trees, washing line poles and mechanical units are scattered around the houses in disorder. Instead of isolating these symbolic, gable-roofed residential buildings, try to create a taste of "living environment" where a various things to scattered in diverse ways. Intention is to set up a vibrant place that overflows with furniture, bicycles, and everything related to the residentiary's life.

The facade is a corrugated stainless mirror sheet that faintly reflects the surrounding nature and building integrate well into the scenery with unique presence. The building wear a different looks in every hour, seasons and the weather. The fickle pattern resembles the colorless sky, suggestive of something more than a mere finishing material of an architecture. Our hope for the residents is to provide a flow feeling of the time in the changing expressions of these houses. These scenes will remain with the people and we are sure they will carry on those memories for future generation.

Study

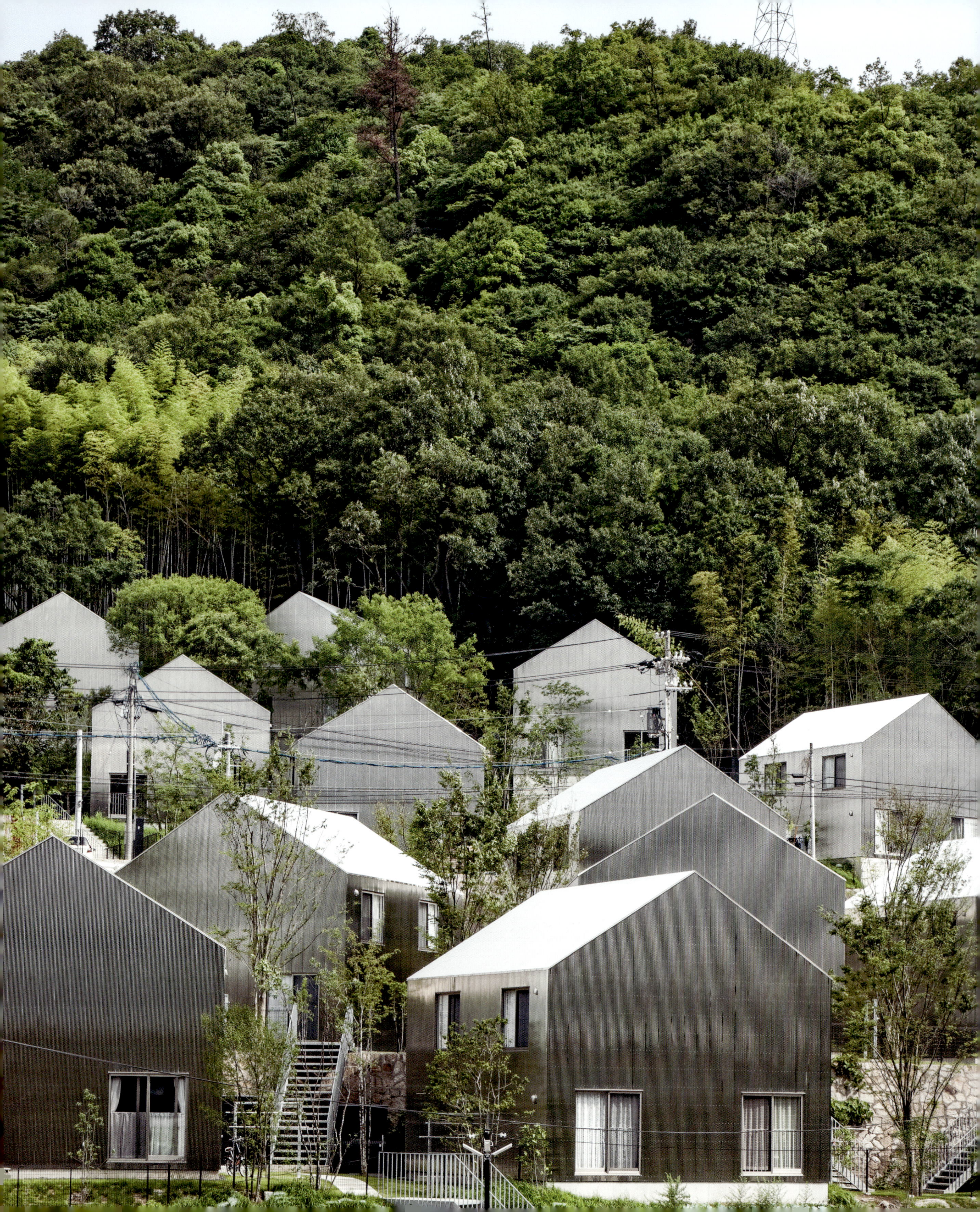

Gable-roofed townhouse (two houses in one unit)　2住戸を一纏めにした家型住居

Path, stairs, handrails, storages, trees, washing line poles and mechanical units are arranged randomly ◁△
各住戸の周りには，路地や樹木や階段，手すり，外部物置，物干フレーム，設備機械などが，あえて整理せずに分布されている

◁ View from southeast　南東より見る

Setonomori Houses　161

Study

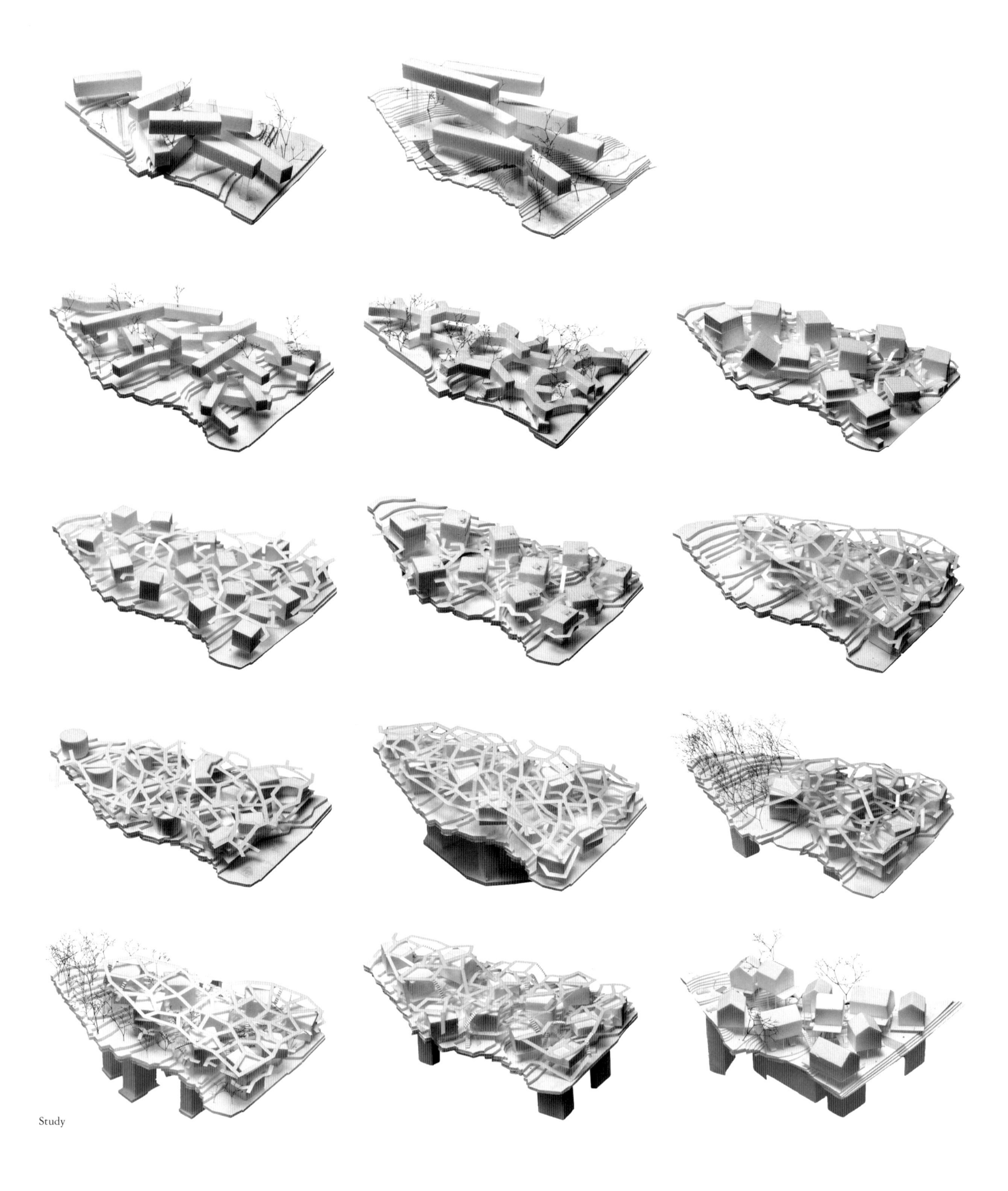

Elevations S=1:200

First floor S=1:200

Second floor

View from inside 部屋からの風景

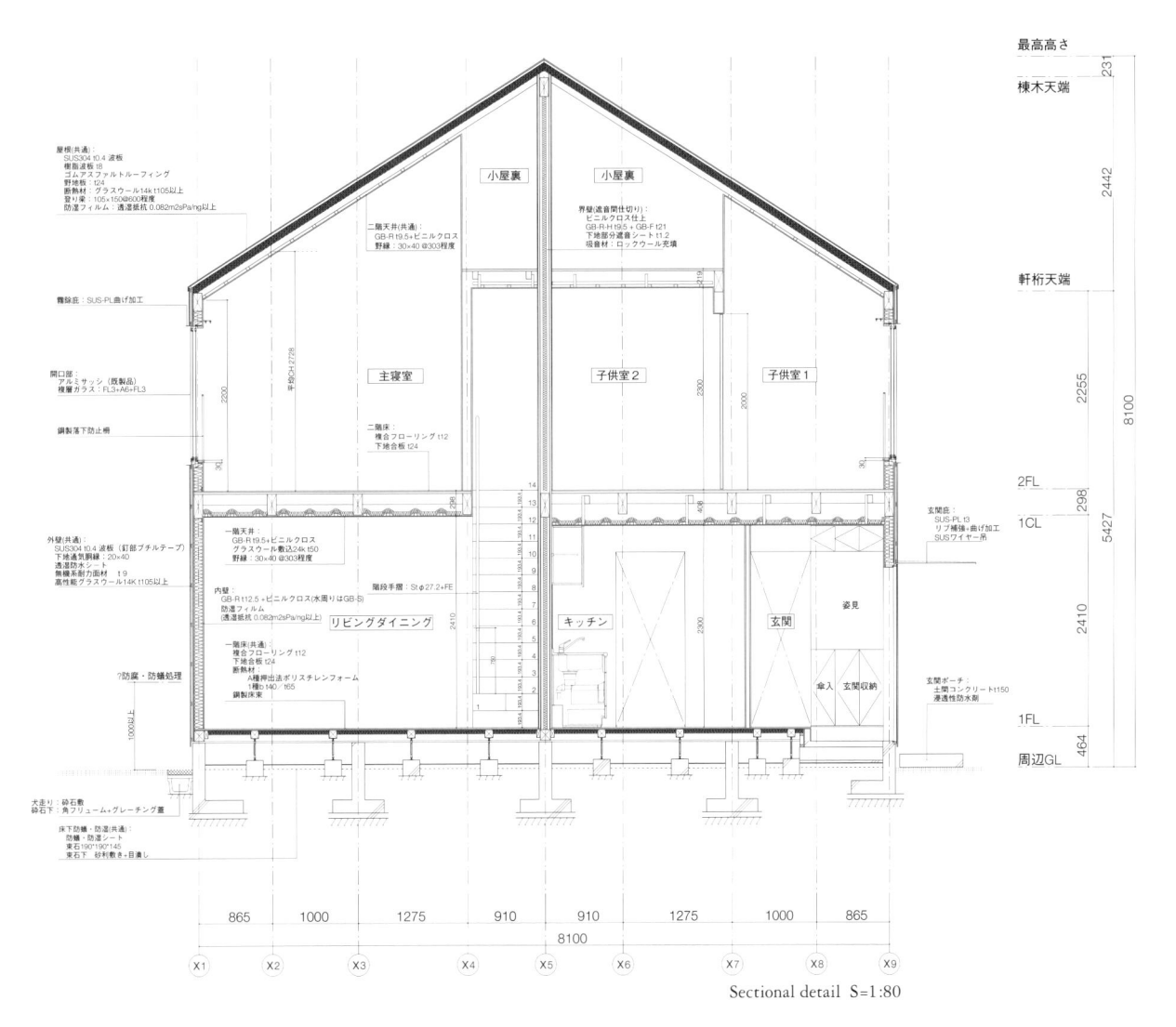

Sectional detail S=1:80

1 ENTRANCE
2 KITCHEN
3 LIVING/DINING ROOM
4 STORAGE
5 WC
6 WASHROOM
7 BATHROOM
8 CHILDREN'S ROOM
9 MASTER BEDROOM

Setonomori Houses

瀬戸内海にほど近い山あいの小都市に建つ26戸の集合住宅。敷地は傾斜地で昔のひな壇造成の痕跡が残る場所である。敷地を訪れたときに印象に残ったのは、この敷地の周囲に点在する民家と背後の山がつくり出す景観であった。それぞれの民家を結びつけるように巡る階段や急な坂道も魅力的だ。それらの周辺状況を引き受けた上で、未来の生活へと繋がる「新しい風景」を構築することを考えた。

周辺の民家のスケールに合わせるように、2住戸を一纏めにした家型の建物13棟が建つ。配置計画は、地形とアクセス、眺望と住棟間に生まれる路地や辻などの関係だけではなく、風景全体を考慮したものとなった。背後の山との連続性を意識して、住棟間には合計100本以上の樹木を植樹している。それはまた適度なプライバシーや領域感を柔軟に生み出す意図もある。

家々の周りには、路地や階段、手すり、外部物置や樹木、物干フレームや設備機械などが、あえて整理せずに乱雑に分布している。象徴的な家型の住棟が物体として孤立するのではなく、様々なものたちが様々に分布する「生活環境」のようなものをつくることを考えた。ここに住人の家具や自転車など生活にまつわるものが溢れ出ることで、生き生きした場所が生まれることを意図した。

外装はステンレス鏡面の小波板で、周囲の緑や空の様子をおぼろげに写し込み、建物が風景の中にとけ込みながら独特の存在感を持つ。その表情は季節や時間や天気によって刻々と変化する。それはもはや建築の仕上げ素材というよりも、そのものが色を持たないゆえに様々な表情をみせる空模様のようである。ここで暮らす人々が、変化する家並みの表情に季節の変化や一日の時の流れを感じてくれればと思う。それは人々の記憶となり、その積み重ねが未来へと受け継がれていくに違いない。

Downward view toward path between units　住戸間にある小径を見下ろす

TAIWAN CAFE
Tainan, Taiwan, 2013 -
CAFE

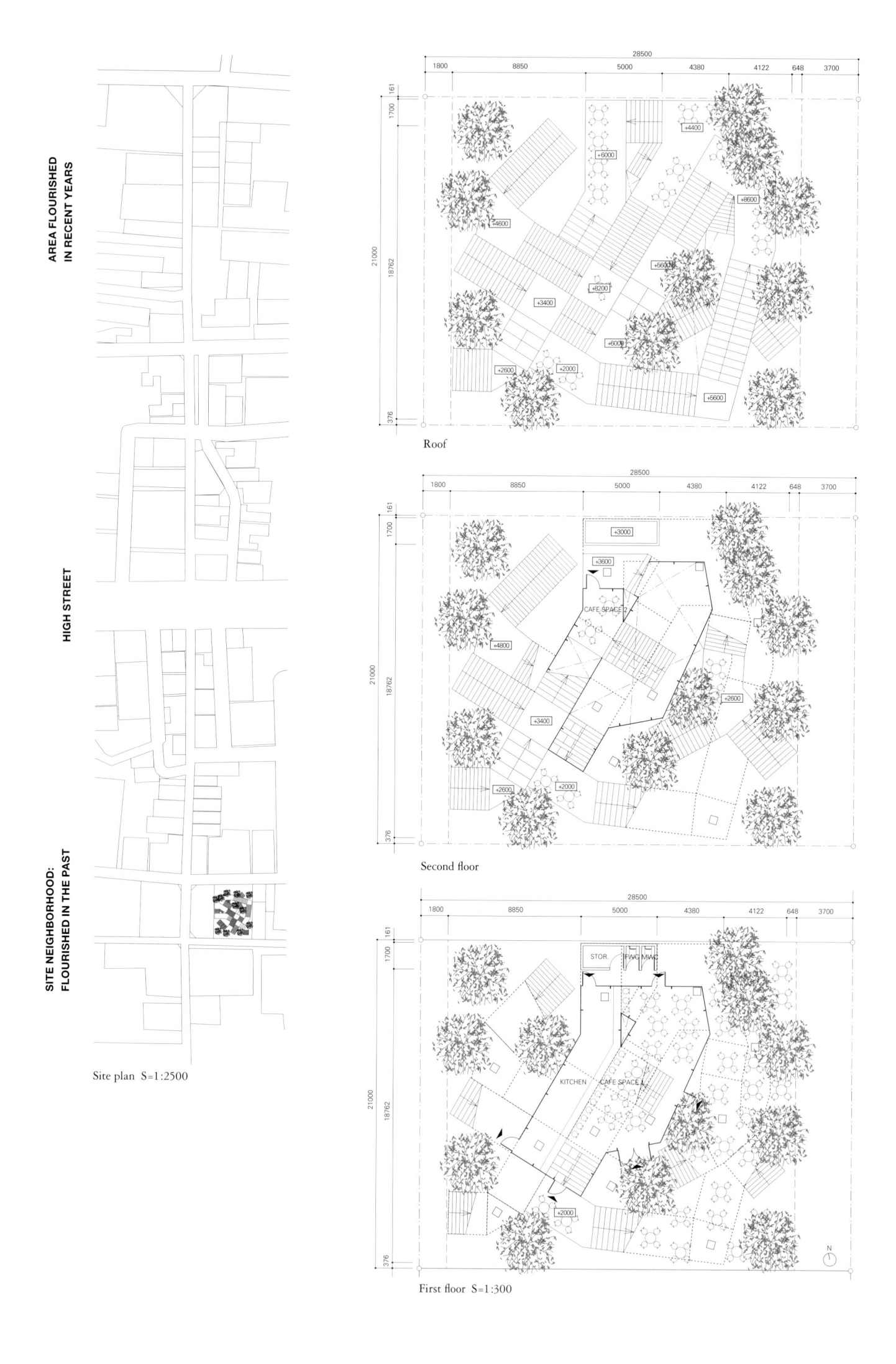

AREA FLOURISHED
IN RECENT YEARS

HIGH STREET

SITE NEIGHBORHOOD:
FLOURISHED IN THE PAST

Site plan S=1:2500

Roof

Second floor

First floor S=1:300

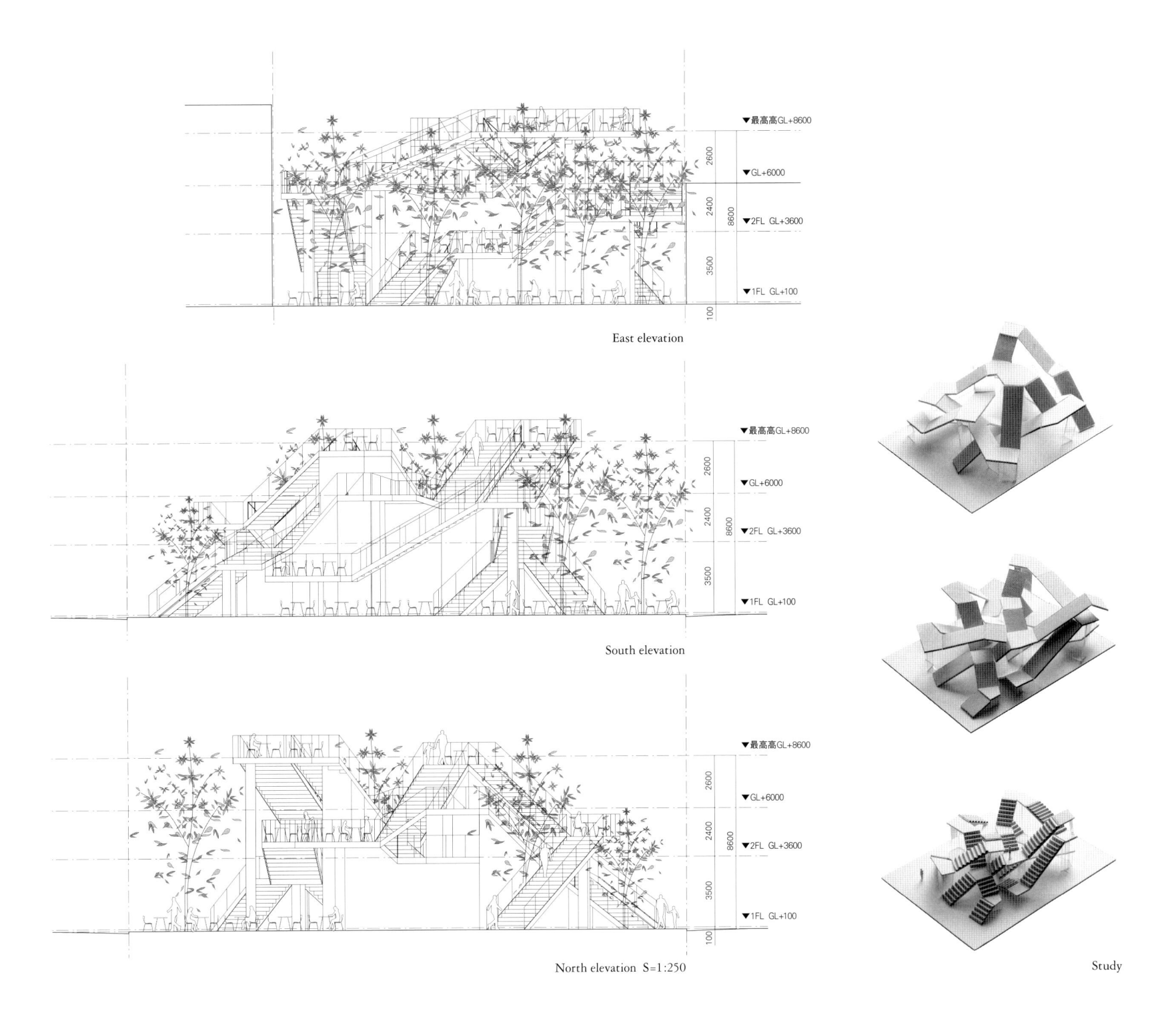

East elevation

South elevation

North elevation S=1:250

Study

BETWEEN ARCHITECTURE, A STREET, A CITY, A PARK AND A BODY

The project is a cafe planned in an urban district of Tainan city, located in the southern Taiwan. The surrounding of the site is a neighborhood once flourished in the past. Recently, there are many stores and cafes emerging for young people at the area on the other side of a high street. An intention of the project was to revitalize the entire surrounding region and to trigger town's rebirth by making a place where people gather on the site. The role for the cafe is projected to play for the first 10 years. Meanwhile, the district is expected to raise its value and the cafe will later be rebuilt into a new facility that matches the elevated worth.

Due to the mid-term plan, the initiating cafe is hoped to provide a distinctive place that cannot be found near the site rather than fulfilling a floor area ratio. That is why the building is made like an extension of a three-dimensional alley, enclosed by tall trees.

Alley spaces in Tainan are attractive. A boundary between a street and a building is vague and people's activities ooze out to a street and generate energy. We aimed at forming a new urban environment that is like a street, like a city, like architecture and like a park by multi-layering the amusing alley spaces.

Furthermore in Taiwan, sunshine is harsh and there is lots of rain. Considering such Taiwan-specific climate, we though of producing a place that is covered by roofs and eaves. The staircase network designed here functions as multi-layered roofs and eaves and provides many places to stay inside and outside.

It is a project as if connecting architecture, a street, a city, a park and a body and is a project containing time that is related to the area's prosperity and the city's vision for the future.

Cafe

建築と路と街と公園と身体の間

台湾の南に位置する台南市の市街地の中に計画しているカフェ。敷地周辺はかつてにぎわいを見せていた地域だが，近年は大通りを挟んだ反対側の地域に若者向けの店舗やカフェが多く展開している。プロジェクトの意図は，この敷地に人が集まる場所をつくることによって，周辺地域全体を活性化させ，街の再生のきっかけとなることである。このカフェの役割は最初の10年と予定されている。その間に地域の付加価値を引き上げることを期待されており，その後は上昇した付加価値にふさわしい新しい施設へと建て替えられる予定である。

上記のような中長期計画に位置づけられている故に，起爆剤としてのこのカフェは容積率を満たすことよりも，敷地周辺には見られない特別な場所をつくり出すことが求められている。高い樹木に囲まれて，立体的な路地の延長のような形で建築がつくられているのはそれ故である。

台南の街は路地空間が魅力的である。路と建築の境界が曖昧であり，人々の活動が常に路ににじみだして活気をつくり出す。そのような豊かな路地空間を立体化することで，路であり，都市であり，建築であり，公園であるような，新しい都市環境をつくり出すことを意図した。

また台湾は日射しが強く，雨が多い。そのような台湾特有の気候を考慮して，屋根一庇で覆われた場所をつくることを考えた。ここにつくられた階段のネットワークが，重層する屋根や庇のように機能して，内部と外部の間にたくさんの居場所をつくり出す。

建築と路と街と公園と身体の間をつなぐようなプロジェクトであり，また地域のにぎわいと街の未来のヴィジョンにもかかわり合う時間を含み込んだプロジェクトともなっている。

Path

Path

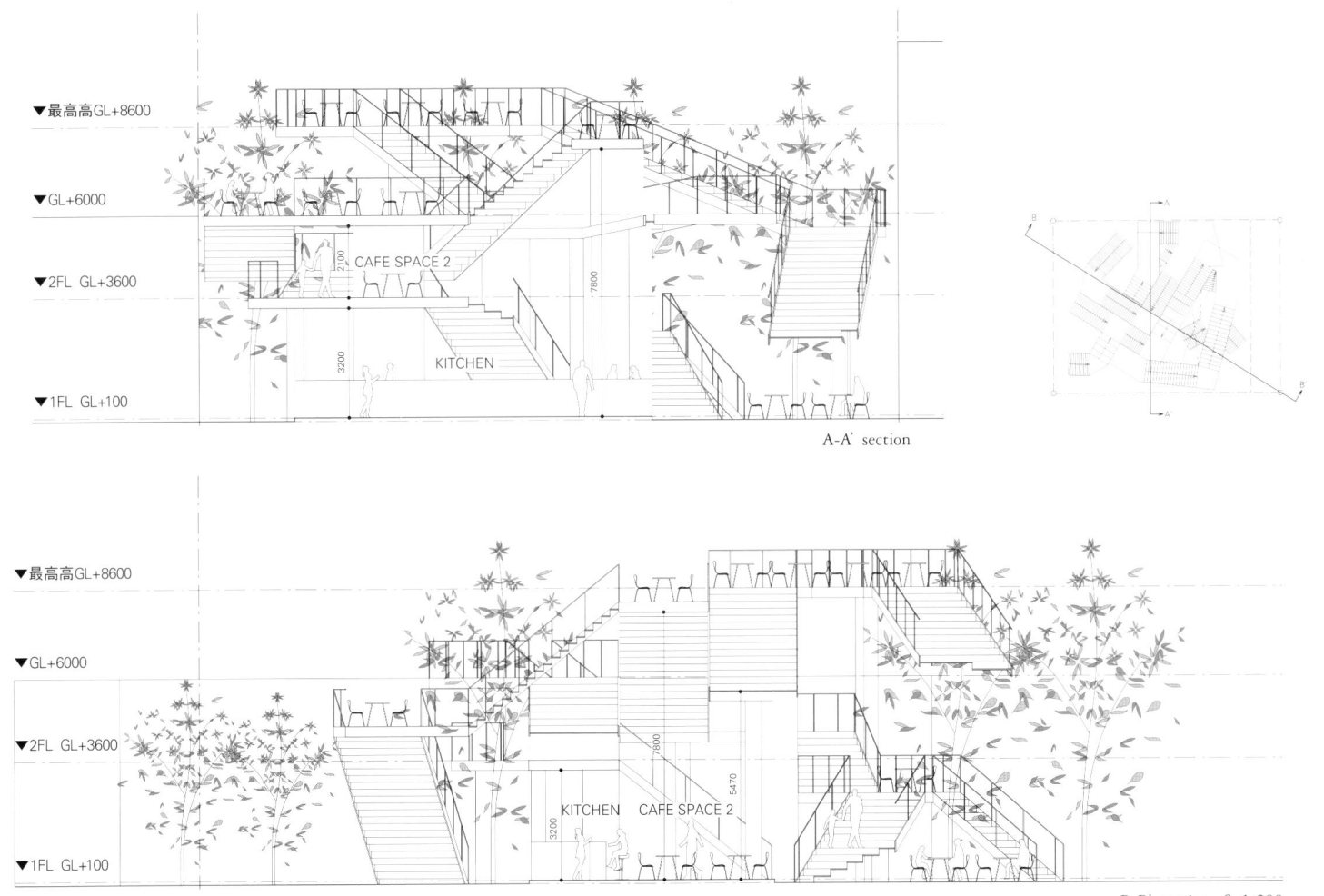

▼最高高 GL+8600
▼GL+6000
▼2FL GL+3600
▼1FL GL+100

CAFE SPACE 2
KITCHEN

A-A' section

▼最高高 GL+8600
▼GL+6000
▼2FL GL+3600
▼1FL GL+100

KITCHEN   CAFE SPACE 2

B-B' section S=1:200

Taiwan Cafe

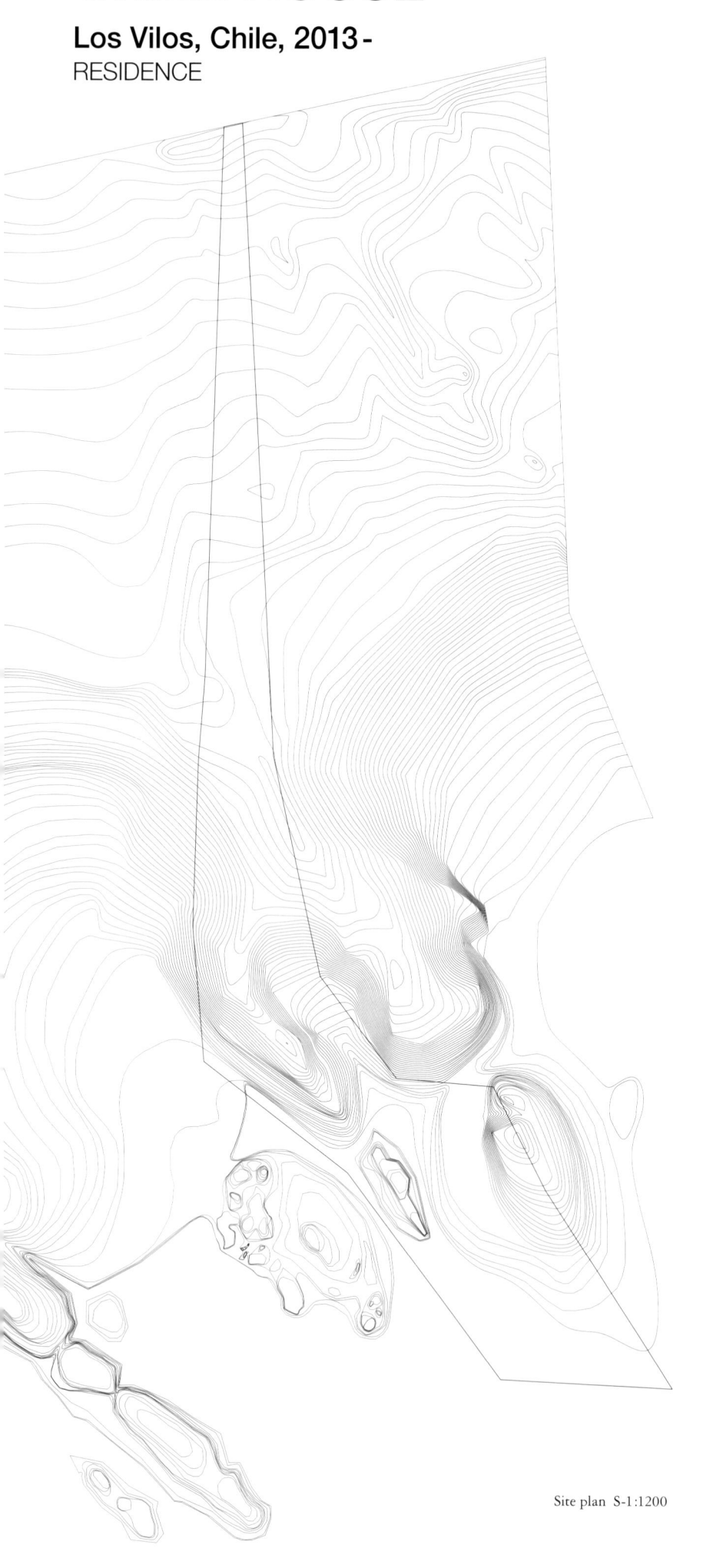

CHILE HOUSE
Los Vilos, Chile, 2013 -
RESIDENCE

This is the vacation house face to the Pacific Ocean, site of a beautiful land in about two hours drive of the Santiago, Chile.

The site is a magnificent cliff that dips into the ocean. When I visited the site, first impression was a dwelling with spaces built into the rocky landscape, a house that allows one to live among the shadows, cast between the rocks and natural cave. Afterwards, prepared models to study with topographical architecture, which included a plan with architectural rock-protrusion; a plan with walls that transform into a rock surface; and a plan for an underground house with only a geometric opening juxtaposed against the rocky landscape.

The result of this study is an architecture with tangling staircases: stacks of numerous steps to create an artificial landform that blend into the surrounding natural rock formations. Mixture of the exterior and interior appears on the terrace and stairs, and it not only become superficial landform but also generate the richness three-dimentional spaces. These layers of steps are also layers of infinite roofs, which are also eaves that protect from the summer sun, and openings that capture the low light of the winter.

Site plan S-1:1200

Massing study

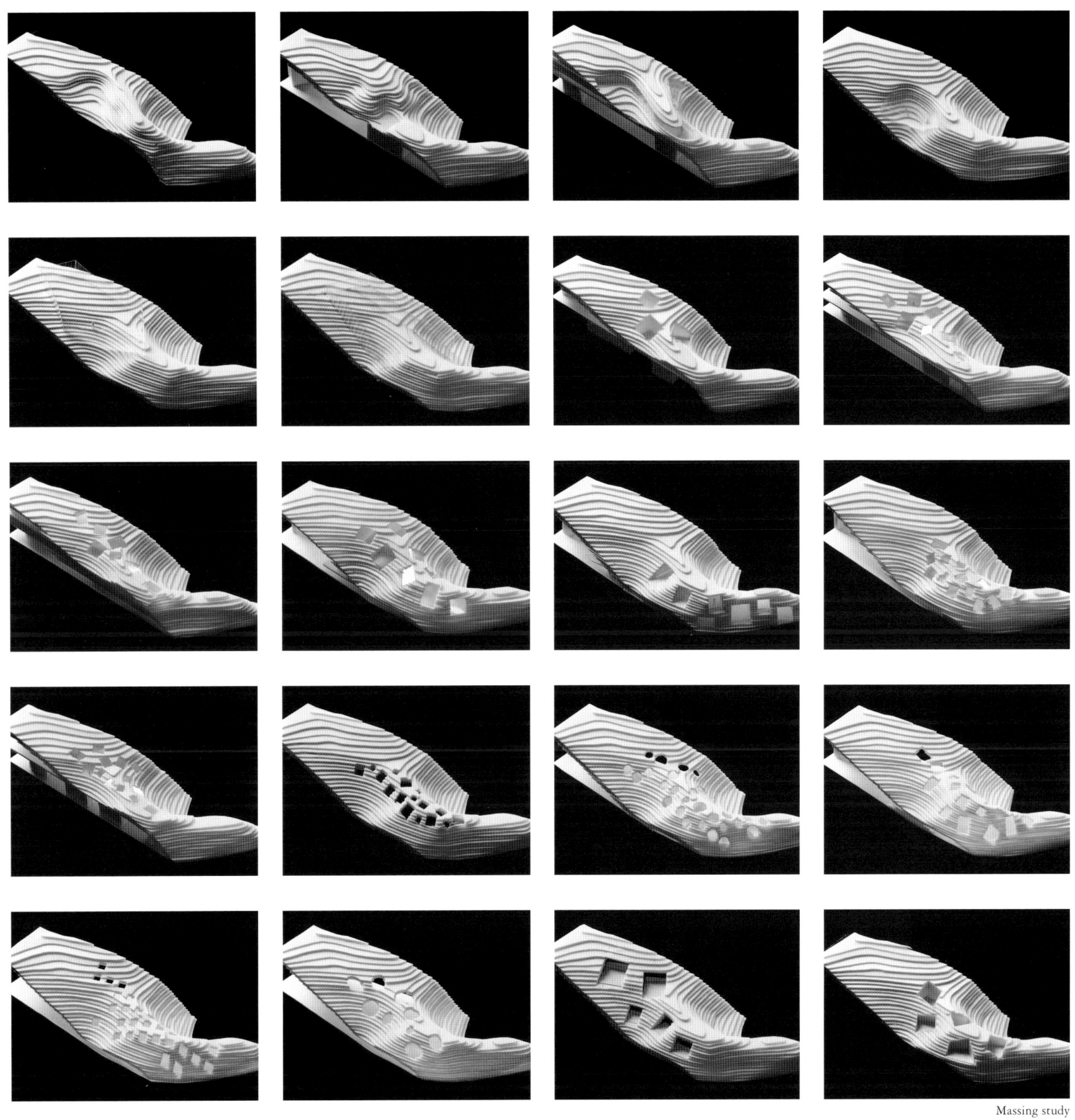

Chile House

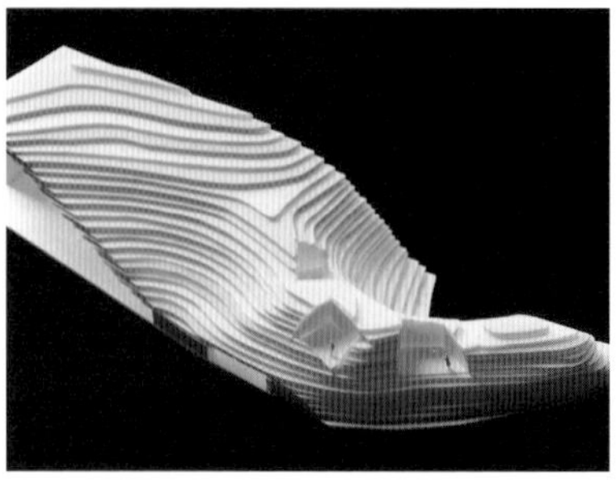
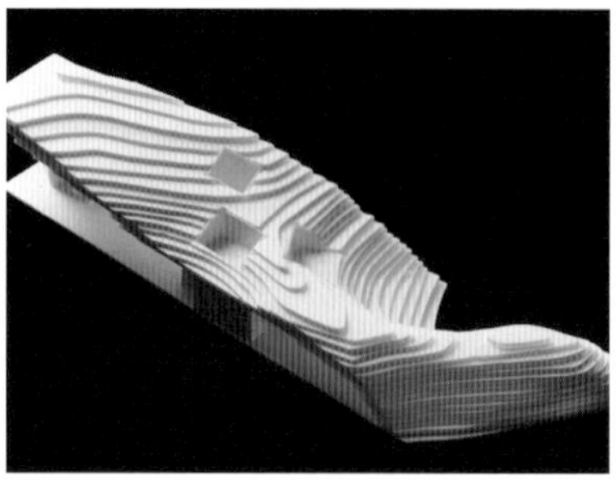
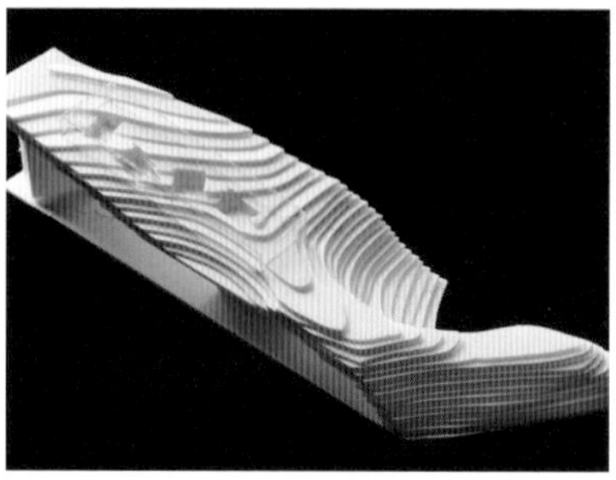
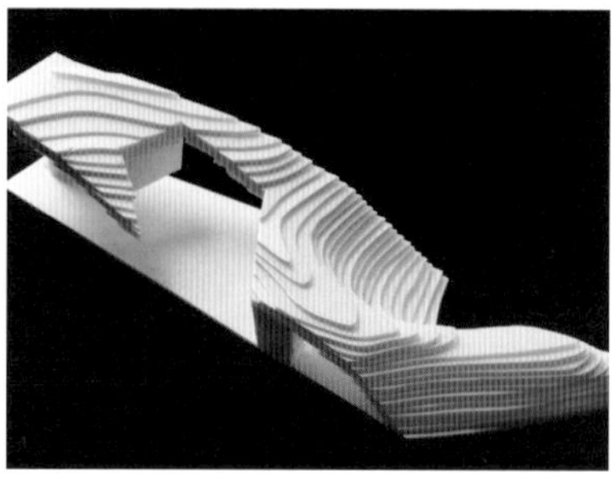
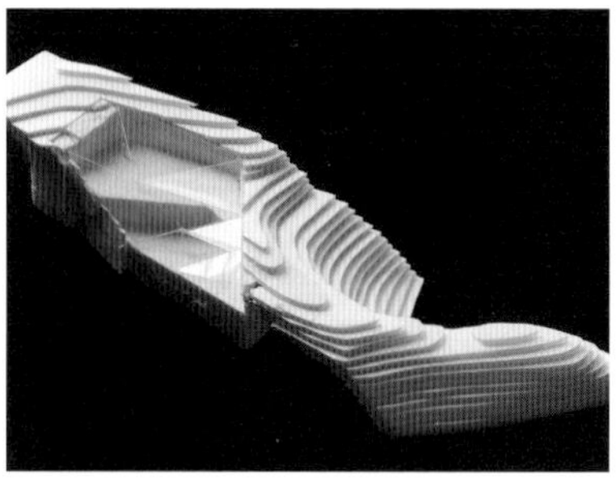
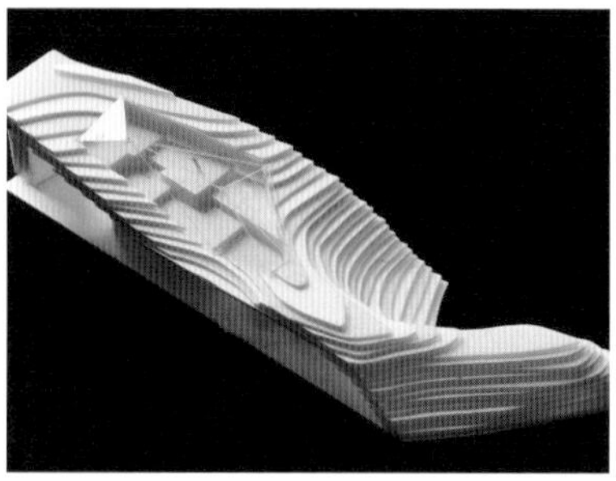
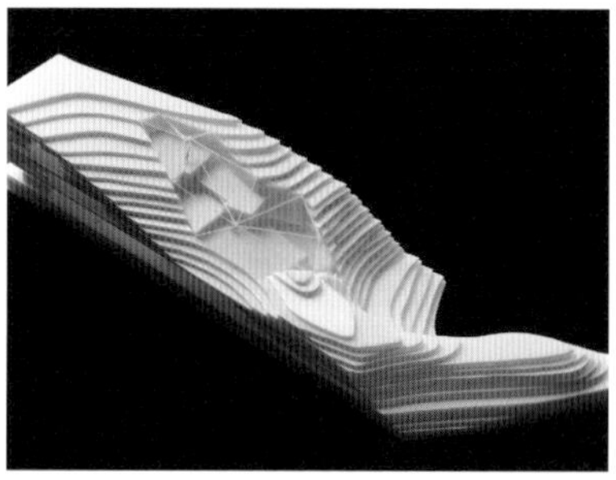
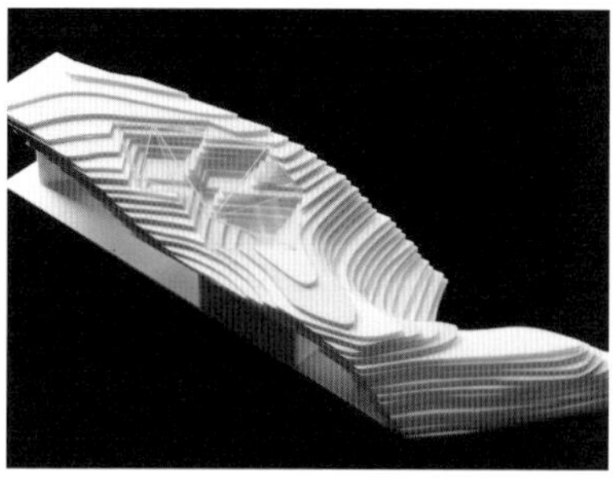
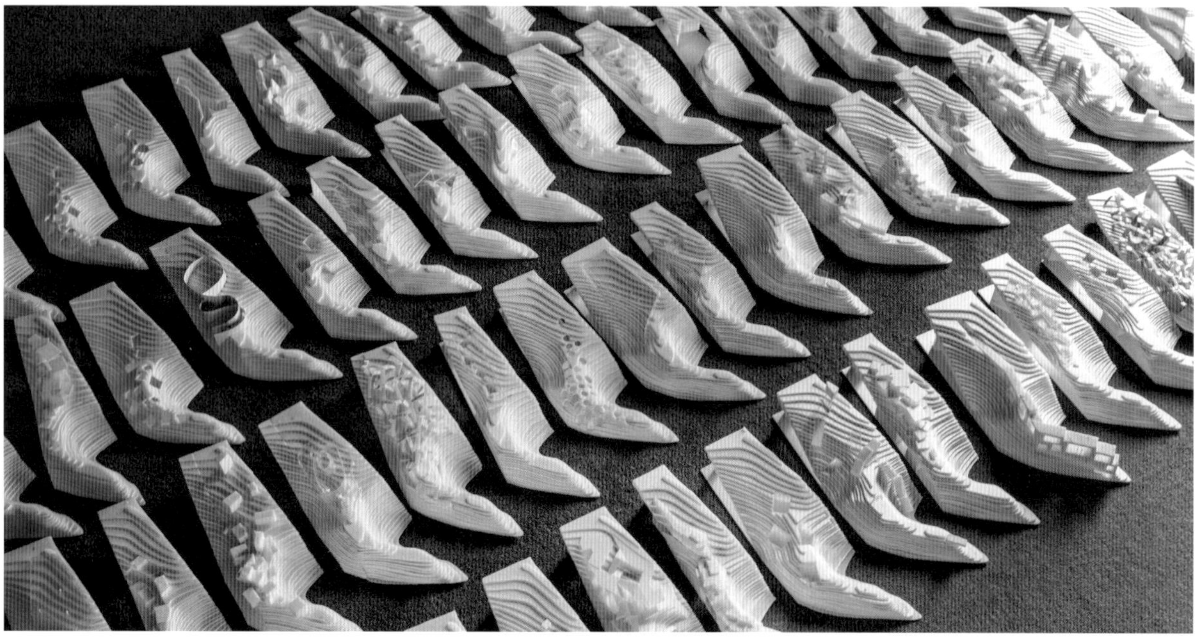
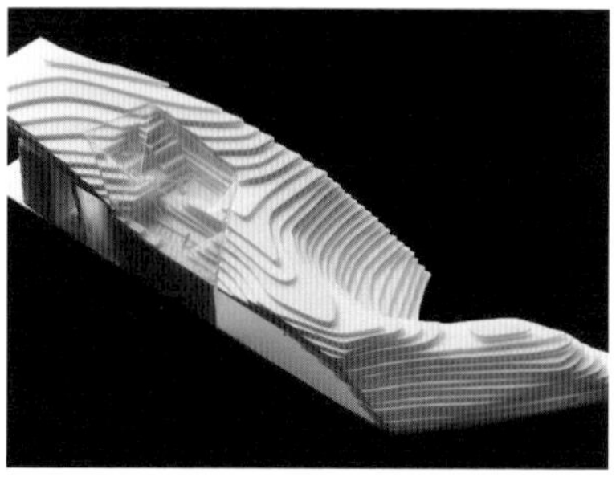
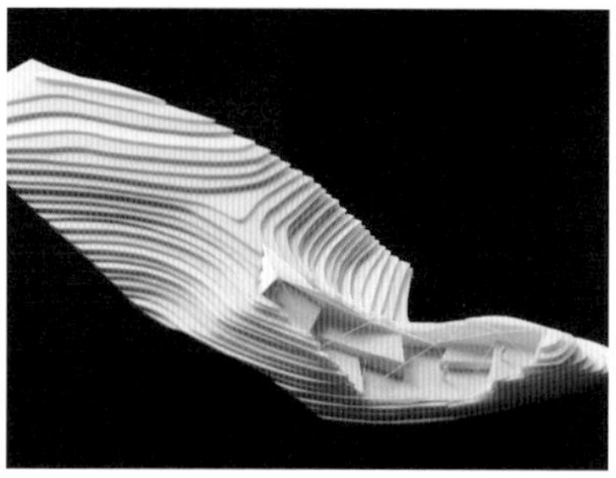
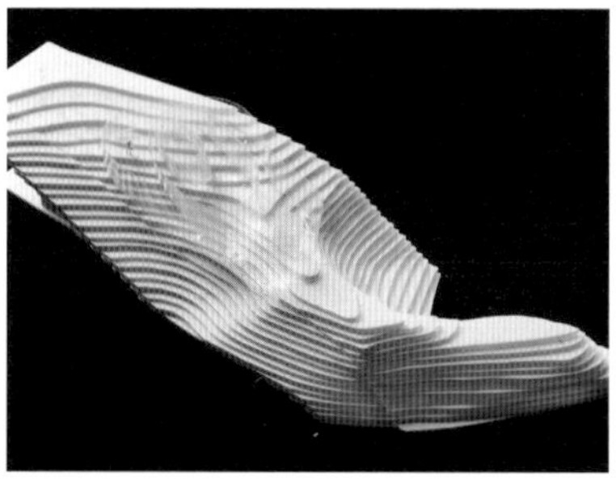
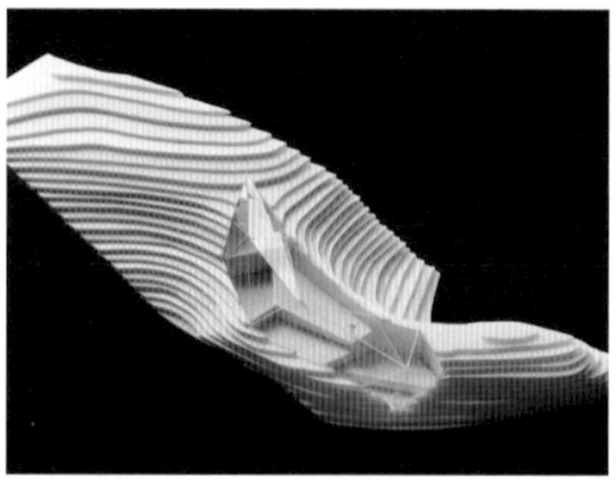
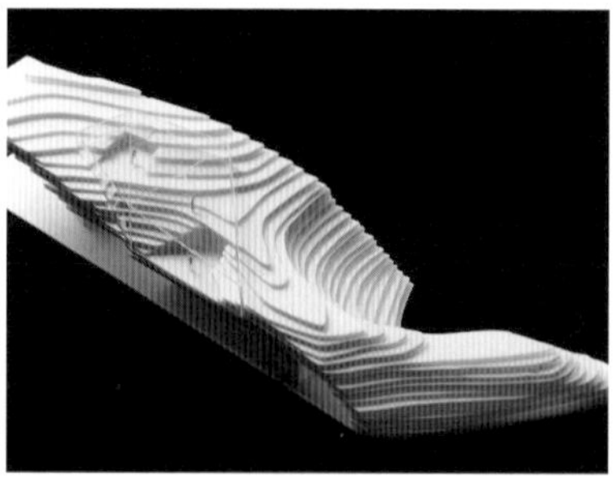
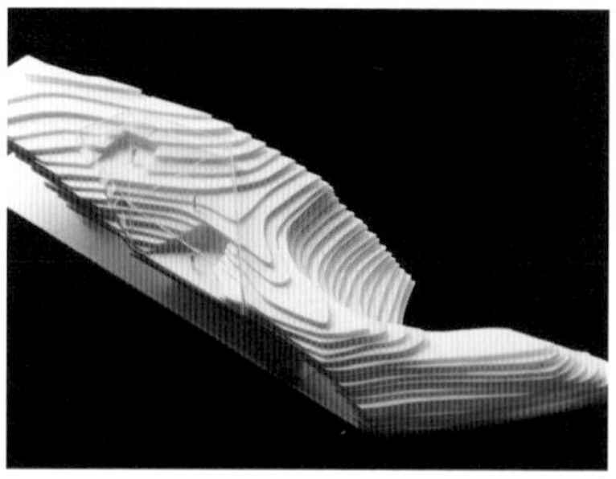

Site

Site

Massing study

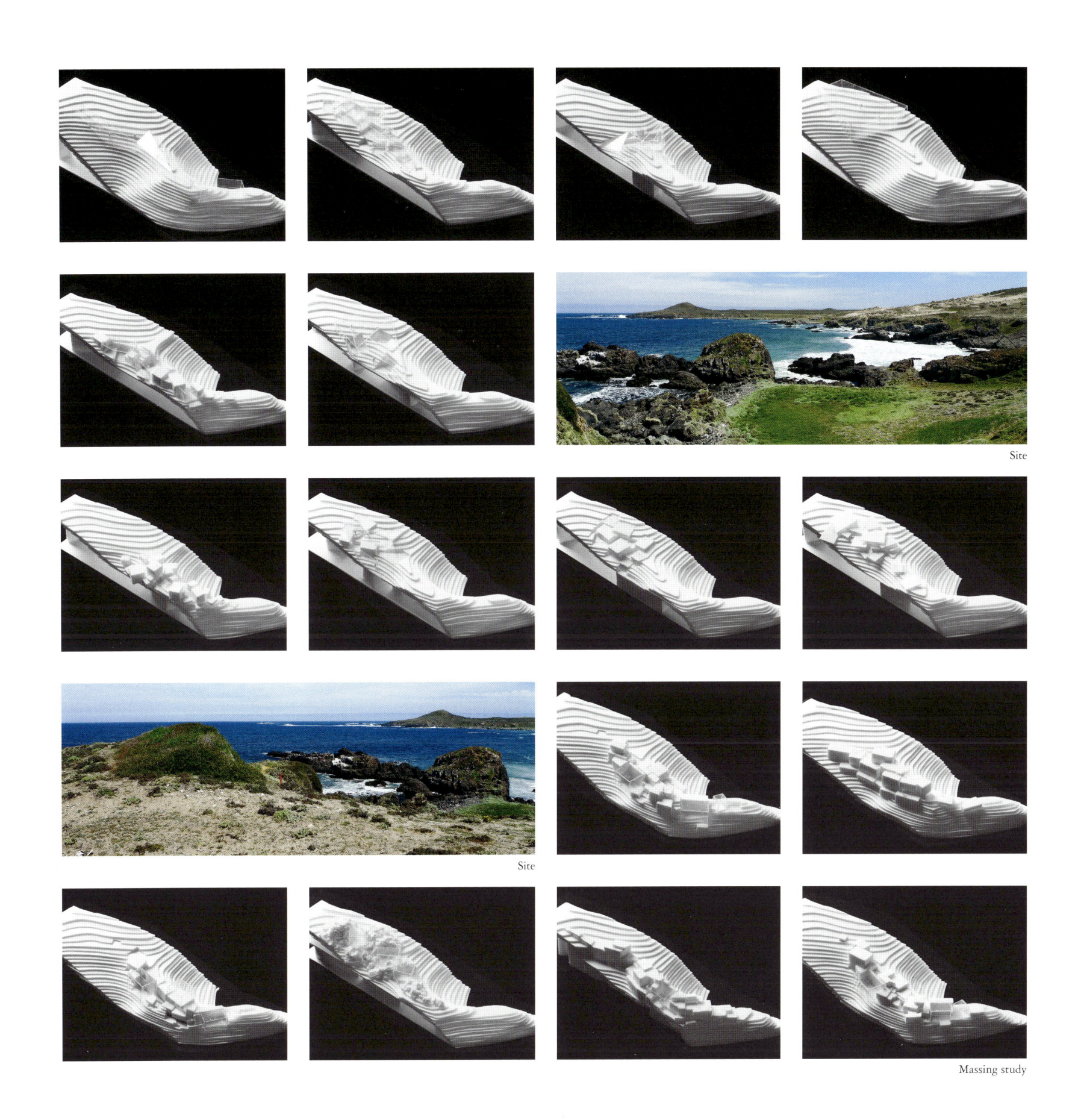

Chile House

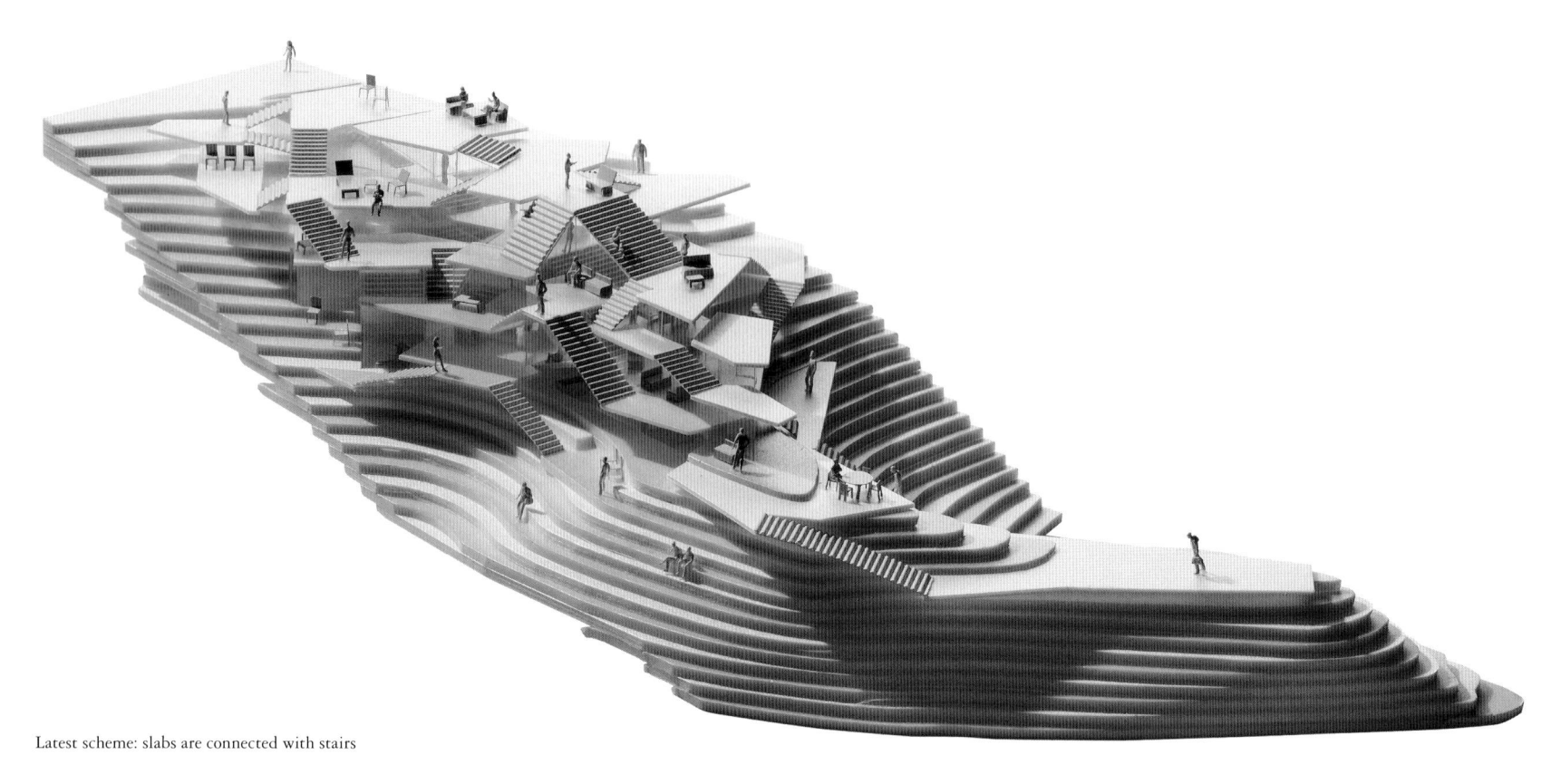

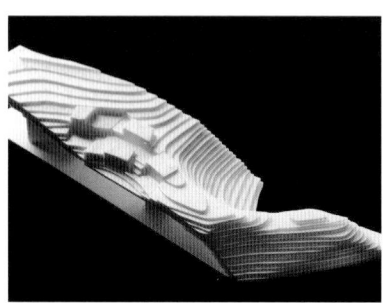

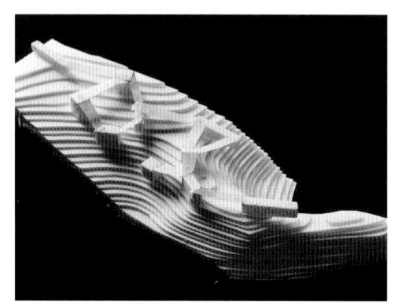

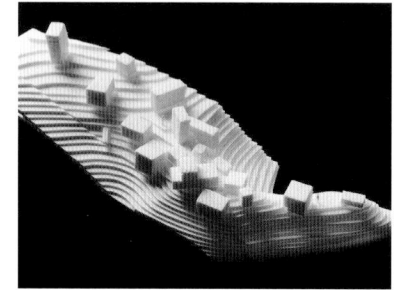

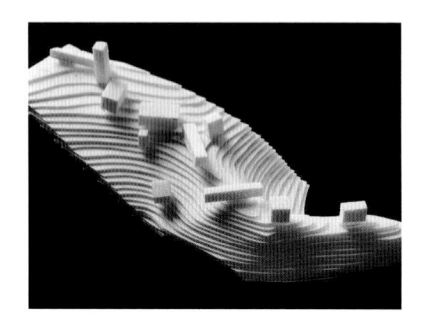

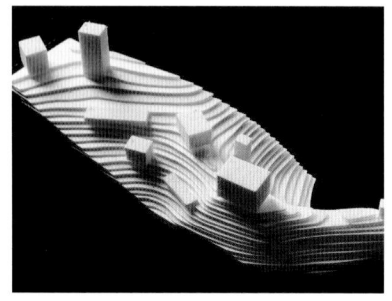

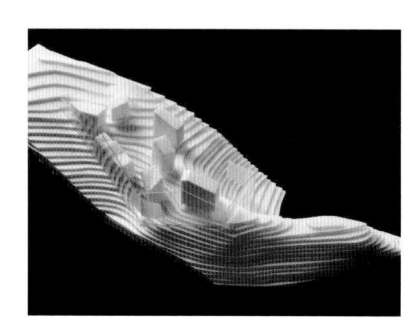

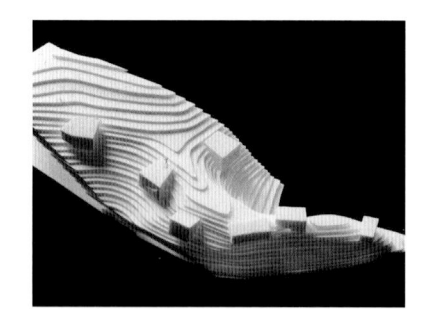

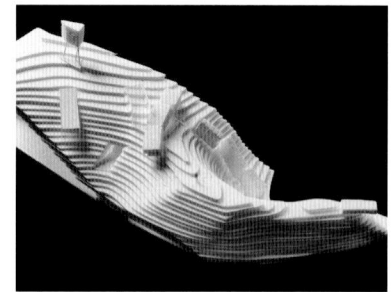

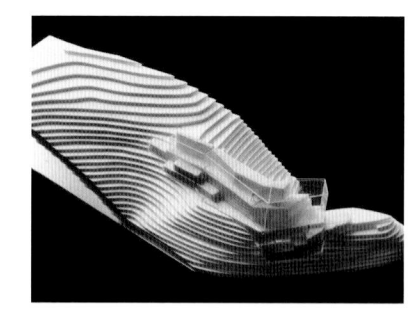

Latest scheme: slabs are connected with stairs

チリ，サンティアゴから車で2時間ほどの太平洋に面した美しい敷地に計画している週末住宅。

敷地は海に向かって落ちていく素晴らしい崖地である。ここを訪れたときに感じた印象は，岩場の地形にとけ込むようにさまざまな場所がつくられていて，あたかも自然の洞窟や岩陰に身を寄せるかのように生活する住宅のイメージだった。そこで岩場が建築的に隆起した案や，壁が岩に変化していく案，または家を地下に埋めてしまい，地上にはただ幾何学的な開口部が岩の地形と対比をなしている案など，地形的な建築をさまざまに試みる模型を制作した。

その中で浮上してきたのは，たくさんの階段が絡み合いながら，無数の段差の地形が生まれ，その人工的な地形が自然の岩場と溶け合うような建築のあり方である。テラスと階段は外部と内部が交錯し，また幾重にも重なる積層感が，単なる表面的な地形を超えて，立体的で豊かで複雑な空間を生み出している。またこれらの段々の重なりは，無数の屋根の重なりでもあり，夏場の日射を遮るたくさんの庇として機能し，また冬場には低い日射を取り込むつくりとなっている。

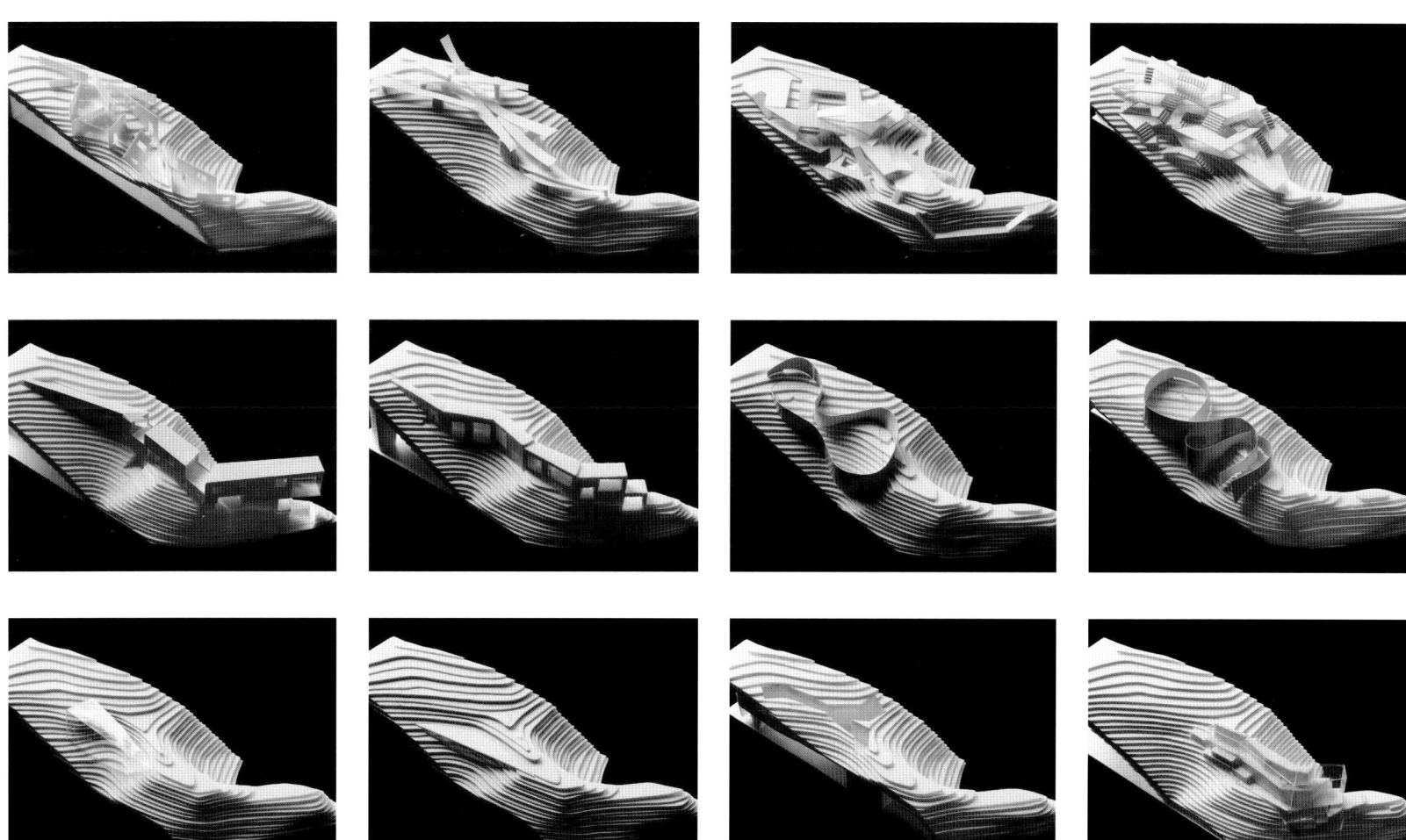

Massing study

SOUK MIRAGE / PARTICLES OF LIGHT

2013 –
COMMERCIAL BUILDING COMPLEX

URBAN SCALE CONCEPT

This project for the new retail zone seeks to participate fully within the larger master plan of a City (confidential).

Located between Education City and Financial Center, the site plays a critical role in the future development of this city.

In order to activate this portion of the site as well as to create a new landmark in the city, the project proposes not only low rise development, but a higher development, visible from far around.

At an urban scale, the shape of the buildings is inspired by the harmonious silhouette of traditional Bedouin tents, anchoring the whole site in this city's cultural heritage.

ARCHITECTURAL CONCEPT

Reinterpreting the vibrant atmosphere and lively qualities of the traditional market, as well as the inherent beauty of vernacular Islamic architecture, the project is composed of a modular structural system of arches. Different sizes of arch modules (2.5, 5 and 10 meters) are stacked one on top of another depending on the program needs and the kind of space required.

This simple system organizes the entire site, providing unity and coherence, as well as a unique and timeless architectural expression.

Courtyard

**THESE TWO OPTIONS SHOW
THE FLEXIBILITY OF THE PROJECT**
The same modular system of arches is used in a low rise development with two high rise gateways at each end of the site. The density of shops gradually decreases toward the center creating a comfortable shaped green area.

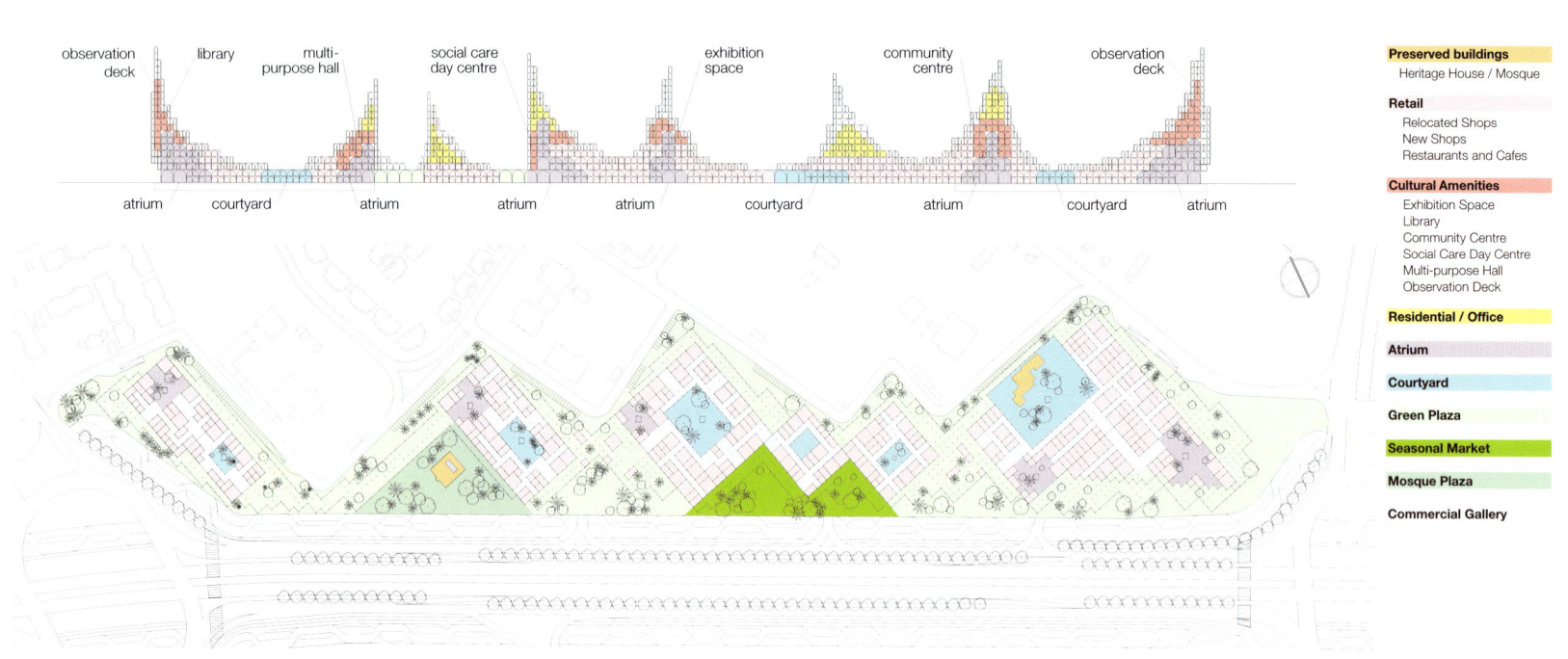

Diagram: program (option A)

Preserved buildings
Heritage House / Mosque

Retail
Relocated Shops
New Shops
Restaurants and Cafes

Cultural Amenities
Exhibition Space
Library
Community Centre
Social Care Day Centre
Multi-purpose Hall
Observation Deck

Residential / Office

Atrium

Courtyard

Green Plaza

Seasonal Market

Mosque Plaza

Commercial Gallery

Aerial view

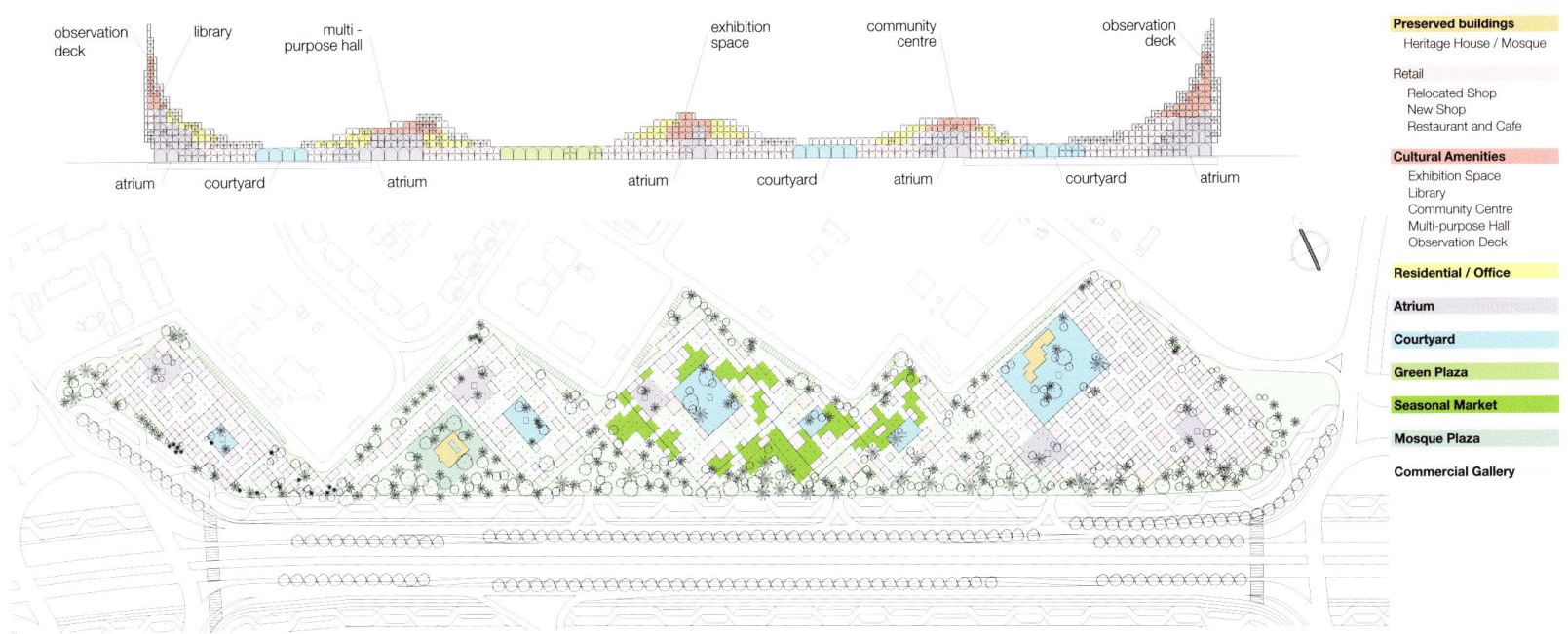

Preserved buildings
Heritage House / Mosque

Retail
- Relocated Shop
- New Shop
- Restaurant and Cafe

Cultural Amenities
- Exhibition Space
- Library
- Community Centre
- Multi-purpose Hall
- Observation Deck

Residential / Office

Atrium

Courtyard

Green Plaza

Seasonal Market

Mosque Plaza

Commercial Gallery

Diagram: program (option B)

Souk Mirage / Particles of Light

Atrium

Commercial gallery

都市スケールのコンセプト

このプロジェクトはある都市の大規模なマスタープランに盛り込もうとしている新たな商業エリアのための計画である。

敷地は学園都市と金融センターに挟まれたところに位置し，将来的にこの都市の発展に重要な役割を果たすと考えられる。

この都市の景色に新たなランドマークを付け加えると同時に，敷地の活性化を狙って，今プロジェクトでは低層の開発だけでなく遠からでも見える高層開発も行う。

都市規模のスケールでは，伝統的な遊牧民が使うテントの美しいシルエットから着想を得て，建物の形態をつくる。それにより，敷地全体をこの都市の文化的伝統に深く根ざしたものとする。

建築コンセプト

伝統的な市場が持つ活発な空気感やいきいきとした性質，またヴァナキュラーなイスラム建築固有の美しさを再解釈し，アーチ型のモジュールを使った構造システムでプロジェクトを構成する。異なるサイズのアーチ型モジュール（2.5，5，10メートル）が，要求されたプログラムや空間の種類に応じて互いに重なりあう。

このシンプルなシステムで敷地全体を構成し一体感と一貫性を持たせ，また同時に独創的で時を経ても色褪せることのない建築の表現をつくり出す。

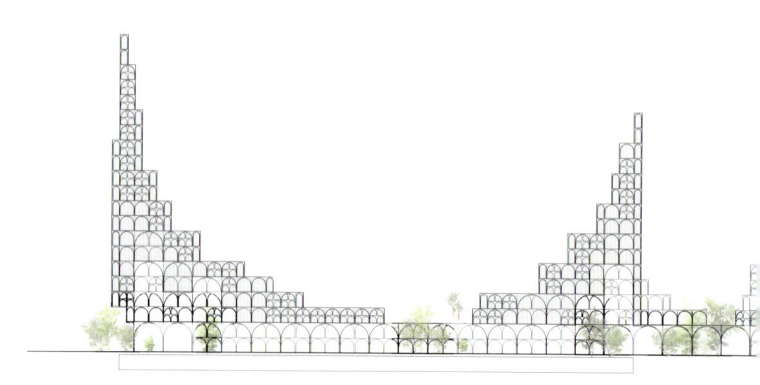

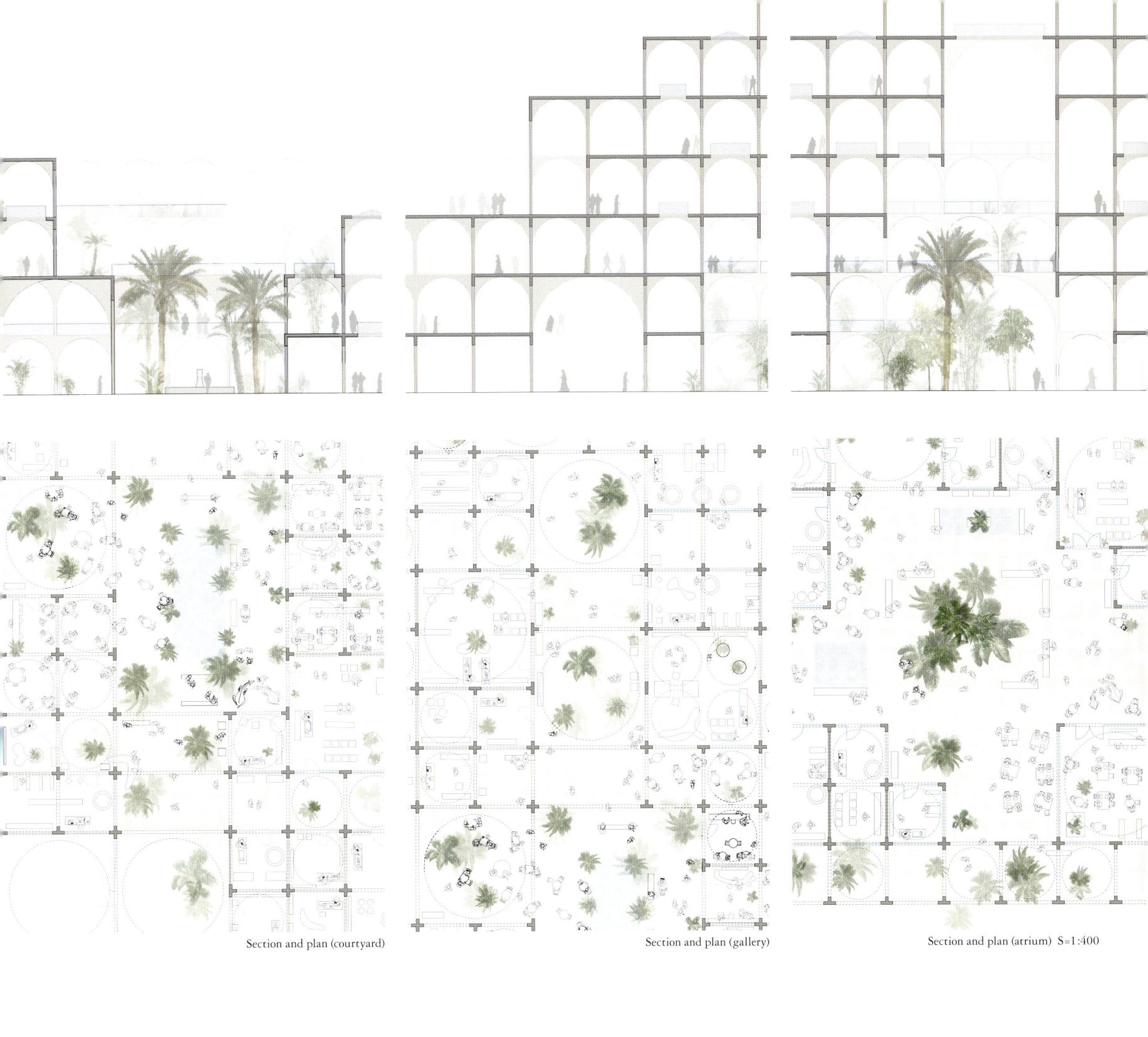

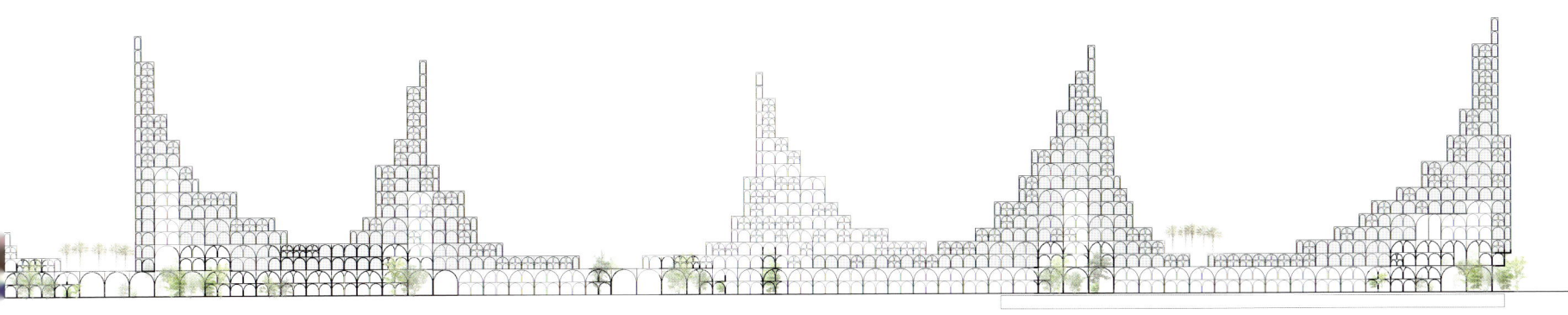

Section and plan (courtyard) Section and plan (gallery) Section and plan (atrium) S=1:400

Longitudinal section S=1:2500

Souk Mirage / Particles of Light

OUTLOOK TOWER

2013 -
OBSERVATORY / WATER PLAZA

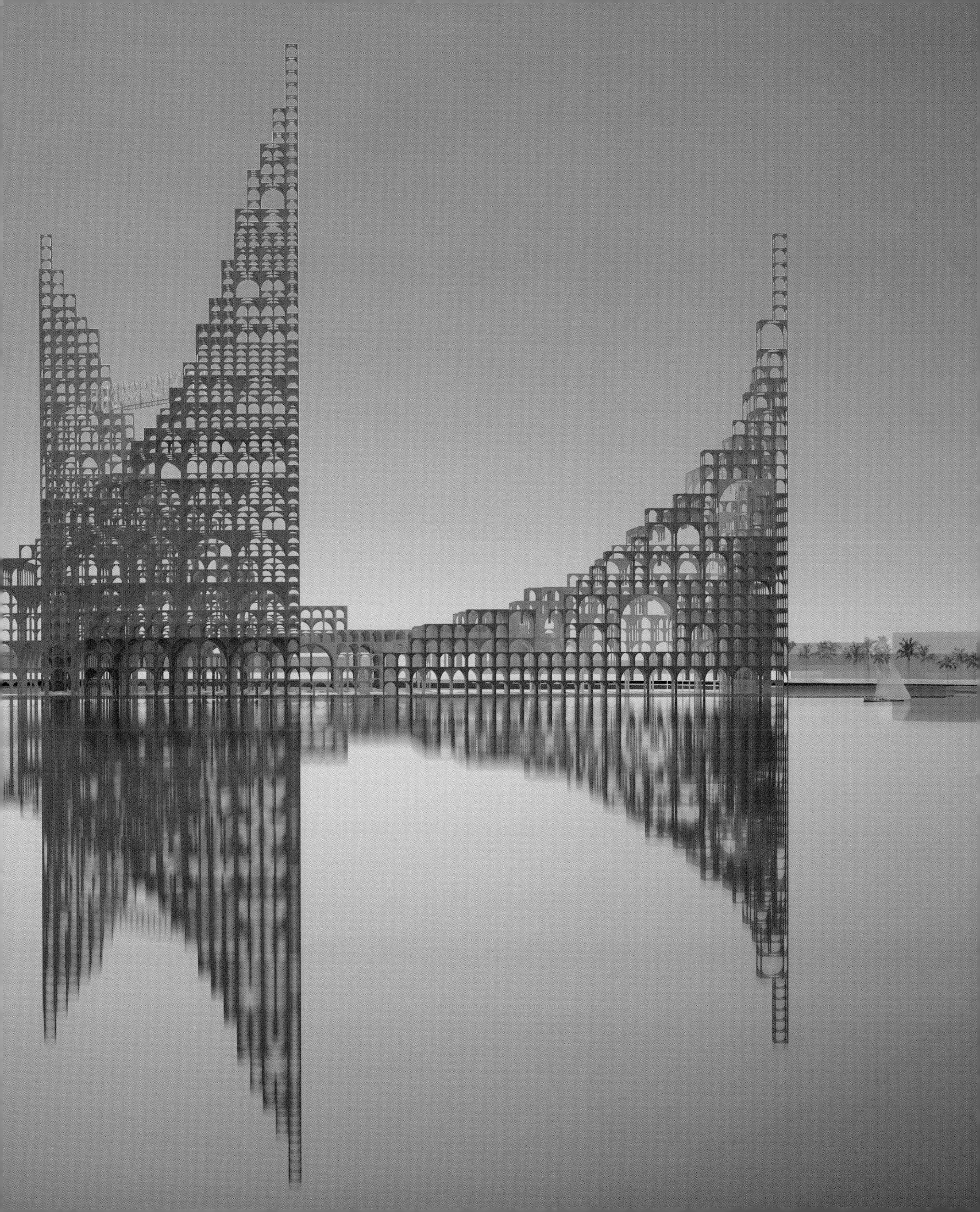

Ground floor

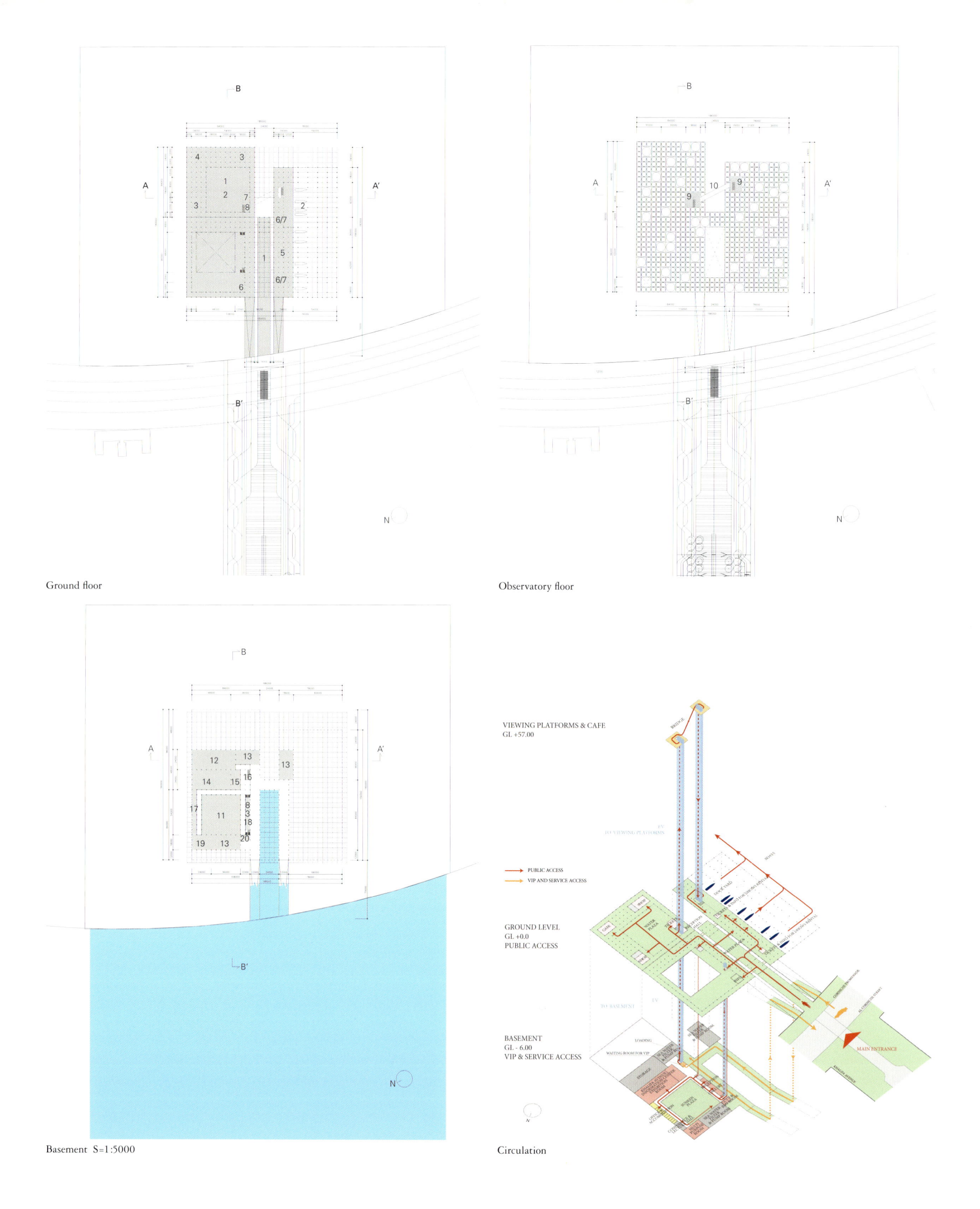

Observatory floor

Basement S=1:5000

Circulation

VIEWING PLATFORMS & CAFE
GL +57.00

→ PUBLIC ACCESS
→ VIP AND SERVICE ACCESS

GROUND LEVEL
GL +0.0
PUBLIC ACCESS

BASEMENT
GL -6.00
VIP & SERVICE ACCESS

184

View from water plaza

1. WATER PLAZA
2. ATRIUM
3. SHOP
4. CAFE
5. DOCK YARD
6. INFORMATION
7. TICKETS
8. RECEPTION HALL
9. VIEWING PLATFORM & CAFE
10. BRIDGE
11. SUNKEN PLAZA
12. STORAGE
13. SEA WATER FILTER PUMP ROOM
14. INFORMATION CENTER / EXHIBITION ROOM
15. CONFERENCE & LECTURE HALL
16. WATING ROOM FOR VIP
17. OFFICE & COMMON WOEK PLACE
18. GALLERY
19. MULTIPURPOSE ROOM
20. CCTV & BMS ROOM

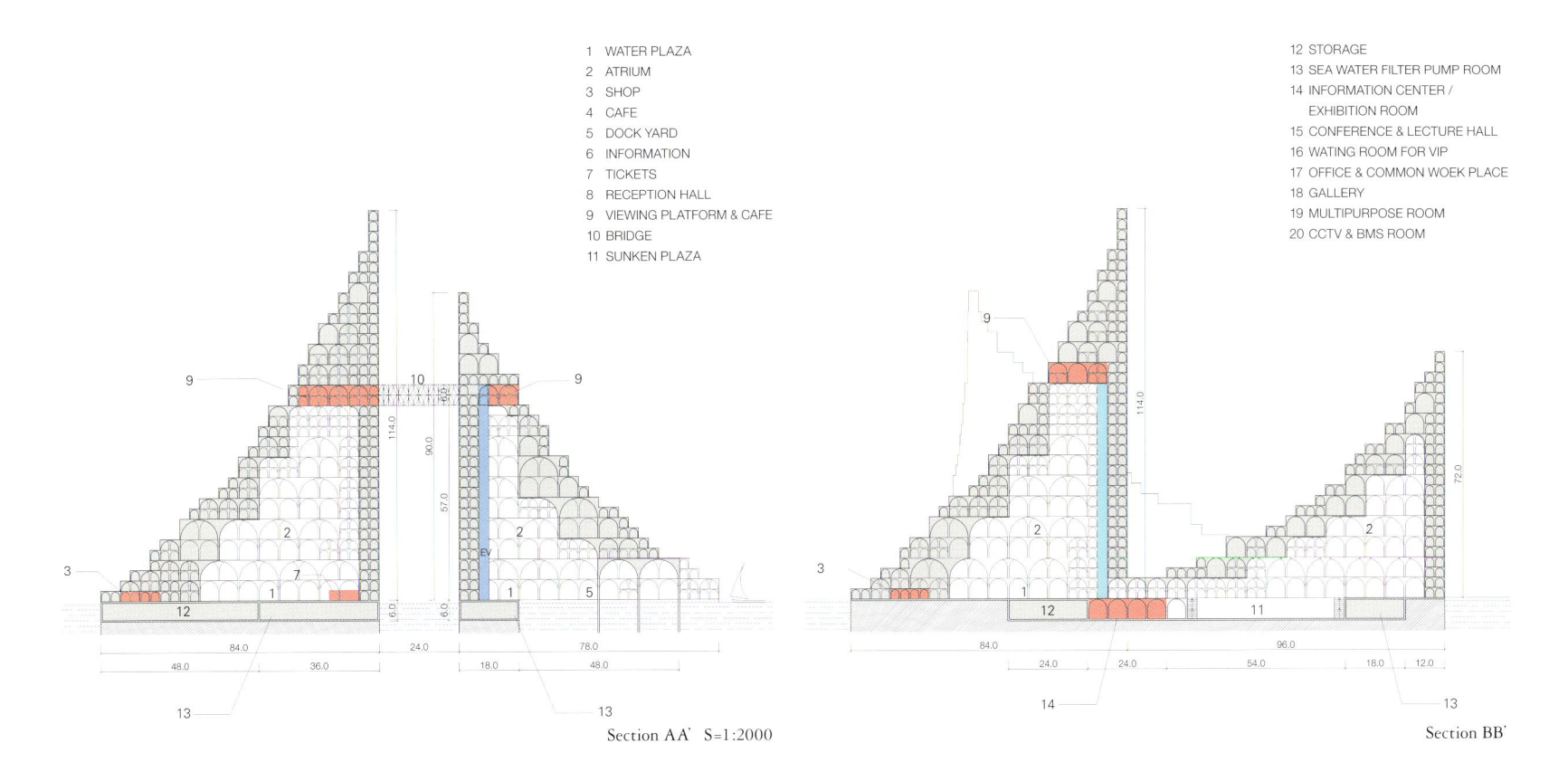

Section AA' S=1:2000

Section BB'

Outlook Tower

Elevation

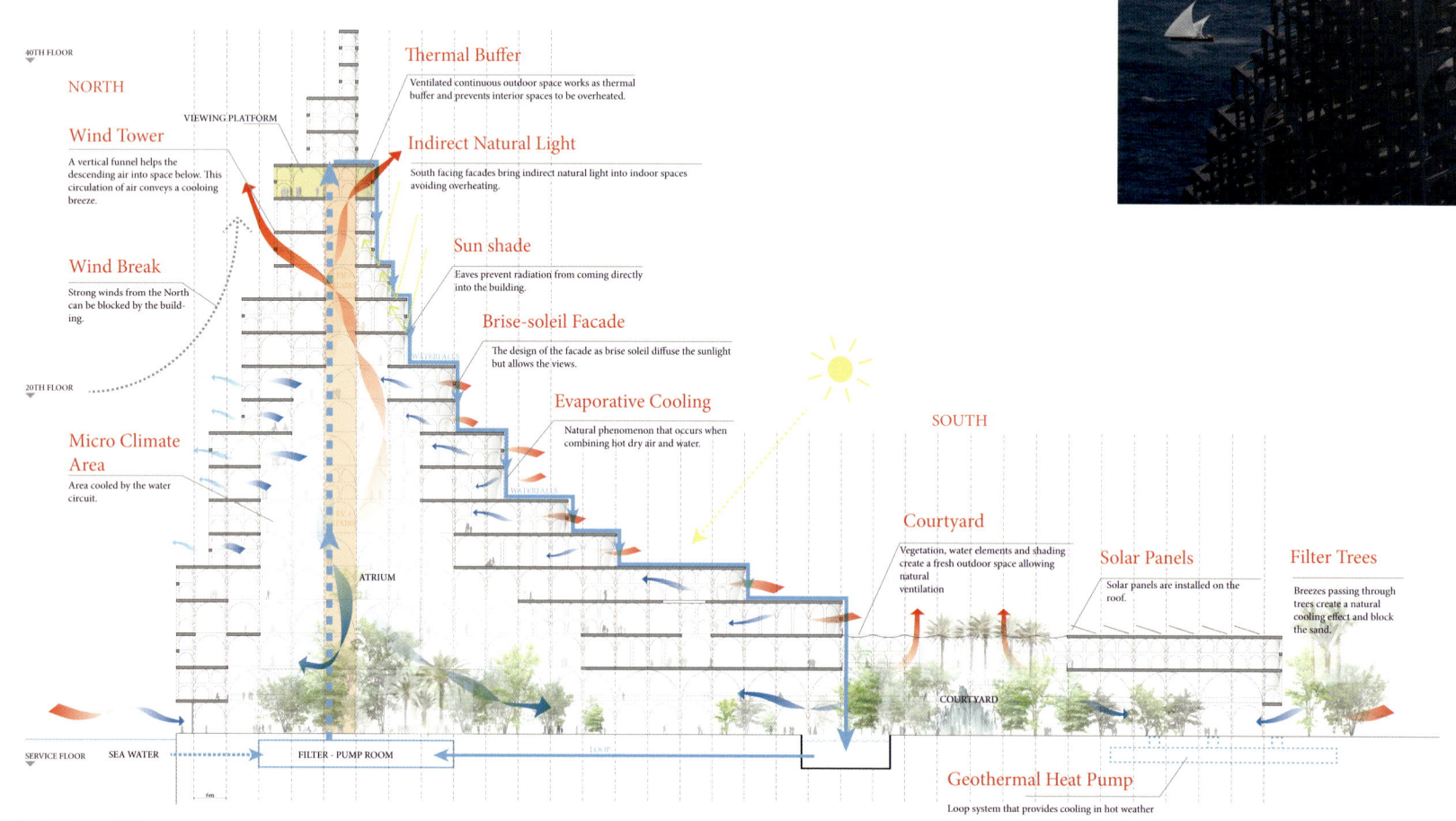

Section S=1:1200

NORTH

Wind Tower
A vertical funnel helps the descending air into space below. This circulation of air conveys a cooling breeze.

Wind Break
Strong winds from the North can be blocked by the building.

Micro Climate Area
Area cooled by the water circuit.

Thermal Buffer
Ventilated continuous outdoor space works as thermal buffer and prevents interior spaces to be overheated.

Indirect Natural Light
South facing facades bring indirect natural light into indoor spaces avoiding overheating.

Sun shade
Eaves prevent radiation from coming directly into the building.

Brise-soleil Facade
The design of the facade as brise soleil diffuse the sunlight but allows the views.

Evaporative Cooling
Natural phenomenon that occurs when combining hot dry air and water.

SOUTH

Courtyard
Vegetation, water elements and shading create a fresh outdoor space allowing natural ventilation

Solar Panels
Solar panels are installed on the roof.

Filter Trees
Breezes passing through trees create a natural cooling effect and block the sand.

Geothermal Heat Pump
Loop system that provides cooling in hot weather

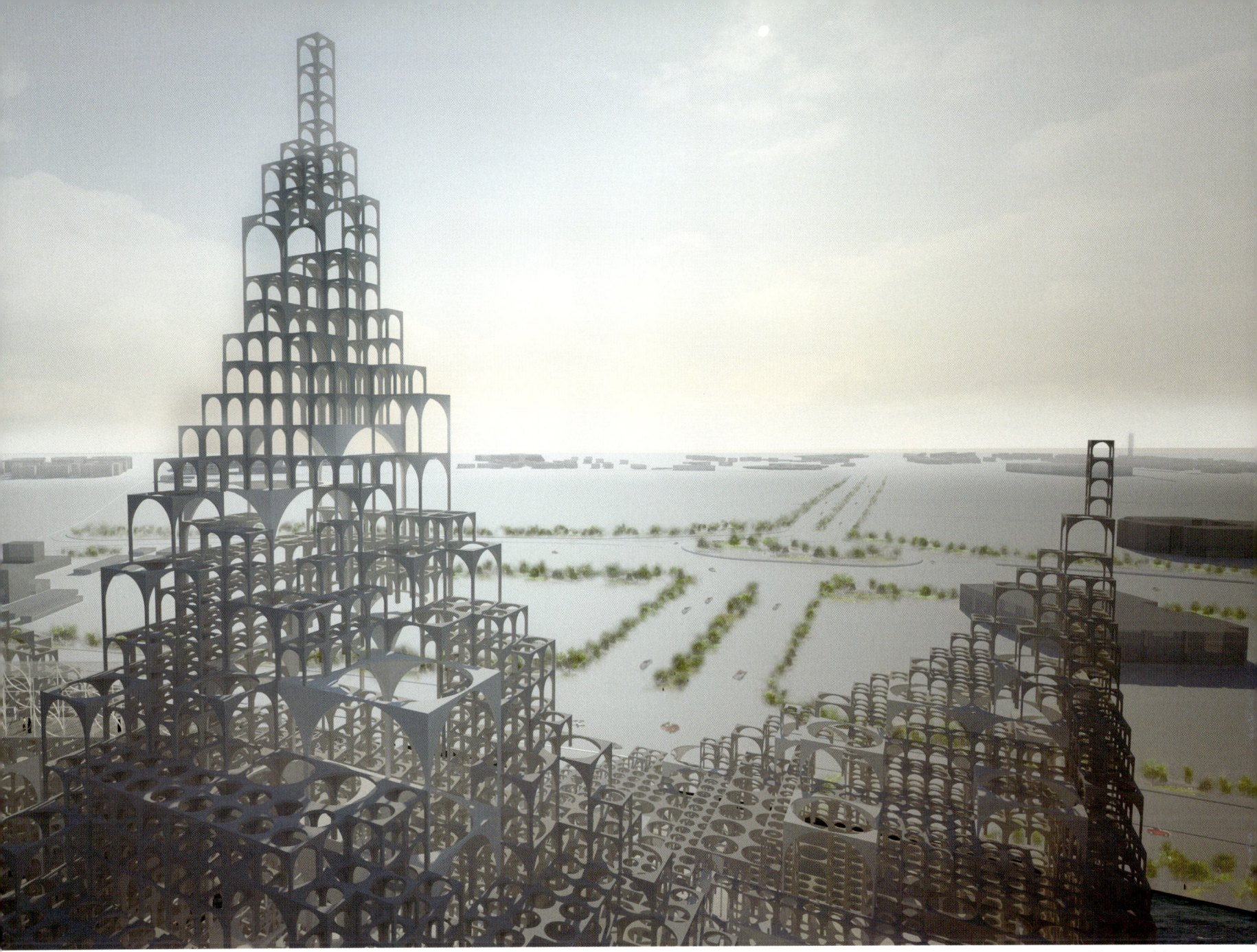

View toward Avenue

URBAN CONCEPT

This project for an Outlook Tower and water plaza seeks to participate fully within the larger master plan of a City (confidential).

Located at the beginning/end of the avenue, Education City and Financial Center in between, the site plays a critical role in the future development of this city.

In order to activate this grand plan as well as to create a new landmark in the city, the project proposes multiple transparent towers, visible from far around and offering views on the most prominent historical and contemporary landmarks in this city.

At an urban scale, the shapes of the buildings are inspired by the harmonious silhouette of traditional Bedouin tents, anchoring the whole site in this city's cultural heritage. From a far, the volumes are perceived as a gateway connecting the Corniche Sea with the mainland while having an overall mirage-like appearance.

ARCHITECTURAL CONCEPT

Reinterpreting the inherent beauty of vernacular Islamic architecture, the project is composed of a modular structural system of arches. Different sizes of arch modules (3, 6 and 12 meters) are stacked one on top of another depending on the program needs and the kind of space required. This simple system organizes the entire site, providing unity and coherence, as well as a unique and timeless architectural expression.

By incorporating multiple waterfalls, instead of one large, different mountains of water are created feeding the avenue.

There will be a wide range waterfalls; smaller on the top to prevent any interference from the wind and larger towards the bottom to create evaporative cooling.

By combining the transparency of the arches with the stepping waterfalls, a dynamic play with light and shadow is created, while appearing mirage-like.

Observatory floor

Water dock

都市コンセプト

これはある都市の都市計画の一部をなすべく提出された展望タワーと水景広場のプロジェクトである。

敷地はアヴェニューの両端に位置し、またその間に学園都市と金融センターがあるので、今後この都市が発展する中で重要な役割を担うと考えられる。

この壮大な計画を活性化させながら、都市の景観に新たなランドマークを生み出すため、今プロジェクトでは多様な透過性を持ったタワーを提案する。タワーは遠く離れた場所からでも見ることができ、同時に素晴しいこの都市の歴史的な、あるいは時代のランドマークへの見晴しを提供する。

都市規模のスケールでは、伝統的な遊牧民が使うテントの美しいシルエットから着想を得て、建物の形態をつくる。遠くから見れば建物のヴォリュームは蜃気楼の様に揺らぎながら、この都市のC型の海岸通りのある海と陸地をつなげる棚のようにも見える。

建築コンセプト

ヴァナキュラーなイスラム建築固有の美しさを再解釈し、このプロジェクトはアーチを用いたモジュール構造を使って構成されている。異なるサイズのアーチのモジュール（3, 6, 12メートル）が、要求されるプログラムと空間のタイプに応じて互いに重なり合っている。このシンプルなシステムで敷地全体を構成し一体感と一貫性を持たせ、また同時に独創的で時を経ても色褪せることのない建築の表現をつくり出す。

一つの大きな滝をつくるよりもいろいろな種類の滝を組み合わせることで、異なる水の山をつくることができアヴェニューを水で満たしてくれる。

滝には様々な大きさがあり、小さいものは風の影響を防ぐために上の方に、大きいものは蒸発による冷却効果を狙って下の方に置かれる。

段々の滝を備えたアーチの透過性を組み合わせ、操作することで、蜃気楼のようなダイナミックな光と影の演出が可能になる。

ALTERNATIVE OPTIONS
FIVE TOWERS

The first alternative option shows the ability for future expansion. Two additional towers are added in front of the original design, to emphasize the gateway. By doing so, perspective and depth is added to the proposal.
The total footprint is 41.000 square meters, allowing more space for additional outdoor activities.

LINEAR TOWERS

For the second alternative option, the composition of the volumes is shifted in a linear way. Multiple towers are organized in one line, which results in a dynamic play of depth and perspective.
The total site footprint is 44.000 square meters, allowing a much larger space for bigger outdoor activities.

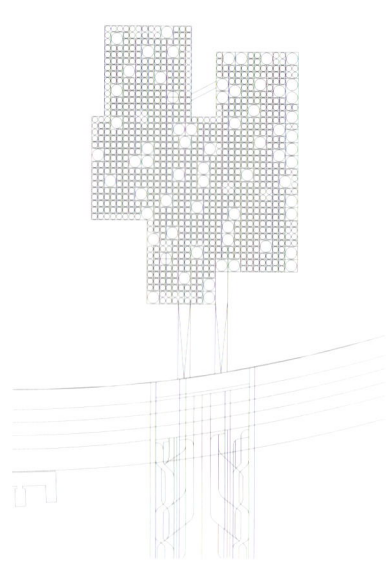

Option A S=1:6000

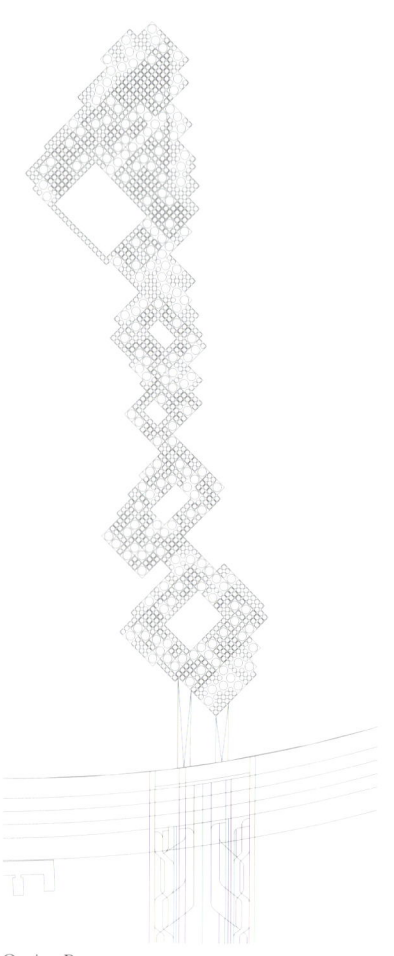

Option B

SOU FUJIMOTO
RECENT PROJECT
LIST OF PROJECTS

HOUSE K
Hyogo, Japan
Design: 2010.07.-11.06.
Construction: 2011.07.-12.07.
Program: residence
Architects: Sou Fujimoto Architects—Sou Fujimoto, principal-in-charge; Yoshihiro Nakazono[ex], Naganobu Matsumura, Aya Tatsuta, Ryota Okada[ex], Naoki Tamura, project team
Consultants: Jun Sato Structural Engineers, structural; Sirius Lighting Office, lighting
Structural system / size: steel frame / 2 stories
Site area: 310.24 m²
Built area: 118.23 m²
Total area: 118.23 m²
P.022-

NUBE ARENA
Las Torres de Cotillas, Spain
Design: 2010.07.-10.08.
Client: Council of Las Torres de Cotillas
Program: auditorium / public space
Architects: Sou Fujimoto Architects—Sou Fujimoto, principal-in-charge; Hideto Chijiwa, Victoria Diemer Bennetzen[ex], Marc Dujon[ex], Nadine de Ripainsel, Andy Yu[ex]; project team
Structural system / size:
steel frame / 4 stories, 2 basements
Built area: 2,935 m²
Total area: 5,344 m²
P.035-

KULTUR PROJEKTE BERLIN
Berlin, Germany
Design: 2010.11.-11.01.
Program: exhibition space
Architects: Sou Fujimoto Architects—Sou Fujimoto, principal-in-charge; Sei Hayashi[ex], project team
Structural system / size: balloon / 1 story
Built area: 2,500 m²
Total area: 2,500 m²
P.040-

LA SMALL HOUSE
Los Angeles, California, U.S.A.
Design: 2010.-
Program: guest house
Architects: Sou Fujimoto Architects—Sou Fujimoto, principal-in-charge; Ryo Tsuchie, project team
Consultants: Ove Arup & Partners Japan Ltd., structural
Structural system / size: hybrid space frame with steel rods and stones / 4 stories
Site area: 668.90 m²
Built area: 13.80 m²
Total area: 24.60 m²
P.032-

NORMANDY RENOVATION PROJECT
Normandy, France
Design: 2011.02.-
Program: residence
Architects: Sou Fujimoto Architects—Sou Fujimoto, principal-in-charge; Ryo Tsuchie, Yibei Liu, Midori Hasuike, project team
Structural system / size: reinforced concrete, timber frame (existing), reinforced concrete (new part) / 4 stories
Site area: 555 m²
Built area: 130.7 m²
Total area: 166.5 m²
P.046-

PUBLIC TOILET IN ICHIHARA
Ichihara, Chiba, Japan
Design: 2011.-12.
Construction: 2012.
Client: Ichihara City
Program: public lavatory
Architects: Sou Fujimoto Architects—Sou Fujimoto, principal-in-charge; Nao Harikae[ex], Naganobu Matsumura, Naoki Tamura, project team
Consultants: Jun Sato Structural Engineers, structural; Archi Build Co.,ltd, mechanical
Structural system / size: steel frame (female), timber frame (male and disabled) / 1 story
Site area: 643.56 m²
Built area: 209.48 m²
Total area: 209.48 m² (female: 203.60m², toilet booth for female: 2.00m², male and disabled: 5.88m²)
P.044-

VITAMIN SPACE ART GALLERY
Guangzhou, China
Design: 2011.-
Construction: 2013.08.-
Client: Vitamin Space
Program: art gallery
Architects: Sou Fujimoto Architects—Sou Fujimoto, principal-in-charge; Shintaro Honma, Aya Tatsuta, Shingei Katsu, Sacha Favre[ex], project team
Structural system / size: reinforced concrete / 1 story
Built area: 453 m² (first phase) / 273 m² (second phase)
Total area: 453 m² (first phase) / 273 m² (second phase)
P.068-

SMALLEST / LARGEST ART MUSEUM
Château La Coste, Aix-en-Provence, France
Design: 2011.-
Program: museum
Architects: Sou Fujimoto Architects—Sou Fujimoto, principal-in-charge; Nao Harikae[ex], Nadine de Ripainsel, project team
Consultants: Jun Sato Structural Engineers, structural
Size: 1 story
Site area: ∞
Built area: 93 m²
Total area: 93 m²
P.064-

TAIWAN TOWER
Taichung, Taiwan
Design: 2011.-14.(est.)
Construction: 2014.-17.(est.)
Client: Urban Development Bureau, Taichung City Government
Program: observatory / museum
Architects: Sou Fujimoto Architects / Fei & Cheng Associates—Sou Fujimoto, principal-in-charge; Naganobu Matsumura, Shintaro Honma, Hideto Chijiwa, Ryo Tsuchie, Masaki Iwata, Keisuke Kiri, Shao feng Chiu, Yibei Liu, Yichen Hsieh, Haruka Tomoeda, Toshiyuki Nakagawa, Midori Hasuike, Weiwei Zhang, Nao Harikae[ex], Mai Suzuki[ex], project team
Consultants: Ove Arup & Partners Japan Ltd., Supertech Consultants, structural; Ove Arup & Partners Japan Ltd., HENG KAI INC., mechanical
Structural system / size: steel frame (partly steel reinforced concrete) / 4 stories, 2 basements
Site area: 4.4 ha
Built area: 10,000 m²
Total area: 12,769 m²
P.054-

BETON HALA WATERFRONT CENTER
Belgrade, Serbia
Design: 2011.-14.(est.)
Construction: 2014.-16.(est.)
Client: Urban Planning Institute of Belgrade
Program: commercial building complex
Architects: Sou Fujimoto Architects / AAA—Sou Fujimoto, principal-in-charge; Nao Harikae[ex], Yoshihiro Nakazono[ex], Hideto Chijiwa, Masaki Iwata, Keisuke Kiri, Sei Hayashi[ex], project team
Consultants: Ove Arup & Partners Japan Ltd., structural and mechanical
Structural system / size:
steel frame / 4 stories, 2 basements
Site area: 92,300 m²
Built area: 22,194 m²
Total area: 34,741 m²
P.048-

RIZHAO CITY CLUB CHINA
Rizhao, Shandong, China
Design: 2011.-13.
Construction: 2012.-13.
Client: Wanji Group
Program: clubhouse
Architects: Sou Fujimoto Architects—Sou Fujimoto, principal-in-charge; Nao Harikae[ex], Aya Tatsuta, project team
Structural system / size:
steel reinforced concrete / 2 stories
Site area: 20,000 m²
Built area: 20,000 m²
Total area: 8,000 m²
P.060-

FUTUROSPEKTIVE ARCHITEKTUR
Kunsthalle Bielefeld, Bielefeld, Germany
Design: 2012.01.-12.04.
Construction: 2012.04.-12.05.
Client: Kunsthalle Bielefeld
Program: exhibition
Architects: Sou Fujimoto Architects—Sou Fujimoto, principal-in-charge; Nao Harikae[ex], Hideto Chijiwa, Masaki Iwata, Keisuke Kiri, Ryo Tsuchie, Nadine de Ripainsel, Aya Tatsuta, Sei Hayashi[ex], Naoki Tamura, Toshiyuki Nakagawa, Mai Suzuki[ex], project team
Size: 3 stories
P.140-

MOUNTAIN HOTEL
China
Design: 2012.02.-
Program: hotel
Architects: Sou Fujimoto Architects—Sou Fujimoto, principal-in-charge; Nao Harikae[ex], Keisuke Kiri, Shingei Katsu, Toshiyuki Nakagawa, project team
Size: 2 stories, 2 basements (entrance hall), 1 story, 1-2 basements (guest house)
Built area: 953 m² (entrance hall), 1,967 m² (guest house)
Total area: 1,582 m² (entrance hall), 2,110 m² (guest house)
P.142-

TAIWAN PAVILION
Tainan, Taiwan
Design: 2012.03.-13.03.
Construction: 2012.10.-13.07.
Client: FU-DU Building Co., Ltd.
Program: pavilion / showroom
Architects: Sou Fujimoto Architects—Sou Fujimoto, principal-in-charge; Nao Harikae[ex], Keisuke Kiri, Shingei Katsu, Nakagawa Toshiyuki, project team
Consultants: FU-DU Building Co., Ltd., structural and mechanical
Structural system / size: steel frame / 1 story
Site area: 1,886 m²
Built area: 1,270 m²
Total area: 750 m²
P.104-

SETONOMORI HOUSES
Coastal Area of the Seto Inland Sea, Japan
Design: 2012.07.-12.10.
Construction: 2012.10.-13.04.
Client: Shipbuilding Company
Program: townhouse
Architects: Sou Fujimoto Architects—Sou Fujimoto, principal-in-charge; Naganobu Matsumura, Shintaro Honma, Ryo Tsuchie, Rie Ikeda[ex], project team
Consultants: Jun Sato Structural Engineers, structural; EOS plus, yamada machinery office, mechanical
Structural system / size: timber frame / 2 stories
Site area: 3,420.79 m² (north area), 2,047.82 m² (south area)
Built area: 916.11 m² (north-south area)
Total area: 1,832.22 m² (north-south area)
P.156-

ARCHITECTURE AS FOREST
SICLI Pavilion, Geneva, Switzerland
Design: 2012.11.-13.03.
Construction: 2013.03.-13.04.
Client: Membre du Comité de la MA
Program: exhibition
Architects: Sou Fujimoto Architects—Sou Fujimoto, principal-in-charge; Hideto Chijiwa, Masaki Iwata, project team
Size: 1 story
P.141-

SERPENTINE GALLERY PAVILION 2013
Kensington Gardens, London, U.K.
Design: 2012.12.-13.04.
Construction: 2013.04.-13.06.
Client: Serpentine Gallery
Program: pavilion
Architects: Sou Fujimoto Architects—Sou Fujimoto, principal-in-charge; Naganobu Matsumura, Shintaro Honma, Hideto Chijiwa, Keisuke Kiri, Ryo Tsuchie, Nadine de Ripainsel, Haruka Tomoeda, Yibei Liu, Midori Hasuike, Minako Suzuki, Marie de France, Andreas Nordström, project team
Consultants: AECOM, structural and mechanical
Structural system / size:
steel frame (@800mm, 400mm grid) / 1 story
Site area: 541 m²
Built area: 357 m²
Total area: 357 m²
P.86-

CENTER OF TRADITIONAL PERFORMING ARTS IN IZUNOKUNI
Izunokuni, Shizuoka, Japan
Design: 2012.12.-13.03.
Client: Izunokuni City
Program: auditorium
Architects: Sou Fujimoto Architects—Sou Fujimoto, principal-in-charge; Masaki Iwata, Toshiyuki Nakagawa, Rie Ikeda[ex], Mizuho Ozawa[ex], Hugh Hsu, project team
Consultants: Ove Arup & Partners Japan Ltd., structural
Consultants: EOS plus, mechanical
Structural system / size: timber frame / 2 stories
Site area: 3,900 m²
Built area: 740 m²
Total area: 860.3 m²
P.134-

JJ99 YOUTH HOSTEL
Tainan, Taiwan
Design: 2012.12.-13.05.
Construction: 2013.06.-13.12.
Client: FU-DU Building Co., Ltd.
Program: hotel
Architects: Sou Fujimoto Architects—Sou Fujimoto, principal-in-charge; Masaki Iwata, Shingei Katsu, Toshiyuki Nakagawa, Hugh Hsu, Rie Ikeda[ex], Mizuho Ozawa[ex], project team
Structural system / size:
reinforced concrete, steel frame / 8 stories
Site area: 517.5 m²
Built area: 400 m²
Total area: 2,612 m²
P.154-

CONNECTICUT POOL HOUSE
Connecticut, U.S.A.
Design: 2012.12.-
Program: pool house
Architects: Sou Fujimoto Architects—Sou Fujimoto, principal-in-charge; Nadine de Ripainsel, Andreas Nordström, Marie de France, Axel Clissen, project team
Size: 1 story
Site area: 1,500 m²
Built area: 200 m²
Total area: 185 m²
P.107-

MUSEUM IN THE FOREST
Taoyuan County, Taiwan
Design: 2012.-13.
Construction: 2014.01-14.08.[est.]
Program: museum
Architects: Sou Fujimoto Architects—Sou Fujimoto, principal-in-charge; Nao Harikae[ex], Masaki Iwata, Keisuke Kiri, Toshiyuki Nakagawa, Rie Ikeda[ex], Hugh Hsu, Minako Suzuki, project team
Consultants: Tomita Structural Design, structural
Structural system / size: reinforced concrete, steel frame / 1 story, 0.5 basements
Site area: 46,578.6 m²
Built area: 531.5 m²
Total area: 728.8 m²
P.130-

GINZA BUILDING
Tokyo, Japan
Design: 2012.10.-
Client: KAWASAKI BRAND DESIGN Inc.
Program: office / residence
Architects: Sou Fujimoto Architects—Sou Fujimoto, principal-in-charge; Keisuke Kiri, Masaki Iwata, Naoki Tamura, Nobuyuki Tejima, project team
Consultants: Jun Sato Structural Engineers, structural; EOS plus, mechanical
Structural system / size: steel frame / 14 stories
Site area: 57.35 m²
Built area: 48.64 m²
Total area: 474.46 m²
P.150-

LOUISIANA CLOUD
Design: 2012.-
Program: urban planning
Architects: Sou Fujimoto Architects—Sou Fujimoto, principal-in-charge; Nao Harikae[ex], Yoshihiro Nakazono[ex], Nadine de Ripainsel, Sei Hayashi[ex], project team
P.128-

TREE SKYSCRAPER
Design: 2012.-
Program: urban planning
Architects: Sou Fujimoto Architects—Sou Fujimoto, principal-in-charge; Nadine de Ripainsel, Sei Hayashi[ex], project team
P.126-

ENERGY FOREST (ENERGY. OIL AND POST-OIL ARCHITECTURE AND GRIDS)
Rome, Italy
Design: 2012.
Construction: 2013.
Client: Fondazione MAXXI
Program: urban planning
Architects: Sou Fujimoto Architects—Sou Fujimoto, principal-in-charge; Tim Bacheller, Marcos Duffo, project team
Structural system: polycarbonate sheet, steel wire
P.122-

CATALUNYA HOUSE
Caldes de Malavella, Spain
Design: 2012.
Construction: 2014.[est.]
Client: Imaestri International Realty Ltd.
Program: residence
Architects: Sou Fujimoto Architects—Sou Fujimoto, principal-in-charge; Tim Bacheller, project team
Structural system / size:
steel reinforced concrete / 3 stories
Site area: 2,414 m²
Built area: 939 m²
Total area: 400 m²
P.112-

21ST CENTURY RAINFOREST ARCHITECTURE
Libreville, Gabon
Design: 2012.-
Client: Agence Nationale des Grands Travaux, Republique Gabonaise
Program: conference center
Architects: Sou Fujimoto Architects—Sou Fujimoto, principal-in-charge; Tim Bacheller, Sacha Favre[ex], Marcos Duffo, Yibei Liu, project team
Structural system / size:
steel reinforced concrete / 5 stories
Site area: 430 ha
Built area: 17,600 m²
Total area: 18,609 m²
P.117-

YUZ MUSEUM
Shanghai, China
Design: 2012.01.-12.12.
Construction: 2013.01.-13.12.
Client: YUZ FOUNDATION
Program: museum
Architects: Sou Fujimoto Architects—Sou Fujimoto, principal-in-charge; Keisuke Kiri, Naoki Tamura, Toshiyuki Nakagawa, Lisa Awazu[ex], project team
Consultants: Shanghai Dushi Architectural Design Institute, structural and mechanical
Structural system / size:
steel reinforced concrete / 3 stories
Site area: 7,963 m²
Built area: 5,950 m²
Total area: 9,854 m²
P.136-

GEOMETRIC FOREST - SOLO HOUSES PROJECT
Cretas, Spain
Design: 2012.-13.
Construction: 2014.[est.]
Client: Solo House Spain S.L.
Program: residence
Architects: Sou Fujimoto Architects—Sou Fujimoto, principal-in-charge; Tim Bachelle, Sacha Favre[ex], Angel Barreno[ex], project team
Structural system / size: timber frame / 2 stories
Site area: 12,240 m²
Built area: 222 m²
Total area: 421 m²
P.100-

TAIWAN CAFE
Tainan, Taiwan
Design: 2013.04.-
Client: FU-DU Building Co., Ltd.
Program: cafe
Architects: Sou Fujimoto Architects—Sou Fujimoto, principal-in-charge; Masaki Iwata, Aya Tatsuta, Shingei Katsu, Toshiyuki Nakagawa, Hugh Hsu, Marie de France, project team
Consultants: RGB Structure, structural
Structural system / size: steel frame / 2 stories
Site area: 598.5 m²
Built area: 309.51 m²
Total area: 121.30 m²
P.165-

SOUK MIRAGE / PARTICLES OF LIGHT
Design: 2013.-
Program: commercial building complex
Architects: Sou Fujimoto Architects—Sou Fujimoto, principal-in-charge; Tim Bacheller, Sacha Favre[ex], Helen Lung[ex], Angel Barreno[ex], Marcos Duffo, project team
Structural system: reinforced concrete
Site area: 130,000 m²
Built area: 64,400 m²
Total area: 83,000 m²
P.176-

CHILE HOUSE
Los Vilos, Chile
Design: 2013.
Construction: 2014.
Client: Interdesign S.A.
Program: residence
Architects: Sou Fujimoto Architects—Sou Fujimoto, principal-in-charge; Tim Bacheller, Marcos Duffo, project team
Structural system: steel reinforced concrete
Site area: 4,400 m²
Built area: 488 m²
Total area: 250 m²
P.170-

OUTLOOK TOWER
Design: 2013.-
Program: observatory / water plaza
Architects: Sou Fujimoto Architects—Sou Fujimoto, principal-in-charge; Masaki Iwata, Aya Tatsuta, Marie de France, Vincent Hecht, Axel Clissen, Andreas Nordström, project team
Size: 40 stories
Site area: 5.4 ha
Built area: 40,000 m²
Total area: 6,000 m²
P.182-

SOU FUJIMOTO

Born in Hokkaido, Japan in 1971.
Graduated from Faculty of Engineering, Department of Architecture (Bachelor's degree of Architecture), University of Tokyo in 1994.
Established Sou Fujimoto Architects in 2000.
-
http://www.sou-fujimoto.net/

SOU FUJIMOTO ARCHITECTS
藤本壮介建築設計事務所

Sou Fujimoto	藤本壮介
Naganobu Matsumura	松村永宜
Shintaro Honma	本間新太郎
Hideto Chijiwa	千々岩秀人
Masaki Iwata	岩田正輝
Keisuke Kiri	桐圭佑
Ryo Tsuchie	土江亮
Nadine de Ripainsel	
Aya Tatsuta	立田彩
Naoki Tamura	田村直己
Shingei Katsu	葛沁芸
Timothy T Bacheller	
Haruka Tomoeda	友枝遥
Toshiyuki Nakagawa	中川俊之
Liu Yibei	刘牟失北
Shao feng Chiu	邱紹峰
Nobuyuki Tejima	手島伸幸
Marcos Duffo Weinstock	
Hsieh Yi Chen	謝宜蓁
Wang Yin-Fan	王吟方
Midori Hasuike	
Vincent Hecht	
Minako Suzuki	鈴木美南子
Hugh Hsu	許昕緯
Axel Clissen	
Jane Luk	陸沛靈
Andreas Nordström	
Marie de France	
Zhang Weiwei	張微偉
Yumiko Nogiri	野桐友美子
Yukari Minemura	峯村裕加里
Izumi Osumi	大隅泉

Cover:
Souk Mirage / Particles of Light
—
English translation:
Lisa Tani: pp.9-20, pp.74-84 / Satoko Hirata: p.47, p.89, p.106, p.131, p.137
Erika Sakai: p.60, p. 68, p.154, p.158, p.170 / Reijiro Sawaki: p.44, p.126, p.128, pp.134-135, p.151
和訳:
原田勝之：p.43, p.67, pp. 125 / 上野黄：p.109, p.119, p.180, p.188
—
Credits:
Photographs
GA photographers:
p.82, Yukio Futagawa / pp.10-11, pp.86-87, pp.90-91, pp.94-95, pp.98-99, p.160, p.191, Yoshio Futagawa
pp.4-5, p.15, pp.22-23, pp.26-27, pp.30-34, p.38, p.68, p.70 middle, p.71, p.93, pp.96-97, pp.100-103, p.106, p.114, pp.130-133, pp.150-151, pp.156-159, pp.161-164, pp.171-175 (except p.173 color photo), Katsumasa Tanaka
pp.50-51, p.64, p.67, pp.144-147, p.149, p.154, p.165, pp.167-169, Yuta Mizoguchi / pp.54-55, Takuya Seki
Iwan Baan: p.45
Sebastiano Luciano: pp.124-125
Except as noted: Sou Fujimoto Architects
-
Sketches, Hand Drawings
Sou Fujimoto
-
Renderings and Architectural Drawings
Sou Fujimoto Architects

SOU FUJIMOTO RECENT PROJECT
藤本壮介 最新プロジェクト

2013年9月25日発行

企画：二川由夫
撮影：GA photographers
印刷・製本：大日本印刷株式会社
制作・発行：エーディーエー・エディタ・トーキョー
151-0051　東京都渋谷区千駄ヶ谷3-12-14
TEL.(03)3403-1581(代)

禁無断転載

ISBN 978-4-87140-684-0 C1052